The Fellowship of the Throne in John's Apocalypse

A Theo-Political Inquiry into Authority and Society and Their Christological Bond

Fabián Santiago

MONOGRAPHS

© 2020 Fabián Santiago

Published 2020 by Langham Monographs
An imprint of Langham Publishing

www.langhampublishing.org

Langham Publishing and its imprints are a ministry of Langham Partnership

Langham Partnership
PO Box 296, Carlisle, Cumbria, CA3 9WZ, UK
www.langham.org

ISBNs:
978-1-78368-763-3 Print
978-1-78368-844-9 ePub
978-1-78368-845-6 Mobi
978-1-78368-846-3 PDF

Fabián Santiago has asserted his right under the Copyright, Designs and Patents Act, 1988 to be identified as the Author of this work.

All rights reserved. No part of this publication may be reproduced, stored in a retrieval system or transmitted, in any form or by any means, electronic, mechanical, photocopying, recording or otherwise, without the prior written permission of the publisher or the Copyright Licensing Agency.

Requests to reuse content from Langham Publishing are processed through PLSclear. Please visit www.plsclear.com to complete your request.

All Scripture translations in this work are the author's own, unless otherwise stated.

Scripture quotations marked NASB are taken from the New American Standard Bible®, Copyright © 1960, 1962, 1963, 1968, 1971, 1972, 1973, 1975, 1977, 1995 by The Lockman Foundation. Used by permission.

Scripture quotations marked NRSV are from the New Revised Standard Version Bible, copyright © 1989 National Council of the Churches of Christ in the United States of America. Used by permission. All rights reserved.

British Library Cataloguing-in-Publication Data
A catalogue record for this book is available from the British Library

ISBN: 978-1-78368-763-3

Cover & Book Design: projectluz.com

Langham Partnership actively supports theological dialogue and an author's right to publish but does not necessarily endorse the views and opinions set forth here or in works referenced within this publication, nor can we guarantee technical and grammatical correctness. Langham Partnership does not accept any responsibility or liability to persons or property as a consequence of the reading, use or interpretation of its published content.

In this fascinating close reading of the biblical text of the book of Revelation, with Oliver O'Donovan's political theology as his exegetical guide, Dr Santiago proposes from his Mexican context a new way forward for an avowedly secular state where over 90 percent of the population are active Christian believers with a rich religious heritage. Bringing together his upbringing and education in Mexico and his theological and biblical studies in London, he argues that the Apocalypse brings to a climax the biblical account of God's kingly rule in which the throne of God, the basis of divine power, is supremely fulfilled through the exalted Christ in a liturgical sociality of the Fellowship of the Throne, which becomes the ultimate horizon for political power. This provides a welcome theo-political challenge to the secular public discourse of not only Mexico but much of the Western world, and a much-needed call to the church to embody the authority of the risen and exalted Christ in today's society.

Rev Richard A. Burridge, PhD
Former Dean and Professor of Biblical Interpretation,
King's College London, UK

This arresting book is theological interpretation of Scripture at work, or as the author would phrase it, *theo-political* engagement with Scripture at work. Santiago weaves deftly through Oliver O'Donovan, John Milbank and William Cavanaugh, and the wider intellectual tradition in which these voices are located, while being resolutely focused on hearing anew the Apocalypse of John as Scripture. The author's contextual location is an added powerful presence throughout, lending extra impact to the reading.

Angus Paddison, PhD
Dean of Faculty,
Department of Theology, Religion, and Philosophy,
University of Winchester, UK

One of the most encouraging developments in theology over the last few decades has been the widening of the perspective by major contributions from the Majority World. Fabian Santiago's detailed and perceptive study of the throne in the book of Revelation contributes immensely to the study of this particular book but also widens the discussion over the importance of the fusion between religion and politics and how the Bible can help us fill out our understanding.

The importance of emphasizing a christological centre for this study on the divine throne highlights the essential nature of biblically directed worship as a starting point for a legitimate political understanding of what the book of Revelation teaches. It turns out that the first political activity is worship and this is what equips the liturgical community for their social, economic and political activities.

Christopher Wigram, PhD
Visiting Lecturer,
London School of Theology
All Nations Christian College
Former International Director, European Christian Mission

Contents

Abstract xi

Acknowledgments xiii

Abbreviations xv

Chapter 1 1
Introduction
   1.1 O'Donovan's Political Theology 5
   1.2 The Apocalypse's Political Theology 11
   1.3 Thesis 19
   1.4 Mode of Inquiry 20
   1.5 Structure 22

Part I: Method

Chapter 2 27
O'Donovan's Theo-Political Hermeneutics
   2.1 Principles for Engaging O'Donovan 30
   2.2 Hermeneutical Framework 33
      2.2.1 YHWH Is King 34
      2.2.2 Human Mediation 38
      2.2.3 Two Cities / Two Rules 40
      2.2.4 Evangelical Mode / Christological Turn 42
   2.3 Theo-Political Implications 46
   2.4 Conclusion 52

Chapter 3 55
The Apocalypse's Narrative
   3.1 How To Navigate the Narrative 57
   3.2 Narrative Unit 1: The Authorized Son of God Dictates
        Messages for Seven Congregations 63
   3.3 Narrative Unit 2: The Throne, the Exalted Lamb and
        the Scroll 65
   3.4 Dis/continuity? 69
   3.5 Negotiating a Way Forward 72
   3.6 Narrative Unit 3: Authority, Liturgy and Sociality in the
        Aftermath of Political Conspiracy 75

3.7 Narrative Unit 4: The Advent of the Holy City and the
     Materialization of the Fellowship of the Throne 83
3.8 The Apocalypse's Plot 85
3.9 Critique from our Reading 86
3.10 Conclusion 89

Part II: Authority

Chapter 4 93
The Exalted Jesus
4.1 The First and the Last as the Son of God 94
    4.1.1 Visionary Argot 95
    4.1.2 A Blend of Divine and Messianic Overtones 98
    4.1.3 Linking Portrayals of the Same Persona 106
    4.1.4 Theological Implications 108
4.2 The Divine Throne Is Also the Lamb's 109
    4.2.1 What the Throne Stands for 110
    4.2.2 The Messianic Lamb 113
    4.2.3 Worship as an Exclusive Divine Prerogative 116
    4.2.4 Theological Implications 118
4.3 The Woman's Child Becomes God's Son 119
    4.3.1 The Advent of the Messiah 120
    4.3.2 The Enthronement of the Messiah 122
    4.3.3 What Does the Dragon's Conspiracy Tell Us? 125
    4.3.4 Theological Implications 132
4.4 The Divine King Speaks Justice 133
    4.4.1 A Collage of Traditions about the King 133
    4.4.2 Divine Prerogatives Ascribed to the King 136
    4.4.3 And the King Said 139
    4.4.4 Theological Implications 140
4.5 Conclusion 142

Chapter 5 143
Models of Authority
5.1 Contemplative Authority: The King Becomes a Philosopher 144
5.2 Coercive Authority: The Return of the "King" 154
5.3 Authority as Judgment 162
5.4 Critique from Divine Authority 175
5.5 Conclusion 183

Part III: Society

Chapter 6 187
   The Liturgical Sociality
      6.1 Archeology and Enactment of Liturgy..................................188
      6.2 Sacred Space 190
          6.2.1 Mediated Presence 197
      6.3 Holy City..199
          6.3.1 Landscapes..200
          6.3.2 Re-building the City..203
          6.3.3 Theological Boundaries...206
      6.4 Liturgical Space as Theo-Political Category 210
      6.5 Mexican Liturgical Space 219
      6.6 Conclusion 221

Chapter 7 223
   Models of Society
      7.1 Ancient Society..224
      7.2 The Church as Society 231
          7.2.1 The Church as Political Society..................................232
          7.2.2 The Church as Post-Political Society 236
          7.2.3 The Church as a Moral Society 244
      7.3 Critique from Liturgical Sociality..247
      7.4 Conclusion 254

Chapter 8 255
   Conclusions
      8.1 "I, John . . . Was in the Isle Called Patmos . . . Was in
          (the) Spirit"..255
      8.2 "The Marriage of the Lamb Has Come".............................256
      8.3 "Who Bore Witness . . . as Far as He Perceived".................257
      8.4 "This Calls for Discernment" 260
      8.5 "If Anyone Has an Ear" 263

Bibliography..267
   A. Primary Sources...267
   B. Secondary Literature...276

Index of Names...295

Index of Subjects...299

Index of Scripture...311

List of Figures

Figure 1. The Apocalypse's Narrative Flow 63
Figure 2. Liturgical Spaces 197

List of Tables

Table 1. Exegetical and theoretical model (Old Testament) 40

Table 2. Exegetical and theoretical model (Old and New Testaments) 47

Table 3. Textual links about the exalted Jesus across the narrative: eyes and mouth 107

Table 4. Textual links about the exalted Jesus across the narrative: seven spirits 107

Table 5. Textual links about the exalted Jesus across the narrative: throne 108

Abstract

From among modern inquiries into what constitutes the political, and within the current environment of hostility towards what the field of theology can offer to its study, Oliver O'Donovan emerges with his unique brand of political theology. His method of inquiry, resourced by Scripture and Christian tradition, and predicated on Christology, offers a construal of authority distilled from the Bible's own account of God's kingly rule as understood within the biblical narrative of salvation history, with momentous implications for the realm of the political, in particular as relates to the categories of authority and society and their interplay. Given O'Donovan's manifest interest in the book of Revelation and the centrality within the book's narrative of themes intrinsic to O'Donovan's political theology, the Apocalypse, we argue, offers the ultimate ground for a discussion about the political in the terms suggested by O'Donovan. In undertaking this exercise, we find that the Apocalypse's own construal of authority is in fact about divine authority conceived around the throne of God, the seat of divine power, which has undergone a christological shift brought about by the exalted Jesus. We then go on to argue that throughout the Apocalypse a correlation gradually becomes apparent between the divine authority and a liturgical sociality defined by the presence of the exalted Jesus. This correlation of divine authority and liturgical sociality which is mediated by the very same exalted Jesus we have called the Fellowship of the Throne. And it is this Fellowship of Throne, we argue, that must now become the ultimate horizon of the political.

Acknowledgments

I would like to thank the King's College London Theological Trust for its gracious generosity in supporting me and my family throughout this project.

I would also like to thank my supervisors Professor Edward Adams and the Rev Professor Ben Quash for allowing this research project to move forward and for their patience and availability throughout its last stages.

Last, but not least, I would like to thank my wife and children for bearing with me throughout this project. In particular, I want to acknowledge my wife Rebeca's efforts in proofreading this document while continuing with all her duties as wife, mother and member of the church.

Τῷ ἀγαπῶντι ἡμᾶς (Rev 1:5)

Fabián Santiago

Abbreviations

ACT/G	Ancient Christian Texts – Greek Commentaries on Revelation
ACT/L	Ancient Christian Texts – Latin Commentaries on Revelation
ANF	The Ante Nicene Fathers, nine volumes
BDAG	A Greek-English Lexicon of the New Testament and Other Early Christian Literature, revised and edited by Danker, based on Bauer's
HALOT	The Hebrew and Aramaic Lexicon of the Old Testament
JSP	Tanakh: Jewish Publication Society
LCL	The Loeb Classical Library
LSJ	A Greek-English Lexicon, compiled by Liddell and Scott, revised and augmented throughout by Jones
NPNF1	The Nicene and Post-Nicene Fathers, First Series, fourteen volumes
NPNF2	The Nicene and Post-Nicene Fathers, Second Series, fourteen volumes
NRSV	The New Revised Standard Version of the Bible
NTA	New Testament Apocrypha, two volumes
OTP	The Old Testament Pseudepigrapha, two volumes

CHAPTER 1

Introduction

As a Mexican Christian with a keen interest in the politics and public life of my country, I find one of the most perplexing paradoxes of contemporary life in Mexico to be the stark contrast between the confessional religious beliefs of the large majority of its citizens and the no less confessional secular creed of the state and those allowed a voice within the public square. This is particularly remarkable when we consider that in the 2010 Mexican census, when asked to name their religion, about 101.3 million individuals (out of 112.3 million) chose to identify with some strand of historic Christianity, thus accounting for 90.2 percent of the total population.[1] Of these, 92.9 million identified themselves as Roman Catholics (i.e. 82.7% of the total),[2] and 8.4 million as Protestants/Pentecostals/evangelicals (i.e. 7.5% of the total).[3] In spite of these figures, and whatever these may reveal about the population,

---

1. Instituto Nacional de Estadística y Geografía (INEGI), *Panorama de las religiones en México*, 3.

2. INEGI, *Panorama de las religiones en México*. It should be said that the particular strand of Roman Catholicism in Mexico has, from the late sixteenth century, been deeply influenced by the cult to the Virgin of Guadalupe, who is regarded as "a Mexican representation of the Virgin Mary, Mother of God" (Brading, *Mexican Phoenix*, 11). This is usually known as *guadalupanismo*. Also, Mexico is the second country, after Brazil, with the world's largest number of Catholics, see Pew Research Centre, *Global Christianity*, 23.

3. INEGI, *Panorama de las religiones en México*, 3. The definition of an evangelical advanced by Timothy Larsen would resonate with the Mexican context, see Larsen, "Defining and Locating," 1–3. It should be noted that our numbers do not include Adventist, Mormons and Jehova's Witnesses, whom the Mexican national statistics office grouped together numbering 2.5 million people (2.6% of the total), see INEGI, *Panorama de las religiones en México*, 3.

at present the law dictates that "El estado mexicano es laico" (the Mexican state is secular).[4]

This contemporary landscape, however, is at odds with the past, since Mexicans have historically tended to embrace a view of reality infused with a concern for the transcendent, as opposed to a purely immanent or secular approach to life. A variety of extant pre-colonial (i.e. pre-Columbian) texts, ironically recovered and preserved by the Spanish, attest to this Mexican "ethos."[5] In fact, when the Spaniards set out in search of new territories overseas after having completed the "reconquista" of Islamic Spain,[6] it was with what could be regarded as a mixed colonial and missionary enterprise in mind.[7] Christianity therefore arrived in Mexico in 1519 in its Roman Catholic iteration.[8] However, this mission into the so called New World was understood to be subject to the colonial interests of the crown of Castile[9] and had been sanctioned by various papal bulls. This framework for a church subservient to the Spanish monarch came to be known as the "patronato real (royal patronage),"[10] and modelled an asymmetrical relationship between church and state that prevailed in independent Mexico from 1821 onwards.[11]

---

4. *Ley de Asociaciones Religiosas y Culto Público*. Texto Vigente (17 Dec 2015). Artículo 3. This document is available at http://www.diputados.gob.mx/LeyesBiblio/pdf/24_171215.pdf.

5. For instance, (a) there is the Mayan *Popol Vuh* with its creation account, see Tedlock, *Popol Vuh*, 63–74; or (b) the Aztec *Codex Chimalpopoca* and its account of the five suns and its cataclysmic eschatology, see Bierhorst, *Codex Chimalpopoca*, 2.2–49; 75.1–78.21; or (c) the foundational narrative of the Aztecs (known as *Crónica Mexicana*) which tells of a journey led by their god Huitzilopochtli which took them to a land where they saw an eagle perched on a cactus eating a snake, the place where Tenochtitlan would be founded, see Alvarado Tezozomoc, *Crónica Mexicana*, 1; or (d) the wisdom literature known as *huehuehtlahtolli* (Nahuatl for "ancient word") with its markedly theological orientation and high view of family life, see Olmos, *Huehuetlahtolli*, 275–495.

6. Elliot, "Spanish Conquest," 149, 152.

7. Elliot, 160–161.

8. See Barnadas, "Catholic Church," 511–540; Chauvet, "misiones franciscanas," 28–48; Alcalá, "misiones de los dominicos," 49–54.

9. Barnadas, "Catholic Church," 512.

10. Barnadas, 512. Rightly so, Barnadas asks "why did the church allow itself to be bound hand and foot to the interests of the Spanish crown?" (Barnadas, 513). Admittedly, according to Luis Medina Ascensio, since 1622 the Holy See attempted to put an end to the patronage, see Medina Ascensio, "La iglesia ante la emancipación," 184–185. For a more favourable view on the "patronato real" see Gutiérrez Casillas, "La organización de la Iglesia," 55–57.

11. See Bethell, "Note on the Church," 231; cf. Lynch, "Catholic Church in Latin America," 528.

In the nascent Mexican state, the Roman Catholic church went from unambiguous establishment in the first Mexican constitution of 1824,[12] to a disestablishment of sorts in the constitution of 1857 that limited church property (and revenue) to premises used only for its own activities.[13] A three-year civil war between so called conservatives and liberals ensued this constitutional shift,[14] and the outcome was a reinforced anticlerical stance within the institutions of the Mexican state.[15] It was during this time that Christianity in its reformed and evangelical modes first emerged in Mexico,[16] but following a further violent revolt in the country,[17] a substantial review of the constitution denied the legislative arm of the government the power to establish any religion,[18] and in effect banished religion from the public square and confined it to the private sphere.[19] Secularism, understood as an autonomous space closed to faith and worship, went on to subsume many areas of national life.[20] If previously it was held that "La enseñanza es libre" (teaching is to be practised in freedom),[21] now this statement was qualified as "La enseñanza es libre; pero será laica la que se dé en los establecimientos oficiales de educación" (teaching is to be practised in freedom, however, education provided by the state must be secular).[22] Furthermore, such is the

---

12. See *Constitución de 1824*, Artículo 3, available online at http://www.diputados.gob.mx/biblioteca/bibdig/const_mex/const_1824.pdf.

13. See *Constitución de 1857*, Artículo 27, available online at https://archivos.juridicas.unam.mx/www/legislacion/federal/historicos/1857.pdf.

14. Bazant, "Mexico from Independence," 459–463.

15. Lynch, "Catholic Church in Latin America," 527–531.

16. Bastian, "La primera ola de la penetración protestante," 296–310; Martin, *Tongues of Fire*, 93–98; Lynch, "Latin America," 409–410.

17. At first, it seems that the immediate reason for the Mexican revolution of 1910–1920 was to put an end to the dictatorial regime of Porfirio Díaz. However, revisionist views advanced alternative theses (e.g. Womack, "Mexican Revolution," 79–82). Still, if Díaz's dictatorship led to the Mexican revolution, why did the Mexican state deepen its secular turn at the end of it? It seems "liberal" strands of the revolution left their anticlerical imprint in the movement, see Womack, "Mexican Revolution," 100, 104–105, 113–114, 140.

18. See *Constitución de 1917*, Artículo 130.

19. See *Constitución de 1917*, Artículo 24.

20. John Milbank's theological account of the genesis (or archeology) of the secular as an autonomous domain or space has proved very useful at this point, see Milbank, *Theology and Social Theory*, 9–18.

21. *Constitución de 1857*, Artículo 3.

22. *Constitución de 1917*, Artículo 3. This goes some way towards explaining why theological education in Mexico is underdeveloped.

state's monopoly and secular grip on the public square that to this day no minister of any religion is allowed to bring his opinion to bear or to participate in any political (and therefore public) act; should such an individual wish to take part in any official or political event they must have first resigned their position as a minister of religion.[23]

Ironically, the unabashed secular stance of the new Mexican constitution went on to give way to "a new form of enlightened despotism, a ruling conviction that the state knew what ought to be done and needed plenary powers to fulfil its mission; Mexicans had to obey."[24] The result was a one-party monopoly of the government for the rest of the twentieth century.[25] With the advent of a democratic change of regime at the turn of the century, expectations were running high for the fulfilment of the so far elusive and seemingly benevolent "enlightened liberal utopia," which to this day remains one of the predominant ideologies in Mexico. Any hopes of its realization, however, have been marred most recently by the return of violence across Mexican territories – in a manner highly reminiscent of pre-Columbian and pagan Aztec practices which have included "flaying"[26] and "human sacrifice"[27] of sorts. These have resulted from the brutal confrontations between drug cartels and have been witnessed once more in the public square.[28]

---

23. cf. *Constitución Política de los Estados Unidos Mexicanos*. Texto Vigente (6 March 2020). Artículo 130. This document is available at http://www.diputados.gob.mx/LeyesBiblio/pdf/1_060320.pdf.

24. Meyer, "Mexico," 157. Equally, the anticlerical stance of the state led to an episode known as *La Cristiada*, a war between the government and a Roman Catholic party in the late 1920s, see Meyer, "Mexico," 167–169.

25. Hamnett, *Concise History of Mexico*, 240–291.

26. Human flaying: "And then, too, he started and began the practice of flaying humans. This was when he sang songs at Texcalapan. Then, to start with, he seized an Otomi woman, who was washing maguey fibers at the river, and flayed her. Then he made one the Toltecs named Xiuhcozcatl wear the skin, and he was the first to wear a *totec* skin." *Codex Chimalpopoca* 9.50–54.

27. Aztecs' liturgical proclivity for human sacrifices, e.g. "[(Year) 1487]. This is when the house of Huitzilopochtli was dedicated in Tenochtitlan. In four years it had been built to the top. And it was dedicated with prisoners who met their death. Here, all told, are the nations: The Tzapoteca dead were 16,000. The Tlappaneca dead were 24,000. The Huexotzinca dead were 16,000. The Tziuhcoaca dead were 24,400. And this includes Cozcacuauhtenanca and people from Mictlancuauhtla. Thus all the prisoners add up to 80,400." *Codex Chimalpopoca* 58.35–42. In this source, the origin of human sacrifice is traced back to Huemac, a ruler of the Toltecs, a group previous to the Aztecs, in the year 1063, see *Codex Chimalpopoca* 9.44–10.5

28. See United Nations Office on Drugs and Crime (UNODC), *World Drug Report 2010*, 237–241.

In some ways it is the incongruous asymmetric correlation between the totalized secular discourse of a political elite and the marginalized voice of a religious majority that drives the present author to inquire into the political from a theological stance. And though a project of this nature may be regarded as irreverent or even heretical by the established Mexican consensus of today, we align most decidedly with theologian Oliver O'Donovan who has argued that the political and the theological have each been artificially guarded against the other by a cordon sanitaire,[29] and that

> the renewed advocacy of political theology in our own time has had as its concern to break out of the cordon sanitaire. [And that] When that advocacy has been at its clearest, it has insisted that theology is political simply by responding to the dynamics of its own proper themes. Christ, salvation, the church, the Trinity: to speak about these has involved theologians in speaking of society, and has led them to formulate normative political ends.[30]

1.1 O'Donovan's Political Theology

In fact it is O'Donovan who has coined the term "political theology" to refer to this method of inquiry ordered from a transparent theological (and therefore confessional) standpoint;[31] a term which

> does not suppose a literal synonymity between the political vocabulary of [Israelite/Christian] salvation and the secular use of the same political terms. It [instead] postulates an analogy – not a rhetorical metaphor only, or a poetic image, but an analogy grounded in reality – between the acts of God and human acts, both of them taking place within the one public history which

---

29. O'Donovan, *Desire of the Nations*, 1–2.
30. O'Donovan, 3.
31. "The best way of describing how I understand my political work is with Anselm's famous programme, 'faith seeking understanding'. It is not only faith's primary object, God, that needs understanding, but the world in which we have to live." Oliver O'Donovan in Shortt, *God's Advocates*, 249.

is the theatre of God's saving purposes and mankind's social undertaking.[32]

More importantly, the political theology O'Donovan has argued for aims at showing "how the political concepts wrapped up in Jewish and Christian speech about God's redemption of the world still had political force."[33] This kind of political theology, he argues, is "an intellectual enquiry located on the horizon of the theology of the church," since "every aspect of theology is a pursuit *of* the church."[34]

As for the particular shape which O'Donovan's political theology has taken over the years, we may here highlight two aspects of it. First, theologically speaking, it began with a christological foundation, the resurrection of Jesus, which in turn developed into a trinitarian framework. The publication of *Resurrection and Moral Order* in 1986 prepared the way for the advent of *The Desire of the Nations* in 1996.[35] In the former book, O'Donovan argues that "[i]n the resurrection of Christ creation is restored and the kingdom of God dawns."[36] In the latter, as its subtitle suggests (i.e. "rediscovering the roots of political theology"), O'Donovan enlarges the historical horizon of that christological event,[37] looking back to ancient Israel, forward to the Spirit-empowered (early) church,[38] and beyond to Christendom, which he

---

32. O'Donovan, *Desire of the Nations*, 2.
33. O'Donovan, *Ways of Judgment*, ix.
34. O'Donovan, 239.
35. According to Nicholas Wolterstorff, "*The Desire of the Nations* is . . . the most important contribution to political theology in our century." Wolterstorff, "Discussion of Oliver O'Donovan's," 100. With reference to the title of the book (i.e. *The Desire of the Nations*), it is arguably an expression derived from Genesis 49:10 LXX: καὶ αὐτὸς προσδοκία ἐθνῶν (literally, "and he [is] the expectation of the nations"). This phrase was interpreted christologically by the church fathers, e.g. Justin Martyr, *Apology* 1.32, 54; Justin Martyr, *Dialogue with Trypho* 52, 120 (ANF/1); Augustine, *Reply to Faustus the Manichaean* 12.42; 22.85, 87 (NPNF1/4); Eusebius, *Ecclesiastical History* 1.6.1–2, 4, 8 (NPNF2/1); Jerome, *Letter* 144.8 (NPNF2/6).
36. O'Donovan, *Resurrection and Moral Order*, 15. This point is revisited and complemented in O'Donovan's first instalment of his trilogy on *Ethics as Theology*. See O'Donovan, *Self, World, and Time*, 91–97. This christological purchase of O'Donovan's theological project safeguards it against "the pathos of modern theology," as Milbank puts it, when theology "surrenders its claim to be a metadiscourse" and "no longer seeks to position, qualify or criticize other discourses," rather it becomes "'positioned' by secular reason," Milbank, *Theology and Social Theory*, 1.
37. In fact, O'Donovan deploys the christological construal "Christ-event" to refer to Jesus's advent, passion, restoration and exaltation. See O'Donovan, *Desire of the Nations*, 133.
38. See O'Donovan, *Desire of the Nations*, 19–20. In *Desire of the Nations* O'Donovan makes explicit links to *Resurrection and Moral Order*. See O'Donovan, *Desire of the Nations*, 19, 30.

construes as "the idea of a professedly Christian secular political order, and the history of that idea in practice,"[39] that is to say, "the idea of a confessionally Christian government, at once 'secular' (in the proper sense of that word, confined to the present age) and obedient to Christ, a promise of the age of his unhindered rule."[40]

The Ways of Judgment followed in 2005,[41] which along with *The Desire of the Nations* may be thought of "as two phases in a single extended train of thought,"[42] since *The Ways of Judgment* "continues the exploration that [*The Desire of the Nations*] began, into how theological and political concepts correspond; but it approaches the correspondence more from the political side."[43] More significantly perhaps, *The Ways of Judgment* observes a threefold structure that mirrors the trinitarian political theology O'Donovan conveys in this book, i.e. judgment (God), representation (Jesus), and communication (Holy Spirit).[44] O'Donovan explains this model as follows:

> In the first place we speak of the God-given right of judgment within the world, and of the church's deference to that right, not usurping the privileged sphere of secular judgment. In the second place we speak of the God-given representative of mankind, and of the church's challenge to all other political representations. And in the third place we speak of the eschatological summons to social communication, and of the church's modeling of communication as life beyond judgment.[45]

Second, hermeneutically speaking, O'Donovan argues that "the hermeneutic principle that governs a Christian appeal to political categories within

---

39. O'Donovan, *Desire of the Nations*, 195.
40. O'Donovan, 195.
41. In the interim the O'Donovans edited *From Irenaeus to Grotius: A Sourcebook in Christian Political Thought 100–1625*, in 1999, and authored *Bonds of Imperfection* in 2004, which was meant to be "an accompaniment" to the previous book, "undertaking more sustained analysis of individual thinkers and more developed arguments about specific issues." O'Donovan and O'Donovan, *Bonds of Imperfection*, 1. Oliver O'Donovan also authored *The Just War Revisited*, published in 2003, and a year earlier, *Common Objects of Love*.
42. O'Donovan, *Ways of Judgment*, x.
43. O'Donovan, x. "If *Desire of the Nations* is the manifesto, *The Ways of Judgment* . . . is both a restatement and an outworking of the earlier book." Bretherton, "Introduction," 268.
44. See O'Donovan, *Ways of Judgment*, v–vi, 239.
45. O'Donovan, 239–240.

the Hebrew Scriptures is, simply, Israel itself. Through this unique political entity God made known his purposes in the world."[46] That is to say, "the governing [hermeneutic] principle is the kingly rule of God, expressed in Israel's corporate existence and brought to final effect in the life, death and resurrection of Jesus."[47] More importantly, since a "political hermeneutic has to yield theology,"[48] it follows that "theology, by developing its account of the reign of God, may recover the ground traditionally held by the notion of authority."[49] This is a key theo-political category recovered by O'Donovan, and was a "central theme of the pre-modern political theology, which sought to find criteria from the apostolic proclamation to test every claim to authority made by those who possessed, or wished to possess, power."[50]

Therefore, O'Donovan's hermeneutic trajectory begins with "a liturgical act in which political and religious meanings were totally fused,"[51] encapsulated in the expression "YHWH is king."[52] In his exegetical framework "Yhwh's authority as king is established by the accomplishment of victorious deliverance, by the presence of judicial discrimination and by the continuity of a community-possession,"[53] where "Yhwh's rule receives its answering recognition in the praises of his people."[54] In fact, "the link which ties the exercise of Yhwh's kingly rule to the praise of his people is that as the people congregate to perform their act of praise, the political reality of Israel is displayed."[55]

Then Jesus appears proclaiming "the 'fulfilling of the time' which had brought the 'Kingdom of God near' (Mark 3:15)."[56] And though what "Jesus had to say about the reign of God was authoritative because it was confirmed

---

46. O'Donovan, *Desire of the Nations*, 27.
47. O'Donovan, 27.
48. O'Donovan, 22.
49. O'Donovan, 19.
50. O'Donovan, 17.
51. O'Donovan, 32.
52. יְהוָה מֶלֶךְ (e.g. Ps 10:16; 29:10; 93:1; 96:10; 97:1; 99:1; 1 Chron 16:31; Exod 15:18; Isa 33:22). See O'Donovan, *Desire of the Nations*, 32. Out of deference to Jewish tradition we will capitalize the transliteration of the name, YHWH. However, we will quote exactly from O'Donovan as he transliterates the name as "Yhwh" in *The Desire of the Nations*, which he then capitalizes in *The Ways of Judgment*.
53. O'Donovan, *Desire of the Nations*, 36.
54. O'Donovan, 47.
55. O'Donovan, 47.
56. O'Donovan, 82.

by an exercise of power that demonstrated it,"[57] "the authority of the Kingdom and its messenger lay in itself, not in the reception that it found."[58] Nonetheless his authority "proved itself by eliciting faith: from the crowds that thronged round, from the sick and their relatives who came for help, and from the disciples who came to learn."[59] O'Donovan observes, however, that "Jesus proclaimed the coming of the Kingdom of God, but the apostolic church did not. [Instead] It told the story of what happened when the Kingdom came: its conflict with the established principalities and powers and its vindication at God's hand through Jesus' resurrection."[60] Therefore, since the church "stood on the other side of that great crisis which [Jesus's] proclamation evoked . . . it claimed continuity with his proclamation, because he, and his message of the Kingdom, had been vindicated."[61] Within this perspective "Pentecost can be seen as the moment at which the church comes to participate in the authority of the ascended Christ."[62] In other words, "Pentecost authorised the church by uniting it with the authorisation of Christ. It belongs, therefore, immediately to the moment of authorisation, Christ's Exaltation."[63]

As a result of the above, O'Donovan argues that "the true character of the church" is as "a political society," so to speak, "ruled and authorised by the ascended Christ alone and supremely; it therefore has its own authority; and it is not answerable to any other authority that may attempt to subsume it."[64] Also, in eschatological terms, "the revelation of the church as *polis*, living immediately under the rule of God, coincides with the revelation of the church as *bride*, in marital fellowship with God. The completion and finalization of political order under the free and worshipping embrace of God's rule coincides with the completion and finalization of social order in complete and uncoerced fellowship with God."[65]

---

57. O'Donovan, 89.
58. O'Donovan, 113.
59. O'Donovan, 113.
60. O'Donovan, 120.
61. O'Donovan, 120.
62. O'Donovan, 162.
63. O'Donovan, 161.
64. O'Donovan, 159.
65. O'Donovan, *Ways of Judgment*, 240.

Overall, O'Donovan's agenda is for "a political theology shaped by the Christ-event" and encompassing two natural spheres for action.[66] On the one hand, it "must criticise existing notions of political good and necessity, not only classical republican notions but imperial and theocratic notions too, in the light of what God has done for the human race and the human soul."[67] To put it another way, "this is political theology in its liberal mode, attacking and overcoming the pretentiousness of the autonomous political order."[68] On the other hand, political theology "has an ecclesiological mode, which takes the church seriously as a society and shows how the rule of God is realised there."[69] It must also argue that the proclamation of the kingdom is not evacuated from any theological construal of Christ.[70] The liberal and ecclesiological modes of political theology may be summed up as follows, "Political theology must have something to say about society and something to say about rule, and the two must be coordinated."[71]

It is here that the book of Revelation's unique voice must be brought into the discussion of the political from a theological standpoint, not least because it sets the terms of the discussion in O'Donovan's own collection of essays on the political,[72] and receives close exegetical and theological consideration in O'Donovan's work in general.[73] The Apocalypse offers the ultimate ground for

---

66. O'Donovan, *Desire of the Nations*, 122.

67. O'Donovan, 122.

68. O'Donovan, 123.

69. O'Donovan, 123.

70. See O'Donovan, 123.

71. O'Donovan, 193. By contrast, Peter Scott and William Cavanaugh provide a framework for and definition of political theology without any explicit christological purchase or orientation: "political theology is . . . the analysis and criticism of political arrangements (including cultural-psychological, social and economic aspects) from the perspective of differing interpretations of God's ways with the world." Scott and Cavanaugh, *Blackwell Companion to Political Theology*, 1. More recently Nicholas Wolterstorff has suggested that "Political theology is not theology with a political cast; it is theology of or about the political, more specifically, theology of or about the state." Wolterstorff, *Mighty and The Almighty*, 2n3.

72. "The opening essay of the collection, 'History and Politics in the Book of Revelation,' forms a programmatic introduction." O'Donovan and O'Donovan, *Bonds of Imperfection*, 3.

73. For example O'Donovan, *Desire of the Nations*, 153–157; cf. Rowland, "Apocalypse and Political Theology," 242–244. It should be noted that the Apocalypse had resourced the work of some modern theologians like Karl Barth and Hans Urs von Balthasar, for instance, see Mangina, "Apocalypticizing Dogmatics," 193–208; equally on Barth and the use of a theological apocalyptic discourse see Lowe, "Why We Need Apocalyptic," 41–53. For aptly introductions to the person, work and legacy of Barth and Balthasar, respectively, see Hardy, "Karl Barth," 21–42; and Quash, "Hans Urs von Balthasar," 106–123.

a discussion of the political, and invites a theo-political inquiry very much in the terms suggested by O'Donovan. Let us then proceed to explain this claim.

1.2 The Apocalypse's Political Theology

In the last vision of the book of Revelation (21:9–22:6) John reports how he is led by an angel and carried in the Spirit to be shown the bride of the Lamb (21:9; see also 19:9, 7). Yet, in a manner characteristic of the book of Revelation, where an image is seamlessly superseded by a different visual symbol,[74] what he sees, looking down from a high mountain is a city coming down from heaven (21:10), a city which he then goes on to describe in detail, both in appearance and in architectural features and dimensions (21:11–23).

Emerging gradually from his description is the liturgical design and focus of this city; it is pictured as a giant cube (21:16) in the manner of the holy of holies of the Solomonic Temple in the times of the Israelite monarchy (cf. 1 Kgs 6:20), the space reserved for the ark of YHWH's covenant (cf. 1 Kgs 6:19; 8:6) in that Israelite economy of sacred spaces (cf. 1 Kgs 6:5).[75] The Apocalypse's holy city is the ultimate totalized sacred space where the presence of the Lord God all-powerful and the Lamb make redundant any perpetuation of the notion of a reserved or private space for divine worship within the economy of a wider space (21:22). What is more, this new undefiled (21:27) sacred space becomes a place of pilgrimage, a beacon for the nations (21:24) drawing in the diffused and humbled (human) political authority, i.e. the kings of the earth, by now dethroned by the divine King (cf. 19:19–21). In fact, this city/holy-of-holies with the radiant presence of God and the Lamb in its midst appears to fulfil, with a liturgical and christological variation, the Isaianic prophecy of restoration of a post-exilic Israel (Isa 60), where YHWH would arise upon them with his visible glory (Isa 60:2), and nations would walk by their light and kings by their brightness (Isa 60:3; cf. 60:11).[76]

---

74. For a theological approach to the sequence of images in the Apocalypse see Balthasar, *Theo-Drama*, 15–17.

75. See Caird, *Revelation of St. John*, 273; Aune, *Revelation 17–22*, 1161–1162; Rowland, "Book of Revelation," 723; Boxall, *Revelation of Saint John*, 304; Beale, *Temple and the Church's Mission*, 23, 370.

76. See Oswalt, *Book of Isaiah Chapters 40–66*, 534. For an analysis of this allusion to Isaiah in the apocalyptic text under discussion, and to ascertain to what extent it resources this

The sequence of images within this last vision, which began with the image of the bride and was then superseded by that of a walled city turned sacred space that is also a place of pilgrimage, moves on to that of a primeval garden or paradise (cf. 2:7).[77] This city-garden has a river flowing through it (22:1–2; cf. Gen 2:10) and a tree of life, the leaves of which are for the healing of the nations (22:2; cf. Gen 2:9; 3:22, 24).[78] Above all, however, this is a city-garden that becomes the locus of the throne of God and of the Lamb (22:1).[79] In fact, the vision comes to an end with these words:

> And the throne of God and of the Lamb will be in it [i.e. the city],
> and his servants will liturgically serve him
> and they will see his face, and his name on their foreheads.
> And the night will not be there,
> and they do not have need of light of lamp neither light of the sun,
> since the Lord God will shed light upon them,
> and they will reign for the ages of ages (Rev 22:3–5).

Whichever way this final vision of the Apocalypse is read, whether à la Victorinus of Petovium,[80] or à la Augustine,[81] it is noticeable that the seer,

---

apocalyptic vision, see Bauckham, *Climax of the Prophecy*, 313–318; Aune, *Revelation 17–22*, 1170–1172; Beale, *Book of Revelation*, 1094–1101.

77. See Beale, *Book of Revelation*, 1109–1111, who comments on the "paradisal city-temple," a thesis he fully develops in Beale, *Temple and the Church's Mission*, 23–26, 66–80.

78. See Barth, *Church Dogmatics* III/1, 280–282.

79. David Aune discusses the (exegetical) "genre" of the throne-vision reports in Aune, *Revelation 1–5*, 276–277; cf. Rowland, "Book of Revelation," 596–598. Aune also observes that "there are six scenes in Revelation that center on the heavenly throne room: (1) 4:2–6:17, (2) 7:9–17, (3) 11:15–19, (4) 14:1–5 . . ., (5) 15:2–8, and (6) 19:1–8." Aune, *Revelation 1–5*, 278. Consequently, the apocalyptic vision under discussion, in particular 22:1–3, does not fit into Aune's exegetical construal, as he implicitly concedes.

80. "For the sevenfold Holy Spirit, when he has passed in revue the events to the last time, to the very end, returns again to the same times and supplements what he had said incompletely. Nor ought we inquire too much into the order of the Revelation. Rather, we ought inquire after the meaning . . ." Victorinus of Petovium, *Commentary on the Apocalypse* 8.2 (ACT/L), third century AD. This hermeneutical device of recapitulation is "perhaps the most important contribution of Victorinus to the interpretation of Revelation," Weinrich, *Revelation*, xxii.

81. "In this book called Revelation, there are indeed many obscure statements, intended to exercise the mind of the reader, and there are only a few statements plain enough in their meaning to enable us to infer the meaning of others from them, and then only with some labour. This is chiefly because John repeats the same things in many different ways, so that he seems to be speaking of different matters whereas he is in fact speaking of the same things in different words." Augustine, *City of God* 20.17, trans. W. R. Dyson.

enabled by the Spirit and deploying different images to narrate it (i.e. a bride, a walled city, a sacred space, a place of pilgrimage, a primeval garden),[82] approaches his subject from the periphery to the centre. And at the heart of this centripetal narration two themes are inextricably intertwined: (1) the divine political authority signified by the throne jointly shared by God and the Lamb, and (2) a liturgical sociality embodied by the servants, whose relationship to the throne exists through the mediation of the Lamb (i.e. the exalted Jesus), whose name is tattooed onto their foreheads. Unique to this economy of power is the fact that, though subservient to the throne, the liturgical sociality is not overwhelmed or sidelined, instead it is brought in to share in the power of the throne and to reign together with the divine authority. This new dynamic of power is what we have called the *koinonia* or *Fellowship of the Throne*.

Admittedly, the Greek noun κοινωνία, which connotes sharing, participation and generosity in addition to fellowship,[83] or communion, association and partnership,[84] does not feature as such in the Greek text of the Apocalypse. However, John calls himself a συγκοινωνός, that is to say, a participant or partner "of the thing in which one shares."[85] In fact, he introduces himself as "your brother and partner [συγκοινωνός] in the affliction and kingdom and endurance in Jesus."[86] Since the liturgical sociality, as we call it, composes a "kingdom" [βασιλεία] (1:6, 9; 5:10), we think "*koinonia*" is a better term than "kingdom of God" (11:15; 12:10) to convey (a) the sharing of the throne between God and the exalted Jesus, and (b) the participation of the Lamb's servants in God's reign, in addition to their enjoying God's generosity in giving his light (see 22:3–5, quoted in full above).[87] Arguably, John presupposes

---

82. On the topic of "theology and representation" see Ward, *Theology and Contemporary Critical Theory*, 1–10.

83. See Danker, BDAG, 552.

84. See Liddell and Scott, LSJ, 970.

85. Danker, BDAG, 952; cf. Liddell and Scott, LSJ, 1666.

86. Rev 1:9; cf. 18:4.

87. The pedigree of the term *koinonia* as a political category is attested in Aristotle's *Politics*, where it features thirty-nine times in total. From the outset Aristotle observes "Since we see that every city [πόλις] is some sort of community [κοινωνία], and that every community is constituted for the sake of some good . . . the community that is most authoritative of all and embraces all the others does so particularly, and aims at the most authoritative good of all. This is what is called the city [πόλις] or the political [πολιτικός] community [κοινωνία]." Aristotle, *Politics* 1.1.1, trans. Carnes Lord. The Greek text has been consulted at *Aristotle's Politica*.

some degree of *koinonia* between the Lamb and his servants as they liturgically serve him (cf. 1:9).[88]

Thus, if this *koinonia* or Fellowship of the Throne, eschatologically discerned by John through the Spirit, is the *telos* or denouement of the narrative of the book of Revelation,[89] it follows that (a) these two themes (i.e. divine authority and liturgical sociality) and their correlation were introduced at an earlier stage in the narrative and are developed throughout; (b) any other major theme (e.g. evil, judgment, justice) or symbol (e.g. the dragon, the beast, the false prophet, the great city) within the narrative becomes subsidiary to these two intertwined and overarching themes; that is to say, their featuring in the narrative ultimately contributes – whether affirming, opposing, questioning, demanding, celebrating and so forth – to the development and materialization of the Fellowship of the Throne; and most importantly, (c) the Fellowship of the Throne, as the seat of power, becomes the ultimate horizon of the political.[90]

This theological construal of the Fellowship of the Throne,[91] which encompasses the two themes of authority and sociality, their correlation, and their orientation to the divine, is by no means exclusive to the book of Revelation. We have identified at least three ancient theo-political traditions predating

---

88. In the rest of the New Testament, *koinonia* as a theological concept that somehow links God the Father and the Son of God (i.e. Jesus), with his disciples or servants is presumed in John 17:21, and is explicitly conveyed in 1 Cor 1:9. Interestingly enough, Augustine links these two ideas (i.e. "koinonia" and "kingdom of God"), as he explains that salvation and everlasting life "cannot be anything else than the kingdom of God, to which fellowship with Christ alone introduces us." Augustine, *On the Merits and Forgiveness of Sins, and on the Baptism of Infants* 1.15 (NPNF1/5); cf. idem, *Letter* 91.3 (NPNF1/1)]. More recently, O'Donovan construes *koinonia* with a markedly ecclesiastic orientation, see O'Donovan, *Ways of Judgment*, 242–243.

89. Were a canonical reading to be deployed, it would follow that this *koinonia* or Fellowship of the Throne is the *telos* or denouement of the grand overarching biblical narrative. As the biblical canon, in particular the New Testament, gradually settled, see for example Athanasius, *Festal Letters* 39.4–6 (NPNF2/4); Augustine, *On Christian Doctrine* 2.8 (NPNF1/2), some church fathers deployed this hermeneutical approach to Scripture, see for example Augustine, *City of God* 20.4, 17. Equally, this hermeneutical approach was presupposed by the earliest commentary on the Apocalypse, written by Victorinus of Petovium in ca. AD 258–260, as noted by William C. Weinrich in ACT/L, xxii–xxiii. Among contemporary practitioners of this reading of Scripture we may highlight the biblical scholar N. T. Wright together with Oliver O'Donovan, for instance. Of the former, see in particular Wright, *New Testament and the People*, 132, 141–143, 456–464; Wright, "Narrative Theology," 189–200.

90. Closer views to our construal of the Fellowship of the Throne may be found in Bauckham, *Theology of the Book of Revelation*, 143; O'Donovan, *Ways of Judgment*, 241.

91. "To make a representation of Christian teaching is to construe it, to commend a version of it which may not be made up but is certainly made." Webster, "Introduction," 7.

John's Apocalypse[92] that deal with these themes in similar ways.[93] They are as follows:

First, the Hebrew/Israelite tradition,[94] that is the theological matrix for the Apocalypse as already alluded to above when we referred to some Old Testament theological motifs. Within this tradition the story of the Exodus in particular is highly relevant, since it relates how YHWH brought the Israelites out of Egypt to make them a kingdom of priests and a holy nation (Exod 19:4–6; cf. Rev 1:6; 5:10), that is to say, a liturgical sociality where he would be their God (Exod 20:2–5; cf. Rev 21:7), their one and only God (Deut 6:4),[95] and therefore, their king (cf. 1 Sam 12:12; Exod 15:18). In this model of divine authority and sociality, Moses mediated communication between (a) YHWH and the people of Israel (e.g. Exod 3:15; 19:8–10; 20:16, 19; Deut 34:10), and between (b) YHWH and the former oppressive human authority, the Pharaoh (Exod 7:1). However, with the establishment of the Israelite monarchy the human king took over some of YHWH's responsibilities towards his people,[96] now ruling over them (1 Sam 8:20; cf. 12:12; 1 Chron 16:31) and fighting their wars (1 Sam 8:20; cf. Exod 14:14, 25; Josh 10:14; cf. Rev 19:11). This explains why at Solomon's accession to the throne, all the assembly of Israel bowed

---

92. Arguably John's *Apocalypse* bears the marks of a mid- to late-first-century AD document, or of an early second-century AD one at the latest. Two main scholarly views on the date of the Apocalypse, the so called Neronian (i.e. AD pre-70) and Domitianic (i.e. ca. AD 95) dates, are still highly contested. A survey of the arguments in favour of each view is offered in Guthrie, *New Testament Introduction*, 948–962; cf. Marshal, Howard, Travis, and Paul, *Exploring the New Testament*, 326–328. J. A. T. Robinson tracks scholarly fashions on the dating of the New Testament documents, including the Apocalypse, for the nineteenth and twentieth centuries. See Robinson, *Redating the New Testament*, 1–12. In particular, he highlights the shift of the scholarly consensus from the Neronian to the Domitianic date at the turn of the past century in the UK, represented by J. B. Lightfoot and R. H. Charles, respectively. See, Robinson, *Redating the New Testament*, 224–226; cf. Wilson, "Problem of the Domitianic Date," 587–589. Ian Boxall has noted, perspicaciously, that "much of the internal evidence is ambiguous, susceptible to interpretations which support datings in the late 60s or early-to-mid-90s." Boxall, *Revelation of Saint John*, 10.

93. An instance of a work on comparative political theology is Lauderville, *Piety and Politics*. In particular, see Lauderville, 3.

94. See O'Donovan's apologia on the right (and wrong) ways of using the Old Testament in political theology in O'Donovan, *Desire of the Nations*, 27–29; cf. O'Donovan, "Response to Gordon McConville," 89–90. For a critique of the confessional character of so-called minimalist/sceptical historical approaches to the history of Israel see Provan, Long, and Longman III, *Biblical History of Israel*, 3–35; cf. Kitchen, *Reliability of the Old Testament*, 1–6, 449–500; Walton, *Ancient Near Eastern Thought*, 15–18.

95. See McConville, *God and Earthly Power*, 20.

96. See O'Donovan, *Desire of the Nations*, 53–56.

down and prostrated/worshipped (?) YHWH and the king (1 Chron 29:20), with Solomon described as sitting on YHWH's throne as king (1 Chron 29:23). This is one instance in the Old Testament where we get very close to the Apocalypse's Fellowship of the Throne.[97]

Second, the Greek theo-political tradition, relevant since John's Apocalypse is addressed to an *ekklesia* (assembly/congregation), a term borrowed from Greek thought in which it was regarded as "the assembly of adult male citizens which had the ultimate decision-making power in a Greek state."[98] In the Apocalypse, it is presumed that the *ekklesia* is in the midst of a polis (city).[99] As for the idea of the polis, this was fundamental in Greek theo-political thought, since it was regarded "a city of gods as well as a city of humankind . . . Spatially, the civic *agora*, the human 'place of gathering', and the *akropolis*, the 'high city' where the gods typically had their abode, were the twin, symbiotic nodes of ancient Greek political networking."[100] This theo-spatial design of the city is made explicit in Plato's works, for instance

> the legislator's first job is to locate the city as precisely as possible in the center of the country, provided that the site he chooses is a convenient one for a city in all other respects too . . . Next he must divide the country into twelve sections. But first he ought to reserve a sacred area for Hestia, Zeus and Athena (calling it the "acropolis"), and enclose its boundaries; he will then divide

---

97. A second instance in the Old Testament, more apocalyptic in nature, is the vision and interpretation recorded in Daniel 7, in particular the vision of the enthronement of one like a son of man by the Ancient of Days (7:13–14) following the previous dethronement of four beasts (7:11–12). In the interpretation of this vision it is "the people of the holy ones of the Most High" who are enthroned (7:27 NRSV). Therefore, what Daniel 7 keeps theologically apart (i.e. the Ancient of Days, like a son of man, the people), Revelation 22:3–5 unites christologically (i.e. God, the Lamb and his servants) in what we call the Fellowship of the Throne.

98. Roberts, *Oxford Dictionary of the Classical World*, s.v. "ekklesia"; cf. Aristotle, *Politics* 2.6.19 (1266a10); 3.11.15–16 (1282a25+); 3.14.4 (1285a10+).

99. See Rev 1:4, 11; 2:1, 7, 12, 18; 3:1, 7, 14. "Much of our political terminology is Greek in etymology," Cartledge, "Greek Political Thought," 11. It should be noted, however, that the Apocalypse draws its theo-political categories mainly from its Israelite/Jewish matrix, in particular the Old Testament, as already observed. For a Christian understanding of *ekklesia* see Weissenrieder, "Contested Spaces in 1 Corinthians," 86–107; Wannenwetsch, *Political Worship*, 137–145.

100. Cartledge, "Greek Political Thought," 14.

the city itself and the whole country into twelve sections by lines radiating from this central point.[101]

Equally important to the design and *politeia* (constitution) of the city was its protection and government, which becomes one of the key themes addressed in Plato's magnum opus, the *Republic*. In fact, it may be argued that in this work Socrates, the lead character construed by Plato, is involved in a quest for the ultimate embodiment of (human) authority, the guardian of the city,[102] culminating with the figure of the philosopher-king.[103] In this Platonic instance of the Greek tradition are included the model of authority (the guardian) and sociality (the polis) and their divine orientation (the acropolis).

Third, there is the Roman theo-political tradition, a version of which the Apocalypse criticizes from a Christian theo-political standpoint in Revelation 13 and 17–19, for instance.[104] However, earlier versions of this Roman tradition distanced themselves from developments within the Greek/Hellenistic tradition, which resulted in the deification of its ruler, the absolute King,[105] and arguably "anticipated the establishment of the official state cult of the emperor, viewing the Roman emperor as a successor of the Hellenistic kings."[106] In particular, one of these earlier versions is Cicero's *On the Commonwealth* (*De Re Publica*), which "was the first, and perhaps the only serious attempt by a Roman to analyze the structure and values of republican government and imperial rule."[107] We find the Ciceronian view of the *res publica* (instead

---

101. Plato, *Laws* 5.745b-c, as translated by Trevor J. Saunders in *Plato: Complete Works*.
102. cf. Plato, *Republic* 2.374d.
103. cf. Plato, *Republic* 5.473c-e.
104. It should be said that John of the Apocalypse was a trailblazer for a Christian theo-political critique of a heretical mode of authority and liturgical sociality (i.e. empire), see O'Donovan, "History and Politics," 30–42. Augustine followed John's steps in his magisterial *City of God*, "a critique of Rome's morality and theology, suggesting that these were shadows of what is true." Phillips, *Political Theology*, 23. John of the Apocalypse could also be described as a pioneer of *Kulturkritik* and Critical Theory from a Christian theological standpoint, if this is basically understood as "the development of analyses of culture and theories of culture," Ward, *Theology and Contemporary Critical Theory*, xii.
105. If compared with the Platonic model of guardians and polis, the Hellenistic model saw the rise of an absolute guardian (the king) who suffocated not just one polis but a network of them; see Garnsey, "Introduction," 401–402.
106. Garnsey, "Introduction," 406. For a more nuanced understanding of this topic, see Price, *Rituals and Power*.
107. Zetzel, *Cicero*, xvii. "The titles of Cicero's twin volumes *de Re Publica* and *de Legibus* betray his ambitions: to do for Roman political theory what his master Plato had done for

of the Greek polis) to be framed in terms of a divine orientation: "Our home is not the one bounded by our walls, but this whole universe, which the gods have given us as a home and a country to be shared with them."[108] Equally, it shows a preference for some degree of participation from each of the actors in his res publican model:

> of the three primary forms my own preference is for monarchy; but monarchy itself is surpassed by a government which is balanced and compounded from the three primary forms of commonwealth. I approve of having something outstanding and monarchic in a commonwealth; of there being something else assigned to the authority of aristocrats; of some things being set aside for the judgment and wishes of the people. This structure has, in the first place, a certain degree of equality . . . it also has solidity . . . There is no reason for revolution when each person is firmly set in his own rank, without the possibility of sudden collapse.[109]

However, the Ciceronian ideal failed to prevent revolution from within,[110] and civil war broke out between Pompey and Julius Caesar, from which the latter emerged victorious.[111] Following Caesar's death Rome witnessed the rise of a new quasi monarchical order embodied by Octavian Augustus,[112] whose *Res Gestae Divi Augusti* was prefaced as follows: "Below is a copy of the achievements of the deified Augustus, by which he made the world subject to the rule of the Roman people, and of the expenses which he incurred for the state and people of Rome, as inscribed upon two bronze columns which have been set up at Rome."[113] In other words, the *Res Publica* imagined by Cicero

---

Greek." Atkins, "Cicero," 489. In connection with this, it has been suggested that Augustine's title of his book, the City of God, "marks a conscious contrast with the Republic of either Plato or Cicero, indeed of both." Chadwick, *Augustine of Hippo*, 129.

108. Cicero, *On the Commonwealth* 1.19.

109. Cicero, 1.69.

110. See Lintott, "Crisis of the Republic," 6. Arguably, Cicero wrote *On the Commonwealth* between ca. 55–51 BC; see Zetzel, *Cicero*, x.

111. Julius Caesar, *Civil War* 3.85–106; see Cassius Dio, *Roman History* 42.18–19; Suetonius, *Deified Julius Caesar*, 35.

112. See Garnsey, "Introduction," 406.

113. Augustus, *Res Gestae Divi Augusti* heading, as translated in Cooley, *Res Gestae Divi Augusti*.

had lost its balance, and its monarchical component had stifled the role of the (legislative) aristocrats and the (judging) people, enabling Augustus to declare: "When I was holding my thirteenth consulship [2 BC], the senate and equestrian order and people of Rome all together hailed me as father of the fatherland."[114] It is precisely Augustus's political and liturgical emergent order and legacy that the Apocalypse critically engages in its visions.

1.3 Thesis

In locating the (apocalyptic) construal of the Fellowship of the Throne within its wider ancient theo-political context, and highlighting the various traditions the Apocalypse drew from (Israelite/Jewish) and critically engaged with (Roman, and indirectly through it, Greek/Hellenist), it follows that our approach to the Apocalypse must be theo-political in nature. Equally, since the Apocalypse anticipates, even in first-century AD Patmos (1:9; cf. 3:12, 20–21), the materialization of the Fellowship of the Throne, this in turn becomes the ultimate horizon of the political. As a result, focusing on the development of the two components of the Fellowship of the Throne (authority and sociality) and their correlation, and ordering a theo-political inquiry based on the terms set out by O'Donovan, this thesis will show that divine authority, as signified by the throne, undergoes a christological shift because of the exalted Jesus. After all, "to speak of divine authority after the resurrection of Christ is to speak of the authority of the exalted Christ."[115] In connection with this, the narrative registers an (ontological) attempt to prevent this shift, and a historical/eschatological challenge by a heretical mode of authority to the christologically re-defined divine authority. In turn, this exegetical analysis will lead to a critical interaction with O'Donovan's model of human political authority and its post-resurrection subsidiary role.[116]

This thesis will go on to show that the liturgical sociality is predicated on the (mediating) presence of the exalted Jesus in its midst despite the absence

---

114. Augustus, *Res Gestae Divi Augusti* 35.1. This title was also granted previously to Julius Caesar, see Cassius Dio, *Roman History* 44.4.

115. O'Donovan, *Resurrection and Moral Order*, 141.

116. See O'Donovan, 127–130; O'Donovan, *Desire for the Nations*, 146–157; O'Donovan, *Ways of Judgment*, 127–148.

of any explicit sacramental discourse, (e.g. baptism and Eucharist),[117] if a minimalistic sacramental view is taken following the New Testament and Augustinian trend;[118] though if marriage (19:7, 9; cf. 18:23) is regarded a sacrament, then this becomes the exception in the Apocalypse's lack of explicit sacramental discourse.[119] As a result this work will argue that this christological cohesion and mediation makes the liturgical sociality subservient only to the divine throne. This exegetical analysis will again lead to a critical interaction with O'Donovan's model of the church as the visible expression of the divine authority,[120] whose institutional form and order is defined by the sacraments.[121]

1.4 Mode of Inquiry

It should be noted that our inquiry is predicated on what may be regarded (at least by some) as the default theological task (i.e. "theology is largely biblical interpretation").[122] Thus, for a practitioner of political theology as Oliver O'Donovan, "if the notion of a 'political theology' is not to be a chimera, they

---

117. With reference to Rev 3:20, Oecumenius (ca. 600 AD) noted "That supper that is with the Lord signifies the reception of the holy mysteries." Oecumenius, *Commentary on the Apocalypse, Third Discourse* (ACT/G). However, slightly earlier than Oecumenius, Apringius of Beja wrote (again, on 3:20) "Our salvation, the Lord Jesus Christ, stands and knocks on the door of our heart. Whoever awakens from his serious sins and will cast away the bond of wickedness and the suffocation of the heart, he will without doubt enter and will eat with him, and he will fill him with the delights or righteousness." Apringius of Beja, *Explanation of the Revelation, Revelation 3*, (ACT/L); cf. Jerome, *Homilies on the Psalms* 9, as quoted in Weinrich, *Revelation*, 54. Since then a variety of interpretations on 3:20 have been advanced. More recently George Caird revived Oecumenius's view, see Caird, *Revelation of St. John* , 58; cf. Boxall, *Revelation of Saint John*, 78. However, alternative views are advocated by Bauckham, *Climax of the Prophecy*, 104–109; Aune, *Revelation 1–5*, 260–261; Rowland, "Book of Revelation," 587; Beale, *Book of Revelation*, 307–309.

118. In the New Testament baptism is clearly prescribed in Matt 28:19 (cf. Eph 4:5); whereas "communion" is expressly prescribed in Luke 22:17–19 and 1 Cor 11:23–26. With reference to Augustine, see for instance Augustine, *Letter 54* 1.1 (NPNF1/1).

119. There is also the reference to the Lord's Day (Rev 1:10), whose keeping O'Donovan would consider a sacrament, see O'Donovan, *Desire of the Nations*, 186.

120. See O'Donovan, *Desire of the Nations*, 158–192; O'Donovan, *Ways of Judgment*, 231–319.

121. See O'Donovan, *Desire of the Nations*, 172.

122. Vanhoozer, *Is there a Meaning*, 9. One of David Ford's twelve thesis for twenty-first century Christian theology affirms that the "study of Scripture is at the heart of theology." Ford, *Shaping Theology*, 243; Ford, "Epilogue," 761.

must be authorised, as any datum of theology must be, from Holy Scripture."[123] Accordingly, since its inception this thesis was conceived as inhabiting the intersection of two fields of knowledge within the wider epistemic horizon of theology (i.e. biblical studies and systematic theology), as attested by the joint supervision it had benefitted throughout from Professor Edward Adams (biblical studies) and the Revd Professor Ben Quash (systematic theology). It is Scripture,[124] in this case the Apocalypse and its many allusions to the Old Testament, which has enabled the inquisitive meeting and interaction between these two disciplines, not least because the church tradition that has nurtured the confessional stance of the present writer acknowledges the centrality and authoritative role of Scripture in personal matters as well as church life.[125] And to close the virtuous epistemological circle, in the words of Karl Barth, "theology is a function of the Church."[126]

However, as already noted, the parting of the ways between biblical studies and systematic theology highlights the challenge for this thesis to bring together what even today some scholars try to keep apart.[127] It should be said

---

123. O'Donovan, *Desire of the Nations*, 15.

124. Alternative construals of Scripture are as follows: (i) "The Word of God is God Himself in Holy Scripture . . . Scripture is holy and the Word of God, because by the Holy Spirit it became and will become to the Church a witness to divine revelation." (Barth, *Church Dogmatics*, I/2, 457); (ii) "*To attest the texts of the Old and New Testaments as 'Scripture' is to make specific claims about this text . . . Scripture is not first a source for historical inquiry, nor a text that delights our literary sensitivities; calling these collected texts 'Scripture' points to its commissioned role in the saving purposes of God.*" (Paddison, *Scripture*, 1 [original emphasis]).

125. Oscar Gutiérrez offers a historical account of how the Bible played a key role in the emergence and shape of protestant and evangelical communities in Mexico since the mid-nineteenth century on, see Gutiérrez Baqueiro, "Influencia de la Biblia," 288–295. For a descriptive theological account of the role of the Bible that resonates with this church tradition see Larsen, "Defining and Locating," 7–9; cf. Bebbington, *Evangelicalism in Modern Britain*, 2–4; Wells, "Evangelical Theology," 608–609. Speaking about his evangelical church tradition, O'Donovan observes that "formal theological study confirmed me in a strong commitment to the Scriptures as the norm of all theology" (Shortt, *God's Advocates*, 265). As for the book of Revelation, the text itself conveys its expected authoritative and normative role within the communities of their addressees, see Revelation 1:3; 22:7, 18–19; cf. Apringius of Beja, *Explanation of the Revelation* 1.3 (ACT/L); Andrew of Caesarea, *Commentary on the Apocalypse* 24.72 (ACT/G); Mangina, *Revelation*, 40–41, 253.

126. Barth, *Church Dogmatics*, I/1, 3.

127. Accounts and confessional (i.e. ideological) reasons as to why to throw a cordon sanitaire around biblical studies in order to protect them from systematic theology are offered, among others, by (1) Green, "Scripture and Theology," 23–43; (2) Hays, "Reading the Bible," 7–11; (3) Paddison, *Scripture*, 122–144. For a critique of the modern construal of a supposedly neutral or objective exegesis of the biblical text see Smith, *Who's Afraid of Postmodernism?*, 31–58.

that this parting of the ways has contributed to some extent to the emergence of the so called theological interpretation of the Bible, whose premises as articulated by Kevin Vanhoozer,[128] for instance, this present writer finds quite sympathetic. More importantly, as suggested by O'Donovan,

> in any branch of theology concepts mediate between the reading of the scriptural text (the lector's task) and the construction of theory (the theologian's). Theory has to respond to the concepts found in Scripture, and its adequacy as theology will be measured by how well it has responded to them. Identifying concepts comes before constructing theory; but it comes after reading the text.[129]

In other words, "it is an *exegetical* task."[130] Accordingly, our inquiry, framed within O'Donovan's terms for a christological political theology, surveys the narrative of the Apocalypse in order to identify the key categories (or concepts) of divine authority and liturgical sociality in order to theologically construe the Fellowship of the Throne, from which we engage with ancient (Plato, Cicero, Augustus) and modern (O'Donovan) construals of authority and society and their correlation. In connection with this, in the course of our work occasional references to the Hebrew and Greek form of some words is made to highlight a particular concept in discussion. When this is the case, we follow the conventions for entries (whether nouns, adjectives or verbs) in dictionaries like HALOT (Hebrew) and BDAG or LSJ (Greek).

1.5 Structure

Having established the two main arguments of this study and explained our mode of inquiry, we now outline the order of our inquiry, which is comprised

---

128. See Vanhoozer, "What is Theological Interpretation," 19–25. In particular, Vanhoozer notes that "Theological interpretation of the Bible . . . is biblical interpretation oriented to the knowledge of God" (Vanhoozer, 24). For other advocates of this hermeneutical movement see Green, "The (Re-)Turn to Theology," 1–3; Hays, "Reading the Bible"; Moberly, "What Is Theological Interpretation," 161–178; Allen, "Theological Commentary," 1–9; Paddison, *Scripture*. For both a critique and a qualified endorsement of this hermeneutical movement see Carson, "Theological Interpretation of Scripture," 187–207.

129. O'Donovan, *Desire of the Nations*, 15.

130. O'Donovan, 16. "Exegetical theology investigates biblical teaching as the basis of our talk about God" (Barth, *Church Dogmatics*, I/1, 16).

of three parts in addition to this introduction (chapter 1) and a conclusion (chapter 8).

Part I will set out the framework for our inquiry, offering in chapter 2 a more detailed account of O'Donovan's exegetical model which shapes his political theology, and which in turn has enabled him to recover the notion of authority, the acknowledgment of which serves to confirm the political identity of a society.[131] Also, we will consider how this model has influenced his reading of the Apocalypse. Chapter 3 will provide the backdrop for our work on the book of Revelation by offering a narrative reading of it through which we shall be able to trace the origin of the expectation, development and materialization of the Fellowship of the Throne.

Part II will present our first thesis, starting with chapter 4 in an exegetical exploration of the Apocalypse's construal of divine authority as the correlation of power and divine status between the one who sits on the throne and the exalted Jesus, where the latter is portrayed as the Son of God, the Lamb, the Messiah and the divine King. In connection with this, we will consider the frustrated attempt to prevent this re-definition of divine authority, and a subsequent challenge to it. For its part, chapter 5 will briefly discuss Platonic (i.e. Greek) and Roman construals of human political authority, two archetypal models that anticipated the idealist and realist "strands of Western political thought,"[132] in order to better understand O'Donovan's and see where it stands in relation to them, and then proceed to a critique of all of them from the standpoint of the Apocalypse's construal of divine authority (i.e. the input provided by chapter 4), as expected from "a political theology shaped by the Christ-event."[133]

Next, part III will consider our second thesis by exegetically examining in chapter 6 the Apocalypse's construal of a liturgical sociality, predicated on the mediating presence of the exalted Jesus, as (a) the re-envisioning of sacral space, and (b) the motif of the holy city, whether in the making or eschatologically materialized. Chapter 7 will briefly explore Platonic and Roman arguments for what unites a community, and then proceed to engage

---

131. See O'Donovan, *Desire of the Nations*, 47.
132. O'Donovan, *Ways of Judgment*, 13.
133. O'Donovan, *Desire of the Nations*, 122.

critically with O'Donovan's model of the church as a political society from Revelation's construal of the liturgical sociality.

Lastly, chapter 8, a conclusion as already mentioned, will bring to a close this theo-political inquiry into the Apocalypse's Fellowship of the Throne.

Part I

Method

CHAPTER 2

O'Donovan's Theo-Political Hermeneutics

The resurgence of political theology at the turn of the millennium,[1] concomitant, it seems, with the failure of the so-called secularization theory,[2] on the one hand, and of the exhaustion of the secular discourse on the other,[3] has been impacted by the emergence of Oliver O'Donovan's project, carried out in close collaboration with his wife Joan.[4] There remain, however, some contemporary voices that claim political theology should retreat back into exile from intellectual and public life,[5] voices with which O'Donovan engages in an apologia for a political theology articulated in the first chapter of *The Desire of the Nations*. In this work he counters some of the objections shaped by "the modern tradition of separating politics from theology,"[6] such as those put

---

1. See de Vries and Sullivan, *Political Theologies*, 3; Cavanaugh, Bailey and Hovey, *Eerdmans Reader*, xvi–xx. For a more comprehensive archeology or genealogy of political theology see Phillips, *Political Theology*, 11–30.

2. Peter Berger's recantation of his secularization theory is conveyed in Berger, "Desecularization of the World," 1–18. For an alternative account of the secular condition see Taylor, *Secular Age*.

3. See Habermas, "Relations Between the Secular," 260. For other voices advocating a postsecular world, see Smith, "Secularity, Globalization," 9; Sigurdson, "Beyond Secularism?," 178–184.

4. The O'Donovans have contributed to the recovery of a Christian tradition on political theology with the publication of their *From Irenaeus to Grotius: A Sourcebook in Christian Political Thought*, a collection of texts from the patristic age to the early modern period.

5. See Ekins, "Secular Fundamentalism," 81.

6. O'Donovan, *Desire of the Nations*, 6.

forward by Mark Lilla, whose view of an immanent history in pursuit of human progress disposes of what he considers as an archaic political theology.[7]

History is precisely what O'Donovan suggests Christian theology must accept "as the matrix in which politics and ethics take form," while setting out to "affirm that it is the history of God's action, not sheer contingency but [imbued with] purpose."[8] O'Donovan points out, however, that "the wisest advocates of political theology have understood that they must find a more objective point of reference for their work than the historical dialectic,"[9] and that "if the notion of a 'political theology' is not to be a chimera, they must be authorised, as any datum of theology must be, from Holy Scripture. Nothing assures us a priori that politico-theological concepts are to be found; the question of their existence must be put to Scripture itself."[10] Therefore,

> theory has to respond to the concepts found in Scripture, and its adequacy as theology will be measured by how well it has responded to them. Identifying concepts comes before constructing theory; but it comes after reading the text, for it is not a matter simply of emphasising key words in the text . . . the words themselves are not the concepts but are like flags on a map which signal their presence. It is an *exegetical* task.[11]

---

7. Lilla, *Stillborn God*, 4–5; cf. Kirwan, *Political Theology*, 3.
8. O'Donovan, *Desire of the Nations*, 12.
9. O'Donovan, 12.
10. O'Donovan, 15.
11. O'Donovan, 15–16. Interestingly enough, O'Donovan's method is but one of several approaches embraced by practitioners of political theology, which according to a taxonomy construed by Elizabeth Phillips may be based on (1) theological understandings of creation, fall and human nature, for example pessimism (Augustine) versus optimism (Aquinas), covenant (Calvin) versus Leviathan (Hobbes, Carl Schmitt); (2) theological traditions (Catholic, Lutheran, Reformed, Anglican, Eastern Orthodox); (3) twentieth-century scholarship, i.e. Political Theology (Johann Baptist Metz, Jürgen Moltmann, Dorothee Sölle), Public Theology (David Tracy, Richard John Neuhaus, Max Stackhouse), and Liberation Theology; and (4) emergent schools of thought, or second generation of political theologies such as Postliberalism (Stanley Hauerwas, Oliver O'Donovan), Radical Orthodoxy (John Milbank, Graham Ward, Catherine Pickstock), and contextual theologies (e.g. replicas of liberation theology in other parts of the world). On this see Phillips, *Political Theology*, 31–54; see also Bretherton, "Introduction," 268, who distinguishes between Augustinian-Reformed, Aristotelian-Thomistic, and Anabaptist/Radical Reformation traditions (or trajectories). A feature of the political theologies developed by O'Donovan and Radical Orthodoxy, for instance, is the inclusion of a genealogy and critique of secular reason, following overarching historico-theological trajectories, see O'Donovan, *Desire of the Nations*, 193–284; O'Donovan and O'Donovan, *Bonds of Imperfection*, 2–14;

Consequently, O'Donovan picks up the concept of authority in Scripture, which he renders hermeneutically as "the reign of God," or "the kingdom of God."[12] In turn, this epistemic move allows him to map political history onto the history of God's reign as conveyed by Scripture, a mapping that frees "modern historicism from its always-disturbing suggestions of arbitrariness."[13] Thus, O'Donovan sees a threefold epistemic benefit in this approach:

(a) "the history of divine rule safeguards and redeems the goods of creation. Divine rule is not the *potentia absoluta* that underlies the bare fact of creation itself, but the *potentia ordinata* which works within the covenant that is established through creation."[14] Accordingly, divine rule makes possible the full realization of any element of creation, and that includes human beings. What is more, "to judge politics in the light of the divine rule is to be assured of its world-affirming and humane character."[15]

(b) If history is the history of God's reign, then we have to rethink our concept or idea of authority. Specifically, our focus moves away from "the authority of institutions" and centres instead on "a human act, the 'political act'... which, performed by one or few on behalf of many, witnesses faithfully to the presence and future of what God has undertaken for all."[16] That is to say, "the political act is the divinely authorised act. A political theology will seek to understand how and why God's rule confers authority upon such acts."[17] The shift from political institutions to the political act in this construal of authority is due to the fact that political institutions, after all, change from time to time, and their shape, according to O'Donovan, depends on God's

---

Milbank, *Theology and Social Theory*; Smith, *Introducing Radical Orthodoxy*, 87–89; Shortt, *God's Advocates*, 103–111, 248–257. For a brief critique of them see Shortt, 61–66, 97, for instance.

12. O'Donovan, *Desire of the Nations*, 17–19.
13. O'Donovan, 19.
14. O'Donovan, 19. According to Alister McGrath, William of Ockham coined these two expressions. The "'absolute power of God' (*potentia absoluta*) refers to the options that existed before God had committed himself to any course of action or world ordering. The 'ordained power of God' (*potentia ordinata*) refers to the order established by God their creator as an expression of the divine nature and character. The 'two powers of God' do not refer to two different sets of options now open to God. Rather, they refer to two different moments in the history of salvation." McGrath, *Christian Theology*, 210.
15. O'Donovan, *Desire of the Nations*, 19.
16. O'Donovan, 20.
17. O'Donovan, 20.

providence.[18] In other words, O'Donovan sees the historical shift that has tied authority to an office or a political institution, in the West, as a consequence of the loss of theological ground by politics. And yet, "a truthful description of the political act, which will establish its conditions, purpose and mode of execution, will also shed light upon political institutions."[19]

(c) If history is the history of God's reign, it "is presented to us as a *revealed* history which takes form quite particularly as the history of Israel. Against this canonical history our understanding of general and universal history as a whole must be measured."[20] Of course, this proposal calls for a (cautious) hermeneutical strategy, in particular when dealing with Israel in the Old Testament, because "the history of a nation, even the history of the ideas that were important to that nation, will not constitute a theology on its own, but only as we trace the truth of God's rule unfolded in the sequence of events and cultural periods of that nation's life."[21]

2.1 Principles for Engaging O'Donovan

It should be noted that this study's pursuit of a theo-political inquiry into divine authority and liturgical sociality guided by O'Donovan's political theology sets itself within the recent scholarly tradition of critical interaction – whether face-to-face and/or written – with O'Donovan's wider-in-scope work on theology, politics and ethics. To mention just three instances of this mode of critical interaction, there are the (editorial and/or face-to-face) critical interchanges between biblical scholars (Old and New Testament scholars), theologians (systematicians, moral and ethicists), political theorists, lawyers and philosophers, on the one hand, and O'Donovan himself, on the other,

---

18. O'Donovan, 20. "Theologians, in pointing to [divine] providence as the source of political authority, understood it as a service of human progress, securing the social world in the face of disintegration and preparing it for its goal in redemption." O'Donovan, *Ways of Judgment*, 134.

19. O'Donovan, *Desire of the Nations*, 20.

20. O'Donovan, 21.

21. O'Donovan, 29.

convened by Linda Woodhead,[22] Craig Bartholomew,[23] and Luke Bretherton,[24] respectively. If we survey these records of critical interaction, we would note the varied routes for engagement with O'Donovan's work, which are broadly speaking set out according to method (e.g. biblical exegesis, hermeneutics) or content (an argument advanced in any of his books), where the contributor offers their respective appraisal and/or critique. Alternatively, the contributor may be focusing on an aspect of O'Donovan's work in order to advance their own point of interest, which may in turn resonate with O'Donovan's theological interests.[25] However, heuristically speaking, it would appear that contributors to these critical engagements (a) approach O'Donovan's work from their area of interest or expertise (e.g. biblical studies, theology, ethics, law studies, political theory, philosophy, etc.), (b) select a book(s), a theme or an idea of O'Donovan's, (c) summarize it, (d) assess it and criticize it, and hopefully (e) are met with a response from him.

As for ourselves, since this thesis was conceived and structured around two key concepts in O'Donovan's political theology (i.e. authority and society and how they are correlated),[26] our own approach and critical engagement with O'Donovan's work follows a rationale which can be conveyed in four principles. First, as is customary in scholarly circles, we have read and become familiar with a wide selection of O'Donovan's scholarly output (as shown in the bibliography at the end of this book, including his "trilogy" *Resurrection and Moral Order*, *The Desire of the Nations*, and *The Ways of Judgment*,[27] on which see §1.1) in order to (a) have a good grasp of O'Donovan's overall (theo-political) thought, (b) attain a deeper understanding of his key theo-political concepts, and (c) understand how his ideas have developed and evolved with time. Second, and as a result, we have provided in the introduction to this work (§1.1) a summary of the key concepts of O'Donovan's political

---

22. As recorded in the August 1998 edition of the journal *Studies in Christian Ethics*. In particular, see Woodhead, "Editorial," ix.

23. As recorded in Bartholomew, Chaplin, Song and Wolters, *Royal Priesthood*. In particular, see Bartholomew, "Introduction," 1–45.

24. As recorded in the 2008 edition of the journal *Political Theology* 9, no. 3. In particular, see Bretherton, "Introduction," 265–271.

25. See for example, Wright, "Paul and Caesar," 173–193.

26. O'Donovan, *Desire of the Nations*, 193.

27. O'Donovan's fondness for triloguies, whether on political theology or theological ethics, comes more transparent in O'Donovan, *Self, World, and Time*.

theology, and in addition, we offer in this chapter (i.e. chapter 2) a more extensive account of O'Donovan's hermeneutics and theo-political model which connects the key concepts of authority and society. Third, equipped with this O'Dovanian theo-political framework, we set in motion our own critical conversation with O'Donovan in the following manner:

(i) Each successive chapter (i.e. chapters 3 to 7) opens with a reference to one of O'Donovan's ideas or concepts on hermeneutics and political theology in order to guide the question to be addressed by that chapter.

(ii) Chapters 3, 4 and 6 develop their own argument from the perspective of the Apocalypse, referring to O'Donovan's ideas or concepts from time to time in order to align and maintain this ongoing conversation with O'Donovan's theo-political framework.

(iii) Chapters 5 and 7, however, provide a more comprehensive account of O'Donovan's view on authority and society. In other words, these chapters allow the reader to hear O'Donovan's voice, while at the same time continuing to provide a space for the present writer's critique of O'Donovan's models of authority and society from the perspective gained in chapters 3, 4 and 6, that is to say, from the perspective of the Apocalypse. To put it another way, an ongoing critical conversation takes place between the voices of the Apocalypse and O'Donovan on the key concepts of authority and society and their correlation; voices, it should be said, mediated by the present writer.[28]

(iv) In addition, since the Apocalypse is regarded as Scripture ($1.4), its critique of O'Donovan's concepts will be given preeminence in our arguments.

Finally, it should be noted that O'Donovan's reading of the Apocalypse has equally been considered as part of our reading list for this thesis, and we refer to it from time to time, and engage with it as part of our wider critique of his

---

28. "As soon as there is mediation, there is interpretation . . . But was there ever a time without interpretation? Will there ever be a time when we don't interpret?" Smith, *Who's Afraid of Postmodernism*, 36.

work. We now turn to offer an extensive account of O'Donovan's hermeneutics and theo-political model on authority and society.

2.2 Hermeneutical Framework

Embedded political theology in revealed history is a feature of the biblical narrative right from the outset. In particular, as biblical scholar Gordon Wenham introduces his exegetical work on the text of Genesis 1–11, he observes that this biblical text "is a commentary, often highly critical, on ideas current in the ancient world about the natural and supernatural world."[29] For instance,

> the tower of Babel story [in Gen 11:1–9], is a satire on the claims of Babylon to be the center of civilization and its temple tower the gate of heaven . . . Babel does not mean gate of God, but "confusion" and "folly." Far from its temple's top reaching up to heaven, it is so low that God has to descend from heaven just to see it![30]

Equally, "it seems that Gen 1–3 takes up the ideas current in the ancient world and comments on them. Gen 1 again affirms the unity of God over against the polytheisms current everywhere else in the Ancient Near East. In particular it insists that the sun, moon, stars, and sea monsters – powerful deities according to pagan mythology – are merely creatures."[31]

Nonetheless, Genesis 1–11 also offers an alternative and constructive theological account of divine and human reality.[32] Perhaps without realizing it, Wenham was stepping into the field of political theology, a view confirmed by biblical scholar J. Gordon McConville,[33] and arguably by theologian William Cavanaugh.[34] In particular, McConville elaborates on this feature of

---

29. Wenham, *Genesis 1–15*, xlvii.
30. Wenham, xlix.
31. Wenham, xlix.
32. Wenham, l.
33. See McConville, *God and Earthly Power*, 23–26.
34. "Humankind was created for communion, but is everywhere divided . . . this opening statement will serve as a somewhat bold summary of the book of Genesis, chapters 1–11 . . . Although at first sight Genesis and [Rousseau's] *The Social Contract* seem to be about quite different tasks, both are similarly engaged with foundational stories of human cooperation and division." Cavanaugh, *Theopolitical Imagination*, 9.

the biblical text that engages critically with its surrounding culture and also offers an alternative theological account of the divine being and the human sociality, thus leading him to develop an Old Testament political theology, which "can be viewed as a critical dialogue with the dominant powers in ancient Israel's world."³⁵ For him this theo-political enterprise "can hardly be understood apart from Genesis and Exodus in particular. The former establishes a relationship between Israel and creation, and between Israel and other nations. The latter tells the archetypal story of the exodus from Egypt, places Israel's covenant with Yahweh, and in the same connection proclaims the first laws."³⁶ As a result, McConville argues, "'the primary history' places Israel in relation to the other nations."³⁷ It is at this point within the flow of the biblical history of Israel that O'Donovan introduces his hermeneutical framework,³⁸ which he construes around the expression יְהוָה מלך (YHWH is king/YHWH reigns, e.g. Ps 93:1).

2.2.1 YHWH Is King

To begin with, this expression does not refer to "the *potentia absoluta* which philosophical theology ascribes to the divine creator on the brink, as it were, of creating, able to bring about this world of meaning that he has brought about but equally able to bring about alternatives."³⁹ On the contrary, presumably in the liturgical context of the First Temple period (as that offered by Psalm 93 for instance) this expression, which is about divine authority, "evokes free action because it holds out to the worshippers a fulfilment of their agency within the created order in which their agency has a place and meaning. Yhwh's kingship is not a creation *ex nihilo* but an act of providence, keeping faith with creation once made."⁴⁰ O'Donovan distils some theo-political implications resulting from this confessional expression: (i) it

---

35. McConville, *God and Earthly Power*, 30.

36. McConville, 30.

37. McConville, 31. In this thesis, McConville and (indirectly) Wenham have balanced a sort of deficit in O'Donovan's biblical survey of Israel's history and its potential for political theology, see McConville, ix.

38. For a scholarly exchange between critics (including McConville) of O'Donovan's reading of the Old Testament and O'Donovan himself, see Bartholomew et al., *Royal Priesthood*, 46–90.

39. O'Donovan, *Desire of the Nations*, 32.

40. O'Donovan, 32.

provided stability to the created geophysical order; (ii) it offered stability to the international geopolitical order in which the nation of Israel played a role; (iii) it fostered the conditions for the social order within Israel sanctioned by law and marked by justice, with a view to protect the most vulnerable people among them: "as Israel is situated among the nations, so are the poor and defenceless situated within Israel. He who cared for the welfare of a servile nation in Egypt cared for the welfare of a servile class in Israel."[41]

More importantly, when the political question in Israel is seen in the light of the claim יְהוָה מֶלֶךְ a number of political terms seem to revolve around the idea of YHWH's kingship. O'Donovan highlights three of them in particular: יְשׁוּעָה (salvation), מִשְׁפָּט (judgment) and נַחֲלָה (possession). To these he adds a fourth term, תְּהִלָּה (praise).[42] In his view, all these terms are relevant for his (exegetical) framework of political theology, and he explains each as follows.

Salvation, which though it connotes a military sense of victory, is usually found in acts of deliverance. Arguably, the Exodus is YHWH's act of deliverance par excellence (Exod 14:13; 15:2). "It is clear that the primary political implication of [salvation] is Israel's power to win military engagements, especially engagements against the odds."[43] O'Donovan sees YHWH's military victories interpreted as חֶסֶד (kindness, favour), as tokens of his unbreakable commitment to his covenant people. Also, his military victories are seen as צֶדֶק (rightness, righteousness), which O'Donovan translates as vindication or justification, because "we are in the fully public realm of a world court."[44] The painful transition into exile, in O'Donovan's view, only intensifies this link, as "the victory that Yhwh promises must inevitably have the force of a public rehabilitation of a disgraced and humiliated people."[45]

Judgment.[46] As king, YHWH works out a righteous judgment (Ps 99:4). "To judge is to make a distinction between the just and the unjust, or, more precisely, to bring the distinction which already exists between them into

---

41. O'Donovan, 33.
42. O'Donovan, 36; O'Donovan, *Ways of Judgment*, 142.
43. O'Donovan, *Desire of the Nations*, 36–37.
44. O'Donovan, 37.
45. O'Donovan, 37.
46. For an extended discussion of this theo-political category see O'Donovan, *Ways of Judgment*, 6–12.

the daylight of public observation."[47] YHWH's judgment is worked out at the individual level as well as at a national and international level (Ps 96:10), and usually has long-term implications. Judgment "is primarily a judicial performance."[48] Besides, O'Donovan thinks that "if history, for Israel, is the telling of Yhwh's acts to future generations, then law is the telling of his judgements, which, once given, are to be handed on."[49]

Possession. For Israel as a people, the land promised by YHWH to them was fundamental to his public order. In fact, "without the consciousness of something possessed and handed on from generation to generation there could be a theology of divine judgments but not a political theology, since it would never be clear how the judgments of God could give order and structure to a community and sustain it in being."[50] Now, YHWH's gift of the land to Israel operated at a corporate level as well as at tribal and familiar level. As well as possessing the land, Israel became YHWH's possession, and Israel also possessed the law. In short, "we may say that the land was the material cause of Yhwh's kingly rule, as judgment was the formal cause and his victories the efficient cause."[51]

Praise.[52] "The link which ties the exercise of Yhwh's kingly rule to the praise of his people is that as the people congregate to perform their act of praise, the political reality of Israel is displayed . . . The gathering of the congregation is the moment at which people's identity is disclosed."[53] To put it another way, it is because Israel was a worshipping community, that they were also a political community. Even individual praises, whatever their original motivation, were encouraged to be made public in the congregation, to be politicized (e.g. Ps 35:18; 40:9–10 MT [40:10 ET]). The scope of praises offered to YHWH went beyond the congregation itself: "some visions of the universal rule of Yhwh envisage a world-assembly of nations in Jerusalem, on the model of Israel's own pilgrim-feasts [Isa 2:3; Mic 4:2]."[54] Of course,

---

47. O'Donovan, *Desire of the Nations*, 38.
48. O'Donovan, 39.
49. O'Donovan, 39.
50. O'Donovan, 41.
51. O'Donovan, 41.
52. For example, Ps 22:4 MT (22:3 ET).
53. O'Donovan, *Desire of the Nations*, 47.
54. O'Donovan, 48.

Israel's were not the only praises recognising YHWH's rule, heaven constantly rendered the praise due YHWH (cf. Ps 50:6).

With reference to the "threefold analysis of divine rule as salvation, judgment and possession," O'Donovan suggests that it "will provide a framework for exploring the major questions about authority posed by the Western tradition."[55] In fact, he formulates two theorems based on this understanding of the expression "YHWH is king": (i) *"Political authority arises where power, the execution of right and the perpetuation of tradition are assured together in one coordinated agency."*[56] If one of those elements is missing or separated from the others, O'Donovan observes, there is no room for authority. At the same time, authority is subject to the changing nature of the social environment it works on. This leads to the second theorem. (ii) *"That any regime should actually come to hold authority, and should continue to hold it, is a work of divine providence in history, not a mere accomplishment of the human task of political service."*[57] O'Donovan points out that every political regime should be seen against the backcloth of God's historical divine rule. To put it another way, political history is mapped onto salvation history.

In relation to Israel's praise of YHWH, O'Donovan formulates a third theorem: *"In acknowledging political authority, society proves its political identity."*[58] In other words, "acknowledgment is the fundamental relation that obtains between a society and its own political authorities. It recognises them – not in the constitutive sense of conferring existence on them by recognition, but in the much more basic sense of simply acknowledging that they are there and that they are theirs."[59] Additionally, praise "is not a constitutive element of political authority alongside the other three. For it is not recognition, or consent, that *constitutes* political authority; yet the presence of political authority is *demonstrated* in recognition."[60]

---

55. O'Donovan, 45.
56. O'Donovan, 46; O'Donovan, *Ways of Judgment*, 142 (emphasis in original).
57. ODonovan, *Desire of the Nations*, 46 (emphasis in original).
58. O'Donovan, 47 (emphasis in original).
59. O'Donovan, 47.
60. O'Donovan, *Ways of Judgment*, 142.

2.2.2 Human Mediation

From the Exodus, leaving Egypt behind, to the settlement of the Promised Land and the charismatic leadership of the Judges, the rise of the Israelite monarchy in particular witnessed a more institutionalised form of mediation of divine authority. "The authority of Yhwh was, like Yhwh himself, imageless. Nobody could represent it. Yet it was shown forth on earth through cataclysmic events, not only of a natural but also of a political order. Human acts as well as earthquake and fire demonstrated his rule among his people. Immediacy and human mediation complemented each other in a delicate balance."[61] Exodus 20:19 makes this point, where Moses was asked to mediate between God and the people of Israel as the former talk to the latter. Yet, O'Donovan asks, "how could immediacy and mediation be understood in a complementary way when the people were no longer at Sinai, when the thunder and lightning and the sound of the trumpet were no longer to be heard? . . . The answer they reach is: Yhwh is immediately present in conquest, his presence is mediated in judgment; and he is present in a kind of concealed immediacy in the law."[62]

Over time, however, the monarchy played a key role in mediating divine authority, since (a) it assumed an institutionalized military function,[63] where the victories of the king, at least in the royal psalms, were understood as "won by Yhwh and granted by him as a favour to the king."[64] (b) As YHWH's representative the king exercised a judicial function. Based on Psalm 101, O'Donovan suggests the king "was required to promise just judgment not only in his own daily assizes, but through making worthy appointments to his household."[65] (c) "The most important thing the monarchy had to offer Israel was the function of continuity, ensuring an unbroken tradition in the occupation of the territory and the perpetuation of the national identity."[66] All in all, "the king marched at the head of Israel's armies, and upheld Israel's identity in its struggles with neighbors and enemies; furthermore, he embodied and

---

61. O'Donovan, *Desire of the Nations*, 49.
62. O'Donovan, 50.
63. See O'Donovan, 53.
64. O'Donovan, 57.
65. O'Donovan, 56–57.
66. O'Donovan, 61.

safeguarded Israel's identity by the careful study of Israel's laws."[67] In addition, as YHWH's son (Ps 2:7) the king played "a role of double representation: he represented Yhwh's rule to the people, ensuring their obedience, and he represented the people to Yhwh, ensuring his constant favour."[68] And yet, within this context, O'Donovan highlights how Israel resisted the temptation of making "an image of Yhwh out of the monarch" once it became a monarchy.[69]

However, the history of the monarchy witnessed "the interaction of kings and prophets. The prophets shared the task of tradition-bearing with the monarch; and, indeed, theirs was the more significant part, since it was through their words that Yhwh himself defined and redefined in each new circumstance the moral content of the tradition to which the kings were answerable. That content was the law."[70] Equally, mediation of God's rule was "also borne in lesser and partial ways by other authorities in Israel, priestly and administrative."[71] Thus, "the priest stood before the altar of YHWH bearing the names of the tribes of Israel on his shoulders, and by his acts of confession, prayer, and sacrifice involved the whole nation in the identity conferred on it by God."[72]

Therefore, as Israel relied on functions of agency or mediation, "it permitted a unitary government subject to the independent authority of Yhwh's law, which had its independent voice in society through the prophetic movement."[73] This in turn leads O'Donovan to formulate a fourth theorem: "*The authority of a human regime mediates divine authority in a unitary structure, but is subject to the authority of law within the community, which bears independent witness to the divine command.*"[74]

Up to this point, O'Donovan's exegetical and theoretical model may be summed up conceptually as follows:[75]

---

67. O'Donovan, *Ways of Judgment*, 157.
68. O'Donovan, *Desire of the Nations*, 61.
69. O'Donovan, 65.
70. O'Donovan, 62.
71. O'Donovan, 123.
72. O'Donovan, *Ways of Judgment*, 157.
73. O'Donovan, *Desire of the Nations*, 65.
74. O'Donovan, 65 (emphasis in original).
75. This table summarizes our own understanding of O'Donovan's model. It should be said that no such table is provided in O'Donovan's books. However, for a scholarly precedent

Table 1. Exegetical and theoretical model (Old Testament)

	Historical Manifestations Over Time		Conceptual
	Immediacy YHWH is King	Mediated YHWH' son	Authority
Political Authority	Salvation/victory	Military function (king)	Power
	Judgment	Judicial function (king)	Execution of right
	Possession (land, law)	Function of continuity (king, prophet, priest)	Perpetuation of tradition
Political Identity	Praise		Society

2.2.3 Two Cities / Two Rules

When the people of Israel looked beyond their borders to witness "the dramatic rise of the Mesopotamian empires,"[76] their vision of how their God related to their neighboring nations was manifest: "Yhwh Elyon is awesome, a great king over all the earth. He subdues peoples under us and nations under our feet [Ps 47:2–3 ET],"[77] which then is balanced "with a further account of Elohim's reign, which declares that 'the princes of the nations shall assemble with the people of the God of Abraham' [Ps 42:9 ET]."[78] In other words, "Israel's awareness of its own distinctness as Yhwh's chosen is held in a careful equilibrium with a hope for co-operation with surrounding peoples."[79] At the international level it was YHWH's rule that "secured the relations of the nations and directed them towards peace" with no "unitary

---

in using these kind of communicative devices in theological work, see Smith, *Introducing Radical Orthodoxy*, 172, 177.

76. O'Donovan, *Desire of the Nations*, 68.
77. O'Donovan, 66.
78. O'Donovan, 66.
79. O'Donovan, 67.

mediator" between them.⁸⁰ "Yhwh's world order was plurally constituted. World-empire was a bestial deformation."⁸¹ From this O'Donovan derives a general statement: "*the appropriate unifying element in international order is law rather than government.*"⁸²

Nonetheless, "the rise of the empires was viewed primarily as a sign of Yhwh's judgment against his people . . . Yet it would have been impossible for a prophet in the classical Yahwist tradition of Judah to make the fall of the city and the abrogation of the covenant the ultimate horizon of his vision."⁸³ Accordingly, this led to the (prophetic) criticism of empire – not a novelty in itself in view of the episode of Babel in Genesis 11, says O'Donovan – which gradually degenerated as the images used by Daniel show (Dan 7). However, in addition to the critique of empire, the exile led to the rise of hope, hope in YHWH's restoration of Israel, which also had a political implication: "the order of the future, when Israel shall return to her home, will be an internationally plural order, free from the unifying constraints of empire. The events of Israel's overthrow by the empire and her subsequent restoration will serve as a lesson and a model by which Yhwh will instruct the nations of the world."⁸⁴

While in exile, however, Israel developed a theological awareness of their new political context as recorded in the letter the prophet Jeremiah sent to the exiled community in Babylon (Jer 29). There we find "two political entities coexistent in one time and space," which may be understood in two ways:

> on the one hand, there are two "cities," the social entities of Israel and Babylon which live side by side; on the other, there are the two "rules" under which Israel finds itself, that of Babylon and that of Yhwh. These two interpretations of the situation make it flexible as a model, capable of illuminating not only the situation in which Israel shared social space with others, but also the situation at home where it sensed its own provisional political institutions as alien to its true calling.⁸⁵

---

80. O'Donovan, 72.
81. O'Donovan, 72.
82. O'Donovan, 72 (emphasis in original).
83. O'Donovan, 69.
84. O'Donovan, 71.
85. O'Donovan, 83. As pointed out by O'Donovan, the theme of the two cities as a result of Israel's exile in Babylon is recast in Christian terms by Augustine in Augustine, *City of God*

Yet, once the exile came to an end, those who returned home still felt in exile there.[86] Even so, O'Donovan suggests this offered a twofold opportunity for Israel, (i) to separate or withdraw "from the idolatrous society in which it has dwelt. To go home will be to affirm that it is still Yhwh's holy people, and so to excite universal wonder at what Yhwh has done through its history."[87] Equally, (ii) it offered the possibility of influencing the imperial power, "offering constructive assistance on the one hand and securing protection for the holy people on the other."[88] The risk of converting this transient possibility into a permanent one required of Israel to "heed prophecy, alert for the culmination of Yhwh's purposes in which the Ancient of Days will entrust his Kingdom to a son of man, who should also represent the people of the saints of the Most High."[89]

2.2.4 Evangelical Mode / Christological Turn

As O'Donovan moves from the Old Testament to the New, he tests whether his model holds up to Jesus's arrival and the announcement of God's kingdom,[90] as recorded in the gospels. To begin with, "what Jesus had to say about the reign of God was authoritative because it was confirmed by an exercise of power that demonstrated it."[91] More importantly, O'Donovan suggests that "Jesus' authority consists in his capacity to bring us directly into contact with God's authority."[92] At the same time, Jesus and his generation lived with the legacy of Israel's exile, which was conveyed theologically in the imagery of the "Two Cities, with their concomitant Two Rules expressing Israel's alienation from its calling," which in turn "gave way to the Two Eras."[93] However,

---

17.4, 16; 18.2; 19.26; idem, *On the Catechising of the Uninstructed* 11.16; 21.37; idem, *Against Lying* 33, (both in NPNF1/3); idem, *Reply to Faustus the Manichaean* 12.36, (NPNF1/4); idem, *On the Psalms* 55.11; 62.3–4; 65.1–4, 7; 87.5–7; 126.2, (NPNF1/8).

86. O'Donovan, *Desire of the Nations*, 83; Wright, *New Testament and the People*, 268–272.
87. O'Donovan, *Desire of the Nations*, 84–85.
88. O'Donovan, 86.
89. O'Donovan, 88.
90. See Wright, *Jesus and the Victory*, 199.
91. O'Donovan, *Desire of the Nations*, 89.
92. O'Donovan, 89.
93. O'Donovan, 93.

Jesus . . . believed that a shift in the locus of power was taking place, which made the social institutions that had prevailed to that point anachronistic. His attitude to them was neither secularist not zealot . . . He did not recognise a permanently twofold locus of authority. He recognised only a transitory duality which belonged to the climax of Israel's history, a duality between the coming and the passing order.[94]

Then, using the same pattern of analysis as for YHWH's reign O'Donovan considers (a) Jesus's works of power, which he identifies primarily as "acts of exorcism and healing" in the gospels: "By comparison . . . [Jesus] treated the fact of Roman occupation casually, with little respect and less urgency. Israel was enslaved to spiritual enemies, and of this its colonial status was, at most, a secondary symptom."[95] However, O'Donovan sees in Jesus's agenda "a statement of true political priorities. Jesus' departure from the zealot programme showed his more theological understanding of power, not his disinterest in it. The empowerment of Israel was more important that the disempowerment of Rome; for Rome disempowered would in itself by no means guarantee Israel empowered."[96] So, Jesus's power addressed "the forces which most immediately hindered Israel from living effectively as a community in God's service, the spiritual and natural weaknesses which drained its energies away."[97]

(b) In line with John the Baptist, Jesus also proclaimed the judgment of God upon Israel, and Gentile people would play a role both as instruments to implement the judgment, and as beneficiaries of it. Jesus showed also a special concern for the non-ruling classes of Israel, the poor and the tax-collectors, which "illustrate[s] clearly enough that Jesus' demonstration of divine judgment was not only to be a matter of forcing divisions [Matt 10:34–36], but of recovering and reconciling the alienated."[98]

(c) In terms of possession, during Jesus's time the law operated as the boundary marker, a source of national identity for the Jew/Israelite in view

---

94. O'Donovan, 93.
95. O'Donovan, 93.
96. O'Donovan, 95.
97. O'Donovan, 95.
98. O'Donovan, 98.

of the Roman occupation.[99] However, Jesus aimed at "making God's law accessible to God's people . . . [as] an interpreter of God's law, [he] believed that national restoration had come through the reappropriation of the law. Yet there was something which set his interpretation apart. Associated with the proclamation of the dawning Kingdom, it acquired a claim of ultimacy."[100]

(d) As for the element of praise in the Yawhistic model, O'Donovan sees its New Testament counterpart in *"the faith with which Jesus was received."*[101] Again, that does not mean those that received Jesus with faith invested him with authority by their response. "The authority of the Kingdom and its messenger lay in itself, not in the reception that it found. But it proved itself by eliciting faith."[102] What is more, "faith in the coming Kingdom, then, implied an act of political recognition directed to Jesus himself . . . In that sense the coming of the Kingdom was proved by the acknowledgment of Jesus as king. Yet that acknowledgment presupposed the recognition of the Kingdom itself; otherwise it would have been a rebellious bid for autonomy against God's rule."[103] As a result, the "Two Kingdoms period, in which Temple without power and praetorium without worship coexisted in some kind of parallel, was declared closed."[104]

Turning to the rest of the New Testament, O'Donovan highlights a hermeneutical challenge to the gospels' consensus: "Jesus proclaimed the coming of the Kingdom of God, but the apostolic church did not."[105] Instead, it "told the story of what happened when the Kingdom came: its conflict with the established principalities and powers and its vindication at God's hand through Jesus' resurrection."[106] It is in this sense that the church may claim continuity with Jesus's proclamation of God's rule because both "he, and his message of the Kingdom, had been vindicated."[107] And yet, O'Donovan sees an extraordinary opportunity for political theology in addressing this

---

99. See Wright, *New Testament and the People*, 237–238.
100. O'Donovan, *Desire of the Nations*, 100–101.
101. O'Donovan, 113 (emphasis in original).
102. O'Donovan, 113.
103. O'Donovan, 117.
104. O'Donovan, 117.
105. O'Donovan, 120.
106. O'Donovan, 120.
107. O'Donovan, 120.

kerygmatic challenge: "if Christian theology as a whole has sometimes allowed the careless or sceptical to conclude that the church changed its proclamation from Kingdom to Christ somewhere around AD 50, it is the special task of political theology to efface that impression."[108] The line of kerygmatic continuity factors in the two roles ascribed to Jesus as (a) the mediator of God's rule, "the role focussed centrally upon the Davidide monarch,"[109] and (b) the representative individual, "who in lonely faithfulness carries the tradition of the people, its fate and its promise, in his own destiny; this was the role of Jeremiah and of his exilic imitators, summing up the tradition of the isolated sufferers in Israel's liturgy."[110] What is more, "when to this formal duality is added the eschatological presence of God's Kingdom, then the two functions are transformed into more than place-holding roles. We must then speak of Christ as the *decisive* presence of God and the *decisive* presence of God's people."[111]

Another christological correlation takes place between the death and resurrection of Jesus, in which "Jesus' death was the overthrow of God's cause at the hands of rebellious Israel; his resurrection was the reassertion of God's triumph over Israel."[112] To put it another way, "it is the resurrection that establishes the authority of the new life. The death, on the other hand, is understood as a severance from the old, destroyed authority, that of law with its twin oppressions of 'the flesh' and 'condemnation.'"[113] The kerygmatic account of Jesus and the kingdom of God, as told by the early church, may be ordered in "four moments" that O'Donovan exegetically identifies as "Advent, Passion, Restoration and Exaltation."[114] This christological turn of the kerygma is construed as the Christ-event where "we found the elements of God's rule: an act of power, and act of judgment and the gift of possession.

---

108. O'Donovan, 123. For a survey of "Kingdom of God" passages in early Christian literature (including the New Testament) see Wright, *Jesus and the Victory*, 663–670.

109. O'Donovan, *Desire of the Nations*, 123.

110. O'Donovan, 123.

111. O'Donovan, 124.

112. O'Donovan, 129.

113. O'Donovan, 128.

114. O'Donovan, 133.

But these elements are presented in the narrative account of a decisive act, an act in which God's rule was mediated and his people reconstituted in Christ."[115]

More specifically, the Christ-event is construed as: (i) advent, which looks back to Christ's pre-existence and to his incarnation as Jesus, and which affirms his role as mediator of God's rule;[116] (ii) passion, which sees the cross of Jesus as judgment on this world;[117] (iii) restoration, which refers to Jesus's resurrection from death and as result to "the overcoming of Israel's sin and the affirmation of Israel's new identity in its representative."[118] Equally, the resurrection of Jesus is both restoration of creation and a signpost to "the time of the world's future."[119] And (iv) exaltation, "undescribable in itself, is clothed in the imagery of royal coronation. The ascended Christ takes his throne, as the Davidide monarch was summoned to do in the ancient psalm (2:1) on the right hand of the divine majesty. The Son of Man is presented before the Ancient of Days and receives the Kingdom."[120] In this politically loaded imagery of the ascension, O'Donovan sees (a) the end of Christ' story, since "it has told of an act of divine rule: power put forth, judgment effected and the gift of communal identity secured. The coronation of Christ expresses the accomplishment of that act as a whole."[121] But also, (b) the exaltation marks the "*foundation* which determines all future time,"[122] and it has set in motion Pentecost. As a result, O'Donovan's exegetical and theoretical model may be updated conceptually, as shown in table 2.

2.3 Theo-Political Implications

O'Donovan goes on to argue that two fundamental implications for political authority and for the church have followed from the exaltation of Jesus, which he encapsulates in this expression: "The kingly rule of Christ is God's own

---

115. O'Donovan, 133.
116. See O'Donovan, 133–136.
117. See O'Donovan, 136.
118. O'Donovan, 141; see also Wright, *New Testament and the People*, 273.
119. O'Donovan, *Desire of the Nations*, 143.
120. O'Donovan, 144. It seems Ps 110:1 fits better than Ps 2:1 into this train of thought.
121. O'Donovan, 145.
122. O'Donovan, 145.

Table 2. Exegetical and theoretical model (Old and New Testaments)

	Historical manifestations over time					Conceptual
	Immediacy YHWH is King	Mediated YHWH's son	Evangelical mode Jesus	Christological turn Christ-event		Authority
Political authority	Salvation/victory	Military function (king)	Works of power	Advent		Power
	Judgment	Judicial function (king)	Proclamation of God's judgment	Passion	Exaltation	Execution of right
	Possession (land, law)	Function of continuity (king, prophet, priest)	Interpretation of law	Restoration		Perpetuation of tradition
Political identity	Praise		Faith	Church		Society

rule exercised over the whole world. It is visible in the life of the church,"[123] and yet, "this awaits a final universal presence of Christ to become fully apparent."[124] On the one hand, "authorities, political and demonic, which govern the world . . . have been made subject to God's sovereignty in the Exaltation of Christ."[125] That is to say, "the terms on which the bearers of political authority function in the wake of Christ's ascension are new terms. The triumph of God in Christ has not left these authorities just where they were, exercising the same right as before. It imposes the shape of salvation-history upon politics."[126] This reauthorization of political authority, as O'Donovan calls it,[127] means that "the authority of secular government [now] resides in

---

123. O'Donovan, 146.
124. O'Donovan, 146.
125. O'Donovan, 146.
126. O'Donovan, *Ways of Judgment*, 4.
127. See O'Donovan, *Desire of the Nations*, 157; O'Donovan, *Ways of Jugement*, 4.

the practice of judgment."[128] To put it in another way, "it means that political authority in all its forms – lawmaking, war-making, welfare provision, education – is to be re-conceived within this matrix and subject to the discipline of enacting right against wrong."[129] What is more, "what Christ's enthronement had effected was to force upon the principalities and powers the alternatives of subjection and outright confrontation and defeat. It had brought in a moment of apocalyptic division."[130] Precisely, "that is the question underlying the book written by John of Patmos."[131]

On the other hand, "the future age now has a social and political presence. A community lives under the authority of him to whom the Ancient of Days has entrusted the kingdom."[132] This is the church, whose true character is, analogously, "a political society,"[133] and as such "it is ruled and authorised by the ascended Christ alone and supremely; it therefore has its own authority; and it is not answerable to any other authority that may attempt to subsume it."[134] This is because "Pentecost authorised the church by uniting it with the authorisation of Christ. It belongs, therefore, immediately to the moment of authorisation, Christ's Exaltation."[135] However, "the political character of the church, its essential nature as a governed society, is hidden, to be discerned by faith as the ascended Christ who governs it is to be discerned by faith."[136] In addition,

> the catholic identity of the church derives from the progress of the Spirit's own mission. It is therefore always larger than its ordered structures, taking its shape from the new ground that the Spirit is possessing. It remains for the church's structures to catch up with this mission, to discern what the Spirit has done,

---

128. O'Donovan, *Ways of Judgment*, 3; cf. O'Donovan, *Desire of the Nations*, 151.
129. O'Donovan, *Ways of Judgment*, 4.
130. O'Donovan, *Desire of the Nations*, 152–153.
131. O'Donovan, 153.
132. O'Donovan, 158.
133. O'Donovan, 159.
134. O'Donovan, 159.
135. O'Donovan, 161.
136. O'Donovan, 166.

and to construct such ordered links of community as will safeguard brotherly love.¹³⁷

Equally, "the sacraments provide the primary way in which the church is ... given institutional form and order ... In these forms we know where the church is and can attach ourselves to it."¹³⁸

By contrast, O'Donovan's reading of the Apocalypse seems to bring out some tension in his overall thought about the church. In fact, his reading bypasses the very first vision of the Apocalypse, which takes place at Patmos in the first-century AD. It seems this hermeneutic move is due to the scant presence of the church in the narrative, which O'Donovan justifies as follows:

> The faithful believer appears in history as an individual ("him who conquers" in the letters to the seven churches) or as a pair (the two witnesses), standing against organized society. The very word "church" is used by John only to designate those equivocal communities which he addresses in his introductory letters. There is, on the face of it, no place for the church catholic on earth.¹³⁹

However, O'Donovan concedes that "this startling silence is not intended as a denial ... What John intends is to direct our eyes to the *source* of this new and real political community."¹⁴⁰

Additionally, O'Donovan establishes a correlation between secular government and the church's mission. "If the mission of the church needs a certain social space, for men and women of every nation to be drawn into the governed community of God's Kingdom, then secular authority is authorised to provide and ensure that space."¹⁴¹ This leads him to explore the interaction between church and secular authorities during Christendom, an era that began for O'Donovan with the Edict of Milan in AD 313, and whose core idea is "intimately bound up with the church's mission."¹⁴² That is to say, "the church's one project is to witness to the Kingdom of God. Christendom is *response* to

---

137. O'Donovan, 169–170.
138. O'Donovan, 172.
139. O'Donovan, "History and Politics," 42.
140. O'Donovan, 42.
141. O'Donovan, *Desire of the Nations*, 146. O'Donovan appeals here to 1 Timothy 2:16.
142. O'Donovan, 195.

mission, and as such a sign that God has blessed it. It is constituted not by the church's seizing alien power, but by alien power's becoming attentive to the church."[143] Thus, "in its primary form . . . the Christendom idea supposes the *vis-à-vis* of church and secular government, as distinct structures belonging to distinct societies and, indeed, distinct eras of salvation-history."[144] We may register here an echo of the "two cities / two rules" model (§2.1.3) that operated in Israel during exile.

Again, O'Donovan's reading of "empire" in the Apocalypse offers a point of contrast with his understanding of the dynamics of the church and the secular authority during Christendom. On the one hand, based on Revelation 12–13, O'Donovan sees empire as an specific "phenomenon of the messianic age, evoked by the triumph of the Christ-child and the restricted dominion of the devil upon earth."[145] As the beast emerges from the sea, so empire imposes order upon chaos; what is more, since the wounded beast was healed (i.e. one of its heads), "empire seems to introduce the promise of resurrection into human affairs."[146] The ideologist of the empire is embodied by the beast from the land, since "the falsely messianic empire must conceal its character with a plausible appearance of true speech."[147] What is more, empire "provides a concrete form in which mankind can give itself, heart and soul, to a community of evil."[148] Equally, "the closure of the market on ideological lines is a sign of the separation of the communities."[149]

On the other hand, in Revelation 17 John managed "to present the political situation of his day from another angle, examining the general features that it shares with empires of the past, yet not withdrawing from the particular claims he has made about the character of empire in the messianic age."[150] Therefore, if "the tyranny of the beast in chapter 13 was exercised through the market,"[151] in chapters 17–18 empire "ruled over nations by exercising

---

143. O'Donovan, 195.
144. O'Donovan, 196.
145. O'Donovan, "History and Politcs," 38.
146. O'Donovan, 36.
147. O'Donovan, 37.
148. O'Donovan, 37.
149. O'Donovan, 38.
150. O'Donovan, 38.
151. O'Donovan, 40.

commercial and cultural monopoly."[152] Fornication with empire is seen as "the surrender of individual integrity in undisciplined and destructive commerce. Empire is not simply an extreme case of unified rule; it is a coalescence of powers that drains integrity from all but the dominant partner."[153] In addition, "the relation between the empire and its client kingdoms is central to the prophet's view of how empire comes to its destruction."[154] Its end comes out from "the force of the resentment which it has engendered."[155] In fact, "the logic of the beast's end and the logic of the Whore's end are the same, predatory power collapsing in on itself."[156] What is more, this "collapse of empire . . . reveals the operation of divine providence," and "the collapse of this messianic empire will reveal the final rule of God's Messiah over history."[157]

In this negative or apophatic criticism, O'Donovan observes that "the paradigm of political activity has been imperial conquest; the permanent political institution, the city, has merely served to sustain and develop the exploitation of imperial dominion by commercial means."[158] However, "the root of any true political order, in which human beings can relate to God and to each other lovingly, is the conspicuous judgment of God."[159] Therefore, "in the concluding sections of the Apocalypse we shall be shown the outline of a new social existence founded upon the judgments of God. This cannot be a product of history, because it is brought about by the judgment of God upon history. It is given from heaven, descending like a bride prepared for the bridegroom,"[160] therefore for O'Donovan the triumph over evil takes place both as "a battle and as an act of judgment."[161]

---

152. O'Donovan, 40.
153. O'Donovan, 41.
154. O'Donovan, 40.
155. O'Donovan, 41.
156. O'Donovan, 41–42.
157. O'Donovan, 42.
158. O'Donovan, 42.
159. O'Donovan, 43.
160. O'Donovan, 43.
161. O'Donovan, 43.

2.4 Conclusion

Set within the (recent) scholarly tradition of critical engagement with O'Donovan's work, which usually takes place on an ad hoc basis, this thesis has framed its engagement with O'Donovan's political theology following four principles: (i) to read as much of O'Donovan's scholarly output (in particular, on political theology) as possible with a view to grasping his overall perspective and key theo-political concepts, (ii) to offer an account of the core elements of his political theology and hermeneutical model that correlates his key concepts of authority and society, (iii) to critique O'Donovan's models of authority and society from the perspective provided by the Apocalypse, and (iv) to refer to his reading of the Apocalypse and offer a critique of it where necessary. As a result, this chapter has focused on the second point, that is to say, it has offered an account of O'Donovan's hermeneutical model and the correlation within it of the key concepts of his political theology (i.e. authority and society).

In this process we have found that the epistemic purchase which O'Donovan finds in Scripture in order to map political history onto God's salvation history has played a key role in the development of his political theology, with the concept of political authority playing an important part. This is understood as the triad made up of power, judgment and tradition, the recognition of which grants a society its political identity. O'Donovan turns the liturgical expression "YHWH is King" into the locus of his hermeneutical framework, the embodiment of political authority as conveyed in biblical history, whether in its unmediated mode or in its mediated one, mainly through the Israelite king. After the Israelite exile, it was Jesus who recovered this claim of political authority as he proclaimed and enacted "the Kingdom of God." The apostolic church, in turn, conveyed this message in christological terms, construed by O'Donovan as the Christ-event played out in four moments (i.e. Advent, Passion, Restoration and Exaltation). It is the church, authorized by the exalted Jesus in Pentecost, who gives political and social expression to the authority of the exalted Jesus, to whom alone it is accountable. Human authority also (e.g. government) is redefined by the exalted Jesus, in the sense that it is now limited to the practice of judgment.

However, this account of political authority seems to be in tension with O'Donovan's reading of the book of Revelation. Though he still reads political history within the framework of salvation history, O'Donovan's political theology of the Apocalypse plays down the political expression of the church within the narrative, and therefore the authority and reality of the exalted Jesus – and his own argument that the church conveys the authority of the exalted Jesus in visible terms. And yet his analysis of empire brings out a conflicting account of the terms for political authority set by the exalted Jesus as he has defined it. His construal of divine judgment, however, is indeed the determining factor that allows the political space for the holy city in Revelation.

CHAPTER 3

The Apocalypse's Narrative

"The ancient writers themselves used, as a matter of instinct, to express truth about the relations of things in narrative," observes O'Donovan, and "in the narrative of their own people's history they discerned truths about the relations of things."[1] This understanding of narrative discourse and the need for a hermeneutics to match is presupposed in O'Donovan's method of theo-political inquiry into Scripture,[2] and with regard to the Old Testament brings him to the conclusion that "the hermeneutic principle that governs a Christian appeal to political categories within the Hebrew Scriptures is, simply, Israel itself."[3] In §1.1 and §2.2 we endeavoured to make transparent the application of O'Donovan's method to Scripture and to highlight how it may apply to the reading of Revelation, but in doing this we must not forget that in this hermeneutical framework narrative is the means of conveying the account (or history in this case) from which a reader/hearer may discern a theo-political truth. "This interconnexion of history and truth the theologian must be prepared to explore with [the reader] . . . [not] simply re-reading the documents in an enterprise of literary exegesis, but finding the truth within the unfolding patterns of the history."[4]

---

1. O'Donovan, *Desire of the Nations*, 29.

2. The narrative condition of Scripture has not been always appreciated, as noted by Hans Frei in Frei, *Eclipse of Biblical Narrative*, 136. On the (re)discovery of the narrative nature of Scripture among biblical scholars and theologians see Barton, "Disclosing Human Possibilities," 53–60.

3. O'Donovan, *Desire of the Nations*, 27.

4. O'Donovan, 29.

As for the Apocalypse, it may be stating the obvious to say that it is a narrative.[5] Jerome's recension of Victorinus's early commentary on the Apocalypse, for instance, regarded the book of Revelation as a narrative,[6] a classification which he makes with no explicit reference to any pre-modern narrative theory.[7] Admittedly, Victorinus's literary instinct, or better Jerome's,[8] is endorsed by more recent commentators on the text. Eugene Boring, for example, says that "the Apocalypse must be grasped as a whole, for it simply cannot be understood verse by verse. It is a narrative, a drama with action and movement that conveys the message of each part within the context of the story in its totality."[9] In the same way, David Barr observes that "because it is all divided up into neat chapters and discrete verses . . . it is easy to miss the most important thing for understanding the Apocalypse: it is a narrative."[10] In fact, narrative approaches to the book of Revelation which draw heavily from narrative theory have become an upward trend, with David Barr and Eugene Boring pioneering it late in the twentieth century, joined later by James Resseguie. Incipient and perhaps programmatic essays by some of them were followed by full exegetical commentaries where a narrative approach dominated,[11] to the point that by 1998 David Barr considered it "unusual for any commentary or major work on the Apocalypse to ignore narrative readings."[12] As regards

---

5. For a quasi mathematical definition of "narrative = story + discourse" see Barthes, "Introduction," 87; Chatman, *Story and Discourse*, 19. For a most comprehensive definition of narrative based on "conditions of narrativity" see Ryan, "Toward a Definition," 28.

6. Victorinus of Petovium, *Commentary on the Apocalypse of the Blessed John* 8.1 (ANF/7). Victorinus's original commentary on the Apocalypse, written in ca. AD 258–260, was revised and amended by Jerome at the beginning of the fifth century AD, approximately. See Weinrich, *Latin Commentaries*, xx–xxi; Bruce, "Earliest Latin Commentary," 354. Presumably, this English translation published originally in 1886 was based on Jerome's recension of Victorinus's commentary. However, "the original of Victorinus remained unknown until 1916 when Johannes Hausleiter discovered the original in *Codex Ottobonian latinus* 3288A (fifteenth century)." Weinrich, *Latin Commentaries*, xxi.

7. By then Plato and Aristotle at least had already formulated some kind of (incipient) narrative theory, cf. Plato, *Republic* 3.392a+; Aristotle, *Poetics*; Aristotle, *Rethoric*.

8. Overall, Jerome seemed to regard most of Scripture as narrative, cf. Jerome, *Letter* 51.4–5; 53.8–9 (NPNF2/6).

9. Boring, *Revelation*, vii.

10. Barr, *Tales of the End*, Kindle edition, location 149.

11. Essays: e.g. Barr, "Apocalypse as a Symbolic"; Barr, "Using Plot to Discern"; Barr, "Waiting for the End"; Boring, "Narrative Christology." Commentaries: Barr, *Tales of the End*; Boring, *Revelation*; Resseguie, *Revelation Unsealed*; Resseguie, *Revelation of John*.

12. Barr, *Tales of the End*, location 79. It should be observed that along with a narrative approach to the Apocalypse, recent surveys of scholarly work on the book of Revelation make

The Apocalypse's Narrative

O'Donovan, he observes that in the Apocalypse "John combines a diastatic emphasis on the difference of God and the opacity of historical events with a narrative of historical revelation that finds the ultimate meaning of human sociality in the rule of Christ."[13]

Therefore, since ancient and modern scholars regard the Apocalypse as narrative, and adopting O'Donovan's hermeneutical method of theo-political inquiry, we now approach the narrative of the Apocalypse where we will discern the origin of the expectation, development and materialization of the Fellowship of the Throne in which the two theo-political categories of authority and society become integrated.

3.1 How To Navigate the Narrative

What does it take for the narrative of the book of Revelation to move from the very first vision John hears and sees in Patmos of someone "like a son of man" (say vision A) to the grandeur of the holy city coming down from heaven and bringing about the materialization of the Fellowship of the Throne (say vision Z)? Clearly, it is not a simple linear movement from vision A to Z,[14] neither in terms of time nor of space, and any account of the narrative of John's Apocalypse must necessarily deal with the still contentious issue of its structure. "How has our author structured or, better said, restructured his source material? This is one of the most debated issues in the scholarly study of Revelation."[15] Gregory Beale, who carried out a survey of various proposals advanced by scholars on this issue, perspicaciously observed that "a blessing and curse of John's Apocalypse are the many commentators who have attempted to interpret the book. This is especially true of the many outlines proposed for its literary structure. The diverse proposals are a maze

---

evident the wide range of other hermeneutical approaches to the Apocalypse used to date; see Witherington III, *Revelation*, 51–64; Paul, "Ebbing and Flowing," 523–531.

13. O'Donovan, "History and Politics," 29.

14. As already mentioned in the introduction to this thesis, a view on a non-linear unfolding of the Apocalypse's visions was held by Victorinus of Petovium in ca. AD 258–260, followed by Augustine in AD 426, at the latest. See Victorinus of Petovium, *Commentary on the Apocalypse* 8.2 (ACT/L); Augustine, *City of God* 20.17. More recently, follow the discussion on this issue in Beale, *Book of Revelation*, 108–151; cf. O'Donovan, "History and Politics," 30.

15. Witherington III, *Revelation*, 18.

of interpretative confusion,"[16] not least because of the varied hermeneutical presuppositions held by the interpreter when they set to the exegetical task.[17]

Richard Bauckham, for example, approaches the text with a particular concern in mind, the oral performance of the text, because the book was originally meant to be read aloud in each one of the congregations it addressed (1:3). Therefore, in his view, "the structure [of the book] must be indicated by clear linguistic markers."[18] He goes on to identify one of those linguistic markers as the expression ἐν πνεύματι (in [the] spirit), which we find in 1:10; 4:2; 17:3; and 21:10,[19] and to consider these references as marking major transitions in the book. If the vision begins when John is in Patmos in the Spirit (1:9–10), then the moment John is taken to heaven in the Spirit (4:1–2) becomes a major transition that takes place with "an inaugural vision of heaven (4–5), from which develops the whole sequence of judgments down to the end of chapter 16."[20]

To this frame of "linguistic markers" Bauckham adds the whole section delimited by the parallel texts 17:1–3 ‖ 21:9–10, and 19:9b–10 ‖ 22:6–9, that become "structural markers delimiting two parallel sections – 17:1–19:10 and 21:9 –22:9."[21] In between, (i.e. 19:11–21:8), "comes a section which must be understood as a single section describing the transition from one to the other."[22] According to this approach the structure of Revelation would be as follows: "(1) the inaugural vision of Christ, including the seven messages to the churches (1:9–3:22); (2) the inaugural vision of heaven (4–5) leading to the sequences of judgment (6–16); (3) Babylon the harlot (17:1–19:10); (4)

---

16. Beale, *Book of Revelation*, 108; cf. Barr, "Apocalypse as Symbolic," 43. It should be noted that this difference between outlines about the structure of the book of Revelation may be detected even in the extant commentaries on the Apocalypse, whether in Latin or Greek, written in the first millennium AD. See Weinrich, *Latin Commentaries*, v–vi; Oden, *Greek Commentaries on Revelation*, location 15–27.

17. See Stanton, "Presuppositions in New Testament," 60–71.

18. Bauckham, *Climax of the Prophecy*, 3.

19. A similar approach, though based on the "literary hinges" ἃ δεῖ γενέσθαι ἐν τάχει ("what has to come about in a short time," Rev 1:1; 22:6), ἃ μέλλει γενέσθαι μετὰ ταῦτα ("which is about to be made after these [things]," Rev 1:19), and ἃ δεῖ γενέσθαι μετὰ ταῦτα ("what has to come about after these [things]," Rev 4:1) is preferred by Gregory Beale, who thinks the book of Daniel (alluded by these literary hinges) has influenced the structure of Revelation. See Beale, *Book of Revelation*, 111, 135–137; cf. Bauckham, *Climax of the Prophecy*, 23.

20. Bauckham, *Climax of the Prophecy*, 4.

21. Bauckham, 4.

22. Bauckham, 5.

the transition from Babylon to the New Jerusalem (19:11–21:8); (5) the New Jerusalem the Bride (21:9–22:9)."[23]

A different structure is postulated by Elisabeth Schüssler Fiorenza, who relies on a source-critical and tradition-critical approach.[24] For her, three criteria stand out as the most important in defining the structure of the book: "[a] the pattern of seven, [b] the two scroll visions and the Christological inaugural visions in 1:12–20 and 19:11–16, [c] the method of intercalation and interlocking, of 'joining.'"[25] Working on this criteria she discerns four major sections in the book: "[i] the inaugural vision and the letter septer (1:9–3:22); [ii] the seven sealed scroll (4:1–9:21; 11:15–19; 15:1, 5–16:21; 17:1–19:10); [iii] the small prophetic scroll (10:1–15:4), and [iv] the visions of judgment and salvation (19:11–22:9)."[26] Hers is a concentric model that follows this pattern:

(a) 1:1–8;
  (b) 1:9–3:22;
    (c) 4:1–9:21; 11:15–19;
      (d) 10:1–15:4;
    (c') 15:1, 5–19:10;
  (b') 19:11–22:9;
(a') 22:10–22:21.

Therefore, "insofar as the center of the pattern is the prophetic scroll, the structure of the book underscores that the main function of Rev. is the prophetic interpretation of the situation of the community."[27] In addition, "Rev. is not chronologically ordered but theologically-thematically conceived."[28]

For his part, David Barr, who subscribes to a narrative approach, looks at the text of Revelation for "the story told. If we look at the Apocalypse in terms of its action (understood as a series of causally connected events) a reasonably clear pattern emerges."[29] He sees "a strong correlation between the beginning

---

23. Bauckham, 6.
24. Fiorenza, *Book of Revelation*, 159.
25. Fiorenza, 174.
26. Fiorenza, 174.
27. Fiorenza, 163.
28. Fiorenza, 163.
29. Barr, *Tales of the End*, location 398.

and the ending – as we expect in a good story."³⁰ This correlation becomes the frame for the three stories John tells. The first story is about "what happened to John on Patmos. In brief, a majestic human being appears to him and dictates seven messages to the angels of seven churches."³¹ The second story takes place when "John is called up to heaven, where he observes a scene at the divine court . . . a slaughtered-yet-standing Lamb opens a divine scroll and reveals its contents."³² In the third story "a cosmic dragon pursues a cosmic woman but is eventually defeated by a cosmic warrior, resulting in the establishment of a wholly new cosmic order."³³ In short, "the first story details what Jesus would say to the seven communities [1–3]; the second story shows what is happening around the divine throne [4–11]; the third story recounts how a heavenly dragon attacks Jesus and his communities [12–22]."³⁴

What is more, Barr regards these three stories as self-contained and, therefore, three separate stories. "Each sequence has its own logic, its own set of characters, its own base locale, and John plays a somewhat different role in each."³⁵ However, Barr concedes that there are connections between these three stories. "These connections have to do with theme . . . and characters rather than with continuous sequential actions."³⁶ In other words, "John's three dramatic actions do not constitute a sequential, unified action. One does not happen before or after the other. They represent alternative tellings of the story of Jesus with a common theme and overlapping characters."³⁷

Now, since "literary works are capable of more than one interpretation,"³⁸ Barr appropriately asks "Are they all valid? Are some valid and others wrong? Are they all wrong?"³⁹ He suggests that "All interpretations that are grounded in what a text actually says are to some degree valid. All interpretations are partial and fragmentary, however, and thus to some degree wrong. But some

---

30. Barr, location 399.
31. Barr, location 490.
32. Barr, location 491.
33. Barr, location 493.
34. Barr, location 496.
35. Barr, location 505. On narrative characters see Abbott, *Cambridge Introduction*, 130–134; on biblical characters see Bloom, *Satan*, viii.
36. Barr, *Tales of the End*, location 571.
37. Barr, location 575.
38. Barr, location 756.
39. Barr, location 760.

have more faults, are more fragmentary and are thus less compelling than others. Or to be positive, some interpretations are more authentic than others."⁴⁰ About the above proposed structures we would highlight the following: first, it is not clear and Bauckham does not explain on what grounds ἐν πνεύματι should be regarded as a marker which first-century AD hearers of the book of Revelation would have identified a priori as they heard the story. In fact, other New Testament documents also feature this expression, for example Paul's letter to the Romans (Rom 2:29; 8:9; 9:1; 14:17; 15:16) and Ephesians (Eph 2:22; 3:5; 5:18; 6:18). However, dividing or ordering these letters according to that particular audio-linguistic marker would hardly make sense to their first-century AD hearers, whether in Rome or Asia Minor, or even twenty-first-century readers for that matter. Arguably the role of audio markers in John's Apocalypse could be fulfilled by the hypotactic expressions that naturally separate and/or link events within the narrative,⁴¹ such as μετὰ ταῦτα ("after these [things]," Rev 1:19; 4:1; 7:9; 9:12; 15:5; 18:1; 19:1; 20:3) or its neuter variant μετὰ τοῦτο ("after these [things]," Rev 7:1), and καὶ εἶδον ("and I saw," Rev 5:1, 2, 6, 11; 6:1, 2, 5, 8, 12; 7:2; 8:2, 13; 9:1; 10:1; 13:1, 11; 14:1, 6, 14; 15:1, 2; 16:13; 17:3, 6; 19:11, 17, 19; 20:1, 4, 11, 12; 21:1).⁴²

Second, in Fiorenza's case, it is hard to see how the vision of the little scroll,⁴³ which features only in 10:1–11, extends beyond the moment of the seventh trumpet being blown (11:15) right through to 15:4. To begin with, the little scroll story is sandwiched between the sixth and seventh trumpets (9:13; 11:15), a pattern equally observed by the previous series of seven, (i.e. the opening of the seals, 6:1–8:1). There we have an intercalation (the whole of chapter 7) between the opening of the sixth seal (6:12) and seventh seal (8:1). In addition, after the seventh trumpet is blown, there is a short series

---

40. Barr, location 761.

41. The adjective hypotactic refers to subordinate words or clauses, "or of writing style more generally, containing a fair amount of subordinated elements." DeMoss, *Pocket Dictionary*, 69.

42. cf. Aune, *Revelation 1–5*, xciii. In addition, Beale's point, in connection with the expression ἐν πνεύματι, that "John used verbal repetition to indicate these broad divisions of the book because oral recitation would require such structural markers, so that hearers would be enabled better to perceive these divisions," (Beale, *Book of Revelation*, 111) still does not resolve the question of why we should prefer ἐν πνεύματι instead of μετὰ ταῦτα or καὶ εἶδον. Beale seems to echo Bauckham, *Climax of the Prophecy*, 23.

43. τὸ βιβλαρίδιον (the little scroll) features three times in Rev: 10:2 (anarthrous), 9, 10; see also *Shepherd of Hermas* 5.3; 8.3.

of three unnumbered portents in heaven (12:1, 3; 15:1), that frame the story of the dragon's hostility towards the woman, her child-messiah and the rest of her offspring.

Third, now turning to Barr's model of three self-contained and synchronous stories, his account severs textual links that show that the seventh event in at least two of the series of seven (i.e. trumpets and bowls) are connected with each other, and with the inaugural vision of the heavenly throne, as follows:[44]

> And from the throne going out **lightnings** [ἀστραπή] and **sounds/noises** [φωνή] and **thunders** [βροντή] (Rev 4:5a; cf. Exod 19:16)

> And **there came about** [γίνομαι] **thunders** [βροντή] and **sounds/noises** [φωνή] and **lightnings** [ἀστραπή] and an **earthquake** [σεισμός] (Rev 8:5; cf. Ps 77:19 [77:18 ET])

> and **there came about** [γίνομαι] **lightnings** [ἀστραπή] and **sounds/noises** [φωνή] and **thunders** [βροντή] and an **earthquake** [σεισμός] and great **hailstone** [χάλαζα] (Rev 11:19)

> and **there came about** [γίνομαι] **lightnings** [ἀστραπή] and **sounds/noises** [φωνή] and **thunders** [βροντή] and a great **earthquake** [σεισμός] came about (Rev 16:18)

Therefore, in addition to thematic and character links between the three stories in Barr's model, we can identify linguistic connections between them.

As for ourselves, since we also take the book of Revelation as a narrative, we suggest dividing it into smaller narrative units with a view to deepening our understanding of the whole story and enabling us to grasp its plot.[45] However, we are aware that, "whereas our concern is to divide the book, John's concern was to bind it together."[46] Equally, we acknowledge that to some extent, we are imposing an external framework onto the text in order to organize the narrative. And though this is mainly a reader's construct, there

---

44. This point is elaborated by Bauckham, though he regards Revelation 8:5 as part of the outcome of the seventh seal, a point still in contention. In addition, he thinks that the seventh seal encompasses the whole series of seven trumpets, and in turn, the seventh trumpet holds the whole series of seven bowls, another point in contention. See Bauckham, *Climax of the Prophecy*, 7–9, 202–207; Bauckham, "Revelation," 1294; cf. Aune, *Revelation 1–5*, xciii–xcv; Beale, *Book of Revelation*, 116–121.

45. See Barthes, "Introduction," 88–89.

46. Barr, "Apocalypse as Symbolic," 43.

are some elements that are intrinsic to the Apocalypse's narrative and which suggest a transition from one part of the narrative to another.

It is in the light of the above that we now proceed to construe our own account of the story and plot of the book of Revelation, seeking out those elements intrinsic to the narrative that may suggest transitions, while allowing the characters, recurrent themes and motifs that bind the story together to achieve their purpose. To that end, we include the following diagram, inspired by Bernard Duyfhuizen's illustration of the "Framed Narratives" concept in the *Routledge Encyclopedia of Narrative Theory*:[47]

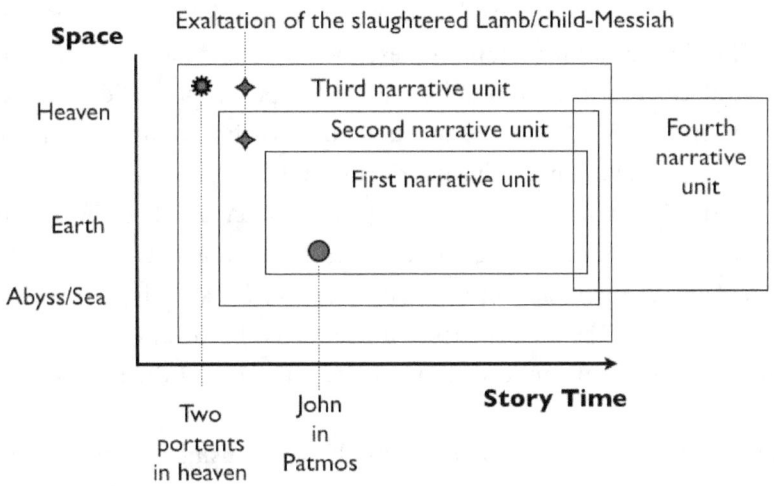

Figure 1. The Apocalypse's Narrative Flow

3.2 Narrative Unit 1: The Authorized Son of God Dictates Messages for Seven Congregations

Our starting point becomes 1:9, which is the point in the text where John begins to report his very first vision.[48] John introduces himself to his (intended) audience as one of them. He will be the narrating voice throughout, but also

---

47. Duyfhuizen, "Framed Narrative," 187.
48. cf. Barr, *Tales of the End*, location 945.

a character. He clearly locates (spatially) the beginning of the story on the island of Patmos, but also finds himself in the Spirit on the Lord's Day (1:10), which signals a temporal and liturgical plane as well. Arguably, this alludes to his theological perspective or point of view on what he is about to tell.[49] Besides, "the use of the past tense is enough to make a narrative subsequent, although without indicating the temporal interval which separates the moment of the narrating from the moment of the story."[50]

John introduces another character, the first one to speak to him, whom he refers to as "like a son of man" (1:13). John first sees this character in the midst of seven golden lampstands, a picture of the space the character inhabits and that has irrupted into John's space. This encounter between John and one "like a son of man" can arguably take place because John was in the Spirit on the Lord's Day. John attempts to describe the appearance of this extraordinary interlocutor from top to bottom, so to speak, using Old Testament allusive language (1:13–16). The encounter overwhelms John (1:17), and it is precisely for this reason that his interlocutor touches and speaks to him. In other words, John's interlocutor has completely broken into John's world, that is, John's space, demonstrating the recurrent interaction between these two spatial planes throughout the rest of the narrative, and arguably culminating with the advent of the holy city from heaven to earth (3:12; 21:2, 10) where it becomes perpetual and leads to the materialization of the Fellowship of the Throne (22:3–5).

In fact, this character introduces himself to John using a narrative name, so to speak (1:17–18), and from that point remains the narrating voice for this first vision, as he orders John to write down and pass on his messages to each of the seven churches in Ephesus, Smyrna, Pergamum, Thyatira, Sardis, Philadelphia and Laodicea (1:11, 19–20) in Asia Minor (1:4), (i.e. the "symbolic" space he inhabits). In his messages, this character ascribes regal and/or messianic titles to himself (e.g. "the Son of God," Rev 2:18; cf. Ps 2:6–9; 2 Sam 7:11–14), and describes himself as exercising divine prerogatives (e.g. "all the congregations will realise that I am the one who examines minds

---

49. See Barr, location 990. On the difference between the narrating voice and the point of view in a narrative, concepts usually misunderstood, see Genette, *Narrative Discourse*, 32, 213; Chatman, *Story and Discourse*, 151–153.

50. Genette, *Narrative Discourse*, 220.

and hearts," Rev 2:23; cf. Jer 17:10; Rom 8:27), he also highlights in a fleeting analeptic move the authority and throne given him by his Father (2:28; 3:5, 21).[51] He anticipates the advent of the new Jerusalem from heaven (3:12), and adumbrates the materialization of the Fellowship of the Throne (3:20–21). This character also professes to know the works of his addressees (2:2, 19; 3:1, 8, 15), and encourages them in their struggle to conquer (2:7, 11, 17, 26; 3:5, 12, 21) so they may receive what he promises them should they succeed. These promises will be fulfilled as the narrative comes to an end. However, these messages dictated to John for the seven churches (2:1–3:21) were addressed to each of the angels of those churches (2:1, 8, 12, 18; 3:1, 7, 14). This demonstrates how two spatial ontological planes remain inextricably intertwined in this vision. And yet, there is no mention of a change in setting.

3.3 Narrative Unit 2: The Throne, the Exalted Lamb and the Scroll

As the narrative goes on, however, a spatial transition is registered. John, presumably still in Patmos, sees a door opened in heaven, a vision then verbalized by his interlocutor as an invitation to go up into his space (4:1). This spatial transition is possible because John is still in the Spirit. The first thing John sees is a throne and one sitting on it (4:2), a visionary setting that will shape John's point of view as he takes up his role as narrator again. While this change of setting acts as a marker moving us on in the narrative, it paradoxically also maintains thematic continuity, since at the end of the previous narrative unit John's interlocutor analeptically refers to his throne and his Father's throne (3:21), precisely the dominant theme in this new vision.[52]

In what follows, John offers a description of the aesthetic and liturgical orientation of this throne vision, beginning with a description of "the one who sits on the throne" (4:2–3), a title or descriptor he coins here and then deploys throughout his narrative (4:9, 10; 5:1, 7, 13; 6:16; 7:10, 15; 19:4; 21:5; cf. 20:11). From this axial point of power John proceeds to introduce the

---

51. On the difference between story time and narrative time, see Genette, *Narrative Discourse*, 34–35, 40; Chatman, *Story and Discourse*, 64.

52. "What the reader is looking for in a plot is a passage from one state to another – a passage to which he can assign thematic value." Culler, "Defining Narrative Units," 139.

heavenly entourage (i.e. characters in the narrative theory argot) that literally surrounds the throne: twenty-four elders and their thrones (4:4),[53] and four composite beings (4:6).[54] Both groups are engaged in a choreographed liturgy shaped by their theological understanding of the one who sits on the throne (4:8–11). This scene proves crucial to how the narrative construes and conveys its point of view.

The liturgical performance described by John becomes an overture to an exaltation scene, which begins with an announcement of a cosmic search for someone worthy of opening a scroll sealed with seven seals, the importance of which is made evident by the fact that it is found in the right hand of the one who sits on the throne (5:1–4). No one but the Lion who had conquered is found to be worthy to carry out this task, John is told (5:5). However, what John sees is a slaughtered Lamb standing in the midst of the throne and its entourage (5:6), not a conquering Lion, according to the words of one elder. Both antithetical descriptors refer to the same ontological being and are kept in tension,[55] a recurrent feature throughout the narrative.[56] From the moment the Lamb takes/receives the scroll from the right hand of the one who sits on the throne, a new choreographed liturgy is enacted by the four composite beings and the twenty-four elders. Their liturgy now turns christological as their song explains why the slaughtered Lamb is worthy to take the scroll and open its seals (5:7–10). At the same time, the exaltation of the slaughtered Lamb generates a proleptic expectation that is going to be replicated in God's new property – an international people meant to be a kingdom and priesthood

---

53. On the symbolic meaning of the number 12 and its multiples like 24 (12 X 2), 12,000 (12 X 1,000) and 144,000 (12 X 12 X 1,000), which when related to persons usually signal God's people (Rev 7:4–8; 14:1, 3; 21:12, 14) see Barr, *Tales of the End*, location 2328; Resseguie, *Revelation of John*, 108–110; Apringius of Beja, *Explanation of the Revelation* 4.4 (ACT/L); Caesarius of Arles, *Exposition of the Apocalypse* Homily 3 (ACT/L); Bede the Venerable, *Exposition of the Apocalypse* 4.4 (ACT/L); Oecumenius, *Commentary on the Apocalypse* Third Discourse (ACT/G); Andrew of Caesarea, *Commentary on the Apocalypse* 4.10 (ACT/G). For alternative views, see Victorinus of Petovium, *Commentary on the Apocalypse* 4.3 (ACT/L); Aune, *Revelation 1–5*, 287–292.

54. The number 4 tends to be related to beings, things or places linked to the earth (Rev 7:1, 2; 9:14; 20:8; cf. 9:15), though 9:13 is the exception; cf. Barr, *Tales of the End*, location 2322; cf. Resseguie, *Revelation of John*, 111; Oecumenius, *Commentary on the Apocalypse* Third Discourse (ACT/G).

55. See Rowland, "Book of Revelation," 602.

56. See Rowland, 622–623.

to rule on earth (5:9–10; cf. 22:3–5). In other words, it looks forward to the Fellowship of the Throne.

At this point, the concentric pattern of the heavenly throne is enlarged when "myriads of myriads and thousands of thousands" of angels join in this liturgical exaltation of the Lamb (5:11–12). The liturgical performance now reaches its climax when every creature in the cosmos gives praise and honour and glory and power to the Lamb as well as to the one who sits on the throne, a liturgy endorsed by both the four composite beings and the twenty-four elders (5:13). What we have witnessed so far in this vision amounts to a political, theological and liturgical shift. At the beginning we saw the throne and the one who sits on it, but now this view is of the Lamb standing by this axial throne and the one who sits on it, and the whole cosmos now locates power in both of them. The rest of the narrative confirms that this political shift is permanent (cf. 6:16; 7:9–10, 17; 22:1, 3). Also, from creation we move to Christology as a theological category underpinning the new liturgy, which is exercised in three stages, focusing on the Creator first, then on the Lamb, and finally on both together.[57]

From this point on (6:1–8:1), the narrative quickens its pace. The Lamb opens one seal after another (6:1, 3, 5, 7, 9, 12; 8:1). And as the first four seals are opened, the earth (or at least a fourth of it) suffers terribly; in particular, a motif relating to some sort of war and its aftermath emerges (6:1–8),[58] which the opening of the fifth seal confirms by introducing the souls of those who have been slaughtered asking for justice or revenge for those who dwell on earth (6:9–10).[59] However, more casualties are expected (6:11). So far, all action is arguably seen from heaven. And yet, the opening of the sixth seal introduces a cosmic commotion that sees heaven split open and rolled back, revealing the one who sits on the throne and the anger of the Lamb throughout the earth, the sight of which neither the elite (whether political, military or otherwise) nor slave or free person can withstand (6:12–17). The finale of this scene is put on hold, and it seems to reach its denouement in a further vision when the narrative is more advanced (cf. 19:11, 17–21). In the

---

57. cf. Andrew of Caesarea, *Commentary on the Apocalypse* 4.10 (ACT/G).

58. In Revelation 6 Jan Fekkes registers symbolic elements of a holy war motif, see Fekkes, *Isaiah and Prophetic Traditions*, 165–166. For the view on the Apocalypse as a sort of Christian war scroll see Bauckham, *Climax of the Prophecy*, 210–237.

59. In our view, this claim is fully met in Rev 19:2.

meantime, John introduces some sort of parenthesis in this narrative flow, which we could define as an embedded micro narrative.

It is about two short visions of God's people. The first vision (7:1–8) highlights the sealing of the twelve tribes of the children of Israel, with 12,000 people per tribe, amounting to 144,000 individuals (7:4; cf. 14:1, 3);[60] whereas the second vision (7:9–17) introduces a large, countless crowd standing in front of the throne and the Lamb, wearing white long robes and holding palm branches. John is told that they come from the great distress (arguably connected to the war motif and its aftermath as previously mentioned) and they have made their robes white in the blood of the Lamb (7:14), which signals that they now form part of the international people bought with the blood of the slaughtered Lamb in the previous vision (5:9).[61] The vision finishes with proleptic images and language that anticipates the happiness and contentment of life in the holy city and the materialization of the Fellowship of the Throne at the end of the narrative (cf. 21:3–7; 22:3–5), with a particular emphasis on the one who sits on the throne setting among them (7:15; cf. 21:3), and the Lamb shepherding them (7:17). Admittedly, when the seventh seal is opened, "there came about a silence in heaven for about half an hour" (8:1).

---

60. "That the 144,000 Israelites are those called to serve God in battle is clear from the form of 7:4–8: a *census* of the tribes of Israel. In the Old Testament a census is always a counting up of the *military* strength of the nation." Bauckham, *Climax of the Prophecy*, 217. cf. Num 1.

61. In the narrative of the Apocalypse, images of God's people across the ages are juxtaposed to convey the point of their christological orientation at the end of the time. Accordingly, the 144,000 of all the tribes of the children of Israel (7:4) are juxtaposed to a countless large crowd "from every nation and tribe and people and language" (7:9) with a markedly Christian orientation (7:14) that adumbrates the Fellowship of the Throne (cf. 7:15, 17). Again, a singular woman (12:1) gives birth to the child-Messiah (12:5), however, the rest of her seed or descendants are "those who keep the commands of God and have the testimony of Jesus" (12:17). Then, the 144,000 are given an explicit Christian orientation in 14:1, 3. Also, there is "the camp of the holy ones and the city that has been loved" (20:9). Once more, in the vision of the (walled) holy city that comes down from heaven, on its twelve gates "names were written, which are the names of the twelve tribes of the children of Israel" (21:12); equally, upon the twelve foundations of the wall of the city "twelve names of the twelve apostles of the Lamb" (21:14). Therefore, if "144,000 is not a quantity" but "a symbol [of God's people]," then to equate the 144,000 (7:4) to the countless international crowd (7:9) is a plausible exegetical move, see Barr, *Tales of the End*, location 2416; cf. Resseguie, *Revelation of John*, 136–138; Beale, *Book of Revelation*, 416–426. For alternative understandings of the similarity of both groups see Caird, *Revelation of St. John*, 94–96; Bauckham, *Climax of the Prophecy*, 215–229. For a view that these are different groups see Aune, *Revelation 6–16*, 439–450; O'Donovan, "History and Politics," 34–35.

The vertiginous pace of the narrative, which climaxed with the cosmic commotion, is paused in terms of story time. Arguably, the reader/hearer may use this pause to digest what has taken place since John began to tell us about the heavenly throne, and may begin to think about a possible plot: (a) harmonious theo-political innovations in heaven, and war and its aftermath on earth, both as a result of the exaltation of the slaughtered Lamb; (b) cosmic commotion because of the great day of the one who sits on the throne and the Lamb's anger; (c) the allusions to the Fellowship of the Throne which has been adumbrated twice; (d) then, silence in heaven.[62]

3.4 Dis/continuity?

What comes next is a series of seven trumpets which are blown by seven angels, one at a time (8:7, 8, 10, 12; 9:1, 13; 11:15). Admittedly, it is not clear in the narrative whether there is continuity or not in terms of the story time. On the one hand, John sees seven angels who stand before God (8:2) – though there had been no previous reference to a group of seven angels,[63] instead John had referred to individual (1:1; 2:1, 8, 12, 18; 3:1, 7, 14; 5:2) or countless angels (5:11; cf. 3:5). He also sees an altar in front of the throne (8:3), that is, in front of God (9:13), under which he had earlier seen the souls of those who had been slaughtered (6:9); he sees the incense associated with the prayers of the holy ones (8:3, 4) featured earlier (5:8), with any vertical motion up to this point appearing to go down from heaven to earth (8:5, 7, 10; 9:1; 10:1; though 9:2–3 and 11:7, 12 prove the exception). At this stage therefore the narrative setting appears to be still located around the heavenly throne, offering some degree of continuity between the series of seven seals and the series of seven trumpets.

---

62. For an alternative interpretation of these apocalyptic visions, yet still with a christological focus, see O'Donovan, "History and Politics," 30–32.

63. Admittedly, there is a motif of "the seven angels" in the book of Revelation, that is to say, (a) the "seven angels" of the seven churches (1:20; cf. 2:1, 8, 12, 18; 3:1, 7, 14; 22:16) who as seven stars are in the right hand (1:16, 20) of "like a son of man" (1:13); (b) the seven angels (οἱ ἑπτά ἄγγελοι) who stand in the presence of God and were given seven trumpets (8:2, 6); (c) the seven angels (οἱ ἑπτά ἄγγελοι) who have the seven blows/strokes/plagues (15:1, 6, 8; 21:9) and coming/going out of the temple (15:6) were given seven golden bowls full of God's wrath (15:7; cf. 16:1; 17:1; 21:9), which each in turn poured out (cf. 16:2, 3, 4, 8, 10, 12, 17); cf. *Tobit* 12.15 (LXX); *1 Enoch* 20, which names "the seven archangels" (20:8); *Life of Adam and Eve (Apocalypse of Moses)* 40.7 (OTP/2).

On the other hand, however, the one who sits on the throne and his entourage (i.e. the twenty-four elders and the four composite beings), recede into the background, so to speak, and the Lamb actually vanishes from this vision. Only the twenty-four elders feature again in a liturgical act at the end of this series (11:16). It would appear that the launch of the series of seven trumpets is influenced in some way by the prayers of the holy ones (8:3–5), which are pictured between the two references to the seven angels. These references to the seven angels help bring about a sense of narrative progression as follows:[64]

> And I saw the **seven** [ἑπτά] **angels** [ἄγγελος] who stand in front of God, and seven trumpets were given to them (Rev 8:2)

> And the **seven** [ἑπτά] **angels** [ἄγγελος] who have the seven trumpets prepared themselves so that they might blow [the trumpets] (Rev 8:6)

In our view, though the narrative does not clearly resolve this ambiguity of whether there is continuity or not between the two series,[65] what is clear is that both the series of the seals and the series of the trumpets are rooted in the earlier vision of the exaltation of the slaughtered Lamb who stands in the midst of the heavenly throne (5:6–10), where the link between the incense and the prayer of the holy ones is introduced for the first time (5:8; cf. 8:3, 4).

As for the series of seven trumpets: the first four wreak havoc on a third of the earth (8:7), sea (8:8), rivers and springs of waters (8:10), and heavenly bodies, meaning sun, moon, stars (8:12).[66] This emphasis on the third part of "something" (cf. Ezek 5:2) denotes a sense of crescendo with respect to the

---

64. This literary device for the construal of a progressive narrative thread is deployed again in the telling of (i) the dragon's downfall (12:7–9 → 20:1–3), and the recounting of (ii) the seven angels bringing the last seven plagues (15:1 → 15:5–6).

65. Bauckham, who favours a clear continuity between the two series, to the point that the seventh seal encompasses the whole series of seven trumpets, "resolves" this ambiguity by appealing to a literary technique known as overlapping or interweaving. For him, the seventh seal includes the throwing of the altar's fire with the censer into the earth (8:5). At the same time, the vision of the seven trumpets begins with the reference to the seven angels in 8:2. This is the overlapping. See Bauckham, *Climax of the Prophecy*, 8–9; cf. Beale, *Book of Revelation*, 460–464. For alternative explanations, see Caird, *Revelation of St. John*, 103–111; Resseguie, *Revelation of John*, 141–143; Aune, *Revelation 6–16*, 494–497, 507–511.

66. For contrasting views on the significance of the "trumpets" see Beale, *Book of Revelation*, 472 (not seeking repentance but punishment) and Caird, *Revelation of St. John*, 112–113 (seeking repentance through punishment); cf. Exod 7:14–11:10; (LXX) *Wisdom of Solomon* 16.

authority exerted on a fourth of the earth by the rider of the pale horse and his companion, which is Death and Hades (6:8), after the fourth seal has been opened (6:7). And yet, the fifth (9:1–12) and sixth (9:13–21) trumpets give way, once more, to the imagery of the war motif.[67] In particular, it is stressed that "those who do not have the seal of God on their heads" become targets (9:4), and that a third of human beings might be killed (9:15). In addition, for the first time in the narrative, the underworld, portrayed as "the abyss" (9:1, 2, 11), becomes the source of this military punishment.

The sixth trumpet gives way to another embedded narrative (i.e. two short visions highly correlated).[68] John himself becomes the protagonist of the first vision as a powerful angel comes down from heaven with a small scroll, and orders him to take it and eat it (10:1–10; cf. Ezek 2:8–3:4). The angel then explains this enactment as the calling and/or commissioning of John to "prophesy to peoples and nations and languages and many kings" (10:11). The second short vision tells of the two witnesses (11:1–14) who prophesy for a limited time with an impressive display of power, but are then killed by the beast that goes up from the abyss (11:7), arguably emulating the fate of their Lord (11:8).[69] However, after three and a half days their corpses are infused with God's breath of life (11:11), and they ascend into heaven in a cloud (11:12). There follows a great earthquake which destroys a tenth of the city and kills seven thousand, with the result that "the others were afraid and gave glory to the God of heaven" (11:13).

---

67. cf. Caird, *Revelation of St. John*, 119.
68. cf. Resseguie, *Revelation of John*, 53.
69. On the identity of the two witnesses, it was suggested they were Enoch and Elijah (e.g. Tertullian, *A Treatise on the Soul* 50 [ANF/3]; Oecumenius, *Commentary on the Apocalypse* Sixth Discourse [ACT/G]; Andrew of Caesarea, *Commentary on the Apocalypse* 10.30 [ACT/G]), Moses or Elisha and Elijah, or Elijah and Jeremiah (Victorinus of Petovium, *Commentary on the Apocalypse* 11.3), the Two Testaments (Caesarius of Arles, *Exposition of the Apocalypse* Homily 8), or "the church that preaches and prophesies on the basis of the two Testaments." (Primasius, *Commentary on the Apocalypse* 11.3, as quoted in Weinrich, *Revelation*, 159; cf. Bede the Venerable, *Exposition of the Apocalypse* 11.3 [ACT/L]). The latter, favoured by modern scholars, has been reinstated as "The OT law demands that a minimum of two witnesses be required for just judgment (Num. 35:30; Deut. 17:6; 19:15). Thus the two witnesses are not two actual individual prophets; rather, they symbolize the corporate prophetic witness of the church." Beale and McDonough, "Revelation," 1119; cf. Aune, *Revelation 6–16*, 603; Bauckham, *Climax of the Prophecy*, 273. What is more, since the witnesses are described as lampstands (Rev 11:4), and a lampstand signified a church (1:20; cf. 2:5), it suggests "there is a role of prophecy and witness for the churches, too." Rowland, "Book of Revelation," 642; cf. Boxall, *Revelation of Saint John*, 164.

The seventh trumpet takes us back to heaven, where loud voices proclaim: "the kingdom of the world has become of our Lord and of his Messiah, and he will rule for the ages of ages" (11:15). This declaration is followed by a liturgical act performed by the twenty-four elders (11:16–18). The series then comes to an end with a vision of God's temple in heaven and the ark of the covenant, and a display of "lightnings and sounds and thunders and an earthquake and great hailstone" (11:19), which rather than signifying a prelude to divine judgment appear to simply echo the liturgical mood of the twenty-four elders.

Overall, and in spite of the discontinuity, it would appear that God's people, the liturgical sociality, whether portrayed explicitly as the holy ones (8:3, 4; cf. 11:18), John's ego (10:8–11), the two witnesses (11:3; cf. 11:18), or allusively as those who have God's seal on their foreheads (9:4), are at the forefront of this vision of seven trumpets. Their prayers are instrumental in the launch of the series of seven trumpets,[70] and their prophetic call and powerful performance, though met with a violent end, are vindicated in anticipation of the theo-political and liturgical finale of the vision (the act of ruling the world now belongs to the Lord and his Messiah, whom the hearer/reader must equate with the one who sits on the throne and the slaughtered-yet-exalted Lamb of the previous vision, a partial unveiling of the Fellowship of the Throne). At the same time, the liturgical performance interprets this theo-political event as God exerting his kingly power while dealing with angry nations, judging the dead, giving his servants their reward, and destroying those who destroy the earth (11:16–18).

3.5 Negotiating a Way Forward

Up to this point in the narrative, John's visionary reports have shown a relatively consistent pattern, where a first vision of someone ("like a son of man," the one who sits on the throne and his entourage, the slaughtered-yet-exalted Lamb) or something (the offering of incense before the throne, symbolizing the prayers of all the holy ones) is followed by a series of seven events, whether numbered or not (seven messages dictated, seven seals opened, seven trumpets blown). Each of these three visions features either an exalted figure

---

70. cf. Beale, *Book of Revelation*, 472.

("like a son of man") or a scene of exaltation (the slaughtered Lamb, the Messiah) in correlation to a senior (political) figure (Father, the one who sits on the throne, the Lord) and his throne, authority, power and kingdom. God's people, the liturgical sociality, also feature repeatedly in each of these visions, and the recurrent call to conquer that is included in each of the seven messages to the churches resonates greatly with the war motif of the seven seals and trumpets in the visions.

Admittedly, what comes next in the narrative shows a remarkable break with the previous pattern, and more importantly, the story time.[71] This sense of an analeptic break-off in terms of story time is magnified by an impersonal narrative voice ("A great portent was seen in heaven . . . and another portent was seen in heaven . . ." 12:1, 3), which is in sharp contrast to John's first-person narration up to this point. There remains however a continuity of the themes of exaltation or the presence of an exalted figure, God's people, and the war motif, though with changes in the discourse. Amidst the changes in the narrative, various events, characters, and themes emerge that hold the narrative together and function as new strands in the story moving the action forward.

(1) There is a short series of three unnumbered portents in heaven (12:1, 3; 15:1), the latter of which leads to the final series of seven, that of the seven bowls (16:1–21). These series connecting with each other in some way contribute to a sense of story time.

(2) As mentioned above (§3.4), a new narrative thread relating to the dragon's downfall emerges between 12:7–9 and 20:1–3, 7–10. Because of the expanse of narrative between these two texts (chs 13–19), the theme of the dragon remains in the background throughout, and the dragon's agents (the sea-beast and the earth-beast, and through them the great city) become active characters in the story wreaking havoc on God's people.

(3) Over the course of several chapters a striking parallelism becomes apparent between the markers that delimit two contrasting visions, one about the great city/prostitute/Babylon,

---

71. cf. Bauckham, *Climax of the Prophecy*, 15; O'Donovan, "History and Politics," 35.

and the other about the holy city/Lamb's bride/new Jerusalem (i.e. 17:1, 3 || 21:9–10; and 19:9–10 || 22:6–9).[72]

(4) The character of the beast that goes up from the sea (13:1) features also several times in this stretch of narrative. We see it in the vision of the seven bowls, where it becomes the "target" of the fifth bowl (16:10), so to speak; again in the vision of the prostitute/great city/Babylon, where it is portrayed as the embodiment of a doomed political dynasty (17:7–13; cf. 17:3), and further on, it features once more in the vision of the divine King (19:19–20), though this time as an individual entity.

(5) The theme/event of the judgment on Babylon the great (14:8) features as part of the vision of the Lamb standing on Mount Zion (14:1–20), the subject of one of the three angelic messages (14:6, 8, 9). We see the great city again in the vision of the seven bowls (16:1–21), where when the seventh bowl is poured out, Babylon is broken into three, while the other cities of the nations simply fall (16:19). Then, beginning in chapter 17 (in particular 17:16), through the whole of chapter 18, and most of the first half of chapter 19, we have an extensive narrative of its fall. In fact, 18:2 uses the exact same expression to refer to the city as 14:8.

Bearing in mind the various narrative threads set out above, it is for the interpreter to negotiate a way forward in order to provide an account of how the narrative unfolds and where transitions, whether temporal or spatial, take place. The risk of severing a narrative thread when choosing to track one character or theme over another remains latent when deciding where to make a narrative partition, however. Interestingly enough, one option preferred by some scholars takes 1 as a starting point, followed by 3, a framework which can accommodate points 4 and 5. However, the resulting exegetical conundrum posed by point 2 in this scenario is not explained satisfactorily in our view, since it remains *split*, that is, unconnected in this

---

72. David Aune provides "a synoptic comparison of the parallel texts that frame these [textual] units," in Aune, *Revelation 1–5*, xcv–xcvii.

account, treated as separate events/stories.[73] For our part, we take point 2 as our guideline,[74] which easily accommodates points 1, 4, and 5, leaving point 3 to take the strain, so to speak. In our opinion this option makes narrative sense, and further exegetical reasons for this *choice* are provided in the next chapter (§4.3.3). At present, however, we continue with our narrative in order to provide an account of its story.

3.6 Narrative Unit 3: Authority, Liturgy and Sociality in the Aftermath of Political Conspiracy

Two consecutive portents in heaven (12:1, 3) narrated in the third person mark the beginning of this new narrative unit. The first portent is a pregnant woman in labour pains (12:1–2), and the second is a dragon standing in front of her, ready to devour her child as soon as he is born (12:3–4). However, the dragon's plot is foiled when the woman's child is taken away towards God and his throne (12:5), bringing about the dragon's downfall and his banishment from heaven (12:7–9). Heaven then celebrates this theo-political display of God's power, and the authority of his Messiah (12:10). The correlation between these two events (i.e. the exaltation of the child-Messiah and the downfall of the dragon), sets in motion a series of characters and events whose nature and fate are gradually revealed as the narrative unfolds (chs 13–19). The telling of the dragon's downfall is later resumed only to reach its anticlimax in the final stop of his downward journey, the lake of fire (20:1–10).

After harassing the woman who has just given birth to the child-Messiah (12:13) without success, the dragon turns his hostility towards the rest of the woman's progeny (i.e. "her seed," 12:17). However, the dragon recedes into the background (or as the narrative puts it later on, he is tied and kept in the

---

73. Broadly speaking, Bauckham follows this option, as we discussed earlier (§3.1). And despite the fact that he deploys the technique known as overlapping or interweaving to explain the narrative threads of the seven angels with seven trumpets (Rev 8:2, 6), and to link them with the seventh seal (8:1) on the one hand, and to link the seventh trumpet (11:15–19) with the seven angels with seven plagues (15:1, 6) encompassing chapters 12–14 on the other, nonetheless, he avoids using this technique to deal with the narrative thread of the dragon's downfall (12:7–9; 20:1–3). See Bauckham, *Climax of the Prophecy*, 8–9.

74. "The parallels between chs. 12 and 20, though the chapters are not identical at every point, suggest that they depict the same events and mutually interpret one another," Beale, *Book of Revelation*, 992.

abyss-prison, see 20:1–3) to give way to the emergence, first, of a fearsome and composite beast from the sea,[75] very similar to himself (13:1), whom he invests with his own power and authority (13:2, 4); and second, of a less fearsome beast from the earth who mimicks him (13:11). The former blasphemes against God and heaven (13:5–6), exerts authority (13:5, 7), makes war against the holy ones and conquers them (13:7),[76] and is worshipped by those who dwell on the earth (13:4, 8); whereas the latter performs signs (13:13) and deceives those who dwell on the earth (13:14);[77] its coercive public liturgy enforces the worship of the sea-beast and its image (13:15–17).

At this point it is worth highlighting that John's narrative temporarily gives way to a shorter counter-narrative, and the narrative's perspective registers a dramatic reversal. Here we find a political authority and a public liturgy from below (i.e. sea/abyss, earth) that unashamedly challenges the authority and liturgy from above (i.e. heaven).[78] In the world order construed by the dragon's agents, it is the dragon and the sea-beast (and its image) who deserve to be worshipped (13:4, 8, 12), rather than one who sits on the throne (because he is the Creator, 4:10–11), or the Lamb (because he was slaughtered, and bought for God, with this blood, a people from "every tribe and language and people and nation," 5:8–14); for them it is the empowered sea-beast (13:2, 4–5) that commands authority from "every tribe and people and language and nation" (13:7), rather than the Son of God (2:18, 26) or God's Messiah (12:10).

The vision of the Lamb standing on Mount Zion (14:1), however, counteracts this theological and liturgical heresy (or counter-narrative). In this vision we see the Lamb together with the 144,000 who have been bought from

---

75. John's allusions to Daniel 7:3–8, 17–25 are almost self-evident, cf. Beale, *Book of Revelation*, 683. However, to account for two beasts coming out from the sea and earth, respectively, George Caird referred to a Jewish tradition about Leviathan, a sea-creature, and Behemoth, an earth-creature, as preserved in *1 Enoch* 60.7–8; *4 Ezra* 6.49–52; and *2 Baruch* 29.4, for instance, cf. Caird, *Revelation of St. John*, 161. Arguably, this tradition seems "an exegesis of Gen 1:21" (Stone, *Fourth Ezra*, 186), in particular, and an elaboration on the Old Testament Leviathan (Isa 27:1; Ps 74:14; 104:26; Job 3:8; 40:25; cf. 1QIsaa 21.8; 4Q380 f3.1) and Behemoth (Job 40:15), in general; cf. Aune, *Revelation 6–16*, 728–729. Interestingly enough, Beale's stance on this is that "The depiction of the two beasts in ch. 13 is based in part on Job 40–41, which is the OT depiction of two Satanic beasts opposing God." (Beale, *Book of Revelation*, 682).

76. cf. Rev 12:17.

77. cf. Rev 12:9.

78. cf. Barr, *Tales of the End*, location 235; cf. Barr, "Apocalypse as a Symbolic," 40; Resseguie, *Revelation of John*, 42–43. O'Donovan calls this form of authority "empire," see O'Donovan, "History and Politics," 36–38.

the earth (14:3; cf. 14:4; 7:4) and whose worship in song before the throne (14:3) is described in a later vision (15:2–4).[79] In this setting three angelic "messages" are proclaimed in midheaven.[80]

The first one relates to an eternal gospel for those who "sit" on the earth and for "every nation and tribe and language and people" (14:6): "Fear God and give him glory, since the hour of his judgment has come; and worship the one who made the heaven and the earth and sea and springs of water."[81] Here there is a marked contrast between the beasts' heresy and the eternal gospel. In other words, the first angel proclaims a return to an orthodox theology that underpins the true liturgy.

The second angel breaks the news that "it has fallen, it has fallen, Babylon the great" (14:8; 18:2). This is the first time in the narrative that Babylon is mentioned, though the descriptor "great" was ascribed, in a previous vision, to the city where the corpses of the two witnesses had been laid out, the same "city" where their Lord had been crucified (11:8). At the end of that same vision, a tenth of the city fell after a great earthquake (11:13). This is another narrative thread that can be tracked in further visions, where Babylon is explicitly referred to as "the great city" (16:19; 18:10, 21).

The third angelic message declares the consequences for those who worship the beast (14:10–11). Since the news about the fate of Babylon is sandwiched between the message of the eternal good news and the message regarding the dire consequences for the worshippers of the beast, it may be argued that a subtle link is established between this city and the worshippers of the beast, which we will see the narrative develop subsequently. These angelic declarations therefore show that the challenge posed by the beasts does not go unnoticed, but that the liturgical polity they have construed is bound for doom.

In fact, from this point forward this is the tone of the narrative (i.e. the time for God's judgment has come). Accordingly, another vision of "like a son of man" shows him leading the reaping of the harvest of the earth (14:14–20),

---

79. cf. Mangina, *Revelation*, 171.

80. Just in this narrative unit, the story registers vertiginous spatial ups and downs, so to speak: from heaven (Rev 12:1, 3, 4) downwards to earth (12:4, 9, 13) and further down to sea (12:12, 18; 13:1), then going up to earth (13:3, 8, 11–14), to Mount Zion (14:1), to the throne (in heaven) (14:3), and down again to midheaven (14:6).

81. Rev 14:7.

while the following vision of another portent in heaven (the third in this unnumbered series) tells of seven angels bringing about the last seven plagues (15–16). As with the vision of the seven trumpets, there is a liturgical prelude (15:2–4). Then one of the four composite beings hand over seven golden bowls full of God's anger to the seven angels (15:7), who in turn pour them out, one after another (16:2, 3, 4, 8, 10, 12, 17). The first four bowls in this series are poured out into the earth, the sea, the rivers and springs of water, and the sun; whereas the fifth is poured out on the beast's throne, which results in his kingdom becoming subsumed in darkness (16:10), and the sixth is poured out on the great river Euphrates. The pouring out of the last bowl into the air leads to a great earthquake that splits the great city into three parts, and causes the cities of the nations to fall (16:18–19).[82]

But is this the end of the story? Not quite. The narrative now focuses on the great city, which is now portrayed as a woman, a high-class prostitute, and elaborates on her judgment. This woman bears the name of Babylon the great (17:1–5; cf. 17.18), and the vision discloses the close bond between her and the beast (17:3, 7).[83] However, the symbolic nature of the beast is interpreted here à la Daniel 7.[84] It stands for some sort of political dynasty, where its seven heads represent both seven mountains and seven kings (17:9),[85] and its ten horns ten kings (17:12). In addition, it seems that the beast in itself stands for one single king (17:11), though this remains unclear. If so, in total the beast stands for a dynasty of eighteen kings.[86]

The beast is bound for destruction, however (17:8, 11; cf. Dan 7:11–12, 26), and the political dynasty it stands for seems to be on the decline: of the

---

82. For a synoptic contrast between the two series of trumpets and bowls, see Aune, *Revelation 6–16*, 498.

83. O'Donovan calls this symbiotic relationship "empire" as well, see O'Donovan, "History and Politcs," 38–42.

84. It should be noted that Rev 17:9–11 interprets in Danielic fashion the vision of the beast in Rev 13. In Daniel 7, after the vision of the four beasts that come out of the great sea (Dan 7:2–12), an interpretation follows, where the beasts stand for four kings that will arise from the earth (Dan 7:17). However, arguably these beasts are also understood as kingdoms (Dan 7:23). In addition, the ten horns of the fourth beast are interpreted as ten kings (Dan 7:24).

85. It remains a possibility that the "seven kings," as a whole, may allude to the founding myth of Rome, with its (legendary) seven kings, and its seven hills; cf. Aune, *Revelation 17–22*, 944–945. On seven (Roman) kings and an eight, represented as statues, and how the latter overthrew some of the former, see Cassius Dio, *Roman History* 43.45.

86. Could *18* (i.e. 6+6+6) be another way to refer to the number of the beast, i.e. 666 (cf. 13:18)?

seven "head-kings," five have fallen, one still stands, and the other has not yet come, and when he does it is only for a short while (17:10).[87] As for the ten "horn-kings," at present (in the story time) these are "kingdomless," but will receive authority for one hour with the beast (17:12) and submit to the beast (17:13, 17). Moreover, these ten soon-to-be-kings, together with the beast-king, will plot against the city-woman and put her to fire (17:16). In other words, since it is in the nature of the beast "to devour" (cf. Dan 7:7, 19, 23; Jer 51:34, 44), so the beast will devour this prostitute-woman as the dragon tried to devour the child of another woman (see 12:4). On the whole, the version of authority enacted by the (corporate) beast militates against the sociality it pretends to support and rule.

Admittedly, the vision of the dirge of Babylon (18:1–19:4), the great city, tells us more of the city as a city with political, economic and social entanglements, which the vision sexualizes and describes as improper relations thus conveying that they are tainted and shaped by what the beasts stand for, as already discussed. The great city is also both a place and a sociality hostile to God's people (18:24; cf. 17:6), and as such she is judged further by God (19:2), an event that fully meets the demand voiced by the souls of those who had been slaughtered when the fifth seal was opened by the Lamb in an earlier vision (6:9). This vision thus provides an additional perspective of the fate of the great city, which arguably amounts to ontological annihilation (18:21).[88]

Next, it is the turn of the beasts, dealt with in the vision of the rider on the white horse (19:11–21), who is portrayed as the ultimate authority personalized (i.e. the divine King). This vision deploys the discourse of justice, conveying it in both agonistic and forensic terms (19:11) on a global scale

---

87. The narrative shies away from identifying each one of the seven head-kings as opposed to, say, identifying each one of the seven churches, a fact to consider in any attempt to clarify what the narrative deliberately mystifies. For a synoptic list of "alternate ways of counting the Roman emperors" see Aune, *Revelation. 17–22*, 947–948. Historically speaking Julius Caesar was quite reluctant to bear the (political) title "king," see Nicolaus of Damascus, *Life of Augustus* 21; Suetonius, *Deified Julius Caesar* 79.

88. Once more, a pattern of progression of the "judgment" that wreaked havoc on the "great city" may be noted. Accordingly, in the vision of the sixth seal, a tenth of the (great) city fell after a great earthquake (Rev 11:13; cf. 11:8); whereas in the vision of the seventh bowl, the great city was split into three parts after a powerful earthquake (16:18–19). In the dirge of Babylon this is portrayed as undergone annihilation (18:21).

(19:15).⁸⁹ Sandwiched between the vision of the fall of the great city and the vision of the divine King, however, we have a short vision about another sexualized yet appropriate (i.e. covenantal) relationship: that of a marriage between the Lamb and his fiancée (19:5–10),⁹⁰ adumbrating the advent of the holy city from heaven (21:2, 9). Returning to the vision of the divinely authorized King (19:16), the rider on the white horse who is also called the "Word of God" (19:13), we find that as he "speaks" the forensic language of justice he effects a judicial verdict on human authority which has by now become complicit in theological delusion and coercive liturgy as enacted by the (sea) beast, the false prophet and their alliance with the kings of the earth (19:19–20; cf. Ps 2:1–3). As a result, the divine King dethrones the beast and de-authorizes the kings of the earth (19:20–21; cf. Dan 7:11, 26; Ps 2:4–12).⁹¹

Interestingly enough, this vision illustrates the conflict between two modes of authority in spatial terms: one from above, heaven (19:11, 14), from whence the rider on the white horse comes, and one from below, sea, from whence the beast comes (implicitly), and earth, from whence the kings come (19:19), with an explicit spatial boundary between them signalled by midheaven (19:17).⁹²

---

89. "And I saw the heaven having being opened; and look, a white horse, and the one who sits on it being called faithful and true, and with justice he judges and wages war." (Rev 19:11). This apocalyptic vision alludes to the mode of authority embodied by the figure of the king in ancient Israel, whose job description, so to speak, was to judge and to wage war on behalf of their people (1 Sam 8:20; cf. 4Q51 8a b.12–13; 1 Sam 8:5). This Old Testament allusion has been ignored by biblical scholars commenting on Revelation 19:11.

90. On marriage as a metaphorical expression of a covenant see Mendenhall, and Herion, "Covenant," 1.1194–1195.

91. *4 Ezra* 11–12 and *2 Baruch* 35–43 (OTP/1), both roughly contemporary with John's Apocalypse, deploy a "Daniel 7" framework to convey each a vision (*4 Ezra* 11.1 – 12.3; *2 Baruch* 35.1 – 37.1), which in turn is explained each à la Daniel 7 (*4 Ezra* 12.10–39; *2 Baruch* 39–40). In fact, *4 Ezra* 12.11 explicitly claims this is a further elaboration of Daniel's vision; cf. Stone, *Fourth Ezra*, 345. More importantly, in both visions and explanations, it is (a) the Lion (*4 Ezra* 11.37)/Messiah (*4 Ezra* 12.31–32) that will judge and destroy the Danielic fourth beast portrayed as eagle (*4 Ezra* 12.32–33), which signified Rome, see Stone, 348; or (b) the vine and fountain (*2 Baruch* 36.3)/Anointed One (*2 Baruch* 39.7) that will convict and kill the Danielic fourth beast portrayed as the great forest (*2 Baruch* 40.1–2), cf. Stone, 368–369. Additionally, in *4 Ezra* 12.3 "the whole body of the eagle was burned"; cf. Daniel 7:11, where the fourth beast is killed and its corpse burnt, which in turn is explained as a forensic act of dethronement (Dan 7:26).

92. In the narrative of the book of Revelation, the combination of the verb καταβαίνω (to move downward, come/go down) followed by the expression ἐκ τοῦ οὐρανοῦ (from heaven) features eight times as follows: (a) the (holy) city comes down from heaven (3:12; 21:2, 10); (b) an angel comes down from heaven (10:1; 18:1; 20:1); (c) fire comes down from heaven (13:13; 20:9); and (d) large hailstones come down from heaven (16:21). However, this combination of terms is never deployed in the vision of the rider on the white horse, i.e. the divine King. Rather, any indication of motion is given (1) to "the armies, which are in heaven, came after

In addition, this scene provides the finale for the vision of the sixth seal, where heaven is rolled up and the elite on earth, led by the kings of the earth, are faced with the anger of the Lamb (6:12–17).[93] What is more, the vision of the rider on the white horse provides a full response to the question posed by the worshippers of the dragon and the beast, who asked: "who [is] similar to the beast, and who is capable to wage war against it?" (13:4).

After that, the narrative analeptically takes us back to the dragon's story. In fact, this new vision of his downfall and demise offers us a new perspective on his persona (20:1–3, 7–10).[94] In the earlier vision of another (i.e. second) portent in heaven, the dragon plotted against the child-Messiah (12:4); in this vision, however, he is portrayed as a someone whose fate discloses that he had conspired politically against a superior power, since he is seized, tied, thrown into an abyss-prison and locked up (20:1–3).[95] And when the prisoner is released (20:7), he deceives the nations (cf. 12:9),[96] and arguably his

---

[ἀκολουθέω]" the rider on the white horse (19:14), (2) to "all the birds that fly in midheaven" to get together (συνάγω) (19:17; cf. Ezek 39:4, 17), (3) to "the beast and the kings of the earth and their armies having been gathered [συνάγω] to make war" (19:19). Therefore, if this passage may be regarded as a "parousia" text ("there is general agreement among commentators that this pericope is a description of the return or Parousia of Jesus Christ" [Aune, *Revelation 17–22*, 1046]), it should be understood as a "presence" as opposed to "arrival or coming," that is to say, the "presence" of the divine King is now evident since heaven has been opened (19:11; cf. 6:14). Precisely this is the point made by a similar vision after the opening of the sixth seal (6:14–17). By contrast, *Apocalypse of Peter* 1 (NTA/2) renders a version of the Parousia developed from Mark 13 and parallels.

93. cf. Fekkes, *Isaiah and Prophetic Traditions*, 166.

94. cf. Beale, *Book of Revelation*, 992.

95. In the Old Testament motif of political conspiracy, a king of Israel or Judah is seized, bound, and imprisoned – in short, dethroned and exiled after an ancient Near Eastern imperial power invades either the northern kingdom of Israel or the southern kingdom of Judah because of the evil done by their respective king in YHWH's eyes, for example 2 Kgs 15:30; 17:1–6. Evidently, the Old Testament pattern of political conspiracy is but an instance of a wider practice in the ancient Near East. For instance, tablet BM 92502 lines ii 32–35, of the so-called Assyrian and Babylonian Chronicles, recorded that "Shutruk-Nahhunte (II), king of Elam, was seized by his brother, Hallushu-(Inshushinak I) (lit. Hallushu, his brother, seized him) and he (Hallushu-Inshushinak I) shut the door in his face. For eighteen years Shutruk-Nahhunte (II) ruled Elam. Hallushu-(Inshushinak I), his brother, ascended the throne in Elam." (Grayson, *Assyrian and Babylonian Chronicles*, 77–78). Kirk Grayson argues that the phrase "shut the door in his face" is perhaps "an Elamite idiom meaning 'he threw him in prison'" (Grayson, 77).

96. In the vision of the sixth trumpet, the nations will trample the holy city for forty-two months (11:2); whereas in the vision of the seventh trumpet, the liturgy of the twenty-four elders reminds us that "the nations were angry, and yet your anger came" (11:18). On the other hand, Babylon, the great city, exerted its influence on all the nations, since "from the wine of the strong desire of her unlawful sexual intercourse she has given to drink to all the nations" (14:8; cf. 18:3). Also, the great city portrayed as a woman "sits" on nations (17:15). Again, all

agents Gog and Magog (cf. Ezek 38:2–6), into gathering for war (20:8; cf. Ezek 38:8–9) against the camp of the holy ones (20:9; cf. 7:1–8), that is the beloved city (cf. 7:9–17). However, the assault on the city is frustrated when fire comes down from heaven and "eats" the dragon's allies (20:9; cf. Ezek 38:22; 39:6), and the dragon is thrown into the lake of fire joining the beast and the false prophet there (20:10). In other words, as this vision takes up again the story of the dragon's political conspiracy and downfall, it provides a summary of what had been happening from the time he unsuccessfully plotted against the child-Messiah (i.e. making war against the holy ones), that is, the rest of the woman's descendants (cf. 12:17). Once more, this vision signals the hostility of the dragon's agents towards God's people as a challenge to "above" (heaven) from "below" (abyss and earth).[97]

At the same time, the story of the dragon's demise encompasses a short throne vision about the vindication of a particular group of people, "the souls of those who have been beheaded/executed because of the testimony of Jesus and because of the word of God" (20:4; cf. 6:9).[98] Presumably in heaven, they (a) are granted justice or judgment or a judicial verdict (20:4), which (b) is materialized as they are brought back to life from death (20:4),[99] and (c) rule with the Messiah for the same length of time as the dragon remains in his abyss-prison (i.e. a cryptic thousand years, 20:4, 6).[100] This vision also adumbrates the Fellowship of the Throne.

---

the nations were deceived by the sorcery/magic of the great city (18:23). When the great city is split into three parts after an earthquake, the cities of the nations fall (16:19).

97. Interestingly enough, the liturgy of those who conquer the beast acknowledges the Lord God all-powerful as "King of the nations" (15:3), hoping that "all the nations will come and worship before you" (15:4).

98. Arguably, these were the people targeted by the dragon and his agents in the narrative, cf. 12:17; 13:7; Pliny the Younger, *Letters* 10.96.2–3.

99. On "the most complex development of resurrection belief in any Jewish or Christian document of the whole period" see Wright, *Resurrection*, 470–476.

100. Two contrasting early views on "a thousand years" are conveyed in Justin Martyr, *Dialogue with Trypho* 2.80 (ANF/1) and Augustine, *City of God* 20.9. Overall, Justin's view is known as pre-millennial or literal, whereas Augustine's view is referred to as a-millennial, inaugurated millennialism, or spiritual, see Aune, *Revelation 17–22*, 1089; Beale, *Book of Revelation*, 972–973. In connection with this, it should be noted the Apocalypse's dealings with the temporal are wilfully cryptic, with its references to time intervals often changing their (face) value: from "42 months" to "1,260 days" (Rev 11:2–3; 12:6; cf. Dan 12:11; *1 Maccabees* 1.54; 4.52–54; *1 Enoch* 74.13), then the more vague "a short time" (Rev 12:12; cf. *Sibylline Oracles* 12.240), to a mysterious "a time and times and a half of time" (Rev 12:14; cf. Dan 7:25;

Immediately after the dragon's demise another throne scene follows (20:11–15; cf. 4:2), in which heaven and earth are personified as animated entities fleeing from the presence of the one who sits on the throne (20:11),[101] but no place was found for them to hide (20:11), anticipating in some way the advent of a new heaven and a new earth (21:1), as the old order had passed away. At this point the dead are judged according to their works (20:12–13), as had been disclosed earlier in the liturgy of the twenty-four elders after the seventh trumpet had been blown: "the time [came] to judge the dead" (11:18). From among the dead, "whoever was not found written in the book of life, that person was thrown into the lake of fire" (20:15), which is defined as the second death (20:14). The names of the worshippers of the beast do not feature in the book of life (13:8; 17:8), whereas the name of the one who conquers is not to be wiped out from the book of life (3:5; cf. 21:27). Interestingly, the "lake of fire" features as a place from below that aligns or submits to what is determined by the throne, as opposed to other "below" places such as the sea, abyss and earth which had shown such hostility to heavenly authority.

3.7 Narrative Unit 4: The Advent of the Holy City and the Materialization of the Fellowship of the Throne

If the certain doom of the brave new world resulting from the dragon's political conspiracy can be seen as the dominant theme in our third narrative unit, the dawning of a new spatial order signals the beginning and is at the heart of the final narrative unit. This new order of things includes the new heaven and new earth (21:1; cf. Gen 1:1; Isa 65:17; 66:22), and in particular, the advent of the holy city (21:2, 10; cf. 22:19), the new Jerusalem (21:2; cf. 3:12; 21:10), the Lamb's bride (21:9; cf. 21:2). To begin with, we are shown the tent of God among humans, and we are told that they will be his people (21:3), that the one who conquers will inherit these things (21:7), that God will be their God, and this person his child (21:7).

12:7), and finally, "a thousand years" (Rev 20:2, 4; cf. 20:6–7; Ps 90:4; Eccl 6:6; *Sirach* 41.4; 2 Peter 3:8; *Epistle of Barnabas* 15.4).

101. cf. Gospel of Thomas 111 (NTA/1).

On the other hand, as already discussed in detail in our introduction to this study, after the vision of the new heaven and new earth (21:1) the narrative closes in to show a series of images that seamlessly supersede one another,[102] beginning with the expectation of a wedding as John is told to look at the bride, the woman/wife of the Lamb (21:9; cf. 19:7, 9; 21:2; 22:17). This bride, however, is then shown to be the holy city coming down from heaven (21:10), which the seer goes on to describe in some detail (21:11–23).[103] As the narrative goes on, the liturgical design and orientation of the city gradually emerges, being portrayed first as a giant cube (21:16) in the manner of the holy of holies of the Solomonic Temple (1 Kgs 6:20), where the "presence" of the Lord God all-powerful and the Lamb make redundant any need of a temple (21:22).[104] However, the representation of the totalized holy of holies is itself superseded by the imagery of the primeval garden or paradise (cf. 2:7; Gen 2:8 MT/LXX), including precious stones (21:18–21; cf. Gen 2:11–12), a river flowing through it (22:1–2; cf. Gen 2:10), and the tree of life (22:2; cf. 2:7; 22:14, 19; Gen 2:9; 3:22, 24).[105]

Above all, the "bride/city/holy-of-holies/primeval-garden" becomes the locus of the Fellowship of the Throne (22:3–5), the divine political authority signified by the throne jointly shared by God and the Lamb, and the liturgical sociality embodied by his servants whose relationship to the throne exists precisely through the mediation of the Lamb, the exalted Jesus (cf. 5:9–10; 7:13–17). They share in the power of the throne and reign together with the divine authority. This new order of things is now a joint venture between the divine authority and the liturgical sociality (22:5; cf. 5:10; 20:4, 6), enabled

---

102. cf. Beale and McDonough, "Revelation," 1150.

103. cf. Beale and McDonough, 1152; cf. Rowland, "Book of Revelation," 722; Aune, *Revelation 17–22*, 1154.

104. cf. Oecumenius, *Commentary on the Apocalypse* Twelfth Discourse (ACT/G).

105. This apocalyptic vision can be seen as mirroring or "reading" Genesis 2:4–25 in reverse, so to speak, beginning with the "marriage" of the man and the woman (Gen 2:18–25) backwards to the tree of life, river and precious stones (Gen 2:9–12) to the garden itself (Gen 2:8), with its overtones that identify it as a sacred space, the place where YHWH God and human beings meet and interact (e.g. Gen 2:16–18, 22; cf. 3:8), and where human beings were meant to flourish (Gen 2:15–16, 18, 22, 24), working and looking after the garden, or better still, serving and guarding it (Gen 2:15; cf. *2 Baruch* 14.18). For a study that explores the overtones "that the Garden of Eden was the first archetypal temple in which the first man worshipped God" (Beale, *Temple and the Church's Mission*, 66), see Beale, 66–80; cf. Wenham, *Genesis 1–15*, 67.

by the exalted Jesus (2:26–28; 3:21; 5:9–10). This is the *telos* or denouement of the narrative of the Apocalypse.[106]

3.8 The Apocalypse's Plot

Since "a narrative without plot is a logical impossibility,"[107] we should consider what the plot of the Apocalypse is. Often plot is equated to story in a narrative, yet narratologists suggest this should not be the case, because plot is "different from story, [which is] the basic chronology of events, out of which something more complex, plot, is constructed."[108] In other words, though "one can speak of 'telling a story', one cannot speak of 'telling a plot.'"[109] According to H. Porter Abbott, plot functions as "a skeletal story, either universal or culturally fabricated, which performs its psycho-social work while cloaked in a diversity of narrative dress."[110] Plot "serves a story by departing from the chronological order of its events, or expanding on some events while rushing through others, or returning to them, sometimes repeatedly . . . [plot is therefore] the artful disclosure of story."[111]

When considering the Apocalypse's plot we must bear in mind that every narrative unit refers explicitly or tacitly to the axial theo-political role of the heavenly throne, and of the one who sits on it. This emblematic embodiment of ultimate power remains stable throughout the narrative.[112] Also, each unit tells us of a single unique authorized agent (whether it is called the Son of God, the Lamb, the Messiah or the divine King, they are one and the same, the exalted Jesus) empowered by the one who sits on the throne, whose authority and exalted status remains correlated to the ultimate locus of power

---

106. If the human being created in the image of God (Gen 1:26–27; 9:6), and arguably, mediating somehow God's image to his creation (cf. 2 Cor 4:4; Col 1:15; Wenham, *Genesis 1–15*, 29–32), were originally meant to rule (Gen 1:26, 28), then we can say the the Apocalypse recovers and redefines this *telos* of the creation story: "Because man is created in God's image, he is king over nature. He rules the world on God's behalf," Wenham, *Genesis 1–15*, 33.

107. Chatman, *Story and Discourse*, 47.

108. Dannenberg, "Plot," 435.

109. Dannenberg, 435; cf. Chatman, *Story and Discourse*, 43.

110. Abbott, "Story, Plot," 43.

111. Abbott, 43.

112. Power (δύναμις) ascribed or linked to, or deriving from God is registered in Rev 4:11; 7:12; 11:17; 12:10; 15:8; 19:1.

throughout the narrative.¹¹³ Also, in each narrative unit there features a liturgical sociality (i.e. the church in each of the seven cities in Asia Minor, all the churches, the holy ones, the servants, the priests, a kingdom) related to, accountable to, and at the same time dependent on, the figure of the exalted Jesus, and through him, on the throne and the one who sits on it. In short, the Fellowship of the Throne is adumbrated in the unfolding of the narrative.

However, this theo-political and liturgical construal is contested in the first three narrative units. Beginning with a subtle reference to Satan's throne (2:13) in the first narrative unit, followed by the emergence of a war motif set in motion by the earth's elite and by the slaughter of the two witnesses in the second narrative unit, to a full-blown theo-political and liturgical construal set in opposition to the heavenly throne in the third narrative unit, which is enacted by (a) the dragon, who conspires against the authorized agent, the exalted Jesus, and arrogates to himself a locus of power; (b) the sea-beast, who is authorized by the dragon; (c) the earth-beast, who enacts a coercive public liturgy on behalf of the sea-beast, and (d) the great city, which epitomizes a sociality sustained by the mode of authority enacted by the beast.

Nevertheless, it is the enactment of orthodox theology and the true liturgy, as performed by the one who sits on the throne, by the Lamb, and the holy city and/or liturgical sociality, that prevails over a heretical construal of power, authority, coercive liturgy and sociality, as narrative unit four magisterially tells us.¹¹⁴

3.9 Critique from our Reading

In a very insightful manner, hermeneutically and theologically speaking, O'Donovan observes that "upon how we read the ecstatic chapter with which Revelation concludes there turns a great deal for our view of John's political perspectives,"¹¹⁵ which is certainly so if, as we noted in §1.2 and now

---

113. Authority (ἐξουσία) was granted to the Son of God (2:18) by his Father (2:26–28), or acknowledged of the Messiah in relation to God's power (12:10; cf. 11:15).

114. For accounts of the Apocalypse's plot by David Barr and James Resseguie, both practitioners of a narrative approach to the book of Revelation, see Barr, *Tales of the End*, location 390–588; Barr, "Apocalypse as a Symbolic," 45; Resseguie, *Revelation of John*, 44–47. It is worth to note the centrality given to the exalted Jesus in both of these accounts of the Apocalypse's plot.

115. O'Donovan, "History and Politics," 44.

evidenced by our rendering of the narrative of the Apocalypse, we see the Fellowship of the Throne as the *telos* or denouement of Revelation's story. This is the case especially because the Fellowship of the Throne is political in its very nature, since it brings together in one reality the theo-political categories of divine authority, signified by the throne jointly shared by God and the exalted Jesus, on the one hand, and the liturgical sociality embodied by the servants who serve the divine authority by the mediation of the exalted Jesus, on the other; both categories which have featured in a christologically coordinated manner throughout the narrative, and which as they converge to offer the *telos* also become the ultimate political horizon. O'Donovan, however, sees the climax of the Apocalypse immediately after the beginning of this final vision rather than at the end.[116] In particular, he highlights two political moments: reconciliation (as God dwells among human beings) and judgment (since there is no place for evil in the new city), which are coordinated by God's word or speech.[117] In a sense this emphasis plays down the Christology of this vision as enshrined in our construal of the Fellowship of the Throne.

However, our greatest point of contention with O'Donovan's reading of the Apocalypse is that he considers there to be scant evidence of the presence of the (corporate) church in its narrative, and instead notes an emphasis on individuality (the one who conquers) or on a pair (the two witnesses).[118] This leads to him bypassing the theo-political significance of the very first vision of the Apocalypse[119] leaving the initial three chapters of Revelation out of his exploration. And yet, on closer inspection it is apparent that the second person plural features in the letters to the seven churches (2:10, 13, 23, 24), and also there is the expression "and all the churches will know . . ." in 2:23, both which imply the wider church. Also, as O'Donovan himself acknowledges, "however equivocal when viewed one by one, those churches add up to *seven*, which . . . points to a catholic unity behind them."[120] This reality of the corporate church we have construed as the liturgical sociality, which we argue for in our chapter 5 from this very first vision, which is then built on

---

116. See O'Donovan, 46–47.
117. See O'Donovan, 46.
118. This was noted in §2.3; cf. O'Donovan, 42.
119. cf. O'Donovan, 30.
120. O'Donovan, 42.

and complemented as we look at another vision. And though we later revisit the issue of how the Apocalypse strikes the balance between the individual and corporate presence of the church in its narrative (§7.3), we note John's use of the expressions "the holy ones" (5:8; 8:3–4; 11:18; 13:7, 10; 14:12; 16:6; 17:6; 18:20, 24; 19:8; 20:9) and "the servants" (1:1; 2:20; 7:3; 11:18; 19:2, 5; 22:3, 6), whom the narrative supposes to exist with some degree of sociality, as evident in the church of Thyatira (2:20; cf. 2:18), the beloved city (20:9), and the holy city (22:3).[121]

A final hermeneutical observation on O'Donovan's reading of the Apocalypse is that though he presupposes the dynamic of recapitulation within the narrative – a move in line with Victorinus or Augustine, with which we concur[122] – he considers only the second half of the narrative (i.e. 12:1–19:21) as pertaining "the messianic age," inaugurated with the ascension of the child-Messiah and correlated to the downfall of the dragon-Satan and its aftermath of immanent authority and idolatrous political order.[123] The first two series of numbered sevens (seals and trumpets) he interprets as belonging to as a historical pre-Christian time, a view which we can only regard as hermeneutically aporetic.[124] For instance, in our view 19:2 is arguably the response to the claim raised by the "souls of those who have been slaughtered because of the word of God and the witness which they have" (6:9). That is "Until when holy and true Master, do you not judge and do justice to our blood from those who dwell on the earth?" (6:10), and therefore, the narrative continuity between 6:9–10 and 19:2 should be considered in any interpretation of this passage. Equally, 20:4, which refers to "the souls of those who have been beheaded because of the testimony of Jesus and because of the word of God," and which is explicitly Christian, should be considered in any interpretation of 6:9–10. With reference to "the two witnesses" of 11:3, these are linked to "their Lord" who "was crucified" (11:8), clearly an allusion

---

121. Interestingly enough, Paul the apostle seemed to understood the holy ones (οἱ ἅγιοι) as an organized society as church (ἐκκλησία), see 1 Corinthians 1:2; 14:33; 16:1; 2 Corinthians 1:1. Also, Paul equates servants (οἱ δοῦλοι) and holy ones (οἱ ἅγιοι) in Philippians 1:1, where the latter are organized to the point to have an episcopal structure with bishops (ἐπίσκοπος) and deacons (διάκονος), all in plural; however, Paul only refers to the Philippians as church once (4:15), and even there in an indirect way.

122. cf. O'Donovan, "History and Politcs," 30.

123. cf. O'Donovan, 35.

124. cf. O'Donovan, 34–35.

to Jesus, which identifies the two witnesses as Christian prophets (11:3), to say the least. In between these two groups (slaughtered souls and two witnesses) we encounter the unashamedly Christian countless multitude who have whitened their clothes in the blood of the Lamb (7:14).

3.10 Conclusion

Following the literary instincts of past and present commentators that regard the book of Revelation as a narrative, and drawing from O'Donovan's method of theo-political inquiry as searching for or discerning truth within a narrative discourse, we have gone on to offer an abridged version of the Apocalypse's narrative, which we have organized into four units by tracing the narrative's own themes, motifs and characters. Equally, showing beforehand that this has been an uneasy exegetical task for biblical scholars, whether ancient or modern, our account of this narrative did not bypass some of the key conundrums in the Apocalypse, in particular whether there is any continuity between the visions of the seven seals and seven trumpets, or more importantly, the two accounts of the dragon's downfall, for which we provided an exegetical framework ignored by biblical scholars commenting on these passages so far.

Additionally, our rendering of the Apocalypse's narrative has highlighted (a) the centrality throughout the narrative of the heavenly throne and the one who sits on it as the embodiment of ultimate power; together with (b) the recurrent figure of the exalted Jesus as the authorized agent empowered by the one who sits on the throne, partaking of his authority and exalted status; (c) the importance of a liturgical sociality, identifiable as the church, the servants, the holy ones, which remains related to the figure of the exalted Jesus throughout. Thus, we been able to articulate a plot of the Apocalypse's narrative, presenting it in theo-political terms as we have found the narrative itself required. There followed a brief critique of O'Donovan's reading of the Apocalypse in contrast to our own, especially in what pertains to the relevance of the church within the narrative, and the christological perspective of the Apocalypse in every respect.

In short, in our own rendering of the Apocalypse's narrative and plot we have found that our construal of the Fellowship of the Throne can be understood as the *telos* or denouement of the narrative of the Apocalypse, a concept which is firmly grounded in the text itself.

Part II

Authority

CHAPTER 4

The Exalted Jesus

"Authority is . . . a central theme of the pre-modern political theology,"[1] observes O'Donovan, who with his agenda for a contemporary political theology has recovered this ancient concern, postulating that any robust political theology authorized by Scripture "must have something to say about society and something to say about rule, and the two must be coordinated."[2] Within this theo-political framework, argues O'Donovan, "to speak of divine authority after the resurrection of Christ is to speak of the authority of the exalted Christ."[3] This is precisely what our rendering of the narrative and plot of the book of Revelation, as seen in the previous chapter, has drawn our attention to: the recurrent feature of the correlation of power between the one who sits on the throne and the authorized agent (i.e. the exalted Jesus).[4] To some extent, the Apocalypse deploys conventional New Testament christological categories to account for this correlation of power, where the authorized

---

1. O'Donovan, *Desire of the Nations*, 16–17.
2. O'Donovan, 193; cf. 15, 22.
3. O'Donovan, *Resurrection and Moral Order*, 141.
4. There is a de facto consensus among biblical scholars as to the use of the theologoumenon "the exalted Jesus" when referring to the portrayal of Jesus in the book of Revelation, for example, "vindicated by the resurrection, Jesus has been exalted to heaven where he now rules." (Barr, *Tales of the End*, location 1148); "Rev. 1:12–20, the vision of the exalted Christ . . ." (Aune, *Revelation 1–5*, 74); "the exalted Christ" (Rowland, "Vision of the Risen Christ," 2); "*in Revelation we have the exalted Christ* . . ." (Dunn, *Christology in the Making*, 91); "the exalted Jesus" (Boxall, *Revelation of Saint John*, 42); "Jesus' exalted status in Revelation" (Hurtado, *Lord Jesus Christ*, 594). As for O'Donovan, he also deploys this theologoumenon in connection with the Apocalypse, e.g. "the Christ revealed and exalted" (O'Donovan, "History and Politics," 43). With reference to explicit exaltation language in connection with Jesus, this was deployed in the New Testament only by Luke (Acts 2:33) and Paul (Phil 2:9).

agent is portrayed as the Son of God,[5] the Messiah,[6] or as both.[7] However, it also puts forward a new christological category, the Lamb,[8] and develops another one further, the divine King.[9] Most importantly, in the Apocalypse every christological category is deployed within a narrative context.

Accordingly, we delve into the Apocalypse in order to consider in more detail its own fourfold christological construal of divine authority, which we have postulated as the correlation of power and divine status between the one who sits on the throne and the exalted Jesus, the primary component of the Fellowship of the Throne. In particular, we will argue that divine authority is conveyed by the exalted Jesus as (i) the Son of God, who enacts fellowship with the liturgical sociality in anticipation of the materialization of the Fellowship of the Throne; (ii) the Lamb, who recovers a sociality for God, so that divine authority re-creates, so to speak, a sociality; (iii) the Messiah, who highlights the value of tradition and affirms a teleological purpose to history; and (iv) the divine King, who clears forensically an ontological space for the advent of the holy polis.

4.1 The First and the Last as the Son of God

In chapter 3 (§3.2) we provided a synopsis of what we have called narrative unit one (Rev 1:9–3:22), where by and large John's interlocutor becomes the main protagonist. In this section of the narrative as soon as this character introduces himself to John (1:17–20), the conversation becomes one-sided and moves into a monologue where he becomes the central character. In what follows we will consider three aspects about this key protagonist.

---

5. e.g. Mark 3:11; Luke 22:70; John 1:34, 49; 5:25; Heb 6:6; 7:3; 10:29; 1 John 3:8; 5:10, 12, 13; cf. Rev 2:18.

6. e.g. Matt 11:2; 16:20; Mark 8:29; Luke 24:26, 46; John 7:41; Acts 8:5; 9:22; Rom 8:35; 9:3; Eph 1:10, 20; 1 Pet 3:15; cf. Rev 11:15; 12:10; 20:4, 6.

7. e.g. Matt 16:16; Luke 4:41; John 11:27; 20:31; Gal 2:20; Eph 4:13. For Jesus as "the Son of God" see John 20:31; Acts 9:20; Heb 4:14; 1 John 4:15; 5:5; 5:20.

8. τὸ ἀρνίον (the Lamb), the diminutive of ἀρήν, is an articled neuter singular noun featuring twenty-eight times only in the Apocalypse, within the New Testament canon (i.e. Rev 5:6 [anarthrous], 8, 12, 13; 6:1, 16; 7:9, 10, 14, 17; 12:11; 13:8; 14:1, 4 [two times], 10; 15:3; 17:14 [two times]; 19:7, 9; 21:9, 14, 22, 23, 27; 22:1, 3). However ὁ ἀμνός ("a sheep over one year old," BDAG 54; or a lamb, LSJ 84) was deployed with an explicit christological referent in John 1:29, 36; cf. Acts 8:32; 1 Pet 1:19.

9. e.g. 1 Tim 6:15; cf. Rev 17:14; 19:16; cf. also Acts 17:7.

4.1.1 Visionary Argot

First, John deploys what may be called a visionary argot to describe, literally from head to foot, the extra-ordinary being he encounters.[10] John refers to his interlocutor as "like a son of man" (Rev 1:13),[11] describing his clothes (1:13),[12] head, hair, eyes (1:14),[13] feet, voice (1:15),[14] right hand, mouth, appearance/face (1:16).[15] That this passage draws from the existing visionary argot is clear when contrasted with descriptions of extra-ordinary beings in other apocalyptic literature.

For instance, in the vision of Daniel 7, the clothes, hair and head of the Ancient of Days are described (Dan 7:9), and John Goldingay comments that "the one advanced in years is visually a human being, but he stands for God . . . Picturing him as an old man suggests someone august, venerable and respected, judicious and wise. There is perhaps an allusion to the notion of God's existing from eternity."[16] Equally, the character that is eventually empowered or authorized in that vision in stark contrast to the four beasts previously dethroned, is referred to "as a son of man" (Dan 7:13). Daniel 10 introduces a "human being" whose clothes (Dan 10:5), body, face, eyes, arms, feet and voice (Dan 10:6) are described in terms that resonate with the description John gives of his interlocutor in Patmos. Yet, the features of this Danielic being "need not indicate that the person *is* God, or represents God."[17]

By contrast, 1 Enoch 106 tells of the unusual aspects of baby Noah, whose body (1 En. 106:2), hair (1 En. 106:2, 10), face (1 En. 106:2, 5), eyes (1 En.

---

10. The head-to-foot description John made of his interlocutor resembles the Danielic vision of a great and huge statue whose appearance was awesome or frightening and whose description went from head to feet (cf. Dan 2:31–33).

11. The same expression is ascribed once more to the same persona, arguably, in Rev 14:14.

12. A similar expression is deployed in Rev 15:6 to refer to the clothes of the seven angels who have the seven plagues.

13. The same phrase used to refer to the eyes of John's interlocutor is deployed in Rev 2:18 with reference to the Son of God, and 19:12 in connection with the divine King.

14. Exactly the same sentence used to refer to the feet of John's interlocutor is deployed once more in Rev 2:18 in connection with the Son of God. Also, the expression used to refer to the voice of John's interlocutor features two more times in Rev 14:2 ("a voice from heaven") and 19:6 ("a voice of a great crowd").

15. The sentence used to refer to the mouth of John's interlocutor is deployed again in Rev 19:15 in connection with the divine King. Also, a similar phrase used to refer to the face/appearance of John's interlocutor is deployed in Rev 10:1 in connection with a mighty angel.

16. Goldingay, *Daniel*, 165.

17. Goldingay, 291.

106:2, 5, 10) and mouth (1 En. 106:3, 11) are described in terms that resonate, to some extent, with descriptions in Daniel and John's Apocalypse of other unusual "human" beings. This baby was thought to be, at first, like the "sons of the angels of heaven" (1 En. 106:5; cf. 106:6, 10, 12).[18] However, Enoch confirms that this is indeed a human baby (1 En. 106:16) destined to "cleanse the earth from the corruption that is on it."[19] On this Enochian portrayal of baby Noah, Loren Stuckenbruck notes that "his special features at birth . . . might lead one to expect that Noah is going to act as a divine agent. Such an impression, however, does not materialise in the [Enochian] *Birth of Noah*. Rather than being an agent of divine activity, Noah's significance is symbolic."[20]

Equally relevant is the contrast between the descriptions made of Joseph and a heavenly being in *Joseph and Aseneth*. On the one hand, when "Aseneth saw Joseph on his chariot,"[21] she described him as "the sun from heaven has come to us on its chariot and entered our house today, and shines in it like a light upon the earth."[22] She also refers to him as a "son of God."[23] On the other hand, when a "man came to her from heaven,"[24] who introduced himself as "the chief of the house of the Lord and commander of the whole host of the Most High,"[25] it is said of him that this was a man "in every respect similar to Joseph,"[26] there follows a description of his face, eyes, hairs and head, hands and feet,[27] in terms that echo those descriptions found in Daniel, 1 Enoch and the Apocalypse as seen above. C. Burchard, who thinks the man from heaven is Michael, comments on this mirrored description that "Michael holds the post in heaven which Joseph holds in Egypt: second only to the supreme ruler. But he is not Joseph, nor does he appear in his guise."[28]

---

18. On other early Jewish traditions about the "Birth of Noah" see Stuckenbruck, *1 Enoch 91-108*, 608–614.
19. *1 Enoch* 106.17 from Nickelsburg and VanderKam, *1 Enoch*, 166.
20. Stuckenbruck, *1 Enoch 91-108*, 608.
21. Joseph and Aseneth 6.1 (OTP/2).
22. Joseph and Aseneth 6.2.
23. Joseph and Aseneth 6.3.
24. Joseph and Aseneth 14.3.
25. Joseph and Aseneth 14.8.
26. Joseph and Aseneth 14.9.
27. Joseph and Aseneth 14.9.
28. See notes k and o on *Joseph and Aseneth* 14.8, 9 (OTP/2).

Another case in point is the Apocalypse of Abraham, which features the angel Iaoel sent to Abraham to strengthen him and bless him (10:3ff). This angel is in "the likeness of a man,"[29] and is also different from Michael.[30] His body, face, hair and head, and clothes (11:2–3) are described in terms that resonate with the accounts we have just considered above in the Apocalypse, Daniel, 1 Enoch and *Joseph and Aseneth*. For instance, "the hair of his head [is] like snow."[31] However, when Abraham is ascended to heaven (15:4) and is asked to recite a song that describes God, the Eternal One, he does not include bodily features like those of the angel Iaoel in his description, apart from his voice being "like a voice of many waters" (17:1; cf. 17:15; 18:2), and a mention to "the light of your face."[32]

Lastly, there is the illustrative Matthean contrast between the "transfigured Jesus" (Matt 17:1–9 || Mark 9:2–9 || Luke 9:28–36) and "an angel of the Lord" (Matt 28:2–4). Once metamorphosed, Jesus's face "shone as the sun, but his clothes became white as light."[33] Also, at some point in this vision (Matt 17:9) Jesus is called "my son" (Matt 17:5 || Mark 9:7 || Luke 9:35) by a voice from the cloud that surrounded Jesus and his companions.[34] As for the angel who descended from heaven (Matt 28:2), "his appearance was as a lightning, and his garment white as snow."[35]

On balance, Daniel, 1 Enoch, *Joseph and Aseneth*, the Apocalypse of Abraham, Matthew's Gospel and John's Apocalypse show that there was a "visionary" argot to describe extra-ordinary beings, whether divine (the Ancient of Days, the Eternal One), human (baby Noah, Joseph, the historical Jesus), angelic (the "man" of Daniel 10, the man from heaven in *Joseph and Aseneth*, Iaoel in the Apocalypse of Abraham, the Matthean angel from heaven), or otherwise ("as a son of man" of Daniel 7). However, the question arises of who depends on whom for their description. Angels are introduced

---

29. Apocalypse of Abraham 10.4 (OTP/1).
30. cf. Apocalypse of Abraham 10.17.
31. Apocalypse of Abraham 11.2.
32. Apocalypse of Abraham 17.19; cf. 17.15, 18.
33. Matt 17:2; cf. Mark 9:3; Luke 9:29; France, *Gospel of Mark*, 351.
34. Wright, *Jesus and the Victory*, 650, 653.
35. Matt 28:3. N. T. Wright discusses the possible echoes of Daniel 7:9 and 10:6 in this Matthean text in Wright, *Resurrection*, 641n30. We may also consider an alternative example in the book of Acts, which tells us how the apostle Paul had a vision of the Lord (Acts 18:9–10) in terms similar to the account it offers of a message given to Paul by an angel (Acts 27:23–24).

as human beings and described as human beings, whereas the Enochian baby Noah is thought to belong to the children of the angels of heaven. For his part, Joseph becomes a model or paradigm to describe a man from heaven.

Also, features ascribed to "like a son of man" in Revelation 1:13–16 are equally ascribed to the Son of God (2:18), angels (whether a group of seven, 15:6, or a powerful one, 10:1), a great crowd (19:6) and the divine King (19:12, 15). Most importantly, in the gospel story of the transfiguration or metamorphosis of Jesus, which Mark's Gospel locates significantly just after the episode of the disclosure of Jesus as the Messiah, Peter, James and John, who witnessed Jesus being metamorphosed, never stop thinking of him as the Jesus they knew rather than as an "angel," in spite of the ephemeral new visible features his persona had adopted in that moment.[36] In other words, it seems clear that we are exegetically authorized to speak about anthropomorphic angelophanies in some of these texts; however, to speak of an angelomorphic Christophany in John's description of his interlocutor, or in Matthew 17, hardly makes exegetical sense.[37]

4.1.2 A Blend of Divine and Messianic Overtones

The choice of visionary argot deployed by John to describe his interlocutor is, for the most part, validated and justified by the latter, who uses some elements of that discourse as he introduces himself to each (angel of the) church. At the same time, however, John's description of his interlocutor seems visually and theologically limited. That is to say, John's interlocutor gradually reveals or discloses names, titles, features, prerogatives and functions of his persona that John was not able to see or grasp in his initial description. In other words, despite being in the Spirit on the Lord's Day, or perhaps because of it, John required a more subtle apocalypse or revelation of the persona of his interlocutor, whose portrayal varies from message to message as it suits,

---

36. cf. Matt 17:1–4; Mark 9:2–5; Luke 9:28–33. In fact, the recension of this gospel episode in the *Apocalypse of Peter* (NTA/2) signals a highly developed Christology, since it refers to Jesus as "my Lord Jesus Christ, our King" (15) as well as "God Jesus Christ" (16). By contrast, in the *Martyrdom and Ascension of Isaiah* (OTP/2) Jesus, located in the seventh heaven, is turned into an angel to enable the seer to worship him (9.31–32; cf. 9.5); Jesus is then metamorphosed into some kind of angel as he descended through the various layers of heaven into earth (10.20–31).

37. For alternative views of a qualified christological angelophany see Rowland, "Vision of the Risen Christ"; Stuckenbruck, "Revelation," 1539; Stuckenbruck, *Angel Veneration*, 271–272

arguably, the particular needs and challenges of his addressees.[38] Specifically, the introductions to Ephesus (Rev 2:1) and Pergamum (2:12) feature a very narrow selection of elements of John's visionary argot to describe his interlocutor. By contrast, the introductions to John (1:17–18), Smyrna (2:8), which is an abridged version of the introduction to John, Philadelphia (3:7) and Laodicea (3:14) are completely different to what John had said previously as he described his interlocutor, which we think further undermines the view that John described an angelomorphic christophany. For their part, the introductions to Thyatira (2:18) and Sardis (3:1) are a mix of new disclosures and old statements of John's previous description of his interlocutor.

Most importantly, these various introductions of the persona of John's interlocutor convey a unique blend of divine and messianic overtones, which are worth highlighting. To begin with, John's interlocutor introduces himself to John as "the first [ὁ πρῶτος] and the last [ὁ ἔσχατος]," an expression claimed only by YHWH in the whole Old Testament corpus, and within it only in the book of Isaiah. These are when (a) YHWH introduces himself as "the first [רִאשׁוֹן] and the last [אַחֲרוֹן]" (Isa 41:4) as he informs the nations that it is he who decides their fate; equally, (b) as the King of Israel, YHWH is "the first and the last" (Isa 44:6) to his people still in exile, and unapologetically claims there is no other God but him, (c) equally YHWH is the "the first and the last" (Isa 48:12) as he reminds his people that he is the creator of heaven and earth and the one who decides the fate of Babylon, his agent in materializing his plan.[39]

This deeply monotheistic divine title which John's interlocutor claims for himself is, however, correlated to and reinterpreted in an equally deep christological fashion which in a way follows a narrative pattern in three stages (1:18): (a) John's interlocutor is "the one who lives," or the living one, however, and somehow, (b) he became dead, and yet (c) "I am the one who lives for the ages of ages," he says. Clearly this is an anomalous grammatical expression that demands a theological explanation in order to make sense. John's interlocutor did not say "I am the one who was alive, became dead," rather he began saying "I am the one who lives and became dead." In Jeremiah 10:10, YHWH , who is regarded as the true God and everlasting King, is

---

38. cf. Hemer, *Letters to the Seven Churches*, 2.
39. cf. 1QIsaa 34.7; 37.12; 40.17; 1Q8 17.2; 4Q57 f24.38; 4Q57 f29.1; 4Q58 3.20.

referred to as "the living God" in stark contrast with the inert and wooden figures or icons feared by other nations. If this is the kind of life implied by John's interlocutor, that is to say, divine and authentic, how he died is not explained at this stage (until Rev 5:9–14; cf. 1:5). Nonetheless, life after death is once more framed in divine terms.

Additionally, in the narrative of Revelation "the one who lives for the ages of ages" is an expression equally ascribed to (a) the one who sits on the throne (4:9, 10); (b) the one "who created the heaven and the [things] in it, and the earth and the [things] in it, and the sea and the [things] in it" (10:6); and (c) God (15:7) – all of them agree with *Tobit* 13:2 and *Sirach* 18:1, theologically speaking. The correlation between these two modes of introduction, the divine predicate (the first and the last) and the story-name ("the one who lives, and became dead, and yet I am one who lives for the ages of ages") is reiterated,[40] though in an abridged version, in the introduction of John's interlocutor to (the angel of) the church of Smyrna (2:8).

What is more, as part of his message to the (angel of the) church in Thyatira, John's interlocutor claims for himself a divine prerogative (2:23) ascribed only to YHWH in the Old Testament. In a passage that looks at both the people of Judah's unfaithfulness and loyalty to YHWH, and the crooked condition of the human heart, it is YHWH who searches the heart and tests the mind (Jer 17:10).[41]

John's interlocutor therefore introduces himself to John with divine predicates ascribed to YHWH in the Old Testament, or God the Creator in the Septuagint. In addition, these expressions are usually deployed, in their alluded contexts, as part of a theological account that argues strongly for monotheism. More importantly, one of these divine phrases is ascribed explicitly to God in the narrative of the book of Revelation. John's interlocutor also claims for himself divine prerogatives ascribed exclusively to YHWH in the Old Testament. It would appear therefore that divine references in the discourse of John's interlocutor as he introduces himself outdoes the visionary argot deployed by John to describe his interlocutor.

---

40. We borrowed the expression "divine predicate" from Aune, *Revelation 1–5*, 101.

41. cf. Allen, *Jeremiah*, 200. Jer 17:10 is alluded in Rom 8:27, where it is given a Christian and pneumatological make-over; it is also alluded to in *2 Baruch* 48.39 with an eschatological orientation.

Equally, John's interlocutor offers an account of his persona invested with messianic authority. For instance, he introduces himself to the angel of the church in Thyatira as the Son of God (2:18) and addresses in particular the teachings of a prophetess nicknamed Jezebel,[42] presumably a leader in this congregation, who seemed to advocate a compromising approach to the surrounding non-Christian heretical public liturgies that shaped life in the city,[43] a theme the narrative further develops through the visions of the beasts and the great city.[44] However, for those who did not embrace her teaching, the Son of God offers a version of the vindication and exaltation he himself received when his Father granted him authority [ἐξουσία] over the nations, as recorded in 2:26–28a (along with 2:18). These texts allude to Psalm 2:7–9,[45] usually regarded as a royal psalm,[46] and in particular, as a psalm referring to the enthronement of a Davidic king,[47] in pre-exilic times.[48] It tells the story of nations in a state of commotion and kings of the land/earth set against YHWH and his anointed [מָשִׁיחַ],[49] as they attempt to tear apart their bonds.[50] However, the one who sits in heaven (i.e. YHWH) speaks in anger, and says that he has poured out his king [מֶלֶךְ] on Zion, his holy mountain.[51] Then, arguably, the king echoes YHWH's decree,[52] in particular, "YHWH said to me: My son you [are], this day I have fathered you."[53]

---

42. The Old Testament Jezebel features in 1 Kings 16:31 – 2 Kings 9:37; cf. 4Q382 f1.3. Interestingly enough, she is also singled out in *2 Baruch* 62.3 (OTP/1) with a similar negative role.

43. Rev 2:20; cf. Aune, *Revelation 1–5*, 191–194; Jones, *Cities of the Eastern Roman*, 83.

44. cf. Rev 13, 17.

45. This allusion to Psalm 2 features in two other visions in the narrative of the Apocalypse (i.e. Rev 12:5 and 19:15).

46. Gunkel, *Psalms*, 23.

47. cf. Mowinckel, *Psalms in Israel's Worship*, 61–63.

48. More recently, John Day and John Collins have argued for a pre-exilic date for this psalm, as opposed to the emergent view that tends to date it in post-exilic times. See Day, *Psalms*, 90–91; Collins, "King as Son," 11–12.

49. When King Saul was still alive, David did not "raise" (i.e. send [שׁלח]) his hand against YHWH's anointed (מָשִׁיחַ), see 1 Sam 24:7, 11; 26:9, 11, 23; cf. 2 Sam 1:14.

50. Ps 2:1–3; cf. Jer 2:20 and 5:5, where God's people tore apart YHWH's bonds; whereas in Jer 30:8, it is YHWH who will tear apart the bonds of those strangers that enslaved them; cf. Ps 107:14; Nahum 1:13.

51. Ps 2:4–6.

52. Ps 2:7–9; cf. 11Q7 f1_2.4–5; 3Q2 f1.1–3.

53. Ps 2:7.

This decree is about the enthronement and/or exaltation of the king by YHWH himself, a political act construed theologically as "the son of God."[54] At this point it is worth highlighting that the theme of YHWH's son (i.e. God's son), as the divinely authorized king can in turn be seen to allude to the historical narrative of 2 Samuel 7, in particular verses 12 to 14. In this passage YHWH promises to establish the kingdom [מַמְלָכָה] of David's seed, that is to say, establish the throne [כִּסֵּא] of his kingdom, and a filial link is affirmed by YHWH: "I will be to him a father and he will be to me a son."[55] As a result, it is recorded that Solomon, David's son, sat on the throne [כִּסֵּא] of the kingdom/reign [מַלְכוּת] of YHWH, as king [מֶלֶךְ].[56]

Returning to our text in Psalm 2, following the enthronement and/or exaltation of YHWH's son, the kings and rulers of the land/earth are asked to consider and serve YHWH with fear, rejoice with trembling, and kiss the son. Failure to do this will result in their destruction.[57] Therefore, in the midst of an orchestrated revolt,[58] YHWH's anointed as king on Zion is ratified as YHWH's son, and thus authorized to exert power over those kings and rulers of the land/earth.[59] In fact, according to David Cline's ideological criticism of Psalm 2, "as far as the psalm is concerned, Yahweh's function as god is to authorize the political authority of the king."[60] In addition, this psalm "is about the king's hopes for military victory over particular rebellious foreign nations."[61]

As for Revelation 2:26–28a where the allusion to Psalm 2 is woven into the message to the church in Thyatira, this has the evocative effect of echoing a story that has been condensed or abridged in the expression "as I [the Son

---

54. Instances of kings claiming divine sonship in the ancient Near East are offered in Walton, *Ancient Near Eastern Thought*, 282; cf. Collins, "King as Son," 10–15.

55. 2 Sam 7:14.

56. 2 Chron 28:5; 29:23.

57. Ps 2:10–12.

58. cf. Kraus, *Psalms 1–59*, 126; Miller, *Interpreting the Psalms*, 88–89.

59. Military campaigns led by David, once he was anointed king over Israel (2 Sam 5:3) and had captured Zion (2 Sam 5:7), illustrate this conflict between YHWH's anointed and the surrounding nations and their kings or leaders, e.g. the Philistines (2 Sam 5:17–25), the Moabites (2 Sam 8:2), the king of Zobah (2 Sam 8:3–4), and the Arameans (2 Sam 8:5–10). A summary of "all the nations" he subdued is provided in 2 Sam 8:11–12.

60. Clines, *Interested Parties*, 252.

61. Clines, 255.

of God] have received [authority] from my Father."[62] Here, in the context of a hostile and external pagan liturgy that creeps into the congregation in the form of a theological heresy advocated by one of their teachers, the one who overcomes this liturgical and theological challenge will be vindicated and empowered by the Son of God, a theme the narrative gradually develops and materializes in the Fellowship of the Throne.[63]

To (the angel of) the church in Sardis, John's interlocutor introduces himself as "the one who has the seven spirits of God" (3:1). The multiplicity of charismata bestowed to a royal figure can be traced back to Isaiah 11:1–5, which refers to the root or branch of Jesse (i.e. King David's father),[64] since "the spirit of YHWH gives the king the skills needed to reign."[65] The multiplicity of charismata bestowed to a messianic figure, and in particular the "spirit of might/power," is a theme developed also in some Second-Temple literature,[66] for example 1 Enoch 49:2–3; 1QSb 5.25; Psalms of Solomon 17:37; Targum Isaiah 11:1–2. Max Turner observes that "some of the 'messianic' passages building from Isa. 11:1–4, and associated ideas, take up the old hopes of the Spirit coming to expression in power (inter alia) through a regal deliverer . . . This means that in this 'messianic' tradition the Spirit is more than simply 'the Spirit of prophecy.'"[67] That is to say, "here the Spirit is as much God's empowering presence as his self-communicating presence."[68]

Also, since the gospels, which introduced Jesus as the Messiah,[69] highlight the role of the Spirit in his conception,[70] baptism,[71] resistance to temptation,[72]

---

62. Rev 2:28a. "John uses his allusions not as a code in which each symbol requires separate and exact translation, but rather for their evocative and emotive power." Caird, *Revelation of St. John*, 25.
63. cf. Rev 5:10; 20:4, 6; 22:5.
64. 1 Sam 16:1; 17:22; cf. Rev 5:5; 22:16.
65. Watts, *Isaiah 1–33*, 209; cf. Kaiser, *Isaiah 1–12*, 256; 1 Sam 16:13; 2 Sam 23:2; Isa 61:1.
66. cf. Turner, *Power from on High*, 114–118.
67. Turner, 117–118.
68. Turner, 118.
69. e.g. Matt 1:1; Mark 1:1; 8:29; Luke 2:11; John 1:17; 20:31.
70. cf. Matt 1:18, 20; Luke 1:35.
71. cf. Matt 3:16; Mark 1:10; Luke 3:22; John 1:32–33.
72. cf. Matt 4:1; Mark 1:12; Luke 4:1.

exorcisms,[73] and healing,[74] they "were more interested in assuring their readers that Jesus was the expected Messiah of the Spirit and that he was so empowered for his mission than they were in explaining what Jesus' endowment at the Jordan contributed to his own life before God."[75] Equally, in some of these events in Jesus's life where the role of the Spirit has been highlighted, Jesus's condition as Son of God is affirmed.[76] In fact, Peter and the author of John's Gospel acknowledged that Jesus was both the Messiah and the Son of God.[77]

In view of the above, the apocalyptic self-description of John's interlocutor as the one who has the seven spirits,[78] whether referring to the multiplicity of charismata in the Isaianic sense, or the role of the Spirit at various stages of Jesus's life (in the gospel tradition), resurrection (in the Pauline sense),[79] and exaltation (in the Lukan sense),[80] is overwhelmingly messianic in its overtones.[81]

A final messianic strand to consider is the expression "the ruler/rule of God's creation" (Rev 3:14),[82] which is deployed by John's interlocutor as he introduces himself to (the angel of) the church in Laodicea. Admittedly, there is a striking parallelism between Revelation 1:5 and 3:14, of which is worth highlighting in both texts (i) the integrity of the witness, and (ii) the political power he exerts on other institutions of power (i.e. the kings of the earth) or the whole of God's creation, which subsumes the institutions of power under this greater dominion. In fact, these two points fit nicely into

---

73. cf. Matt 12:28.

74. Contrast Matt 12:28 with Luke 10:9.

75. Turner, *Holy Spirit*, 35.

76. e.g. Conception: Luke 1:35. Baptism: Matt 3:17; Mark 1:11; Luke 3:22; John 1:34. Satanic temptation: Matt 4:3, 6; Luke 4:3, 9. Exorcisms: Matt 8:29; Mark 3:11; 5:7; Luke 8:28.

77. Matt 16:16; John 20:31; cf. Matt 26:63; Mark 1:1; Luke 4:41; John 11:27.

78. cf. Barr, *Tales of the End*, location 1115.

79. e.g. Rom 1:4.

80. Acts 2:33.

81. For an alternative view that regards "the seven spirits" as another way of referring to the seven angels see Aune, *Revelation 1–5*, 33–35, 219; which when read with Aune, *Revelation 17–22*, 1053, an aporia emerges. Aune *presupposes* his view on the Qumranic approach to angels as spirits, yet there is no such phrase ("seven spirits") in the Qumranic corpus.

82. Admittedly, this expression may equally be translated as "the beginning of God's creation," as done, inter alios, by Aune, *Revelation 1–5*, 254–257; Beale, *Book of Revelation*, 297–301.

the message to the church in Laodicea. That is to say, the integrity of John's interlocutor (i.e. Jesus the Messiah), is in stark contrast to the works of the "addressee," who is "neither cold nor hot" (3:15); equally, the political power John's interlocutor exerts is further developed in his account of how he became empowered (3:21).[83]

Martin Hengel has suggested that Revelation 3:21 exhibits a different development of "all the statements [in the New Testament] that speak of a sitting or a being of the exalted Christ 'at the right hand of God,'"[84] which in his view "are directly or indirectly dependent upon Ps. 110:1."[85] Therefore, in Revelation 3:21 "the term 'at the right hand' is missing; in its place the communality of throne between the Father and the exalted Son is emphasized, which brings as a correlate the common throne of those who overcome,"[86] which is precisely the Fellowship of the Throne in a nutshell. David Aune also points out that a "distinctive feature of this allusion to Ps 110:1 is that it is placed in the mouth of the exalted Jesus."[87]

Most importantly, in our view both Revelation 3:14 and 3:21 seem to allude, at least thematically, to Isaiah 9:5–6, where the concept of rule/dominion [מִשְׂרָה / (LXX) ἀρχή] is linked to the messianic motif of "the throne of David and his kingdom" (Isa 9:6). Isaiah 9 begins with a note of hope as oppression and war, pictured as darkness, come to an end followed by joy and peace. As opposed to "an unfaithful monarch [in Isaiah 7] whose shortsighted defensive policies will actually plunge the nation into more desperate straits, there is lifted up the ideal monarch who, though a child, will bring an end to all wars and establish an eternal kingdom based upon justice and righteousness."[88] As a result, instead of "the bar across their shoulders" (i.e. the rod of the oppressor), the rule/dominion rests upon the shoulders of the Davidic Son. "Who is this person through whom God intends to bring war to an end and

---

83. In line with the Israelite construal of the "Son of God" (2 Sam 7:12–14), Solomon sat on his father's throne, see 1 Kgs 2:12, 2:24; cf. 1 Kgs 3:6; 8:20, 25; 1 Chron 29:33; 2 Chron 6:10, 16. On this motif see also 2 Kgs 13:13, where Jeroboam sat on the throne of Joash.

84. Hengel, *Studies in Early Christology*, 133.

85. Hengel, 133, cf. Aune, *Revelation 1–5*, 263.

86. Hengel, 134.

87. Aune, *Revelation 1–5*, 263.

88. Oswalt, *Isaiah Chapters 1–39*, 241; cf. 1QM 17.5–8, a Qumranic passage that resonates with these Isaianic themes, where the angel Michael, instead of the Davidic son, is granted the rule/dominion (משׂרה).

establish true freedom upon the earth? Evidently, he is a royal person (note the references to a kingdom, government, and throne), yet he is never called king."[89] What is more, some Second Temple literature features the concept of the "ruler/master of God's creation,"[90] for example Judith 9:12; 3 Maccabees 2:2; 6:2; Testament of Abraham 16:2.

Turning to our apocalyptic texts, the rule/ruler of God's creation, who sits in his Father's throne, embodies a christological materialization of (Isaianic) royal and messianic expectations, blended with a Second-Temple discourse that portrays God the creator as the master and King of the creation, which he governs with compassion. Most importantly, this authorized agent shares in the throne of his Father. In fact, Aune rightly observes that "the theological significance of this use of a *bisellium* [i.e. a double-throne] in 3:21 is the equality that it presumes between those who share such a throne."[91] In addition, since Revelation 3:14 is, arguably, an abridged version of 1:5, this authorizes us, exegetically speaking, to replace our catchword "John's interlocutor" with the more transparent expression "Jesus the Messiah."

4.1.3 Linking Portrayals of the Same Persona

A third and final point to make on the words of John's interlocutor (i.e. the Son of God or Jesus the Messiah) is that they set the textual (and theological) bases for links to alternative portrayals of his persona in the rest of the narrative of the Apocalypse. In particular, (a) there is a textual link that begins with John's description of his interlocutor, goes through John's interlocutor's self introduction, and ends with John's account of the vision of the divine King. Perhaps this is better appreciated as shown in table 3 (below). Also, (b) there is another textual link beginning with John's interlocutor as he introduces himself to the church in Sardis, which in turn is picked up by John as he describes the Lamb in a later vision. Again, let us juxtapose these two texts for a better appreciation of this point (table 4 below).[92]

---

89. Oswalt, *Isaiah Chapters 1–39*, 244; cf. Kaiser, *Isaiah 1–12*, 212.
90. cf. Bauckham, *Jesus and the God of Israel*, 9.
91. Aune, *Revelation 1–5*, 262.
92. cf. Rowland, "Book of Revelation," 603.

Table 3. Textual links about the exalted Jesus across the narrative: eyes and mouth

Speaker/Narrator	Text	Referring to
John	And his eyes as flaming fire (1:14)	John's interlocutor
	and from his mouth a sharp double-edged sword coming out (1.16)	
John's interlocutor	The one who has the sharp double-edged sword (2:12)	Himself
	The one who has his eyes as flaming fire (2:18)	Himself as Son of God
John	And his eyes as flaming fire (19:12)	The divine King
	and from his mouth comes out a sharp sword (19:15)	

Table 4. Textual links about the exalted Jesus across the narrative: seven spirits

Speaker/Narrator	Text	Referring to
John's interlocutor	the one who has the seven spirits of God (3:1)	Himself
John	And I saw . . . a lamb standing as having been slaughtered having seven horns and seven eyes which are the seven spirits of God having been sent away into all the earth (5:6)	The Lamb

However, (c) a link more subtle in nature develops around the figure correlated with the (divine) throne, linking John's interlocutor with both the Lamb and the child-Messiah. This is as follows:

Table 5. Textual links about the exalted Jesus across the narrative: throne

Speaker/ Narrator	Text	Referring to
John's interlocutor	as I too conquered and sat down with my Father in his throne (3:21)	Himself
Every creature	To the one who sits on the throne and (to) the Lamb (5:13; cf. 6:16; 7:9, 10, 17)	The Lamb
Anonymous	and he was taken away, her child, towards God and towards his throne (12:5; cf. 12:10)	The child-Messiah
John	and the throne of God and (of) the Lamb will be in it (22:3; cf. 22:1)	The Lamb

4.1.4 Theological Implications

On balance, narrative unit one offers us John's description of his interlocutor using a special discourse, which we have referred to as visionary argot, usually deployed to speak about extra-ordinary beings, whether divine, angelic, human or otherwise in nature. John's interlocutor goes further, introducing himself to John and to others deploying a discourse with divine and messianic references, which in turn justifies, to some extent, the visionary argot used by John. We have also identified John's interlocutor as Jesus the Messiah, whose own introductions of himself set the textual (and theological) bases to link him to other portrayals of his persona featured in subsequent visions in the narrative. In addition, we register aspects of the christological shift undergone by the divine authority as (i) God the Father authorizes and/or enthrones the Son (i.e. John's interlocutor); (ii) the latter is given authority and allowed to sit on his Father's throne; (iii) Jesus the Messiah currently exerts some divine prerogatives; (iv) he bears divine (e.g. the first and the last) and messianic titles (e.g. the Son of God).

More importantly, this christological mutation of the divine authority offers us a frame to understand this vision (§3.2) as an enactment of the the fellowship between the Son of God and the liturgical sociality, which in turn adumbrates the Fellowship of the Throne. The Son of God's eagerness to have fellowship with the sociality is aptly illustrated at the end of this vision, as a desire to share a meal with them (Rev 3:20). As O'Donovan puts it, "the sharing of food may constitute shared meal, a sign of fellowship; as a sign of fellowship, the meal may be an affirmation of common understanding or purpose; as an affirmation of purpose, it may be a pledge of loyalty, and so on."[93] Thus, divine authority mediated christologically looks after God's sociality, sustains it, gives it a *telos* (the one who conquers), and judges it as well (all the churches will know that I am the one who examines minds and hearts). We may say the exalted Jesus allows for the flourishing of the fellowship, since "the power of politics is a socially formed power that operates to maintain social form. Loss of form means depoliticization, and depoliticization means loss of power."[94]

4.2 The Divine Throne Is Also the Lamb's

The synopsis we provided of narrative unit two (§3.3) highlighted the aesthetic and liturgical orientation of the vision which extends from Revelation 4 to 5. In particular, we noted how the narrative begins with a description of the heavenly throne and the one who sits on it, and then ends with a Lamb standing next to this throne and the one who sits on it, both being acknowledged by the whole cosmos as the new locus of power, moving from creation to Christology in terms of the theological categories that underpin this cosmic worship. The narrative also describes a concentric expansion of the heavenly entourage made of twenty-four elders, four living creatures and countless myriads of angels, all of them joined by every creature in the cosmos in a rhapsodic liturgy jointly worshipping the one who sits on the throne and the Lamb.[95] Precisely, we would now like to explore in some depth three aspects of this account of the divine authority and its christological shift.

---

93. O'Donovan, *Ways of Judgment*, 250.
94. O'Donovan, 234.
95. By contrast, the *Martyrdom and Ascension of Isaiah* (OTP/2) offers a seven-layered view of heaven where the seer ascends from the first to the seventh heaven (7.13 – 9.42), culminating with the vision of the Lord (i.e. Jesus, 9.5) and the angel of the Holy Spirit praising the Father of the Lord (9.40; 10.1–6).

4.2.1 What the Throne Stands for

The purpose of a sacred space in the midst of the people of Israel, whether construed as a tent or temple, was that YHWH would have a "place" to dwell among them.[96] Now, that sacred space was divided into two parts, the holy of holies and the holy place.[97] Within the holy of holies was the ark of the testimony/covenant with two golden cherubim located on top of it.[98] As time passed by the ark came to be regarded both (i) as YHWH's mobile throne when Israel engaged in battle, since it was referred to as "the Ark of the Covenant of YHWH Zebaoth who is enthroned on the cherubim,"[99] and (ii) as a sign of YHWH's presence in the midst of his people to save or deliver them from their enemy.[100] Eventually, the ark was installed in the holy of holies of the Solomonic temple,[101] and by the time of the prophet Isaiah, after the fall of Samaria to Assyria,[102] and during the siege of Jerusalem,[103] King Hezekiah of the kingdom of Judah came to the temple to pray,[104] saying "YHWH God of Israel, who is enthroned on the cherubim, You yourself are God, you alone, to all the kingdoms of the earth. You made the heaven and the earth" (2 Kgs 19:15 || Isa 37:16; cf. 1QIsaa 30:20–21).

With reference to the theological construal of the Son of God (§4.1.2), it is worth highlighting how this theological frame of political empowerment was linked, historically and theologically, to YHWH and his throne, since it was YHWH who was understood to be the "real" King of Israel.[105] Accordingly, David said "from all my sons . . . YHWH . . . chose my son Solomon to sit on the throne of the kingdom of YHWH over Israel."[106] To which the chronicler added that "Solomon sat on the throne of YHWH as king instead of David, his father" (1 Chron 29:23; cf. 1 Kgs 1:46). As a result, it may be said that

---

96. Exod 25:1–2, 8; 1 Kgs 6:1, 12–13; cf. 4Q11 f24_30i.1.
97. Exod 26:33; cf. 4Q11 f30ii_34.7–8.
98. Exod 25:22; 26:33–34; 40:21; cf. Num 7:89; 1 Kgs 8:6–7; 4Q22 27.33.
99. 1 Sam 4:4; cf. 2 Sam 6:2; 1 Chron 13:6.
100. 1 Sam 4:3.
101. 1 Kgs 8:6–7; 2 Chron 5:8–9; cf. 1 Kgs 6:19.
102. 2 Kgs 18:9–12.
103. 2 Kgs 18:17–37.
104. 2 Kgs 19:14.
105. cf. Isa 44:6.
106. 1 Chron 28:5; cf. 2 Sam 7:12–14.

the "Son of God,"¹⁰⁷ personified by Solomon at that time, sat on YHWH's throne.¹⁰⁸ In fact, when Solomon was crowned, "all the assembly [of Israel] bowed down [קדד] and prostrated themselves [חוה] before YHWH and the king."¹⁰⁹ Scott Hahn observes that "this is an extraordinary and unprecedented acknowledgment of the remarkable closeness between God and his earthly representative, the king."¹¹⁰ And yet, when the ark of the covenant was brought into the newly built temple,¹¹¹ the Son of God (i.e. Solomon) declared that YHWH alone was God,¹¹² and along with the people of Israel he offered a sacrifice to YHWH.¹¹³ In other words, no divine status was granted to the Davidic Son of God in spite of sitting on YHWH's throne.

It is thus that a cluster of theo-political concepts associated to YHWH and his throne,¹¹⁴ and visually conveyed by the ark of the covenant, were formed over time (a) affirming a monotheistic view of YHWH, that he alone is God;¹¹⁵ (b) stating that YHWH created the heavens and the earth;¹¹⁶ (c) declaring that YHWH is king over all the earth;¹¹⁷ and therefore that (d) YHWH judges;¹¹⁸ (e) that he transcends time,¹¹⁹ (f) that he is located in heaven,¹²⁰ and yet (g) the ark of the covenant signalled YHWH's presence in the midst of his people to save or deliver them from their enemy;¹²¹ and finally, (h) that a human being was authorized to sit on YHWH's throne.¹²²

At the same time, more dynamic, and at times mystifying portrayals of YHWH and his throne also developed over time, featuring in the visions of

---

107. cf. 2 Sam 7:12–14; Ps 2:6–9; 89:19–20, 26–27.
108. cf. Ps 45:7 [45:6 ET].
109. 1 Chron 29:20.
110. Hahn, *Kingdom of God*, 97.
111. 1 Kgs 8:1–6.
112. 1 Kgs 8:60.
113. 1 Kgs 8:62–63.
114. Eskola, *Messiah and the Throne*, 63.
115. 2 Kgs 19:15; Isa 37:16; cf. 1QIsaa 30.20–21.
116. 2 Kgs 19:15.
117. Ps 47:3; 99:1; 103:19; cf. Zech 14:9.
118. Ps 9:4, 7.
119. Lam 5:19.
120. Ps 103:19.
121. 1 Sam 4:3–4.
122. 1 Chron 28:5; 29:23; cf. 2 Sam 7:12–14; 1 Kgs 1:46.

prophets and seers, such as those by Micaiah son of Imlah,[123] Isaiah son of Amoz,[124] the priest Ezekiel son of Buzi,[125] and Daniel from the tribe of Judah,[126] presumably an Israelite "of royal descent and of the nobility."[127] Arguably, all these visions are alluded to in greater or lesser extent in the narrative of the book of Revelation, in particular in what we have called narrative unit two (§3.3).[128] Micaiah, Isaiah and Ezekiel's visions are alluded to to some extent in Revelation 4, whereas Daniel's vision is alluded to mainly in Revelation 5, in particular, in relation to the motif of someone other than the Ancient of Days being granted unmatched political authority but whose source is symbolized by the throne of the Ancient of Days.[129]

Throughout the narrative of the Apocalypse, the throne still retains most of the theo-political aura of the Old Testament construal around it. It "represents an axis mundi, that is, the immovable center of all reality."[130] In particular, the throne is the throne of God,[131] or his throne,[132] and as result the narrative construes a periphrastic expression for God as "the one who sits on the throne."[133] Also, the one who sits on the throne is acknowledged as the creator of all things, and worshipped as such by the heavenly entourage.[134] The throne of God is also presumed to be the source of political power,[135] and therefore, God reigns.[136] What is more, the judicial prerogatives of the divine throne are equally stressed.[137] In contrast with all these elements of continuity with

---

123. 1 Kgs 22:8, 19–23.

124. Isa 1:1; 6:1–4.

125. Ezek 1:3; 1:1–28; 10:1–22.

126. Dan 1:6; 7:1–14.

127. Dan 1:3 JPS Tanakh translation.

128. cf. Beale and McDonough, "Revelation," 1098–1099.

129. cf. Aune, *Revelation 1–5*, 332–338. Incidentally, "Second Temple throne visions were often modelled on the visions of the Old Testament prophetic writings." Eskola, *Messiah and the Throne*, 65. In fact, Eskola provides a survey of throne visions featuring in Second Temple literature, see Eskola, 71–123; cf. Bauckham, *Jesus and the God of Israel*, 165–172.

130. Stuckenbruck, "Revelation," 1545.

131. Rev 7:15; cf. 22:1, 3.

132. Rev 12:5; cf. 1:4.

133. Rev 4:9, 10; 5:1, 7, 13; 6:16; 7:10, 15; 19:4; 21:5; cf. 4:2, 3; 20:11.

134. Rev 4:9–11.

135. cf. Rev 12:5, 10.

136. Rev 11:17; 19:6; cf. 15:3.

137. Rev 20:12–13; cf. 11:18; 16:5; 18:8, 20; 19:2.

the Old Testament, however, is the main theological innovation of the ownership of the throne being claimed by "the Son" (3:21) / Lamb (22:3), a shift also registered in liturgical terms as both God and the Lamb are worshipped on equal terms (5:13–14; 22:3). We will come back to this in our third point.

4.2.2 The Messianic Lamb

In the the narrative of the book of Revelation the seven-seal scroll becomes the means of cosmically singling out the uniqueness of the Lamb as the only one found to be worthy of opening it (5:1–5). It is this uniqueness which qualifies him to stand next to (5:6), and receive worship jointly with the one who sits on the throne (5:13–14). We have noted (§3.3) that as the first five of the seven seals were opened by the Lamb (6:1, 3, 5, 7, 9), a motif relating to some kind of war and its aftermath gradually emerges, which is met by the heavenly disclosure of the one who sits on the throne and the wrath of the Lamb (6:12–17) after the sixth seal is opened. Also we postulated (§3.6) that the vision of the divine King (19:11–21) provides a suitable denouement for the suspense and tension built up by the consecutive opening of the scroll's seals. Thus, the taking of the scroll from the right of the one who sits on the throne and the opening of its seals had been the means of introducing us to a different perspective of reality where God's and the Lamb's wrath is manifest, though forensically dispensed by the divine King.[138] All these are divine prerogatives symbolized by the scroll, and in some way explain why such a high-profile person, so to speak, was required for the task of opening the seals.[139]

Admittedly, the cosmic search for someone worthy of taking the scroll and opening its seals (5:2–3) registers some polemic and messianic overtones, especially since it is declared that "no one was capable in heaven nor on earth nor even under the earth" (5:3), and this in a world that did indeed consider the Roman emperor as unique among his contemporaries.[140] However, it is

---

138. We have observed (§3.6) that the job description for the (divinely authorized) king was to judge and fight the wars, according to 1 Sam 8:20; cf. Rev 19:11. Later on in the narrative, the Lamb is called the "King of kings" (Rev 17:14; 19:16).

139. For alternative views on the scroll, see, inter alios, Bauckham, *Climax of the Prophecy*, 243–257; Beale, *Book of Revelation*, 339–348; O'Donovan, "History and Politics," 30–32.

140. cf. Josephus, *War of the Jews* 3.401–402 (3.8.9); consider also the idealized view of a king conveyed in *1 Esdras* 4.2–3.

someone other than Caesar who will eventually share in God's throne and worship (5:13; 22:3), those divine prerogatives signalled by the scroll. This person is introduced first as "the Lion, who is from the tribe of Judah" (5:5), then as "the root/shoot of David" (5:5), and finally, as the slaughtered Lamb (5:6). Echoing the evangelical genealogy of "Jesus the Messiah, the son of David, the son of Abraham,"[141] the apocalyptic genealogy of the slaughtered Lamb is traced back firstly to the tribe of Judah, whose portrayal as a lion alludes to Genesis 49:9 (where Judah is successively portrayed as a lion's cub, a lion, and a lioness); and then to David and his descendants, whose portrayal as a root and/or shoot alludes to Isaiah 11:1,[142] which admittedly refers to the shoot that comes out from the stump of Jesse, David's father.[143] Interestingly enough, it is Jesus who explicitly declares: "I am the root and the descendant/family of David."[144]

Both texts alluded to here are invested with messianic overtones.[145] However, the picture of Judah as a (regal) lion did not feature in these two instances,[146] though the image of an explicit messianic lion features in other literature.[147] Most important, however, is the theological construal of the Lamb, who is introduced for the first time in the narrative of Revelation "as having been slaughtered" (5:6; cf. 5:12; 13:8). Again, the Old Testament offers some possibilities for an account of the origin of the image of a slaughtered lamb. One is clearly the Passover story, where an unblemished lamb or young sheep (Exod 12:5) was slaughtered [שחט] at twilight (Exod 12:6),[148] and its blood spread over the doorframe of the house where the roasted meat of that

---

141. Matt 1:1; cf. Luke 3:31, 34.

142. cf. 1QIsaa 10.20; 4Q161 f8 10.11; 4Q285 f7.2.

143. cf. 1 Sam 16:1; 17:22.

144. Rev 22:16.

145. Messianic overtones attached to Gen 49:9 are recorded in *Testament of Judah* 1.6; 17.5 (OTP/1). As for Isa 11:1–5, its messianic overtones were noted in §4.1.2.

146. cf. Bauckham, *Climax of the Prophecy*, 181.

147. e.g. 1QSb 5.29, a document that also contains allusions to Isa 11:2, 4; and *4 Ezra* 11.36–37; 12.31–34, where the messianic lion destroys the (Roman imperial) eagle, a Jewish expectation in sharp contrast to Josephus's view of Roman imperial rule, cf. Josephus, *War of the Jews* 3.400–402 (3.8.9). On the origin of the eagle as a symbol of the Roman imperial army see Pliny the Elder, *Natural History* 10.5.

148. In Exodus 12 only, are different Hebrew terms used to refer to the lamb meant to be slaughtered: שֶׂה ("small livestock beast, a sheep or a goat," Exod 12:3–5); כֶּבֶשׂ ("young ram," Exod 12:5); and צֹאן ("a single animal from the flock [of sheep or goats]," Exod 12:21; cf. 12:32, 38); cf. HALOT 1310, 460, 992–993, respectively.

lamb was eaten (Exod 12:7–8). In this way, those meeting within that house would be spared the death of any firstborn male as YHWH passed over that place because of the blood (Exod 12:12–13). Israelites were meant to celebrate the Passover perpetually (Exod 12:14).

Other images of a slaughtered lamb are associated with a sin offering to be made following an unintentional breaking of YHWH's commands (Lev 4:32–33), or with a guilt offering for the cleansing of a leper (Lev 14:11–13, 25), for instance. And yet, the image of a slaughtered lamb or sheep was transferred to a human person, YHWH's servant, whose suffering and death is described, among other images, as that of "a sheep [on its way] to slaughter" (Isa 53:7).[149] Second Temple literature developed further the image of a sheep/lamb,[150] however, after a survey of this literature, Loren Johns concludes that "there is no evidence . . . to establish the existence of anything like a recognizable redeemer-lamb figure in the apocalyptic traditions of Early Judaism."[151]

As to the messianic Davidic genealogy of the Lamb, as seen above, it is further elaborated in the portrayal of his persona. He has seven horns (5:6), for example, and in the narrative of the book of Revelation a horn signals a form of institutionalized political power (17:12), usually royal status, a usage in agreement with Old Testament and other Jewish literature.[152] More importantly, messianic overtones are also ascribed to the Israelite symbol of the horn, as suggested by the prayer of Hannah,[153] or Psalm 132:17. In fact, messianic overtones relating to the horn of Israel took a christological turn in the evangelical prophecy of Zechariah as recorded in Luke's Gospel.[154] What is more, since ten horns stand for ten kings in the narrative of the Apocalypse (17:12), it is all the more conspicuous to underline that the Lamb has seven horns, that is to say, he "has complete power."[155] In fact, he is called "King of kings" (17:14; cf. 19:16), precisely in the same vision where ten horns stand for ten kings. The messianic overtones of the Lamb's horns are closely tied up

---

149. Other Old Testament possibilities are explored in Johns, *Lamb Christology*, 127–148.

150. e.g. *1 Enoch* 89–90.

151. Johns, *Lamb Christology*, 106; cf. Caird, *Revelation of St. John*, 74.

152. e.g. 2 Sam 2:10; Dan 7:24; 8:20–21; 4Q51 2a d.34; 6Q7 fl.1–2; 1QM 1.4; *Sirach* 47.11; cf. *1 Maccabees* 2.48.

153. 1 Sam 2:10; cf. 4Q51 2a d.34. This text is further elaborated in *Odes* 3.10 LXX.

154. Luke 1:69.

155. Resseguie, *Revelation of John*, 119.

with the equally messianic expression "the seven spirits of God" ascribed to the Lamb, which we discussed earlier (§4.1.2). In short, the Lamb is portrayed as having "Power, knowledge and the Spirit."[156]

With reference to the Lamb "as having been slaughtered" (5:6), the result of a violent death (i.e. by "his" blood, 5:9), he was able to buy or acquire as property [ἀγοράζω] for God, from every tribe and language and people and nation (5:9). It should be said that this is partly the language of the marketplace. In fact the verb ἀγοράζω means "to acquire things or services in exchange for money," or "to secure the rights to someone by paying a price."[157] And ἀγορά is the feminine noun that means marketplace.[158] Again, the Old Testament provides some instances of this kind of "transaction," where one person buys a people for someone else or for himself. On the one hand, Joseph bought [קנה] the land and people of Egypt for Pharaoh (Gen 47:20, 23). On the other hand, YHWH bought [קנה] a people for himself (Exod 15:16; Ps 74:2), the Israelites, who once in exile, he would buy back (Isa 11:11).[159] It seems, then, that the Lamb has claimed and fulfilled a divine expectation.

4.2.3 Worship as an Exclusive Divine Prerogative

Third, since the Lamb has made a transaction, that is to say, has bought an international people for God (5:9), which in turn become a liturgical sociality (a kingdom and a priesthood) that will rule on earth (5:10), he is therefore worthy to take/receive the scroll and open his seals (5:9), and also worthy to be granted or to claim, and exercise, exclusive prerogatives ascribed to God and his throne. Because of this, he is worshipped, first on his own (5:8–12), and then alongside the one who sits on the throne (5:13–14; cf. 22:3).

In the Apocalypse, the two main terms deployed to convey "worship" are (i) προσκυνέω,[160] at times preceded by πίπτω (to fall) in order to emphasize

---

156. Barr, *Tales of the End*, location 2581.
157. BDAG 14; cf. LSJ 13.
158. BDAG 14.
159. Equally, other New Testament documents allude to this image of a people bought for God, e.g. 1 Cor 6:20; 7:23; 2 Pet 2:1.
160. Meaning "to express in attitude or gesture one's complete dependence on or submission to a high authority figure, (fall down and) worship, do obeisance to, prostrate oneself before, do reverence to, welcome respectfully" (BDAG 882; cf. LSJ 1518; Hurtado, *Lord Jesus Christ*, 38). It features twenty-four times in Rev: 3:9; 4:10; 5:14; 7:11; 9:20; 11:1, 16; 13:4 (two times), 8, 12, 15; 14:7, 9, 11; 15:4; 16:2; 19:4, 10 (two times), 20; 20:4; 22:8, 9.

a complete devotion,[161] and (ii) λατρεύω (render cultic service).[162] These are precisely the two terms the Septuagint deployed to translate the Hebrew terms חוה (to bow, worship) and עבד (to work, serve), which feature in the covenantal charter between YHWH and the people of Israel. In that context YHWH is recognized as the God of the Israelites who had taken them out of their Egyptian slavery (Exod 20:2), therefore there should be no other gods before YHWH (Exod 20:3). More importantly, they should not bow down (חוה) to them or serve (עבד) them (Exod 20:5).[163] However, some Israelites like King Ahab (1 Kgs 16:31) and his son King Ahaziah (2 Kgs 22:54), and many in the northern kingdom of Israel (2 Kgs 17:16) did indeed bow down (חוה) and serve (עבד) Baal, breaking the terms of the covenant (cf. 2 Kgs 17:34–35), which in turn resulted in them being led into Assyrian exile (2 Kgs 17:23). Also, as mentioned before, when Solomon was declared king over Israel, all the assembly (of Israel) bowed down (קדד) and prostrated/worshipped (חוה) YHWH and the king (1 Chron 29:20). Afterwards, Solomon sat on YHWH's throne as king (1 Chron 29:23). However, when YHWH's temple was "consecrated," King Solomon declared "YHWH God of Israel, there is no God like you in heaven and on earth" (2 Chron 6:14). Therefore, no one in the Old Testament could have claimed worship on equal terms with the divine being (i.e. YHWH) and his throne despite being enthroned or authorized by him.[164] During Second Temple Judaism, this link between monotheism and exclusive worship only accentuated.[165]

By contrast, the Davidic, messianic, royal, and Spirit-empowered Lamb is worshipped by the whole cosmos along with the one who sits on the throne,

---

161. cf. Rev 4:10; 5:14; 7:11; 11:16; 19:4, 10; 22:8.

162. BDAG 587; cf. LSJ 1032. The term features two times in Rev 7:15; 22:3.

163. cf. Exod 23:24; Deut 4:19; 5:9; 8:19; 11:16; 17:3; 2:5; 30:17. In the New Testament, προσκυνέω and λατρεύω feature together in this sense only in Matt 4:10 and Luke 4:8, precisely when Jesus replied to Satan "You will worship the Lord your God and only to him you will serve."

164. Not even the Danielic "like a son of man" (a visionary figure reinterpreted as the people of the holy ones of the Most High), who was authorized by the Ancient of Days (Dan 7).

165. cf. Bauckham, *Jesus and the God of Israel*, 152, 164; Hurtado, *Lord Jesus Christ*, 37. However, two textual traditions stand out against this otherwise mainstream understanding. (i) *1 Enoch* 48.5; 49.3; 62.5, about the enthronement and worship of the Enochian son of man, cf. 45.3; 51.3; and (ii) *Ezekiel the Tragedian* 68–89 (OTP/2), about the enthronement of Moses. On the former, Bauckham seems to concede (Bauckham, *Jesus and the God of Israel*, 171) whereas Hurtado resists that move (Hurtado, *Lord Jesus Christ*, 39); on the latter, Bauckham disregards that claim (Bauckham, *Jesus and the God of Israel*, 167).

as he claims, as a result of his violent death, the divine prerogatives signalled by the seven-sealed scroll (Rev 5:13–14; cf. 4:8–11). Larry Hurtado notes that "it would be difficult to imagine a more direct and forceful way to express Jesus' divine status."[166] And he adds, "Revelation 5, therefore, affirms that standard for the proper pattern of worship of the recipients of the book."[167] That is to say, "the elaborate description of 'binitarian' worship in Revelation 5 surely was intended to reinforce in the strongest terms the early-Christian practice of including Jesus with God as recipients of worship on earth."[168] In addition, the narrative puts across the theological assertion that ownership of the throne is followed by worship, and the best expression of this, is arguably Revelation 22:3, our basic text for the construal of the Fellowship of the Throne, as noted in the introduction to this thesis. Equally, the narrative of the Apocalypse makes the case for the legitimate object of worship against counterfeit ones. That is to say, God (the one who sits on the throne) and the Lamb are the only legitimate recipients of worship, as opposed to the dragon (13:3–4), the (first) beast and its image (13:3–4, 8, 12, 14–15; 14:9, 11; 16:2; 19:20), or any angel (19:9–10; 22:8–9). What is more, those who wrongly seek or receive worship from other creatures, fare badly in the denouement of the narrative (19:20; 20:10).

4.2.4 Theological Implications

The taking of the scroll and opening of its seals allows the Lamb to exercise divine prerogatives associated with the theological construal of the divine throne and he is worshipped along with God on equal terms, which demanded a new theological understanding of monotheism from the Apocalypse's readers. The exalted Jesus portrayed as the Lamb, who is of Davidic lineage, has complete power and is endowed with messianic multiplicity of charismata. In this way the christological shift undergone by the divine authority becomes transparent. However, the Lamb was slaughtered, that is to say, he suffered a violent death in order to recover for God a sociality who is in turn a liturgical kingdom. So (divine) authority re-creates, so to speak, a sociality. This is the origin (genesis or archeology) of the apocalyptic *politeia* or *res publica*,

---

166. Hurtado, *Lord Jesus Christ*, 592–593.
167. Hurtado, 593.
168. Hurtado, 593.

which we have called the Fellowship of the Throne. Thus, as O'Donovan puts it, "the church is the locus of social renewal and recovery. It summons created fellowship back from judging to acting, back to open sociability from hardened political identities. The church as the 'end' of political community is the matrix within which the created shape of human sociality emerges into view."[169]

Also, this was a market transaction, and market transactions, according to O'Donovan, "are also communications. The market itself, the community of transaction, belongs to neither party alone but to the two parties together; it is not exchanged between them, but held in common."[170] The narrative implies that this was a voluntary market transaction by the Lamb, "they are called voluntary because the first principle in these transactions is voluntary."[171] More importantly, "the notion of representation in the Western political tradition is grounded on the relation of redeemed humanity to Christ, the representative of all humanity in his death and glorification."[172]

4.3 The Woman's Child Becomes God's Son

We have previously noted (§3.5, §3.6) that throughout the Apocalypse's narrative we find a narrative thread woven around the dragon's conspiracy to prevent the enthronement of the child-Messiah, or to dethrone him, which in turn leads to the dragon's downfall. We also pointed out that this correlation between the exaltation of the child-Messiah and the downfall of the dragon sets in motion events and engenders characters whose nature and fate are gradually revealed within the narrative (Rev 12–20).

In line with the above, we will now focus on that correlation of events between the exaltation of the child-Messiah and the downfall of the dragon, narrated in Revelation 12 and 20:1–10. In particular, we want to consider (i) how the narrative frames this episode in messianic terms, (ii) what the narrative tells us about this child-Messiah, and (iii) what the downfall of the dragon tells us about the child-Messiah. We will then assess this account's contributions to the apocalyptic construal of divine authority.

---

169. O'Donovan, *Ways of Judgment*, 241.
170. O'Donovan, 247.
171. Aristotle, *Nicomachean Ethics* 5.2 (1131a+).
172. O'Donovan, *Ways of Judgment*, 157.

4.3.1 The Advent of the Messiah

Revelation 12 is about two portents or signs in heaven (12:1, 3). The first of them relates to a pregnant woman in the midst of labour pains (12:1–2), whereas the second portent is about the dragon-serpent that stands in front of the woman in labour waiting to devour the child as soon as it is born (12:3–4). However, the dragon's plans are frustrated when the male-child is taken away towards God and his throne (12:5). The dragon-serpent continues to harass the woman that had just given birth (12:13), but when his plans are again frustrated, he becomes angry and redirects its hostility towards the rest of the woman's descendants ("her seed," 12:17).

Clearly, the two portents in heaven are inextricably intertwined in this micro-narrative, the contours of which allude to Genesis 3, featuring the fatal encounter of a crafty serpent (נָחָשׁ) and the primeval woman (אִשָּׁה) in the garden. In the Genesis narrative the woman was deceived by the serpent and did what was forbidden for the primeval human beings to do.[173] Because of this, YHWH set enmity between the serpent and the woman,[174] and between their respective "seeds" (זֶרַע).[175] In addition, the woman is told that the toil/pain of conception or pregnancy would be enormous, and that in pain/toil she will bear her children.[176]

The identity of the woman in the Apocalypse narrative enlightens the identity of the child she is expecting. The celestial bodies that she wears (i.e. the sun [ἥλιος], moon [σελήνη] and twelve stars [ἀστήρ]),[177] seem to allude to Joseph's dream in which the sun (שֶׁמֶשׁ), moon (יָרֵחַ) and eleven stars (כּוֹכָב) bowed down to him,[178] a dream which his father understood as referring precisely to himself, Joseph's mother, and (eleven) brothers – with Joseph

---

173. Gen 3:13; cf. 2:16–17.

174. This allusion to the enmity between the serpent and the woman, engineered by YHWH, to some extent relativizes the emphasis put by some scholars on the so called (cosmic) "combat myth" as the mythological framework that underpins this micro narrative. See Aune, *Revelation 6–16*, 669–674; cf. Pataki, "Non-Combat Myth," 268–272. In our view, any (military) engagement is but periphrastic, and neither God nor the Lamb engage directly in war with the dragon in the narrative of the book of Revelation, as the script of the ancient myths do, whether Ugaritic or Hebrew.

175. Gen 3:15.
176. Gen 3:16.
177. Rev 12:2.
178. Gen 37:9.

presumably counting as the twelfth star.¹⁷⁹ And since it was customary to refer to someone's family as including father, mother, brothers, and all the house of their father,¹⁸⁰ it may be said that Joseph's dream referred to "the house of Jacob,"¹⁸¹ (i.e. "the children of Israel.")¹⁸² Joseph's dream therefore can be seen as foretelling that someone from the house of Jacob, as conveyed by sun, moon and (twelve) stars, would be exalted, and the whole house of Jacob would acknowledge the exalted status or condition of one of their members.¹⁸³ Therefore, as the apocalyptic woman wears the "garments" or symbols of the house of Jacob they simultaneously point forward to the exaltation of one of them, and presumably her portrayal as a woman about to give birth points to the child to whom she is soon to give birth.¹⁸⁴

The portent of the pregnant woman alludes also to Isaiah 7:14, which features the sign (אוֹת) given by the LORD (אֲדוֹן) to King Ahaz through the prophet Isaiah, about a young woman (עַלְמָה) who is pregnant and bearing a son who would be named Immanu-El (עִמָּנוּ אֵל), "with-us-God." The Isaianic sign is part of YHWH's response to the house of David in view of the imminent threat of invasion by both King Rezin of Aram and King Pekah of Israel.¹⁸⁵ In this context the sign is meant to reassure both the king and people of Judah that such a political threat would not be materialized,¹⁸⁶ instead another imperial power would in fact take over (the northern kingdom of) Israel (i.e. the king of Assyria).¹⁸⁷ Because of this, the apocalyptic sign of the pregnant woman seems to point also to God's protection for and/or

---

179. Gen 37:10; cf. Wenham, *Genesis 16–50*, 352, 358.

180. cf. Josh 2:18.

181. Gen 46:27; cf. Ps 114:1.

182. Exod 19:3.

183. Thus, Pharaoh set Joseph over all the land of Egypt (Gen 41:41), and so the Egyptians were ordered to kneel before him (Gen 41:43); then, Joseph's brothers – admittedly only ten of them (Gen 42:3)— came to Egypt and bowed before him, presumably acknowledging his status as "the ruler of the land," (Gen 42:6) though they did not know that such a ruler was indeed Joseph (Gen 42:8). And when Joseph revealed his true Israelite identity and blood ties to his brothers (Gen 45:1–4), he asked them to tell his father that in fact it had been God who put him as "lord of all Egypt." (Gen 45:9)

184. *Testament of Naphtali* 5 and *Testament of Abraham [B]* 7 (both in OTP/1), inter alia, are instances of a motif of exaltation linking sun, moon and stars with Old Testament patriarchs; cf. Beale and McDonough, "Revelation," 1122.

185. Isa 7:2.

186. Isa 7:1, 7, 10–12. cf. Oswalt, *Isaiah Chapters 1–39*, 194.

187. Isa 7:17–20.

deliverance of his covenantal people (as implied by the allusion to the house of David) by means of the child that the woman will give birth, who "is about to shepherd all the nations with a rod made of iron" (12:5). Equally, it may be argued that this child-Messiah would mediate God's presence in the midst of his covenantal people (cf. 1:13, 20; 2:1), a point elaborated in §6.2.1, though with a different hermeneutical framework.

Interestingly enough, in the Matthean birth narrative of Jesus the Messiah, David's son, Abraham's son,[188] a woman, Mary, was found to be pregnant by the Holy Spirit.[189] And when she gave birth to a son,[190] named Jesus because he was to save his people from their sins,[191] the whole event was seen as the fulfilment of Isaiah 7:14, which is quoted in full from the LXX with just a minor variant.[192] In addition, when King Herod, who at the time was the ruler of the Jews on behalf of the Roman Empire,[193] heard that the king of the Jews (i.e. the Messiah), had been born,[194] he tried to kill him.[195] As a result, the child's mother fled to Egypt along with her husband and son, where they remained until Herod's death.[196]

4.3.2 The Enthronement of the Messiah

Revelation 12:5 stands out as a text christologically dense and rich in Old Testament allusions. For that reason it is worth quoting it in full:

> And she gave birth [τίκτω] to a male [ἄρσην] son [υἱός],[197]

---

188. cf. Matt 1:1.
189. Matt 1:18; cf. Rev 12:2.
190. Matt 1:25; cf. Rev 12:5.
191. Matt 1:21.
192. Matt 1:22–23.
193. Josephus, *Antiquities of the Jews* 14.381–385 (14.14.4); 15.194–201 (15.6.7).
194. Matt 2:1–4.
195. Matt 2:16.
196. Matt 2:13–15; cf. Rev 12:6. Oecumenius (sixth century AD) interpreted the woman of Revelation 12:1–2 as Mary, construed in Nicean theological fashion as "the mother of God" instead of the historical Mary of the gospels, see Oecumenius, *Commentary on the Apocalypse* Sixth Discourse (ACT/G). For their part, Hippolytus (third century AD), followed by Victorinus of Petovium, understood this apocalyptic woman as the Church, see Hippolytus, *Treatise on Christ and Antichrist* 61 (ANF/5); Victorinus of Petovium, *Commentary on the Apocalypse* 12.1 (ACT/L).
197. In Isaiah 66:8 Zion (צִיּוֹן) is portrayed as a woman that birthed her sons; cf. Isaiah 49:1; 66:7; Micah 4:10. For his part, Paul the apostle referred to "the Jerusalem above" as "our mother [μήτηρ]" (Gal 4:26).

who is about to shepherd [ποιμαίνω] all the nations [ἔθνος] with a rod [ῥάβδος] made of iron.[198]

And yet, he was taken away [ἁρπάζω], her child, towards God[199]

And towards his throne.[200] (Rev 12:5)

Here Oecumenius rightly registered allusions to Psalm 2:7–9,[201] whose "story" we have previously discussed (§4.1.2) when we looked at how John's interlocutor introduced himself to the church in Thyatira as the "Son of God" (Rev 2:18) and reminded them of his own authorization by his Father (2:26–28). We noted that Psalm 2:7–9 conveys the theological construal of the Son of God along with 2 Samuel 7:12–14. At this point we would add that (i) Psalm 2:7 informs that "YHWH said to me: 'My son [בֵּן] you [are], this day I beget [יָלַד] you,'" whereas Revelation 12:5a says a woman (she) gave birth a male son; (ii) Psalm 2:8 informs that YHWH would give (to his son) nations (גּוֹי) as his possession, whereas Revelation 2:5b says that the son is about to shepherd all nations;[202] (iii) Psalm 2:9 informs that YHWH's son would break (רעע) them (i.e. nations) with a scepter/rod (שֵׁבֶט) of iron, as Revelation 12:5b loosely says.

Because the woman's child is taken to God and to his throne, this "ascension" or "enthronement" is theologically framed with the construal of the Son of God, as the allusion to Psalm 2 indicates.[203] To put it another way, the

---

198. cf. Ps 2:7–9.

199. In the Old Testament, Enoch was taken (לקח) to God (אֱלֹהִים) (Gen 5:24), whereas Elijah was going up (עלה) to heaven (שָׁמַיִם) (2 Kgs 2:1); cf. Deut 30:12; Jer 51:53; Ezek 8:3; (LXX) *Wisdom of Solomon* 4.10–11. In the New Testament, Philip was taken away (ἁρπάζω) by the Spirit of the Lord (Acts 8:39), whereas Paul, was arguably taken away (ἁρπάζω) to the third heaven (2 Cor 12:2) or paradise (2 Cor 12:4).

200. YHWH's throne was in heaven (Isa 66:1; Ps 11:4; 103:19; cf. 1 Kgs 22:19) according to Jesus (Matt 5:34; 23:22) and others (Acts 7:49; Heb 8:1; cf. Rev 4:2) in the New Testament. However, as part of the expectation of Israel and Judah's return from exile (Jer 3:14–15, 18), Jerusalem would be renamed as "YHWH's throne" (Jer 3:17).

201. cf. Oecumenius, *Commentary on the Apocalypse* Seventh Discourse (ACT/G).

202. When David was anointed king over Israel, he was reminded of an oracle from YHWH concerning him, that he would shepherd (רעה) YHWH's people of Israel, that is to say, that he would be a ruler (נָגִיד) over Israel; see 2 Sam 5:2 || 1 Chron 11:2. And yet, YHWH was David's shepherd, arguably (Ps 23:1). And when Israel would return from exile, YHWH would be like a shepherd to them (Jer 31:10).

203. cf. Victorinus of Petovium, *Commentary on the Apocalypse* 12.3 (ACT/L); Beale, *Book of Revelation*, 639–642; Caird, *Revelation of St. John*, 150–151; Boxall, *Revelation of Saint John*, 180–181; Mangina, *Revelation*, 151–152; contra Aune, *Revelation 6–16*, 689.

woman's child becomes God's Son in the Davidic and messianic tradition of the term. Earlier (§4.2.1) we considered the cluster of theo-political concepts ascribed to God's throne in connection with the Lamb (5:6, 13). Here we can conclude that as the woman's child becomes God's Son sharing in God's throne, divine status and prerogatives also ensue his exaltation. Clearly, the apocalyptic construal of divine authority elaborates its depth and scope as it piles up previous theological images and concepts associated to the Son of God (2:18) and the Lamb (5:6, 8, 12, 13).

What is more, the heavenly proclamation that follows the throwing of the dragon from heaven (12:10–12), expands the level of divine authorization of the woman's child, since it highlights "the authority [ἐξουσία] of his Messiah [χριστός]," that is to say, God's Messiah (12:10; cf. 11:15; 19:1–2). Here again Old Testament allusions play a part. On the one hand, there are echoes of what is known as the "song of Moses" in Exodus 15, which celebrates how YHWH, who is portrayed as a man of war or warrior,[204] threw Pharaoh's chariots and his army into the sea,[205] so that "they went down into the depths like a stone."[206] The song focuses on YHWH's strength (עֹז), might (זִמְרָה) and salvation (יְשׁוּעָה) or deliverance displayed in that victory over Pharaoh (and his army),[207] who was at times portrayed as a dragon in prophetic oracles.[208] In the light of that salvation or deliverance, the song also declares that YHWH will reign forever and ever.[209]

On the other hand, it is another Old Testament "song" – in fact, a prayer – that of Hannah, that helps us further understand the link between God and the empowerment of his anointed or "the authority of his Messiah"

---

204. Exod 15:3. On the usage of this expression see Josh 17:1; Judg 20:17; 1 Sam 16:18; 17:33; 2 Sam 17:8; Isa 3:2 and Ezek 39:20. On its appropriation by YHWH, see Isa 42:13.

205. Exod 15:4; cf. 15:19.

206. Exod 15:5.

207. Exod 15:2, 4, 19. See how Isa 12:2 and Ps 118:14 echo Exod 15:2.

208. See Ezek 29:3; 32:2.

209. Exod 15:18; cf. Mic 4:7; Ps 10:16. It should be noted that the "song of Moses" is explicitly alluded to in Rev 15:3 as part of a doxology predicated partially on the allusion to that victory of YHWH over the Egyptian Pharaoh and his army, who were climactically defeated in the sea, in an unsurpassable display of divine power. Miriam, Moses's elder sister, replicated exactly this song, see Exod 15:21. Additionally, the tradition of a song ascribed to Moses features in Deut 31:22, 30; 32:44; whereas in the Septuagint, it features additionally in *2 Maccabees* 7.6; *4 Maccabees* 18.18. For other Jewish literature that refers to this tradition, see Josephus, *Antiquities of the Jews* 2.346 (2.16.4); and Philo, *On Husbandry* 81; Philo, *On the Change of Names* 182.

(12:10) as the text puts it. As recorded in 1 Samuel 2:1–10, Hannah's prayer communicates her rejoicing in YHWH's salvation (יְשׁוּעָה) or deliverance after becoming pregnant following years of infertility that had caused her to be verbally abused,[210] and giving birth (ילד) to a son (בֵּן),[211] who in turns she gives to YHWH for his service.[212] Hannah's story resembles that of the apocalyptic pregnant woman who gives birth to a son who is then taken to God and his throne.

As Hannah celebrates YHWH's response to her prayer for a son,[213] she introduces a key motif which the books of Samuel, as a whole, then develop, which is the theological construal of the Son of God,[214] and in particular, the relationship between YHWH and his anointed in terms of empowerment.[215] Hannah pictures a conflict between YHWH and his adversaries where the latter would be shattered and YHWH would thunder in heaven;[216] and where YHWH would judge the ends of the land/earth, give strength (עֹז) to his king (מֶלֶךְ), and exalt the horn (קֶרֶן) (i.e. power), of his anointed (מָשִׁיחַ).[217] In this way a correlation of power is established and affirmed between God, the source of power, and his Messiah, the new locus of power, conveyed by the authority the latter indisputably exercises.

4.3.3 What Does the Dragon's Conspiracy Tell Us?

The advent of the Messiah and his divine authorization (i.e. ascension) leads us to consider its "reversed counterpart," the downfall of the dragon. To begin with, why does the dragon try to "kill" the child-Messiah? And, what does the dragon's conspiracy say about the Messiah's enthronement? Let us explore in some depth an answer to these questions.

---

210. 1 Sam 2:1; cf. Isa 25:9; Ps 14:7; 53:7.
211. 1 Sam 1:2, 6, 7, 20.
212. 1 Sam 1:11, 28; 2:11.
213. 1 Sam 1:10–11, 19; cf. 1 Sam 2:20–21.
214. A secularized version of it is preferred by scholar Robert Gordon, as "Davidic royal ideology." See Gordon, *1 & 2 Samuel*, 26; Gordon, *I & II Samuel*, 78–81.
215. cf. 1 Sam 16:3, 12, 13; 2 Sam 2:4; 5:3, 17; 7:8–16; 12:7; 22:51; 23:1.
216. 1 Sam 2:10.
217. cf. Fokkelman, *Narrative Art*, 105; Gordon, *1 & 2 Samuel*, 26.

First, within the whole canonical New Testament corpus the word δράκων (dragon) features only in the book of Revelation,[218] and then within the narrative of the Apocalypse we find it only in the second half. The Septuagint deploys the noun δράκων for the Hebrew term תַּנִּין which features fourteen times in the Old Testament,[219] and is variously translated as dragon, sea-monster or serpent.[220] Thus, it may be argued that God created the great (גָּדוֹל) dragons (תַּנִּין) in the sea,[221] and that the dragon is invited to praise YHWH.[222] However, there is a strand of tradition where the mythical dragon embodies some sort of force hostile to YHWH/God; accordingly, (a) YHWH kills/slays (הרג) the dragon;[223] (b) YHWH pierced (חלל) the dragon;[224] (c) God broke (שבר) the heads of the dragons;[225] (d) YHWH will trample (רמס) on the dragon.[226] Moreover, the dragon features as a political symbol of ruthless and/or voracious imperial power, whether referring to the king of Babylon (Nebuchadrezzar),[227] or the king of Egypt (Pharaoh).[228]

At this point it is worth noting that at present there is a scholarly consensus that regards the Old Testament imagery of the dragon-serpent as being "imported" from Ugaritic mythopoeia, in particular, the *Ugaritic Baal Cycle*,[229]

---

218. The term δράκων features thirteen times in the narrative of the Apocalypse, i.e. Rev 12:3, 4, 7 (two times), 9, 13, 16, 17; 13:2, 4, 11; 16:13; 20:2.

219. Gen 1:21; Exod 7:9, 10, 12; Deut 32:33; Isa 27:1; 51:9, 34; Ezek 29:3; 32:2; Ps 74:13; 91:13; 148:7; Job 7:12.

220. HALOT, 1764.

221. Gen 1:21.

222. Ps 148:7.

223. Isa 27:1.

224. Isa 51:9.

225. Ps 74:13.

226. Ps 91:13.

227. Jer 51:34. The record of Nebuchadnezzar's first year in tablet BM 21946 obverse lines 15–20 is a case in point: "The first year of Nebuchadnezzar (II): In the month Sivan he mustered his army and marched to Hattu. Until the month Kislev he marched about victoriously in Hattu. All the kings of Hattu came into his presence and he received their vast tribute. He marched to *Ashkelon* and in the month Kislev he captured it, seized its king, plundered [and sac]ked it. He turned the city into a ruin heap. In the month Shebat he marched away and [returned] to Bab[ylon]." (Grayson, *Assyrian and Babylonian Chronicles*, 100). In connection with this, the Babylonian King Hammurabi, in his preface to his laws, regarded himself literally as "the dragon of the kings" (Richardson, *Hammurabi's Laws*, 33n4).

228. Ezek 29:3; 32:3.

229. On this see the texts and translations offered by Gibson, *Canaanite Myths and Legends*; and Smith and Pitard, *Ugaritic Baal Cycle*.

as opposed to a Babylonian import,[230] as originally thought.[231] In particular, it is striking to see the extent of the similarity between the Ugaritic dragon-serpent with seven heads,[232] and the apocalyptic dragon-serpent described as "having seven heads and ten horns, and upon its heads seven crowns."[233] We may also say that, matching up to the pedigree of the Hebrew and Ugaritic symbol of the dragon-serpent,[234] the apocalyptic dragon seems to share in the tradition of hostility towards the Creator, as in the Old Testament, and to the self-appointed king, as in the Ugaritic myth.

Second, and more importantly, we will now consider the actions of the dragon. To begin with, the dragon tries to swallow or devour (κατεσθίω) the woman's child.[235] The portrayal of King Nebuchadnezzar in Jeremiah 51:34, as already mentioned, helps us to understand the political nature of this foiled plot told as follows:

> "Nebuchadnezzar, King of Babylon, ate me,
>   he crushed me
> He set me an empty vessel
>   He swallowed [עלב] me like a dragon [תַּנִּין]
> He filled his belly with my luxury
>   He rinsed me (out)" (Jer 51:34)

---

230. For example, the fight between Marduk against Tiamat as conveyed in the *Enuma Elish*. See the translation provided by Dalley, *Myths from Mesopotamia*.

231. Gibson, *Canaanite Myths and Legends*, 7–8; Day, *God's Conflict with the Dragon*, 4–7. Yet, other possibilities are explored in Aune, *Revelation 6–16*, 682–685.

232. cf. CTA 3.3.34–39 / KTU 1.3 III 37–42. Mark Smith and Wayne Pitard argue, though cautiously, that Yam (or Yamm), the dragon (or Tunnanu), and the twisty serpent all refer to the same mythological entity. See Smith and Pitard, *Ugaritic Baal Cycle*, 253–258.

233. Rev 12:3.

234. The degree to which a resonance between the apocalyptic dragon-serpent and some Greek mythological stories may be established is a matter that rests on the (Greek) mythical source considered, e.g. (the shortest) Hesiod, *Theogony* 918–920; *Works and Days* 769–772; *Homeric Hymns* 3.300–304, 308–309, 351–354; (the longest) Hyginus, *Stories* (see Trzaskoma, Smith, and Brunet, *Anthology of Classical Myth*). Therefore, if the view of *the Homeric Hymns* prevail, Apollo killed the dragon to clear any threat to his project of building an altar for himself and of having a group of priests to attend to it; whereas if Hyginus's version is considered, Apollo killed the dragon to claim a prophetic monopoly in the area (arguably Delos).

235. Rev 12:4, which has been interpreted, for instance, as (a) "to subject [Jesus] to death" (Victorinus of Petovium, *Commentary on the Apocalypse* 12.2 [ACT/L]); (b) "its primary reference is certainly to the crucifixion" (Caird, *Revelation of St. John*, 150); (c) "all the devil's efforts to tempt Chris during his ministry and to kill him, from his birth until the end of his ministry" (Beale, *Book of Revelation*, 637).

...

> "And I will punish Bel in Babylon
> And bring out from his mouth the thing he swallowed
> [עׇלְבֽ]" (Jer 51:44)

Jeremiah 51 is an oracle against Babylon, it conveys YHWH's message of vengeance to repay them (Jer 51:6) for all the evil (רָעָה) they have done in Zion (Jer 51:24). In fact, the above text (Jer 51:34) are words spoken by Zion (Jer 51:35) recalling the fall of Jerusalem to King Nebuchadnezzar and his Babylonian army. If we consider the king of Judah as a Davidic Son of God,[236] who ruled over Jerusalem,[237] (i.e. Zion),[238] we may be able to stretch the political imagery a bit further and suggest that the Babylonian dragon "swallowed" the Davidic Son of God, that is to say, the Babylonian dragon dethroned the Davidic Son of God.[239] However, in what seems a reversal of the exile by YHWH (Jer 51:44), Walter Brueggeman notes that "the monster-god-empire [i.e. Bel] is forced to relinquish the city of Jerusalem and is not free to devour it. Yahweh has snatched the life of Zion out of the mouth of empire."[240] After all, the Old Testament considers YHWH to be King on Zion.[241]

The political nature of the dragon's plot becomes more evident when the narrative thread of his downfall (Rev 12:7–9; 20:1–3) is brought into the discussion, as we proposed in §3.5. Here the dragon being seized, bound, imprisoned, then released and found organising an attack reflects to a certain

---

236. cf. Jer 22:2; 1 Kgs 12:20; 14:21; 2 Kgs 8:19; 2 Sam 7:12–14.

237. e.g. 1 Kgs 14:21; 22:42.

238. e.g. 2 Kgs 19:21; Isa 30:19; Ps 135:21; cf. Ps 2:6.

239. cf. 2 Kgs 25:4–9; Jer 24:1. The political nature of this imagery is attested in one of the foundational texts of classical Greek as follows: "But Rhea was subject in love to Cronos and bore splendid children, Hestia, Demeter, and gold-shod Hera and strong Hades, pitiless in heart, who dwells under the earth, and the loud-crashing Earth-Shaker, and wise Zeus, father of gods and men, by whose thunder the wide earth is shaken. These great Cronos swallowed [καταπίνω] as each came forth from the womb to his mother's knees with this intent, that no other of the proud sons of Heaven should hold the kingly office amongst the deathless gods. For he learned from Earth and starry Heaven that he was destined to be overcome by his own son, strong though he was, through the contriving of great Zeus." Hesiod, *Theogony*, 453–465; cf. Aune, *Revelation 6–16*, 686–687.

240. Brueggemann, *Commentary on Jeremiah*, 480.

241. e.g. Isa 24:23; 52:7; Jer 8:19; Mic 4:7; Zech 9:9; cf. Ps 2:6.

extent an Old Testament motif of political conspiracy,²⁴² in which the king of Judah or Israel is seized, bound, and imprisoned – in short, dethroned and exiled following the invasion of an ancient Near Eastern imperial power brought about as a result of the evil done by them in YHWH's eyes.²⁴³ For instance, Hoshea, son of Elah, who conspired (קשר) a conspiracy (קֶשֶׁר) on Pekah, son of Remaliah, smote (נכה) him, killed (מות) him, and became king (מלך),²⁴⁴ over Israel in his stead.²⁴⁵ However, because of the evil (רַע) he had done,²⁴⁶ the king of Assyria went up and made him a servant (עֶבֶד) of his,²⁴⁷ a vassal. Yet, the king of Assyria found Hoshea had been involved in a conspiracy (קֶשֶׁר), and so had him restrained (עצר) and bound (אסר) him in the house (בַּיִת) of prison (כֶּלֶא).²⁴⁸ Then the king of Assyria besieged Samaria, took it over and sent its inhabitants into exile.²⁴⁹

Or consider Jehoiachin, who became king over Jerusalem for three months only.²⁵⁰ Because he had done evil (רַע) in the eyes of YHWH,²⁵¹ when King Nebuchadnezzar came to Jerusalem,²⁵² he took (לקח) Jehoiachin and sent

---

242. Evidently, the Old Testament pattern of political conspiracy is but a recurrent conflict in the ancient Near East. For instance, tablet BM 92502 lines ii 32–35, of the so-called *Assyrian and Babylonian Chronicles*, recorded that "Shutruk-Nahhunte (II), king of Elam, was seized by his brother, Hallushu-(Inshushinak I) (lit. Hallushu, his brother, seized him) and he (Hallushu-Inshushinak I) shut the door in his face. For eighteen years Shutruk-Nahhunte (II) ruled Elam. Hallushu-(Inshushinak I), his brother, ascended the throne in Elam." (Grayson, *Assyrian and Babylonian Chronicles*, 77–78). Grayson argues that the phrase "shut the door in his face" is perhaps "an Elamite idiom meaning 'he threw him in prison'" (Grayson, 77).

243. To my knowledge, no scholar has proposed this hermeneutical framework to understand the dragon's fall in the Apocalypse.

244. 2 Kgs 15:30.

245. 2 Kgs 17:1. A conspiracy or rebellion à la Hoshea is attested in tablet BM 92502 lines i 12–18 of the so-called *Assyrian and Babylonian Chronicles*: "For fourteen years Nabu-nasir ruled Babylon. (Nabu)-nadin-(zeri), his son, ascended the throne in Babylon. The second year: (Nabu)-nadin-(zeri) was killed in a rebellion. For two years (Nabu)-nadin-(zeri) ruled Babylon. (Nabu)-shuma-ukin (II), a district officer (and) leader of the rebellion, ascended the throne. For one month and two days (Nabu)-[shu]ma-ukin (II) ruled Babylon. (Nabu)-mukin-ze[ri], the Amukkan[ite], removed him from the throne and seized the throne (for himself)." Grayson, *Assyrian and Babylonian Chronicles*, 72.

246. 2 Kgs 17:2.

247. 2 Kgs 17:3.

248. 2 Kgs 17:4.

249. 2 Kgs 17:5–6; cf. tablet BM 92502 lines i 23–30, of the so-called *Assyrian and Babylonian Chronicles* in Grayson, *Assyrian and Babylonian Chronicles*, 72–73.

250. 2 Kgs 24:6, 8.

251. 2 Kgs 24:9.

252. 2 Kgs 24:11.

him into exile (גלה) to Babylon.[253] Zedekiah was then made king (מלך) in Jehoiachin's stead,[254] and reigned (מלך) eleven years in Jerusalem,[255] presumably as a vassal. However, he also did evil (רע) in the eyes of YHWH,[256] and rebelled (מרד) against the king of Babylon,[257] who in turn besieged Jerusalem,[258] and finally invaded it again.[259] And though Zedekiah attempted to escape,[260] he was seized/caught (תפש) and brought to face the king of Babylon, who spoke his judgment (מִשְׁפָּט).[261] Zedekiah's children were slaughtered in front of him; then, Zedekiah was made blind, bound (אסר) with bronze fetters (נְחֹשֶׁת) and sent to Babylon,[262] where he was put (נתן) in the house (בַּיִת) of oversight (פְּקֻדָּה) until the day of his death.[263] As for Jehoiachin, in the thirty-seventh year of captivity/exile (גָּלוּת), he was lifted (נשׂא) from the house (בַּיִת) of prison (כֶּלֶא) by the new king of Babylon,[264] or he was lifted (נשׂא) and brought out (יצא) from the house (בַּיִת) of prison (כְּלִיא),[265] and he was given a throne (כִּסֵּא) from above the thrones of the kings that were with him in Babylon.[266]

This Old Testament motif of political conspiracy plotted by a vassal or minor ruler against a superior imperial power – an evil event in YHWH's

---

253. 2 Kgs 24:12, 15.
254. 2 Kgs 24:17.
255. 2 Kgs 24:18.
256. 2 Kgs 24:19.
257. 2 Kgs 24:20; cf. tablet BM 25127 line 29 in Grayson, *Assyrian and Babylonian Chronicles*, 89; Wiseman, *Chronicles of Chaldean Kings*, 53. Or tablet BM 21901 lines 31–33 in Grayson, *Assyrian and Babylonian Chronicles*, 93; cf. Wiseman, *Chronicles of Chaldean Kings*, 59.
258. 2 Kgs 25:1–2.
259. 2 Kgs 25:8–22; cf. tablet BM 21946 Reversed lines 11–13 of the so-called *Assyrian and Babylonian Chronicles* in Grayson, *Assyrian and Babylonian Chronicles*, 102; cf. Wiseman, *Chronicles of Chaldean Kings*, 73.
260. 2 Kgs 25:4.
261. 2 Kgs 25:6; Jer 39:5.
262. 2 Kgs 25:7; Jer 39:6–7; 52:10.
263. Jer 52:11.
264. 2 Kgs 25:27.
265. Jer 52:31.
266. Jer 52:32. The motif of political conspiracy was also enacted in the Graeco-Roman world as, for instance, when Aristobulus, a "king" (βασιλεύς) (presumably of the Jews) resisted Roman rule, yet he was overcome and shut up (ἔργω) in Rome (from where he had escaped previously). And though later on Julius Caesar released him from his chains or imprisonment (δεσμός), he eventually was poisoned by some people linked to Pompey; cf. Josephus, *War of the Jews* 1.171–174 (1.8.6), 183–184 (1.9.1).

eyes – features also in the oracle against the king of Babylon as recorded in Isaiah 14:4–23, in particular the sequence of grandiose claims and downfall in verses 12–15, which according to John Day and Brevard S. Childs echoes a Canaanite myth.[267] A twist in this motif of the imprisonment of a (minor) king by a superior political power is also provided by the so-called "Isaianic Apocalypse" (Isa 24–27),[268] in particular, Isaiah 24:21–23, to which Enochic Judaism (i.e. 1 Enoch 10:4–6, 11–13) appears to offer a variant, or perhaps, a development,[269] where heavenly beings are bound, imprisoned and punished, a pattern already observed in Isaiah 24:21–22.

Altogether, whether it is an evil and conspiratorial king who is seized, bound, imprisoned and exiled by a superior imperial power, and therefore dethroned; or whether a king's grandiose claims in an attempt to usurp the control of the heavenly council which lead to his being cast down to the bottom of the pit (Isa 14:12–15); or both the host of heaven and kings of the land being imprisoned in a dungeon-pit for many days as punishment from YHWH (Isa 24:21–23), the core elements of this intriguing political Old Testament motif powerfully resonate with Revelation 20:1–3, 7–10, which depicts how the dragon is seized, bound and imprisoned ("dethroned") and exiled from heaven.

In Revelation, the dragon's attempt à la Nebuchadnezzar to swallow the woman's child who becomes God's Son, followed by the dragon's downfall in the manner of ancient Near Eastern and Old Testament patterns of an unsuccessful political conspiracy (i.e. being dethroned, seized, bound and imprisoned by a superior [imperial] power), allows us to conclude that the dragon attempted to prevent the woman's child becoming God's Son in order to claim for himself the prerogatives associated to God's throne, as the narrative has been gradually disclosing. In fact the apocalyptic dragon tries to do what the (historical) Babylonian "dragon" did – to dethrone the Davidic son of God, and to claim for himself the prerogative of authorising or enthroning a puppet king (Rev 13:2) that would serve his imperialistic interests rather

---

267. Day, *Yahweh and Gods*, 170–174; Childs, *Isaiah*, 126.
268. Phrase borrowed from Millar, *Isaiah 24–27*, 1. For its part, R. E. Clements prefers the expression "the Apocalypse of Isaiah," see Clements, *Isaiah 1–39*, 196.
269. cf. Nickelsburg, *1 Enoch 1*, 221–222, 224–225.

than God's salvific, kingly and messianic agenda (12:10), a new theo-political construal from which a new sociality would emerge (12:11).

Precisely, the dragon's hidden and heretical agenda is materialized in the emergence of the sea beast (13:1), which the dragon authorizes (13:2, 4), the earth beast (13:11), and indirectly through the sea/abyss beast (17:3, 7, 8), the great city (17:1, i.e. Babylon, 16:19; 18:10, 21). Together they construe a political authority sustained by a coercive public liturgy that involves the worship of the first beast (13:12), and implicitly requires the worship of the one who authorizes (i.e. the dragon) (13:4). In addition, the dragon becomes a subtle locus of evil as it unsuccessfully attempts to prevent the enthronement of the Messiah. Because of this, it is the exalted Jesus who locates evil, and it is the dragon who embodies a particular mode of evil, an evil predicated on a political conspiracy to prevent the woman's child to become God's Son.

4.3.4 Theological Implications

The advent of the Messiah conveyed through a succession of allusive images going from the primeval woman at odds with the primeval deceiver, then the house of Jacob, one of whom would become exalted, to the prophetic sign about Immanu-El in the midst of his people to protect or deliver them, and finally the evangelical story of the incarnation – all these images account for the value of tradition in society. In fact, "the continuity of tradition," observes O'Donovan, is "foundational to the political task."[270] In other words, "without the consciousness of something possessed and handed on from generation to generation there could [not] be . . . a political theology, since it would never be clear how the judgments of God could give order and structure to a community and sustain it in being."[271]

With reference to the theological transition from woman's child to God's Son usually known as ascension or exaltation, going from earth to heaven, from womb to throne, it provides a ground to affirm the teleological orientation of history. As O'Donovan suggests, "there is an important place in Christian thought for the idea of 'history', using the term as it is widely used in philosophy and theology to mean, not mere events on the one hand, but their inherent significance and direction which makes them intelligible

---

270. O'Donovan, *Ways of Judgment*, 181.
271. O'Donovan, *Desire of the Nations*, 41.

and narratable."²⁷² So, (divine) authority vindicates the past, and protects the course of history and the liturgical sociality along with it (i.e. "the rest of the woman's offspring," Rev 12:17) from being hijacked by a capricious immanent "force" (the dragon) and emptied of its transcendent referent, losing its eschatological horizon.

4.4 The Divine King Speaks Justice

In narrative unit three (§3.6) we provided a synopsis of the apocalyptic vision of the rider on the white horse (19:11–21) and argued that it portrays the divine King deploying the discourse of justice in both agonistic and forensic terms on a global scale. At present we would like to expand this analysis, focusing on three aspects of the vision: (i) the allusions to Old Testament tradition used to describe the apocalyptic king, (ii) the divine prerogatives ascribed to this king, and (iii) how his discourse confirms his exalted status.

4.4.1 A Collage of Traditions about the King

The opening verse of this vision can be translated as follows:

> And I saw the heaven having been opened
> And look, a white horse
> And the one who sits on it being called faithful and true,
> And with justice [δικαιοσύνη] he judges [κρίνω] and wages war [πολεμέω] (Rev 19:11)

Here we would note that this text alludes to the mode of authority embodied by the figure of the king in ancient Israel. When the Israelites contemporaneous with the prophet Samuel, in their desire to emulate the prevailing political model of authority in surrounding nations, asked for the appointment of a king, they put forward the following job description: "our king [מֶלֶךְ] will judge [שׁפט] us and go out [יצא] before us and fight/wage [לחם] himself our wars [מִלְחָמָה]."²⁷³ And though no explicit reference is made to his judging

---

272. O'Donovan, *Resurrection and Moral Order*, 55.
273. 1 Sam 8:20; cf. 4Q51 8a b.12–13; 1 Sam 8:5. "I am . . . the mighty king . . . I made the land speak with justice and truth" (*Hammurabi's Laws*, P21, P22 in Richardson, *Hammurabi's Laws*, 41). Overall, it seems commentators on the Apocalypse have overlooked this allusion to 1 Sam 8:20 in connection with the responsibilities of a king (i.e. to judge and wage war); cf. Walton, *Ancient Near East Thought*, 278.

with justice, we can confidently argue that it was presupposed. After all, this was a nation that had been given the following command when leaving Egypt: "with justice [צֶדֶק] you will judge [שפט] your neighbour."[274] It should be noted that as the narrative of 1–2 Samuel unfolds, this political institution (i.e. the king) was reframed as the theological construal of the Son of God (2 Sam 7:12–14), which we have already looked at in this chapter (§4.1.2) and which adds to our understanding of John's interlocutor's own self-introduction as the Son of God (Rev 2:18).

However, even though David, already anointed (משח),[275] fought (לחם) the wars (מִלְחָמָה),[276] and his son Solomon as king (מֶלֶךְ) judged (שפט) doing justice (מִשְׁפָּט),[277] there is no (textual) evidence of a historic king able to fulfil the expectations or match the profile as originally set out for the king of Israel. By contrast, YHWH remained the unsurpassed judge: "for you uphold my right and my case, you sit on the throne to judge [שפט] [with] justice [צֶדֶק]."[278] YHWH also waged war on behalf of his people. When the Israelites were exiled from the promised land, the prophet Zechariah let them know that "YHWH will go out [יצא] and fight against [לחם] the nations."[279] In fact, we are told that the nations would declare that "YHWH is King."[280] All in all, the evident failure of various kings in living up to this job description resulted in YHWH being confirmed as the ultimate king that judges with justice and fights on behalf of his people.

Despite the shortcomings of the historical Israelite kings, Israel continued to foster a tradition about the ideal king in theological and eschatological terms. Accordingly, the king, as portrayed in Psalm 45,[281] presumably a love song addressed to the king, is asked to gird (חגר) the sword (חֶרֶב) on his thigh (יָרֵךְ),[282] and to ride (רכב) on the word (דָּבָר) of truth (אֱמֶת) and humil-

---

274. Lev 19:15; cf. Deut 1:16.
275. cf. 1 Sam 16:3, 12–13.
276. e.g. 1 Sam 18:17; 19:8; 2 Sam 8:10; 21:15; 1 Chr 18:10; 19:17.
277. e.g. 1 Kgs 3:28.
278. Ps 9:5 (9:4 ET); cf. 9:9 (9:8 ET); 96:13; 98:9.
279. Zech 14:3; cf. Exod 14:14.
280. 1 Chr 16:31; cf. Ps 10:16; 97:1; 99:1.
281. "Interestingly, in ... Psalm 45 ... the context is that of the king as a warrior, something which scholars have hitherto not noticed," Day, *Psalms*, 104.
282. Ps 45:4 (45:3 ET); cf. Rev 19:15, 16. "The king was the head of the armed forces; and in the ancient world divine aid was expected in battle. Accordingly, it is not surprising to find

ity of justice (צֶדֶק);²⁸³ his arrows are for the enemies of the king (מֶלֶךְ);²⁸⁴ he is called אֱלֹהִים (i.e. a god), and his throne (כִּסֵּא) is forever and ever;²⁸⁵ the rod/sceptre (שֵׁבֶט) of his kingdom (מַלְכוּת) being a sceptre of uprightness (מִישׁוֹר).²⁸⁶ Besides, there is a marriage which takes place between the king and the queen consort (שֵׁגַל),²⁸⁷ and the king's sons are installed as princes (שַׂר) in all the earth (אֶרֶץ).²⁸⁸

What is more, this tradition was expanded in one of the oracles of the prophet Isaiah about a descendant of King David, a shoot (חֹטֶר) from the stem (גֶּזַע) of Jesse (יִשַׁי),²⁸⁹ the father of David.²⁹⁰ This descendant would judge (שפט) the poor (דַּל) with justice (צֶדֶק),²⁹¹ smite (נכה) the earth with the rod (שֵׁבֶט) of his mouth (פֶּה),²⁹² and kill (מות) the wicked (רָשָׁע) with the breath (רוּחַ) of his lips (שָׂפָה).²⁹³ He would be girded with justice (צֶדֶק) and faithfulness (אֱמוּנָה) like belts around his loins.²⁹⁴ This king would enable a new sociality to be made up of the returned people of God who had been in exile.²⁹⁵

Now turning to our apocalyptic vision, we find each of these three strands of tradition present in the text: (i) a historicized strand – the requested king who would judge and wage war; (ii) a theologized strand – the quasi-divine king who would ride on truth and justice, defeat his enemies, celebrate his marriage to his queen and empower his children; and (iii) an eschatological strand – the expected Davidic king who would smite the earth and kill the wicked armed with justice and trust, and who would set up a new sociality. All these traditions converge and are actualized in the apocalyptic figure of the rider on the white horse, whose christological identity is skilfully interwoven

---

that a number of royal psalms have a battle context." Day, *Psalms*, 93.

283. Ps 45:5 (45:4 ET); cf. Rev 19:11.
284. Ps 45:6 (45:5 ET); cf. Rev 19:21.
285. Ps 45:7 (45:6 ET); cf. Rev 19:16.
286. Ps 45:7 (45:6 ET); cf. Rev 19:15.
287. Ps 45:10-12 (45:9-11 ET); cf. Rev 19:6-9.
288. Ps 45:17 (45:16 ET); cf. Rev 20:4, 6.
289. Isa 11:1; cf. Rev 5:5; 22:16.
290. cf. 1 Sam 16:1, 10; 2 Sam 23:1; Ruth 4:22; 1 Chr 10:14; 29:26.
291. Isa 11:4; cf. Rev 19:11.
292. Isa 11:4; cf. Rev 19:15.
293. Isa 11:4; cf. Rev 19:21.
294. Isa 11:5; cf. Rev 19:11.
295. cf. Isa 11:11-16.

into this vision, in particular his sharing in the features of the Son of God,[296] as noted in §4.1.3. Equally, he shares in the identity of the Lamb, who is unapologetically identified with the divine name "King of kings and Lord of lords" (17:14), which the rider on the white horse also bears (19:16). Additionally, the rider is called the Word of God (ὁ λόγος τοῦ θεοῦ), a christological title used in the Gospel of John arguably conveying Jesus's divine pre-existence.[297]

What is more, the messianic aura of this apocalyptic portrayal of the king is reinforced as the vision takes up the motif of the political conspiracy of the kings of the earth against YHWH's anointed which features in Psalm 2 (§4.1.2). In particular, Psalm 2:1–3, which seems to be alluded to in Revelation 19:19, introduces the scene of a worldwide conspiracy, where nations and peoples, kings of the earth and rulers discuss how to subvert YHWH and his anointed's rule over them. Of course, the allusion to Psalm 2:6–9 in Revelation 19:15 serves to confirm the theological role Psalm 2 plays in this vision.[298] The Apocalyptic vision also re-enacts the Danielic scene of dethronement of the beast and its punishment by fire where "the beast was seized and with it the false prophet . . . The two living [ones/creatures] were thrown into the lake of fire, which keeps burning with sulphur" (Rev 19:20). In Daniel 7, the fourth beast that came out from the sea "was put to death, and its body destroyed and given over to be burned with fire" (Dan 7:11 NRSV), which was then followed by the exaltation of "like a son of man" (Dan 7:13–14).

4.4.2 Divine Prerogatives Ascribed to the King

As regards to the divine prerogatives exerted by this king, the rider on the white horse leads the heavenly army: "and the armies – who [are] in heaven – it [sic] came after him on white horses, having put on [clothes] made of fine linen, white, clean" (Rev 19:14). This depiction takes us back to Joshua's encounter with the prince/leader/general (שַׂר) of YHWH's army (צָבָא) on the eve of the battle of Jericho (Josh 5:13–15);[299] it is significant because the figure

---

296. cf. Rev 1:14, 16; 2:12, 18; 19:12, 15.

297. See John 1:1–3, 14; cf. 17:5; Irenaeus, *Against Heresies* 1.9.3; 1.10.3; 3.11.8 (ANF/1); Eusebius, *Ecclesiastical History* 1.2.3; 5.28.5 (NPNF2/1). Equally, see discussions on the meaning of ὁ λόγος in Barrett, *Gospel According to St. John*, 149–156; Carson, *Gospel According to John*, 111–118.

298. cf. Beale and McDonough, "Revelation," 1144.

299. cf. 11Q11 5.8.

of the general of a king's army features throughout the Old Testament,[300] and because the closeness of this figure to the king is presumed. Also, we must not forget that the king is expected to lead the army.[301] Further pre-apocalyptic references to the heavenly army include Micaiah's vision about a people left without a king (1 Kgs 22:17) in which he saw YHWH sitting on his throne, and all the army (צָבָא) of heaven (שָׁמַיִם) standing on his right and on his left (1 Kgs 22:19); also, Ezra's prayer in which he speaks of the army of heaven worshipping YHWH (Neh 9:6),[302] and in Second Temple Judaism, Enochic Judaism features God leading a heavenly army in 1 Enoch 1:3–4.[303] It is clear from these references that no ordinary human being could be expected to lead the army of heaven, and that if the rider on the white horse leads the heavenly army,[304] then he must in some way share in this divine prerogative as king.

Revelation 19:15 further describes the rider on the white horse in terms of the task he undertakes as "he treads the vat of the wine of the wrath of God's anger" (cf. 14:19–20).[305] Here we can discern an allusion to Lamentations 1,[306] though in this case it is the kingdom of Judah and the city of Jerusalem that experience the day of his fury/burning (חָרוֹן) anger (אַף) (Lam 1:12) when "the Lord [אֲדֹנָי] has trodden [דרך] as in a wine-press [גַּת] the virgin [בְּתוּלָה] daughter [בַּת] Judah [יְהוּדָה]" (Lam 1:15 NRSV, where the city is personified as a woman). The imagery in Revelation 19:15 is clearly the same, and yet it is the rider taking on the divine prerogative of treading "the vat of the wine of God's anger," which in both passages involves the destruction of the mighty

---

300. e.g. Judg 4:2; 1 Sam 12:9; 1 Kgs 1:19; 16:16; 2 Kgs 5:1; 1 Chr 27:34; 2 Chr 33:11; 11Q19 62.5; cf. Oecumenius, *Commentary on the Apocalypse* Tenth Discourse (ACT/G).

301. cf. 2 Sam 11:1; 1 Chr 20:1. In addition, the dynamics of the relationship between the king and the general of his army are illustrated in 2 Sam 12:26–31.

302. This theologoumenon of a heavenly army worshipping God features in *2 Enoch* 17 (OTP/1).

303. cf. *1 Enoch* 1.9; Jude 14–15.

304. For a non-angelic understanding of the heavenly army see Caird, *Revelation of St. John*, 244; cf. Victorinus of Petovium, *Commentary on the Apocalypse* 19.1 (ACT/L). For an angelic or not nature theory see Beale, *Book of Revelation*, 960–961; and for a view as an angelic heavenly army see Aune, *Revelation 6–16*, 1059–1060.

305. cf. Isa 63:1–6, in particular the allusion to 63:2–3 signified by the garment of the rider on the white horse: "having put on a garment having been dipped in blood" (Rev 19:13); cf. Aune, *Revelation 17–22*, 1057; Beale and McDonough, "Revelation," 1143.

306. In passing, note the echoes of Lamentations 1 in Revelation 18 regarding the fall of the great city, and in 19:11–21, which is about the fate of the city's elite.

people (אַבִּיר) in the midst of the "city" together with its (military) elite (cf. Rev 19:11–21).

Perhaps the most important of the prerogatives of the rider on the white horse is the fact that he wears the divine name: "And he has on the robe and on his thigh a name having been written: 'King of kings and Lord of lords'" (Rev 19:16; cf. 17:14). Of which we can say the following:

First, "King of kings" was a superlative eastern imperial title ascribed to the Babylonian Nebuchadnezzar (Ezek 26:7; Dan 2:37; 4Q112 f3ii 6.5; Dan 3:2 LXX; Dan 4:37b LXX) and the Persian Artaxerxes (Ezra 7:12) or Xerxes (Josephus, *Antiquities of the Jews* 11.123 (11.5.1)).[307] However, in Daniel 4:37 LXX, Nebuchadnezzar ascribes this title to God himself, which other Jewish literature then picks up, as attested in 2 Maccabees 13.4; 3 Maccabees 5.35; 1 Enoch 9.4; 84.2; Philo, *Cherubim* 99; *Decalogue* 141; *Special Laws* 1.18; 4Q381 f76 77.7; 4Q403 f1i.34; 4Q405 f4 5.2. Also, early Christian literature continues its use, e.g. Tertullian, *Against Marcion* 1.4 (ANF/3). And yet, Aristotle (Greece) and Cicero (Rome) regarded their respective leading god as the king of other gods and kings as well.[308]

Second, "Lord of lords" was also a superlative title ascribed to YHWH in Deuteronomy 10:17,[309] which is also combined with the title "God of gods."[310] In fact, this is elaborated in the doxology of Psalm 136, which begins praising YHWH (Ps 136:1), next the "God of gods" (Ps 136:2),[311] and then the "Lord of lords" (Ps 136:3).[312] In addition, this title features in Psalm 135:26 LXX; Daniel 4:37 LXX; 1 Enoch 9:4; 4Q381 f76_77.14; and later on, in Justin Martyr, *Dialogue with Trypho* 16 (ANF/1) – as it quotes Deuteronomy 10:16–17.

Third, a theological combination of these titles is used in the human and angelic doxologies of Daniel 4:37 LXX and 1 Enoch 9:4, where it is declared "You are God of gods, and Lord of lords, and King of kings." A theological progression appears to have taken place at the time of Jewish subjugation to foreign imperialistic powers, a trend which early Christian tradition maintained.

---

307. See also Cassius Dio, *Roman History* 37.6.2; 49.41.1; cf. Beale, "Origin of the Title," 618; Aune, *Revelation 17–22*, 954–955.
308. See Aristotle, *Politics* 1.2.7 (1252b); Cicero, *On the Commonwealth* 1.56.
309. cf. 4Q128 f1.23; 4Q138 f1.5; 4Q151 f1.17; 8Q4 f1.7; XQ1 1.24.
310. cf. 1Q13 f20.1; 4Q128 f1.23; 4Q151 f1.17; 8Q3 f17_25.8; 8Q4 f1.7; XQ1 1.24.
311. cf. 11Q5 15.6.
312. cf. 11Q5 15.7.

For example, 1 Timothy 6:15; Origen, *Against Celsus* 8.4 (ANF/4); *The Divine Liturgy of Mark* 14 (ANF/7); John of Damascus, *An Exact Exposition of the Orthodox Faith* 4.15 (NPNF2/9); *Letter of Agatho, Pope of Old Rome, to the Emperor* (NPNF2/14).

Finally, because of the above, it is all the more striking that the Lamb is now referred to in the following terms: "the Lamb . . . is Lord of lords and King of kings" (Rev 17:14). "No doubt, the use of this divine title . . . is merely another way in which the author of Revelation expresses the absolute deity and kingship of the messianic Lamb."[313] Equally striking is that the rider on the white horse wears this imperial divine name tattooed on his thigh (i.e. "King of kings and Lord of lords," 19:16). With this christological orientation it would continue to be used by a whole body of early Christian literature, for example Irenaeus, *Against Heresies* 4.20.11 (ANF/1); Tertullian, *On the Resurrection of the Flesh* 23 (ANF/3); Cyprian, *Treatise 12* 2.30 (ANF/5); Lactantius, *Divine Institutes* 4.12(ANF/7); *The Divine Liturgy of James* 16 (ANF/7); Origen, *Commentary on the Gospel of John* 2.4(ANF/9); John Chrysostom, *Homilies on 1 Thessalonians* 6 (NPNF1/13); Theodoret, *Dialogues* 1; idem, *Letters* 146 (both in NPNF2/3); Hilary of Poiters, *On the Trinity* 4.8 (NPNF2/9); Ambrose of Milan, *Exposition of the Christian Faith* 3.3.17 (NPNF2/10).

4.4.3 And the King Said . . .

The divine King, who is also the Word of God (Rev 19:13) "speaks" the forensic language of justice conveyed in agonistic terms. In other words, his discourse effects a judicial verdict on human authority complicit in theological delusion and coercive intimidation, as enacted by the (sea) beast and the false prophet, respectively (19:20–21; cf. Psalms of Solomon 17.24 [OTP/2]). The pattern of someone being seized and thrown into a place of confinement as a result of taking part in a doomed political conspiracy has already featured in the story of the dragon's fall (§4.3.3), where we saw it implied the dragon's "dethronement". Allusions to Daniel 7 as noted above (§4.4.1),[314] especially

---

313. Beale, "Origin of the Title," 619; cf. Beale, *Book of Revelation*, 881–882.

314. Both *4 Ezra* 11–12 and *2 Baruch* 35–43 (OTP/1) each deploy a framework (*4 Ezra* 11.1 – 12.3; *2 Baruch* 35.1 – 37.1), which is explained à la Daniel 7 (*4 Ezra* 12.10–39; *2 Baruch* 39–40). In fact, *4 Ezra* 12.11 explicitly says that this is a further elaboration of Daniel's vision. More importantly, in both visions and explanations, it is the "Anointed One"/Messiah (*4 Ezra*

7:26 (NRSV) with its scene of judgment where the fourth beast, arguably, is dethroned and consumed by fire, help us establish that what takes place here is also a scene of dethronement or de-authorization of human authority,[315] which in turn locates ultimate authority in heaven. In addition, as noted earlier (§3.3; §4.2.2), this vision links in with the sequence of the opening of the seven seals of the scroll (6:1–12), in particular bringing to an end the event following the opening of the sixth seal (6:12–17). Also, the vision of the rider on the white horse restates, though with a different set of images, what the blowing of the seventh trumpet had conveyed theologically (i.e. "the kingdom of the world has become of our Lord and of his anointed/Messiah," Rev 11:15).

The result of the above is that the King-Logos judicially clears the (ontological) space for the materialization of the Fellowship of the Throne, which will take place with the advent of the holy city as a new heaven and new earth are fashioned by the Creator (21:1–22:5). In this sense we may say that as the Logos "speaks," a new cosmic/liturgical order is effected out of the chaos or anarchy represented by the alliance of heresy, coercion, and (human) authority, reflecting thus the creation story of Genesis.[316] This is re-creation through justice.[317]

4.4.4 Theological Implications

There are two implications worth highlighting at this point. The first is that, despite the imperial overtones implied by the figure and portrayal of the divine King, he does not obliterate human authority per se (cf. Rev 21:23–24). Instead, the supremacy of the divine King over any human authority fosters a relationship of accountability from the human towards the divine, where allegiance to any form of theological delusion and coercion will inevitably

---

12.31–32; *2 Baruch* 39.7), whether envisioned as a lion (*4 Ezra* 11.37) or as the vine and fountain (*2 Baruch* 36.3), who will judge and destroy "the eagle"/fourth beast (*4 Ezra* 12.32–33), or convict and kill "the great forest"/fourth beast (*2 Baruch* 40.1–2). Interestingly enough, in *4 Ezra* 12.3, "the whole body of the eagle was burned."

315. It should be noted that the first Israelite king was "dethroned" by YHWH, and his forensic verdict was communicated as "word of God," so to speak, by the prophet Samuel to the dethroned King Saul, see 1 Sam 15:28.

316. e.g. Gen 1:1–3.

317. In contrast, Origen took a more inward and soteriological stance as he commented on this apocalyptic text, see Origen, *Commentary on the Gospel of John* 2.4 (ANF/9).

render impossible the flourishing of any human sociality and also determine the viability of that authority. In part, this explains the implosion of the great city, that ultimate mode of sociality sustained by theological delusion and coercion. The second is that, war as a way of exerting power is subverted by the divine King. In this vision, war becomes forensic rather than militaristic. There is no military engagement, instead the King "speaks" his discourse which effects justice through "capital death," that is to say, dethronement or disempowerment. Thus, as O'Donovan points out, "the word of God . . . effects what it signifies."[318] The absence of military violence is made evident by the spatial gap between the two parties in conflict, instead of a battlefield we see the heaven opened, and birds fly in midheaven as the kings come from the earth. In addition, this mode of apocalyptic war enables re-creation instead of bringing about destruction, it gives way to the advent of the holy city, and the materialization of the Fellowship of the Throne.

All in all, the portrayal of the divine King presupposes a correlation of power between the one who sits on the throne and the rider on the white horse. As we have seen, the various strands of Old Testament tradition on the king, whether historical, theological or eschatological in nature, are alluded to in this vision and contribute to make this correlation evident. However, this apocalyptic king is also invested with divine prerogatives, the most important of which is his wearing of the divine name, which along with the other (christological) name (i.e. the Word of God), reinforces his divine status. In addition, the various apocalyptic portrayals of the exalted Jesus as Son of God, Lamb and Messiah converge in this depiction of the divine King. What is more, included among his divine prerogatives is his forensic discourse, conveyed in agonistic terms, which affects the dethronement or disempowerment of human authorities predicated on unorthodox theology and liturgy. As a result, the King-Logos makes possible the advent of a new sociality (i.e. the holy city) and the materialization of the Fellowship of the Throne as he speaks.[319]

---

318. O'Donovan, *Ways of Judgment*, 13.

319. A portrayal of Christ as king, in what seems a millenarian reading of apocalyptic passages coming after this vision (i.e. Rev 20–21), features in *Apocalypse of Elijah* 5.36–39 (OTP/1).

4.5 Conclusion

In this chapter we have scrutinized the various categories used throughout the Apocalypse to communicate the central theme of a correlation of power and divine status between the one who sits on the throne and the authorized agent, which we have argued emerges from our narrative reading of the book of Revelation. These categories included (a) the Father and the Son of God, (b) the one who sits on the throne and the Lamb, and (c) God and the child-Messiah. All these theological construals of the exalted Jesus converge in the portrayal of the divine King, whose prerogative is to bear the doxological and imperialistic divine name "King of kings and Lord of lords," which also presupposes this correlation of power. We have found that the exalted Jesus is empowered with authority (as Son of God and Messiah) and shares in God's throne (as ruler of God's creation, the Lamb and the child-Messiah), which in turn allows him to be worshipped on a par (as the Lamb) with the one who sits on the throne. In this account, the Son of God enacts fellowship with the liturgical sociality in anticipation of the materialization of the Fellowship of the Throne; also, the slaughtered Lamb enables the constitution of a liturgical sociality consecrated to God the Father by a market transaction, while the fact that he was slaughtered becomes the feature on which his being worshipped alongside God is predicated. Equally, the advent of the Messiah and his ascension affirm the value of tradition and infuse history with a teleological orientation.

In this chapter we have also taken a closer look at the theo-political challenge to the exalted Jesus posed by the dragon, who attempted to prevent the christological shift in the divine authority through a political conspiracy, as inferred by the allusions to an ancient Near Eastern/Old Testament motif. The dragon's challenge then continued in the shape of an alternative mode of authority, which developed a coercive public liturgy leading to the worship of the beast and the dragon rather than the worship of God or the Lamb. Human authority allied itself to this theological delusion and coercive liturgy signalled by the beast and the false prophet until the appearance of the divine King, who as the Word of God speaks justice, brought about the dethronement and disempowerment of this twisted mode of authority. We have also established that it is through the divine King-Logos's discourse that the advent of a new liturgical sociality and the materialization of the Fellowship of the Throne is made possible.

CHAPTER 5

Models of Authority

In his *The Ways of Judgment* O'Donovan perspicaciously observes that "there can be no sensible deliberation as to whether we shall or shall not have such a thing as political authority. It is something we simply stumble upon."[1] This may help explain the various and varying models of political authority postulated by both ancient and modern thinkers over time (including O'Donovan). In fact, the Apocalypse's construal of divine authority as the correlation of power between the one who sits on the throne and the exalted Jesus, as discussed in chapter 4, erupted in a world familiar with theo-political accounts of authority characterized by either (a) their speculative nature, such as Plato's ultimate guardian in the *Republic*, within the Greek tradition, or by (b) the more pragmatic approach of the Roman tradition, such as Cicero's revisionist take on Plato in his *Res Publica* or the emperor Augustus's own self-glorifying *Res Gestae Divi Augusti*.[2] In some way these archetypal construals of authority anticipated, or perhaps even set the terms for, an ongoing conversation between the idealist and realist "strands of Western political thought,"[3] as O'Donovan puts it, whose key ideas are wisdom and rationality (contemplative government) as opposed to coercion (coercive government), each

---

1. O'Donovan, *Ways of Judgment*, 128.
2. The allusions to the Greek and Roman tradition were anticipated in the introduction to this work.
3. O'Donovan, *Ways of Judgment*, 13; cf. O'Donovan, *On the Thirty-Nine*, Kindle edition, location 1996+.

representing differing methods of enacting judgment,[4] which in O'Donovan's view has become the new downsized office of any human authority.[5]

In what follows we will briefly explore the prototypes of contemplative (Plato) and coercive (Cicero and Augustus) theo-political accounts of authority, whose basic tenets will in turn allow us to better understand O'Donovan's construal of human authority as judgment in the light of the exalted Jesus. And, having explored these two ancient poles of political thought, and ascertained where O'Donovan stands in relation to them, we will allow the Apocalypse's construal of divine authority to deliver its own critique, as already anticipated in chapter 4. After all, as noted in the introduction to this thesis, "a political theology shaped by the Christ-event . . . must criticise existing notions of political good and necessity, not only classical republican notions but imperial and theocratic notions too, in the light of what God has done for the human race and the human soul."[6]

5.1 Contemplative Authority: The King Becomes a Philosopher

According to O'Donovan, "The emphasis laid by idealist thinkers on the intellectual character of political action is not due solely to Plato's famous thesis about philosophers and kings,"[7] though an understanding of it is undoubtedly crucial. Written in the late fourth century BC,[8] Plato's *Republic* is still regarded by some scholars as his magnum opus and as the most influential document of his whole corpus.[9] In this theo-political dialogue, Socrates, the lead character construed by Plato,[10] embarks on a quest for the meaning of

---

4. cf. O'Donovan, *Ways of Judgment*, 13–15.

5. cf. O'Donovan, *Desire of the Nations*, 151; O'Donovan, "Government as Judgment," 209; O'Donovan, *Ways of Judgment*, 3.

6. O'Donovan, *Desire of the Nations*, 122.

7. O'Donovan, *Ways of Judgment*, 7; cf. *Ways of Judgment*, 14, 236; O'Donovan, *Desire of the Nations*, 198; O'Donovan, *On the Thirty-Nine*, location 2006.

8. Schofield, "Approaching the Republic," 199; Brandwood, "Stylometry and Chronology," 110–112. Contra: Lane, "Socrates and Plato," 157–160.

9. cf. Fine, *Oxford Handbook of Plato*, 4; Ferrari, *Cambridge Companion to Plato's Republic*, xvi.

10. On the so-called "Socratic problem," the fact that Socrates is mostly known to us through Plato's writings, see Lane, "Socrates and Plato," 155–157, 160–162.

justice after challenging the received wisdom on this subject as summarized by Simonides and echoed by Polemarchus, that is "it is just [δίκαιος] to give each what is owed to him."[11] The method of investigation chosen for this inquiry looks first at the whole in order to then focus on a part,[12] and leads Socrates and his interlocutors to imagine a city in order to explore "what sort of thing justice [δικαιοσύνη] is in a city and afterwards look for it in the individual, observing the ways in which the smaller is similar to the larger."[13]

The city imagined by Socrates,

> comes to be because none of us is self-sufficient, but we all need many things . . . And because people need many things, and because one person calls on a second out of one need and on a third out of a different need, many people gather in a single place to live together as partners [κοινωνός] and helpers [βοηθός]. And such a settlement [συνοικία] is called a city [πόλις].[14]

As a result, Socrates proposes, "let's create [ποιέω] a city [πόλις] in theory [λόγος] from its beginnings. And it's our needs [χρεία], it seems, that will create it."[15] This imagined sociality is at first a modest and frugal city content with some basic and practical crafts.[16] However, Glaucon pushes their imagination further to construe a luxurious city whose demands for more crafts, commodities and, in particular, land belonging to its neighbour, will inevitably lead them to war [πόλεμος].[17] "We won't say yet whether the effects of war are good or bad but only that we've now found the origins of war. It

---

11. Plato, *Republic* 1.331e. This view of justice is usually known as "distributive justice," cf. Wells and Quash, *Introducing Christian Ethics*, 139–140.

12. cf. Plato, *Republic* 2.368d-e. It should be said, however, that at this point in the narrative of the *Republic*, Socrates and his friends had already agreed that "justice [δικαιοσύνη] is virtue [ἀρετή] and wisdom [σοφία] and that injustice [ἀδικία] is vice [κακία] and ignorance [ἀμαθία]." Plato, *Republic* 1.350d; cf. O'Donovan, *Ways of Judgment*, 6.

13. Plato, *Republic* 2.369a.

14. Plato, *Republic* 2.369b-c.

15. Plato, *Republic* 2.369c.

16. Glaucon, one of Socrates's interlocutors in this dialogue, contemptuously calls this city a "city for pigs." However, Socrates still regards it as "the true [ἀληθινός] city [πόλις]," that is to say, "the healthy [ὑγιής] one." See Plato, *Republic* 2.372d-e.

17. Plato, *Republic* 2.373a+.

comes from those same desires that are most of all responsible for the bad things that happen to cities and the individuals in them."[18]

This subtle transition from a Socratic true/healthy city to a Glauconian luxurious city becomes a decisive turning point in the unfolding of the dialogue, since it allows Socrates to highlight the city's need for an army, "which will do battle with the invaders in defense of the city's substantial wealth and all the other things we mentioned."[19] Having established the need for an army Socrates then considers the recruitment of those who will guard the city: its guardians, gradually elevating the concept of what and who might become the ultimate guardian of the city.[20] Socrates's construal is of a member of an aristocratic elite in whom "philosophy, spirit, speed, and strength must all, then, be combined in the nature of anyone who is to be a fine and good guardian of our city."[21] In addition, he proposes a traditional (Greek) education for the guardians, which includes "physical training for bodies and music and poetry for the soul."[22] Socrates pursues at great length the subject of what may be the music and poetry suitable for the training of the guardian,[23] and his deliberations on this issue serve in turn to highlight the importance he gives (and with him Plato) to the provision of an orthodox (pagan) theological education for the guardians,[24] as he declares his aim to be ensuring that the "guardians will be as god-fearing and godlike as human beings can be."[25]

Within this guardian elite Socrates defines a hierarchy based on aristocratic (the best) and gerontocratic (the oldest) criteria,[26] thus creating a distinction between complete and auxiliary guardians, the latter appointed to support the former.[27] The need for this differentiation was previously argued for when discussing the role of the guardian as judge, given the higher

---

18. Plato, *Republic* 2.373e.
19. Plato, *Republic* 2.373e-374a.
20. cf. Plato, *Republic* 2.374e+; cf. O'Donovan, *Desire of the Nations*, 148.
21. Plato, *Republic* 2.376c. The necessity of an aristocratic pedigree of the guardian is best advocated by a Phoenician story retold by Socrates in Plato, *Republic* 3.414c-415c.
22. Plato, *Republic* 2.376e.
23. cf. Plato, *Republic* 2.376e-3.403c.
24. e.g. Plato, *Republic* 2.378e-379c, 382e.
25. Plato, *Republic* 2.383c.
26. cf. Plato, *Republic* 3.412c.
27. cf. Plato, *Republic* 3.414b.

qualities required for that responsibility.²⁸ In spite of their status as an elite the Socratic guardians are called to live a radically communal, modest and frugal life,²⁹ becoming a sort of tax-funded bureaucracy whose most important responsibility appears to be the guarding of "their education [παιδεία] and upbringing, for if by being well educated they become reasonable men, they will easily see these things for themselves."³⁰ What is more, though unusual for their time, women are also to be trained as guardians on exactly the same terms as their male counterparts,³¹ with the proviso that "women are weaker than men."³² And so, just as the men, they "must strip for physical training, since they'll wear virtue or excellence instead of clothes. They must share in war and the other guardians' duties in the city and do nothing else. But the lighter parts must be assigned to them because of the weakness of their sex."³³

Crucially, Socrates establishes a correlation between the polity (πολιτεία) or political constitution that frames the flourishing of the imagined city and the nature of the guardians appointed to rule over city. In his words,

> Until philosophers [φιλόσοφος] rule as kings [βασιλεύω] or those who are now called kings [βασιλεύς] and leading men genuinely and adequately philosophize [φιλοσοφέω], that is, until political [πολιτικός] power [δύναμις] and philosophy [φιλοσοφία] entirely coincide, while the many natures who at present pursue either one exclusively are forcibly prevented from doing so, cities will have no rest from evils . . . nor, I think, will the human race. And, until this happens, the constitution [πολιτεία] we've been describing in theory will never be born to the fullest extent possible or see the light of the sun.³⁴

---

28. cf. Plato, *Republic* 3.409+; 4.434b.
29. cf. Plato, *Republic* 3.416c-417b.
30. Plato, *Republic* 4.423e.
31. cf. Plato, *Republic* 5.451d-457c.
32. Plato, *Republic* 5.455d. Julia Annas observes that "some have thought of Plato as the first feminist, because he sees no reason why women should be barred from activities that men do, while others have seen in him a deeply anti-feminist strain, holding that women are worth thinking about only to the extent that they can be socially reconstructed as men." Annas, *Plato*, 49.
33. Plato, *Republic* 5.457a.
34. Plato, *Republic* 5.473c-e.

As the dialogue goes on, Socrates expounds on each side of this correlation.

On the one hand, a guardian is construed from the outset as someone who would "be by nature philosophical,"[35] that is to say, "a lover of learning and wisdom."[36] Now, according to Socrates true philosophers are those "who love the sight of truth."[37] This is an epistemological category that Socrates associates with knowledge as opposed to opinion, which is a lesser form of understanding,[38] whereas knowledge is "a power, the strongest of them all."[39] The philosophical nature of the guardians "must be without falsehood – they must refuse to accept what is false, hate it, and have a love for the truth."[40] To fit in with this profile a guardian should be "by nature good at remembering, quick to learn, high-minded, graceful, and a friend and relative of truth, justice, courage, and moderation,"[41] and would also be expected to learn calculation and arithmetic,[42] geometry,[43] solid geometry,[44] astronomy,[45] and dialectic.[46] Only after having reached "maturity in age and education" would the guardian be entrusted the city.[47]

On the other hand, however, the guardian-philosopher would depend on "a constitution [πολιτεία] that suits him. Under a suitable one, his own growth will be fuller, and he'll save [σῴζω] the community [κοινός] as well as himself."[48] As for the nature of the constitution itself, Socrates had described it earlier as taking one of two possible forms, if "one outstanding man emerges

---

35. Plato, *Republic* 2.375e.
36. Plato, *Republic* 2.376b.
37. Plato, *Republic* 5.475e.
38. cf. Plato, *Republic* 5.476c-d. A third and lesser category than both knowledge and opinion is ignorance, cf. 5.478b-d. In book 7 of the *Republic* Plato goes into great detail regarding his epistemological categories, which may be summed up as follows, going from highest to lowest, so to speak: (i) intellect, which encompasses (a) knowledge and (b) thought; (ii) opinion, which includes (a) belief and (b) imaging; and (iii) ignorance. See Plato, *Republic* 7.533e-534a.
39. Plato, *Republic* 5.477d.
40. Plato, *Republic* 6.485c.
41. Plato, *Republic* 6.487a.
42. cf. Plato, *Republic* 7.525a+.
43. cf. Plato, *Republic* 7.527c+.
44. cf. Plato, *Republic* 7.528a+.
45. cf. Plato, *Republic* 7.528e+.
46. cf. Plato, *Republic* 7.532a+.
47. Plato, *Republic* 7.532a+.
48. Plato, *Republic* 6.497a.

among the rulers, it's called a kingship [βασιλεία]; if more than one, it's called an aristocracy [ἀριστοκρατία]."⁴⁹ Either way, "none of the significant laws of the city would be changed, if they followed the upbringing and education we described."⁵⁰ However, Socrates conceded that "none of our present constitutions is worthy of the philosophic nature [of the guardian], and, as a result, this nature is perverted and altered . . . But if it were to find the best constitution . . . it would be clear that it is really divine [θεῖος] and that other natures and ways of life are merely human [ἀνθρώπινος]."⁵¹ Socrates here gives an eschatological orientation to this construal, stating that "at whatever time the muse of philosophy controls a city, the constitution we've described will also exist at that time, whether it is past, present, or future."⁵²

This brings us to the motif of ascension and exaltation of the philosopher-king, though here it is education that authorizes or empowers the guardian to rule and save the city. This motif is introduced within the context of a story, the famous Platonic story of the cave:

> Imagine human beings living in an underground, cavelike dwelling, with an entrance a long way up, which is both open to the light and as wide as the cave itself. They've been there since childhood, fixed in the same place, with their necks and legs fettered, able to see only in front of them, because their bonds prevent them from turning their heads around. Light is provided by a fire burning far above and behind them. Also, behind them, but on higher ground, there is a path stretching between them and the fire. Imagine that along this path a low wall has been built, like the screen in front of puppeteers above which they show their puppets.⁵³

---

49. Plato, *Republic* 4.445d. It should be noted that Herodotus, *Histories* 3.80–82 (LCL) is regarded as the text that "presents the earliest example of comparative constitutional analysis (though the term *politeia* does not itself occur in the passage)." Winton, "Herodotus, Thucydides," 108. There, the three basic forms of a *politeia* are (i) the best democracy (δῆμος), (ii) the rule by the few (ὀλιγαρχία), and (iii) the rule by one (μόναρχος), see Plato, *Republic* 3.82.1.

50. Plato, *Republic* 4.445d-e.

51. Plato, *Republic* 6.497b-c; cf. 1 Pet 2:13.

52. Plato, *Republic* 6.499d.

53. Plato, *Republic* 7.514a-b. James K. A. Smith discusses a contemporary adaptation of this Platonic story, which he regards as "one of the most ancient of philosophical images" in Smith, *Who's Afraid of Postmodernism*, 15–18.

As the story goes on, we are told that "there are people along the wall, carrying all kinds of artifacts that project above it,"[54] and that the prisoners can only see "the shadows that the fire casts on the wall in front of them,"[55] and as a result, they "would in every way believe that the truth is nothing other than the shadows of those artifacts."[56] Here Socrates raises the key question: "Consider, then, what being released from their bonds and cured of their ignorance would naturally be like, if something like this came to pass."[57] This question introduces the turning-point in the story. "When one of them was freed and suddenly compelled to stand up, turn his head, walk, and look up toward the light, he'd be pained and dazzled and unable to see the things whose shadows he'd seen before."[58] And yet, this person would now be in a position to see "more correctly."[59] What is more, "if someone dragged him away from there by force, up the rough, steep path, and didn't let him go until he had dragged him into the sunlight,"[60] then after some time adjusting his vision he would be able to "see things in the world above . . . he'd see shadows more easily, then images of men and other things in water, then the things themselves."[61] After a while, he would "be able to see the sun, not images of it in water or some alien place, but the sun itself, in its own place, and be able to study it."[62]

Socrates deploys a hermeneutics of epistemology in order to interpret the story, as follows:

> The visible realm should be likened to the prison dwelling, and the light of the fire inside it to the power of the sun. And if you interpret the upward journey and the study of things above as the upward journey of the soul to the intelligible realm . . . [or] knowable realm, the form of the good is the last thing to be seen, and it is reached only with difficulty. Once one has seen

---

54. Plato, *Republic* 7.514b.
55. Plato, *Republic* 7.515a.
56. Plato, *Republic* 7.515c.
57. Plato, *Republic* 7.515c.
58. Plato, *Republic* 7.515c.
59. Plato, *Republic* 7.515d.
60. Plato, *Republic* 7.515e.
61. Plato, *Republic* 7.516a.
62. Plato, *Republic* 7.516b.

it, however, one must conclude that it is the cause of all that is correct and beautiful in anything, that it produces both light and its source in the visible realm, and that in the intelligible realm it controls and provides truth and understanding, so that anyone who is to act sensibly in private or public must see it.[63]

Socrates then argues that "the power to learn is present in everyone's soul and that the instrument with which each learns is like an eye that cannot be turned around from darkness to light without turning the whole body,"[64] and that in effect, this instrument "cannot be turned around from that which is coming into being without turning the whole soul until it is able to study that which is and the brightest thing that is, namely, the one we call the good."[65] If so, education "isn't what some people declare it to be, namely, putting knowledge into souls that lack it, like putting sight into blind eyes."[66] Rather, it is "the craft concerned with doing this very thing, this turning around, and with how the soul can most easily and effectively be made to do it."[67] That is to say, education "takes for granted that sight is there but that it isn't turned the right way or looking where it ought to look, and it tries to redirect it appropriately."[68]

Most importantly, as founders of the city, Socrates and his interlocutors commit themselves "to compel the best natures . . . to make the ascent and see the good."[69] But once this has been done they expect these people "to go again to the prisoners in the cave and share their labors and honors, whether they are of less worth or of greater."[70] This is because the law's concern is "to contrive to spread happiness throughout the city by bringing the citizens into harmony with each other through persuasion or compulsion and by making them share with each other the benefits that each class can confer on the community."[71] Socrates and his interlocutors explain this rationale to their elite as follows: "we've made you kings in our city and leaders of the swarm,

---

63. Plato, *Republic* 7.517b-c.
64. Plato, *Republic* 7.518c.
65. Plato, *Republic* 7.518c-d.
66. Plato, *Republic* 7.518b.
67. Plato, *Republic* 7.518d.
68. Plato, *Republic* 7.518d.
69. Plato, *Republic* 7.519c.
70. Plato, *Republic* 7.519c.
71. Plato, *Republic* 7.519e.

as it were, both for yourselves and for the rest of the city. You're better and more completely educated than the others and are better able to share in both types of life."[72] And "because you've seen the truth about fine, just, and good things, you'll know each image for what it is and also that of which it is the image. Thus, for you and for us, the city will be governed . . . by people who are awake rather than dreaming."[73]

It is within this hermeneutical framework therefore that a sort of epistemological ascension and exaltation, or as Socrates put it, "of turning a soul from a day that is a kind of night to the true day – the ascent to what is, which we say is true philosophy" is made possible.[74] And though the answer to his question as to "how such people will come to be in our city and how – just as some are said to have gone up from Hades to the gods – we'll lead them up to the light?"[75] has in a sense already been addressed in their explanation of the regime of education and physical training that the guardians should undergo, Socrates and his interlocutors proceed to map out in detail the ground a would-be philosopher-king should cover in the manner of a selection process. (i) "Calculation, geometry, and all the preliminary education required for dialectic must be offered to the future rulers in childhood";[76] (ii) in their youth they should undergo "compulsory physical training, for during that period, whether it's two or three years, young people are incapable of doing anything else, since weariness and sleep are enemies of learning."[77] (iii) Then, "from the age of twenty, those who are chosen will also receive more honors than the others. Moreover, the subjects they learned in no particular order as children they must now bring together to form a unified vision of their kinship both with one another and with the nature of that which is."[78] (iv) Once "they have reached their thirtieth year, you'll select them in turn from among those chosen earlier and assign them yet greater honors. Then you'll have to test them by means of the power of dialectic, to discover which of them can relinquish his eyes and other senses, going on with the help of

---

72. Plato, *Republic* 7.520b.
73. Plato, *Republic* 7.520c.
74. Plato, *Republic* 7.521c.
75. Plato, *Republic* 7.521b-c.
76. Plato, *Republic* 7.536d.
77. Plato, *Republic* 7.537b.
78. Plato, *Republic* 7.537c.

truth to that which by itself is."⁷⁹ Five years from then, "you must make them go down into the cave again, and compel them to take command in matters of war and occupy the other offices suitable for young people, so that they won't be inferior to the others in experience."⁸⁰ (v) Finally,

> at the age of fifty, those who've survived the tests and been successful both in practical matters and in the sciences must be led to the goal and compelled to lift up the radiant light of their souls to what itself provides light for everything. And once they've seen the good itself, they must each in turn put the city, its citizens, and themselves in order, using it as their model. Each of them will spend most of his time with philosophy, but, when his turn comes, he must labor in politics and rule for the city's sake, not as if he were doing something fine, but rather something that has to be done.⁸¹

Following on from this figurative exaltation, Socrates envisions a kind of apotheosis for the guardian who did well: "having educated others like himself to take his place as guardians of the city, he will depart for the Isles of the Blessed and dwell there. And, if the Pythia agrees, the city will publicly establish memorials and sacrifices to him as a daemon, but if not, then as a happy and divine human being."⁸²

In brief, the Platonic construal of human authority, with its aristocratic and gerontocratic bent, contemplates the epistemological ascension of the guardian, through an arduous educational regime in pursuit of wisdom (*sophia*) which leads to his final empowerment as ruler of the city (*polis*). This immanent attainment of wisdom (*sophia*) is to be shared with others through education (*paideia*), and will be for the benefit the whole city. And yet, this model of authority must work together with a divine constitution (*politeia*) that reflects the philosophical nature and education of the city's guardians, and whose realization appears to be charged with eschatological expectation.⁸³

---

79. Plato, *Republic* 7.537d.
80. Plato, *Republic* 7.539e.
81. Plato, *Republic* 7.540a-b.
82. Plato, *Republic* 7.540b-c.
83. The thesis that Plato later gave up this construal of authority (i.e. the king-philosopher), is discussed in Schofield, *Saving the City*, 31–50.

5.2 Coercive Authority: The Return of the "King"

In contrast with the deeply speculative nature of the Platonic construal of human authority, Roman political thought was characterized by a more pragmatic approach in general. "The contrast between Roman practice, learning by example, and Greek theory, learnt from books, runs through much Roman writing."[84] And Cicero clearly aligns himself with this Roman perspective in what is arguably regarded as "the first, and perhaps the only, serious attempt by a Roman to analyze the structure and values of republican government and imperial rule,"[85] his *On the Commonwealth*. Thus, he observed "I think that the men who lead these cities by their counsel and authority should be considered far wiser than philosophers who have no experience at all of public life."[86] And yet, he self-consciously wrote *On the Commonwealth* in the light of Plato's *Republic*,[87] though his dialogue is much shorter and more narrow in its focus.[88] His work was well received among his contemporaries,[89] helped perhaps by its historicized approach consciously choosing "not to offend anyone by launching into the events of my own time."[90] Above all, Cicero seemed to frame his dialogue in very patriotic and stoic terms, for example, "since our country provides more benefits and is a parent prior to our biological parents, we have a greater obligation to it than to our parents."[91]

As in Plato's *Republic*, Cicero sets up a conversation, though in his case it takes place between past Roman historical characters who after an initial discussion on the possible meaning of an astronomic phenomenon ("what

---

84. Wiedemann, "Reflections of Roman," 518.

85. Zetzel, *Cicero*, xvii. "Explicit theorizing was not a Roman characteristic" (Wiedemann, "Reflections on Roman," 517).

86. Cicero, *On the Commonwealth* 1.3; cf. Quintilian, *Instituto Oratoria* 12.2.30.

87. e.g. Cicero, *On the Commonwealth* 2.3, 21–22, 51; 4.4; cf. 1.65, 68. This does not diminish Cicero's own contribution in view of "the wealth of evidence for Cicero's wide reading in Greek philosophy and history, and his easy familiarity with philosophical concepts . . . as well as his outstanding ability to organize ideas and arguments." Atkins, "Cicero," 477.

88. cf. Zetzel, *Cicero*, 13–17. In turn, O'Donovan explores Augustine's reading and critique of Cicero's *Res Publica* in O'Donovan, "Political Thought," 52–60; cf. O'Donovan, *Just War Revisited*, 12.

89. "Your books on the Republic are in universal vogue." Cicero, *Epistulae ad Familiares* (*Letters to his Friends*) 8.1.4, as translated by Shuckburgh. cf. Atkins, "Cicero," 498.

90. Cicero, Letters to his brother Quintum 3.5.

91. Cicero, *On the Commonwealth* preface fragment 2.

the meaning is of the second sun which has been reported in the senate?"),[92] turn their attention to political matters ("why in one commonwealth there are two senates and almost two peoples?")[93] in order to address the more pressing question of what "the best organisation [*status*] of the state [*civitas*] [might] be."[94] An answer is immediately offered declaring that "by far the best condition of the state was the one which our ancestors [*maiores*] had handed down to us."[95] This statement discloses the key role played by tradition in Roman thought and life in general, where "the aristocrats represented their ideal as inherited; [and] they made frequent appeal to an amalgam of moral and constitutional precedents which they described as *mos maiorum*, 'the custom of the ancestors.'"[96] More importantly, this answer shows that Roman theo-political thought, as mediated by Cicero, gives priority to the constitution (*politeia* or *res publica*) as opposed to the concept and/or embodiment of authority, whether this be a warrior, king or philosopher, in stark contrast with Plato and his guardian of the city (polis or *civitas*). This order of things remains a recurrent feature throughout the dialogue, as seen above (§5.1), and sets the terms of the discussion for what follows in the Ciceronian dialogue.

Accordingly, Cicero offers a sort of Aristotelian definition of what the *res publica* (i.e. commonwealth/constitution) might be:[97] "the commonwealth [*res publica*] is the concern [*res*] of a people [*populi*], but a people is not a group of men assembled in any way, but an assemblage of some size associated with one another through agreement on law and community of interest."[98] This definition, which "is of great importance both in [the *res publica*] itself and in subsequent European political theory,"[99] in turn leads Cicero to postulate that

> every people [*populus*] ... every state [*civitas*] ... every commonwealth [*res publica*] ... needs to be ruled [*rego*] by some

---

92. Cicero, *On the Commonwealth* 1.15.
93. Cicero, *On the Commonwealth* 1.31.
94. Cicero, *On the Commonwealth* 1.33. "Frequently the phrase *status civitatis*, 'organization/condition/form of the state' is a synonym for res publica." Zetzel, *Cicero*, xxxviii.
95. Cicero, *On the Commonwealth* 1.34; cf. Polybius, *Histories* 1.1.5.
96. Atkins, "Cicero," 481.
97. cf. Zetzel, *Cicero*, 18n53. Cicero's definition "is comparable to Aristotle's description of the *polis* as a κοινωνία πολιτῶν (*Pol.* 3.3), but Aristotle's state is an agglomeration of individual citizens, while [Cicero]'s belongs to the *populus* viewed as a single whole" Zetzel, 128.
98. Cicero, *On the Commonwealth* 1.39a.
99. Zetzel, *Cicero*, 127.

sort of deliberation [*consilium*] in order to be long lived. That deliberative function, moreover, must always be connected to the original cause which engendered the state; and it must also either be assigned to one person or to selected individuals or be taken up by the entire population. And so, when the control of everything is in the hands of one person, we call that one person a king [*rex*] and that type of commonwealth a monarchy [*regnum*]. When it is in control of chosen men, then a state is said to be ruled by the will of the aristocracy. And that in which everything is in the hands of the people is a "popular" state that is what they call it.[100]

Cicero concedes that none of these types of *res publica* is perfect, though anyone may be better than the other.[101] In fact, he surveys the pros and cons of each in turn,[102] and though he toys with the idea of monarchy as his personal choice,[103] in the end he favours a mix of the three types of commonwealth, which could be considered a fourth type,[104] where a balance can be struck between equality and solidity or stability, so "there is no reason for revolution when each person is firmly set in his own rank, without the possibility of sudden collapse."[105]

Cicero then goes on to provide a biography of the Roman *res publica*, showing this commonwealth "as it is born, grows up, and comes of age."[106] He begins with the commonwealth established by Romulus in the founding of the city of Rome,[107] a monarchy where all power was concentrated in himself as king,[108] though he did set up a prototype of the senate, a council [*consilium*] known as "Fathers" whose role it was to offer advise to the ruler.[109] At his death, Romulus was divinized and hailed as "a god and a god's son,

---

100. Cicero, *On the Commonwealth* 1.41-42.
101. Cicero, *On the Commonwealth* 1.41-42.
102. cf. Cicero, *On the Commonwealth* 1.43ff.
103. cf. Cicero, *On the Commonwealth* 1.54, 69.
104. cf. Cicero, *On the Commonwealth* 1.45, 69; 2.65.
105. Cicero, *On the Commonwealth* 1.69; cf. 2.57.
106. Cicero, On the Commonwealth 2.3.
107. cf. Cicero, *On the Commonwealth* 2.4.
108. cf. Cicero, *On the Commonwealth* 2.5, 14, 15.
109. cf. Cicero, *On the Commonwealth* 2.14, 15, 17, 23, 43, 50.

the King and Father of the Roman City."¹¹⁰ Afterwards, successive kings were supposed to have been selected according to "virtue and wisdom ... not a royal pedigree,"¹¹¹ each contributing to the crafting of the Roman *res publica*.¹¹² Cicero chronicles how as time passed the king metamorphosed into a tyrant,¹¹³ leading to his expelling and to a change in the *res publica*, now taking a more aristocratic outlook, with the senate playing a major role:¹¹⁴

> our ancestors, who, when they could no longer endure the power of a king, created annual magistrates [*magistratus*] on the principle of making the senate [*senatus*] the perpetual supreme council [*consilium*] of the republic [*res publica*] ... They established the senate as the guardian [*custos*], and president, and protector of the republic; they chose the magistrates to depend on the authority [*auctoritas*] of this order, and to be as it were the ministers of this most dignified council; and they contrived that the senate itself should be strengthened by the high respectability of those ranks which came nearest to it, and so be able to defend and promote the liberties and interests of the common people [*plebs*].¹¹⁵

Cicero's strand of res publicanism became a casualty in the aftermath of the civil war between Pompey and Julius Caesar.¹¹⁶ The latter's victory and subsequent violent death set in motion a constitutional change that culminated with Octavian's victory over Mark Antony at Actium,¹¹⁷ which saw "the centralization of all [*omnis*] authority [*potentia*] in the hands of one

---

110. Livy, *History of Rome* 1.16, as translated by Benjamin Oliver Foster (LCL); cf. Cicero, *On the Commonwealth* 2.17, 20; Cicero, *Catilinarian Orations* 3.2. However, Livy himself recorded an alternative historical account to Romulus's death in Livy, *History of Rome* 1.16; equally, Augustine offers a theo-political critique of Romulus's presumed apotheosis in Augustine, *City of God* 3.15.

111. Cicero, *On the Commonwealth* 2.24. This seems to echo Plato's construal of the guardian of the polis.

112. cf. Cicero, *On the Commonwealth* 2.27, 37.

113. cf. Cicero, *On the Commonwealth* 2.45–49, 51.

114. cf. Cicero, *On the Commonwealth* 2.56; cf. Atkins, "Cicero," 478.

115. Cicero, *pro Sestio* 137 (Perseus/UChicago).

116. cf. Cicero, *Letters to Brutus* 1.15; Rawson, "Aftermath of the Ides," 489–490; Atkins, "Cicero," 486–487.

117. cf. Tacitus, *Histories* 1.1; Augustus, *Res Gestae* 25.2.

man [*unus*],"¹¹⁸ so the Romans "reverted to what was, strictly speaking, a monarchy,"¹¹⁹ despite Cicero's hopes that young Octavian would seek a return to the sort of *res publica* he had advocated.¹²⁰ This change in the Roman *res publica* may be regarded as the return of the king (à la Romulus).

The *Res Gestae Divi Augusti* (RGDA) gives information about this new model of political authority, offering "an invaluable insight into the political ideology of the Augustan era, in the words of Augustus himself,"¹²¹ with "the implicit message that the Roman empire was in the best possible condition, through the actions of one man, Augustus, who had solved all the problems, and who ruled in the interests of all through his *auctoritas* and virtues, without infringing sovereignty of the senate and the people of Rome."¹²² By contrast, a century or so later,¹²³ Tacitus would observe that

> Octavian [had] presented himself as a consul, and as a man satisfied to hold tribunician authority in order to safeguard the people. Then, by seducing the military with donatives, the masses with grain allowances, and everybody with the pleasure of peace, he gradually increased his powers, drawing to himself the functions of Senate, magistrates, and laws. He met no resistance.¹²⁴

As J. A. Crook put it, "from 30 B.C. onwards, the whole Roman world found itself in the grasp of a single ruler, possessing all power and making all decisions, except insofar as he might choose to leave some of them to others."¹²⁵

---

118. Tacitus, *Histories* 1.1; cf. Florus, *Epitome of Roman History*, preface 4–8.
119. Cassius Dio, *Roman History* 52.1.1.
120. cf. Cicero, *Letters to Brutus* 1.15.
121. Cooley, *Res Gestae Divi Augusti*, 2. Cooley divides the text of the *Res Gestae Divi Augusti* into fourteen sections as follows: (1) heading; (2) the aftermath of the Ides of March (1–2); (3) Augustus's successes in warfare and triumphal celebrations (3–4); (4) powers rejected and offices accepted (5–7); (5) re-ordering society (8); (6) religious honours for Augustus (9–12); (7) the closure of the Gates of Janus (13); (8) honours for Augustus via his sons (14); Augustus's donations to the people of Rome and to his veteran soldiers (15–18); (9) Augustus and the City of Rome: buildings, triumphal commemorations, spectacles (19–23); (10) Augustus's gifts to the gods (24); (11) Augustus's *Res Gestae*: suppression of Rome's internal enemies (25); (12) Rome's empire and influence throughout the world (26–33); (13) the pre-eminence of Augustus (34–35); (14) appendix – summary of Augustus's expenditure. See Cooley, *Res Gestae Divi Augusti*, 102–278.
122. Cooley, *Res Gestae Divi Augusti*, 36.
123. It has been suggested that the *RGDA* was written in ca. AD 13–14; cf. Cooley, 42–43.
124. Tacitus, *Annals* 1.2.
125. Crook, "Augustus," 113.

Nonetheless, it is worth highlighting some key aspects of Augustus's theo-political self-account, which resonate with O'Donovan's view on "the legitimating theory of the Roman empire, by which senate and people were said to confer powers upon the Caesar,"[126] though the manipulative means used to attain this were openly denounced by Tacitus, as seen above. First, Augustus stresses his own initiative to muster an army at his personal expense in order to liberate the state (i.e. the *res publica*), from an oppressive faction,[127] in the aftermath of the violent death of his adoptive father, Julius Caesar.[128] This action opened the door for him to become part of the senate,[129] in which he rose to become its highest ranking member (*princeps senatus*) until his death,[130] and from which he accrued *de jure* power (*potestas*) for life.[131] He also painstakingly details ways in which he complied with the senate's authority (*auctoritas*),[132] while at the same time regarding himself as the leader (*princeps*).[133] "This was not an official title . . . nor it did bestow particular powers, but was adopted by Augustus to indicate his leading role in the state."[134] Arguably, his liberating campaign achieved a favourable outcome with his victory at Actium,[135] which was celebrated by Virgil in an epic poem, where the event is invested with cosmic proportions.[136]

Augustus's *Res Gestae* is a theo-political document fixated on the war (*bellum*) motif,[137] and his victories are "the achievements . . . by which he made the world subject [*subicio*] to the rule [*imperium*] of the Roman people."[138] War (*bellum*), fought by his own army (*exercitus*), therefore becomes his

---

126. O'Donovan, *Ways of Judgment*, 187.
127. cf. Augustus, *Res Gestae* 1.1.
128. cf. Cooley, *Res Gestae Divi Augusti*, 104–111.
129. cf. Augustus, *Res Gestae* 1.2.
130. cf. Augustus, *Res Gestae* 7.2; cf. Cooley, *Res Gestae Divi Augusti*, 134.
131. e.g. Augustus, *Res Gestae* 10.1; cf. 6.2; 34.1.
132. e.g. Augustus, *Res Gestae* 20.4; cf. 12.1.
133. cf. Augustus, *Res Gestae* 13.1; 30.1; 32.3.
134. Cooley, *Res Gestae Divi Augusti*, 160.
135. cf. Augustus, *Res Gestae* 25.2. "Actium constitutes a potent and enduring turning point in the course of Roman history and indeed of Western civilization." Gurval, *Actium and Augustus*, 1; cf. Cassius Dio, *Roman History* 51.1.1–2.
136. cf. Virgil, *Aeneid* 8.671–728.
137. cf. Augustus, *Res Gestae* 1.4; 2; 3.1; 4.1; 15.1; 24.1; 25.1, 2; 26.3; 27.3; 32.2; 34.1.
138. Augustus, *Res Gestae* heading.

political tool of choice, another way of legitimizing his power:[139] "The Pannopian peoples had never had an army [*exercitus*] of the Roman people come near them before I became leader. I made them subject [*subicio*] to the rule [*imperium*] of the Roman people."[140] In fact, Augustus claims "I extended the territory of all those provinces of the Roman people which had neighbouring peoples who were not subject to our authority [*imperium*],"[141] bringing to mind Ovid's words claiming that "The land of other nations [*gens*] has a fixed boundary: [but] the circuit of Rome is the circuit of the world."[142] Thus, wars by land and sea were ensued by victory,[143] and Augustus regarded himself a victor (*victor*).[144]

Because of these victories Octavian was granted a new name by the senate, the name of Augustus,[145] which Ovid explained as follows:

> Augustus alone bears a name that ranks with Jove supreme. Holy things are by the fathers called august: the epithet august is applied to temples that have been duly dedicated by priestly hands: from the same root come augury and all such augmentation as Jupiter grants by his power. May he augment our prince's empire and augment his years, and may an oaken crown protect your doors. Under the auspices of the gods may the same omens, which attended the sire, wait upon the heir of so great a surname, when he takes upon himself the burden of the world.[146]

---

139. "It was the achievement of Augustus to create a volunteer, professional army, its size determined by himself, 'depoliticize' it, and establish for it an ethos of loyalty to himself and the 'divine family.'" (Crook, "Augusts," 114). Another "'brute fact' about the power of Augustus [was] his overwhelming predominance in resources. The figures he gives in the *Res Gestae* suffice to show that the resources he directly had and personally controlled, from the start . . . made it inconceivable for any alternative paymaster to arise, capable of supporting any notable army against him." (Crook, 115).

140. Augustus, *Res Gestae* 30.1; cf. 30.2.

141. Augustus, *Res Gestae* 26.1.

142. Ovid, *Fasti* 2.683–684, translated by James George Frazer (LCL).

143. Augustus, *Res Gestae* 3.1; 13.

144. Augustus, *Res Gestae* 24.1.

145. Augustus, *Res Gestae* 34.2.

146. Ovid, *Fasti* 1.609–616; cf. Augustus, *Res Gestae* 7.2; 11; 12.2; 21.1. "His official name henceforth was Imperator Caesar Augustus. Both names indicated that the bearer was uniquely favoured by the gods for the service of Rome." Price, "Place of Religion," 822; cf. Cooley, *Res Gestae Divi Augusti*, 261–262.

In a similar theo-political vein, Augustus came to be regarded as Chief Priest (*pontifex maximus*),[147] that is to say, the "head of the most prestigious college of pontifices, who were in charge of overseeing state cult,"[148] with his priestly functions becoming "an important part of his self-representation... They conveyed the message that Augustus was a crucial intermediary with the gods in securing their support for Rome."[149] Above all, however, Augustus concluded his theo-political document noting that "the senate and equestrian order and people of Rome all together hailed me as father of the fatherland [*pater patriae*]."[150] The political, theological and filial implications of this title were commented on by Strabo,[151] Ovid,[152] and Cassius Dio,[153] respectively, making clear that "the grant of this title to Augustus was not simply just another meaningless honour, but that it had multiple legal and religious resonances and evoked the idea of someone acting as a saviour, patron and god."[154] To this we may add Crook's observation that the "ruler in the imperial period had the role, also, of supreme and ultimate judge."[155] It is perhaps inevitable therefore that Augustus's deification and ascension would be written into Roman sources after his death.[156]

In brief, the mode of authority anticipated by Romulus, timidly considered by Cicero, and embodied to the full by Augustus as leader and father of his people, was finally also invested with mediating power between the people of Rome and the gods. This model of authority also centred on war and military

---

147. Augustus, *Res Gestae* 7.3; cf. 10.2.

148. Cooley, *Res Gestae Divi Augusti*, 134. "The religious position of the emperor [in Rome] was thus central and pervasive but also diffuse... a range of rituals incorporated the living emperor." Price, "Place of Religion," 837. However, according to Price, this did not amount to an imperial cult, as was the case in the eastern part of the empire, see Price, 845–847; cf. Cassius Dio, *Roman History* 51.20.6–8.

149. Cooley, *Res Gestae Divi Augusti*, 135. On the role of a pontifex see Price, "Place of Religion," 824–830.

150. Augustus, *Res Gestae* 35.1.

151. Strabo, *Geography* 6.4.2.

152. Ovid, *Fasti* 2.127–132.

153. Cassius Dio, *Roman History* 53.18.3.

154. Cooley, *Res Gestae Divi Augusti*, 275. Crook noted that another "aspect of Augustus' *de facto* power... is his role as the universal patron, the sole source of benefits." Crook, "Augustus," 115.

155. Crook, "Augustus," 122.

156. Deification: Cassius Dio, *Roman History* 56.41.9. Ascension: Suetonius, *Deified Augustus* 100.4.

victory as essential theo-political tools, and spearheaded a political tradition that has come to be labelled "realist," presenting itself "as the advocate of necessary force; yet its [more modern] sombre account of human possibilities may sometimes contain a confession of shame in the face of necessity, a sense of tragedy about the cutting-short of reasonable interaction,"[157] which was certainly not a feature of the Augustan discourse.

5.3 Authority as Judgment

The contrasting of these two ancient models of authority (*sophia* and *paideia* versus *bellum* and *subicio*) juxtaposed with the Apocalypse's own construal of divine authority as seen in chapter 4, highlight the relevance of O'Donovan's understanding of human political authority, which takes into account ancient models, yet considers how these and all other construals of human authority have been redefined by Christ. In fact, he presents a dense theological theorem which affirms that "in the resurrection of Christ creation is restored and the kingdom of God dawns,"[158] with the corollary that "the authority of secular government resides [solely] in the practice of judgment."[159] This is because of "the reign of Christ in heaven,"[160] which now "forbids human rule to pretend to sovereignty, the consummation of the community's identity in the power of its ruler."[161] Obviously, both theorem and corollary require further unpacking.

First, starting off with more of an ontological line of inquiry, O'Donovan argues that creation, in its make-up, order and coherence, has been renewed and vindicated by the resurrection of Jesus, and that an ordered creation aligned with its Creator entails a *telos* and *genus* within which a space is open for freedom.[162] Creation "is free because it has a given order to respond to in attention or disregard, in conformity or disconformity, with obedience or with rebellion."[163] This given allows O'Donovan to single out hu-

---

157. O'Donovan, *Ways of Judgment*, 15.
158. O'Donovan, *Resurrection and Moral Order*, 15
159. O'Donovan, *Ways of Judgment*, 3.
160. O'Donovan, "Goverment as Judgment," 209.
161. O'Donovan, *Ways of Judgment*, 4; cf. O'Donovan, *Desire of the Nations*, 151.
162. cf. O'Donovan, *Resurrection and Moral Order*, 31–37; cf. O'Donovan, *On the Thirty-Nine*, location 697+.
163. O'Donovan, *Resurrection and Moral Order*, 37.

man beings' unique role within the created order based on Psalm 8: "man's ordering-to-flourish as its ruler is a necessary condition for the rest of creation to fulfil its own ordering. His rule is the rule which liberates other beings to be, to be in themselves, to be for others, and to be for God."[164] However, O'Donovan observes that the psalmist's description of the grandeur of the human being is yet to be realized according to the writer to the Hebrews, who alluding to Psalm 8 points out "but now we do not yet see all things subjected to him."[165]

It is precisely the writer of Hebrews who sees in Jesus's progression from incarnation to exaltation,[166] "and in the order of the world to come, the vindication and perfect manifestation of the created order which was always there but never fully expressed."[167] This allows O'Donovan to introduce the idea of redemption predicated on the created order as noted above, an idea that implies "the recovery of something given and lost."[168] Thus,

> when we ask what it is that was given and lost, and must now be recovered, the answer is not just "mankind," but mankind in his context as the ruler of the ordered creation that God has made; for the created order, too, cannot be itself while it lacks the authoritative and beneficent rule that man was to give it.[169]

This "world-order restored in Christ" O'Donovan declares "objective reality."[170] O'Donovan also argues for the idea of history with an eschatological orientation, by which he means "not mere events on the one hand, but their inherent significance and direction which makes them intelligible and narratable."[171] That is to say, "the eschatological transformation of the world is neither the mere repetition of the created world nor its negation. It is its fulfilment, its *telos* or end. It is the historical *telos* of the origin, that which creation is intended for, and that which it points and strives towards."[172]

---

164. O'Donovan, 38.
165. Heb 2:8 NASB.
166. Heb 2:9.
167. O'Donovan, *Resurrection and Moral Order*, 53.
168. O'Donovan, 54.
169. O'Donovan, 54–55.
170. O'Donovan, 101.
171. O'Donovan, 55.
172. O'Donovan, 55.

It should be noted that together with the christological objective reality of a restored creation there is a corresponding pneumatological subjectivity in which the Spirit "makes the reality of redemption, distant from us in time, both *present* and *authoritative*;"[173] and that the Spirit "evokes our *free* response to this reality as moral agents."[174] But there is only one reality on which the authority of redemption and our freedom to respond depend, "the reality of a world redeemed, which is both apart from us (in Christ once for all) and immediately engages us (through the Spirit here and now)."[175]

As we have seen, the concept of authority is implicit in O'Donovan's theorem in relation to the objective reality of the restored ordering of creation, which in fact provides us with its epistemological context (i.e. the ontological fact of one reality), that O'Donovan introduces as an overarching definition of authority. For O'Donovan authority is "*an event in which a reality is communicated to practical reason by a social communication.*"[176] Thus, authority "gives practical direction," "is mediated," and "depends on the communicative event, as another's personal presence, activity or word, written or spoken, affords the agent a new perception of reality that is needed for effective action."[177] And because God is the source of all kinds of authority,[178] O'Donovan distinguishes among various types of authorities, in particular, (a) four immediate natural authorities (i.e. beauty, age, community and strength),[179] all of which "have the capacity, as we encounter them in individuals, in human institutions and in the natural world, to inspire and order our actions in distinctive ways";[180] (b) the authority of truth, "to which any form of critical reflection turns";[181]

---

173. O'Donovan, 102.

174. O'Donovan, 102.

175. O'Donovan, 109.

176. O'Donovan, *Self, World, and Time*, 53; cf. O'Donovan, *On the Thirty-Nine*, location 1991+.

177. O'Donovan, *Self, World, and Time*, 53. O'Donovan himself acknowledges this is an update on his previous definition of authority as the objective correlate of freedom. Since "freedom is a *wider category* than authority . . . my phrase was too loose to make a satisfactory definition. Not every exercise of freedom is, directly at least, a response to authority." O'Donovan, *Self, World, and Time*, 53; cf. O'Donovan, *Resurrection and Moral Order*, 122; O'Donovan, *Ways of Judgment*, 68.

178. Rom 13:1.

179. O'Donovan, *Ways of Judgment*, 131; O'Donovan, *Resurrection and Moral Order*, 124.

180. O'Donovan, *Resurrection and Moral Order*, 124.

181. O'Donovan, 125; cf. O'Donovan, *Ways of Judgment*, 131.

(c) obviously divine authority, especially when "we admit that the created order is in disarray, that our perception of it is blinded by sin, and that we find its history aimless and mystifying";[182] and (d) political authority, which we will elaborate on later.

Second, and as a result of the restoration of the created order, the post-resurrection role of human authority is redefined and reduced solely to the political act of judgment as understood by O'Donovan from a biblical and theological perspective. On the one hand, O'Donovan traces the institution of judgment back to Scripture and the pre-monarchical times of the judges of Israel;[183] through the time of the monarchy when the king administered justice,[184] to post-exilic times when judgment became an eschatological expectation.[185] However, O'Donovan concedes that this line of exploration runs the risk of misrepresenting the Old Testament evidence about authority, since

> it would fail to account for the two great figures on whom so much reflection is focussed, those of Moses and David. The one, as deliverer and lawgiver, stands behind the judges of Israel; he is the source of their authority, not of their number. The other, as the recipient of a personal covenant with YHWH, underpins the identity of the people as a whole.[186]

On the other hand, it is on the apostle Paul's teaching that O'Donovan founds the theological purchase for his corollary on human authority. In particular, Romans 13:1, 4:

> Let every soul/person be subject to [the] empowered authorities,
> For there is no authority if not from God
> But those that exist have been appointed/put in place by God.
>
> For a minister/agent of God is to you, for the [common] good[187]

---

182. O'Donovan, *Resurrection and Moral Order*, 127; cf. O'Donovan, *Ways of Judgment*, 131.

183. e.g. Judg 2:16, 18; 3:10; 1 Sam 7:15.

184. cf. 1 Sam 8:6, 20.

185. e.g. Isa 16:5; to which O'Donovan adds Isa 42:1, 4; cf. O'Donovan, *Ways of Judgment*, 3.

186. O'Donovan, *Ways of Judgment*, 3; cf. 157, 190. On the role of the king and other mediators in Israelite society see O'Donovan, *Desire of the Nations*, 49–66, which we have also analysed in §2.1.2.

187. cf. Wannenwetsch, "Liturgy," 76.

> But if you do evil/wrong, be afraid!
> For he does not carry the sword without purpose
> For a punishing minister/agent of God is, with reference to the wrath of the one who does evil.

In O'Donovan's view, this is a deeply subversive text when the role of authority is considered, whether in the light of Israelite (the king as Son of God), Greek (Plato's philosopher-king) or Roman (Romulus, or Octavian as Augustus/Maximus Pontifex/Pater Patriae) traditions.[188] That is to say, "Paul's conception stripped government of its representative, identity-conferring functions, and said nothing about law. He conceded, as it were, the least possible function that would account for its place within God's plan."[189] This is because "God had conferred his sovereignty upon his Christ,"[190] and as a result, "the higher goods of mankind's social destiny have been looked after in the proclamation of Christ; only the lower goods of judgment need concern earthly princes,"[191] that is to say, "the secular princes of this earth, shorn of pretensions to our loyalty and worship, are left with the sole function of judging between innocent and guilty."[192] What is more, for "Paul, no less than for John of Patmos, there is only one political society in the end, which is the new Jerusalem; sovereignty is to be found there and nowhere else,"[193] which we will argue is more exactly portrayed in terms of its political structure through the Apocalypse's construal of the Fellowship of the Throne (§3.7).

It should be noted, however, that O'Donovan's post-resurrection iconoclastic approach to authority is intended to provide a new theo-political framework. In other words, "it means that political authority in all its forms – lawmaking, war-making, welfare provision, education – is to be re-conceived within this matrix and subject to the discipline of enacting right against wrong."[194] For instance, in his *The Just War Revisited*, O'Donovan argues that

---

188. cf. O'Donovan, *Deisre of the Nations*, 148.

189. O'Donovan, "Government as Judgment," 209; cf. O'Donovan, *Ways of Judgment*, 4; O'Donovan, *Desire of the Nations*, 151.

190. O'Donovan, *Ways of Judgment*, 4.

191. O'Donovan, 4.

192. O'Donovan, "Government as Judgment," 209.

193. O'Donovan, *Ways of Judgment*, 4; cf. 5; cf. O'Donovan, *Desire of the Nations*, 156; O'Donovan, "History and Politics," 44–47.

194. O'Donovan, *Ways of Judgment*, 4–5.

armed conflict may be sanctioned as an exceptional act of judgment within the new terms for political authority. "Judgment in war was extraordinary in that it arose out of the failure of all ordinary means, but ordinary in that it was governed by the same principles as the ordinary means."[195] Therefore, each authority involved in "the pursuit of war must be in a judicial spirit, acting as though one is not merely defending one's own interests but deciding an issue between claimants."[196]

However, this theo-political framework has an inbuilt eschatological limitation because it understands political authority as belonging to the realm of the secular, which, if understood in the light of the Apocalypse, can only claim legitimacy in the interim time between the exaltation of Jesus, which presupposes his resurrection, and the materialization of the Fellowship of the Throne.[197] In fact, based on 1 Peter 2:12, O'Donovan laconically refers to secularity as "an idea situated in relation to the expected 'day of visitation,'"[198] in stark contrast to the modern conception of secular as a domain that "had to be instituted or *imagined*, both in theory and in practice."[199] The role of political authority within the unfolding drama of salvation history is therefore to be understood as that of ministers/agents of God who as they perform their judicial duty attest to "the coming reality of God's own act of judgment."[200] Thus, in anticipation of that day of visitation, judgment is understood as "*an act of moral discrimination that pronounces upon a preceding act or existing state of affairs to establish a new public context.*"[201]

---

195. O'Donovan, *Just War Revisited*, 19.

196. O'Donovan, 23; cf. O'Donovan, *Ways of Judgment*, 225–226. For a critique of judgment within O'Donovan's construal of political authority see Biggar, "Defining Polical Authority," 278–283.

197. If the *terminus a quo* is used retrospectively, then Milbank's definition of the secular may apply, i.e. "The *saeculum*, in the medieval era, was not a space, a domain, but a time – the interval between fall and eschaton where coercive justice, private property and impaired natural reason must make shift to cope with the unredeemed effects of sinful humanity." Milbank, *Theology and Social Theory*, 9.

198. O'Donovan, "History and Politics," 35.

199. Milbank, *Theology and Social Theory*, 9. On the "secularist dogmas of our time" O'Donovan considers "the role of secularism as an operative rule of intellectual procedure meant to govern the possibilities of thought *a priori*." O'Donovan, *Ways of Judgment*, 237.

200. O'Donovan, *Ways of Judgment*, 5.

201. O'Donovan, 7.

Third, political authority operates within the dynamics of a non-reciprocal relationship. To use the Pauline discourse: the minister/agent of God exerts authority and the subject submits to them. This asymmetric relationship of authority-obligation is referred to as the "paradox of political subjection,"[202] still a conundrum for modern political theory, according to O'Donovan,[203] since its reality remains a very ordinary experience in which we respond as subjects out of freedom rather than compulsion or spontaneity,[204] and often with awe.[205] Within this liberal model (liberal because of its aura of freedom),[206] the subject acknowledges a bearer of authority whom they support through the paying of taxes,[207] and whose demands they discern, since "the duty of obedience carries with it the right and duty to decide what constitutes obedience at any given point."[208]

More importantly, since the political authority is meant to seek the common good (as in the Aristotelian construal),[209] it "must command the authority of right."[210] That is to say, it must allow for the existence of the community, and for every member to participate in it (as we will argue the Fellowship of the Throne does). "Here, we may say, is the only fundamental and inalienable human right that can be thought of, at once subjective and objective: the right of society as such, the right of each member of society to be social."[211] Equally, a sustainable common good must recognize the need of a society for its own identity, which in turn leads to the development of its tradition. "Tradition is 'what is established'; and 'what is established' is not the past, but the present as determined by the past."[212] However, O'Donovan suggests that power

---

202. O'Donovan, 128.

203. O'Donovan, 127.

204. cf. O'Donovan, 129.

205. cf. O'Donovan, 132–133.

206. O'Donovan's construal of a liberal society is explained in O'Donovan, *Desire of the Nations*, 252–271; also see Chaplin, "Political Eschatology," 265–308.

207. cf. O'Donovan, *Ways of Judgment*, 135; Rom 13:6.

208. O'Donovan, 136.

209. cf. Aristotle, *Politics* 3.13.20 (1248b5+); though for Augustine "the highest and truest common good" is God, see Augustine, *Letter* 137.17 (NPNF1/1).

210. O'Donovan, *Ways of Judgment*, 139.

211. O'Donovan, 139. For a taxonomy of the various meanings of the term right (*ius*) elaborated by Hugo Grotius (with explicit allusions to Aristotle and Cicero), see Grotius, *Right of War and Peace* 1.1, in O'Donovan and O'Donovan, *From Irenaeus to Grotius*, 797–801.

212. O'Donovan, *Ways of Judgment*, 139.

is required in order to materialize this construal of political authority. "If a representative agency has no power to act decisively, it cannot command the authority to require action of us."[213] These three elements, already anticipated in §2.2.2 and §2.2.4, are integrated in a theorem as follows: "Political authority arises where power, the execution of right, and the perpetuation of tradition are assured together in one coordinated agency."[214]

O'Donovan then moves on to consider the ancient question of what kind of constitution – Greek *politeia* (§5.1) / Roman *res publica* (§5.2) – best suits this construal of authority, beginning with the more fundamental issue of legitimacy. "Legitimate rulers are not merely representative rulers; they meet *legal* conditions for their representative status; they have an entitlement to exercise political authority."[215] In a response that discloses his own concrete historical context O'Donovan suggests that "rulers are legitimated on the basis of *popular election*."[216] This move unsurprisingly forces O'Donovan to draw on the modern concept of democracy, which differs greatly from its homonym in ancient classical Greece.[217] Here O'Donovan explicitly presupposes that a "liberal democracy" results in a "liberal government,"[218] and he considers two components to be necessary to this process: (a) the electoral system for legitimation, and (b) some sort of list of "real and felt needs of society" among which he highlights "the obligation of government to natural and divine law."[219] Despite its manifest shortcomings, O'Donovan presents a cautious apologia for democracy as still suitable for the West at this juncture.[220]

In the same constitutional vein and drawing on Marsilius of Padua (who in turn was influenced by Aristotle), Montesquieu and John Locke, O'Donovan argues for the familiar triad of powers of government (i.e. the executive, the judicial and the legislative), as compounding political authority.[221] The

---

213. O'Donovan, 141.
214. O'Donovan, 142; cf. O'Donovan, *Desire of the Nations*, 46.
215. O'Donovan, *Ways of Judgment*, 165.
216. O'Donovan, 166. When the modes of legitimation, say, of the current British prime minister (e.g. David Cameron in 2013) and the Chinese President (e.g. Xi Jinping in 2013) are contrasted, O'Donovan's context becomes more evident.
217. cf. O'Donovan, *Ways of Judgment*, 166.
218. cf. O'Donovan, 168.
219. O'Donovan, 167–168.
220. cf. O'Donovan, 171–178.
221. cf. O'Donovan, 186–188.

main issue in relation with this approach is the "differentiation of political powers,"[222] where, according to O'Donovan, the power originally invested with the authority to convey judgment (i.e. that of the monarch) is sanctioned and delegated to the judiciary (in itself a judicial act). This division of power O'Donovan sees anticipated in ancient Israel,[223] and is also recognized by early modern theory as "a dialectical distinction of two institutional powers *within the one general function of judgment*, the first power to create and maintain courts, the second power to hear cases and give judgments on them."[224] In this arrangement of powers the rule of *sub judice* was introduced to ensure "that the two powers function in a properly dialectical relation to each other, the first power not intervening in court cases and the second power not making judgments of general policy."[225]

Next, a Thomistic innovation that allowed for *lex humana* (i.e. positive law) in addition to divine law (whether natural or revealed), legitimated the making of law by political authority in order to solve "matters otherwise left unresolved" while remaining within the scope of divine law.[226] This then became the ground for the so-called third power, the legislature, whose role is to mediate the people's voice to the first power, so to speak, and to legislate.[227] O'Donovan warns against an extreme version of this third power where it is regarded as a prerequisite for any political community, a view that equates law with legislation. Though law was before any political community in the Christian tradition, legislation comes after it.[228] Also, since the executive (first) power is not subservient to the judicial (second) and legislative (third) powers, nor does the executive operate as a last resort when the two others are unable to function, O'Donovan conceives the first power as an ordinary power of prospective judgment whose function is "*to judge conditions as they arise, and provide for the further judgment of any occurrence that requires it,*

---

222. O'Donovan, 187.
223. cf. O'Donovan, 190–191.
224. O'Donovan, 191.
225. O'Donovan, 192.
226. O'Donovan, 188; cf. Aquinas, *Summa Theologica* 11–1.96.
227. O'Donovan, 194–195.
228. cf. O'Donovan, 189; cf. 199.

so that courts and legislature may be presented with their proper business in an orderly fashion."[229]

Additionally, in this "account of the just constitution of government,"[230] O'Donovan considers how this mode of political authority may relate to counterparts in other nations. This is a question O'Donovan addresses endorsing Hugo Grotius's theo-legal framework where "the international sphere is already law-governed of itself, being regulated by the law of God, natural and revealed, as well as by customary *ius gentium*, prior to any treaty and convention."[231] O'Donovan suggests that Grotius's framework should include an explicit link between the (national) political authority and international institutions and principles rather than to any elusive world-wide authority or government, a recurrent aspiration in the history of ideas.[232] In particular, the idea of a world government "is an abstract idea: the government of a people with no internal relations of mutual recognition. A people with no relations has no identity, and the government of those with no identity has no legitimacy."[233]

One of these international institutions, according to O'Donovan, is the United Nations (UN), whose role was to some extent anticipated by the papacy in former times in the history of Christendom.[234] "The popes were conceived as constituting a kind of international tribunal that could pronounce authoritatively on matters of right between sovereigns where no domestic right prevailed. Controversially, this could include a claim to pronounce on constitutional right, the power to depose rulers whose possession of rule was radically defective."[235] For instance, Pope Gregory VII (ca. 1030–1085) arrogated the prerogative "that he may depose Emperors,"[236] and indeed he deposed a king.[237] However, today's United Nations' express purposes, which

---

229. O'Donovan, 201.
230. O'Donovan, 211.
231. O'Donovan, 211.
232. cf. O'Donovan, 212–214.
233. O'Donovan, 214.
234. cf. O'Donovan, 216.
235. O'Donovan, 215–216.
236. Gregory VII, *Dictatus Papae* 12, in O'Donovan and O'Donovan, *From Irenaeus to Grotius*, 242.
237. cf. Gregory VII, *Letter 8.21*, in O'Donovan and O'Donovan, *From Irenaeus to Grotius*, 245.

are framed within the secular[238] both in terms of time and domain,[239] do not "claim to pronounce on the legitimacy of the states that comprise it."[240] In spite of this, O'Donovan regards the UN as an international quasi-authority, "an agent of earthly politics, introducing an international point of reference that is to frame the decisions of national governments."[241] Precisely the sort of international authority that "assists national governments in exercising each of the three powers of government, judicial, legislative, and provisionary, though without assuming the full exercise of any of them."[242]

Fourth, and most problematical, is the question of how a political authority enacts judgment. For O'Donovan this is arguably the most fundamental issue when considering the gap between divine and human modes of enactment. For instance, O'Donovan observes that in the creation account of Genesis, God speaks and it is done, whereas for a political authority the materialization of judgment is yet to be seen. "The word of God carries the power of God within itself; to echo the old phrase from sacramental theology, it effects what it signifies. But can the human word effect what it signifies?"[243] This question takes us back to the two poles of tradition anticipated by the Greek (*sophia* and *paideia*) and Roman (*bellum* and *subicio*) models, elaborated further by Marsilius of Padua, influenced by Aristotle, and by John Wyclif whose ideas resonate with Plato's. Aristotle poses the dilemma of whether those bearing arms "with a view to ruling in the case of those who disobey and with a view to [defending the city against] outsiders who attempt to do them injustice,"[244] should also be those who make "decision[s] concerning things advantageous and just in relation to one another."[245] He is in fact contemplating the practical compatibility of both tasks required by the city.[246] As seen above (§5.1), Plato's

---

238. The fourfold purpose of the United Nations as enshrined in its charter 1.1 is available at https://www.un.org/en/sections/un-charter/chapter-i/index.html.

239. Though O'Donovan stresses the UN's secular orientation as time, in our view its charter is confessional within the secular as domain; cf. O'Donovan, *Ways of Judgment*, 217.

240. O'Donovan, *Ways of Judgment*, 217.

241. O'Donovan, 218.

242. O'Donovan, 220.

243. O'Donovan, 13.

244. Aristotle, *Politics* 7.8.7 (1328b10+). Interestingly enough, the first task in the Aristotelian city was the priesthood (ἱερατεία), i.e. the attention paid to the god, Aristotle, 7.8.7.

245. Aristotle, *Politics* 7.8.7.

246. cf. Aristotle, *Politics* 7.9.4+ (1329a+).

guardian was required first to protect the luxurious city and make war, then to rise to the role of judge, and then finally to serve as a philosopher, all these responsibilities within the spectrum of the guardian. For his part Augustus (§5.2) did not hesitate in relying on *bellum* to exert *subicio*.

However, in the fourteenth century AD Marsilius of Padua reinstated Aristotle's view and proposed that "since the sentences of the judges against injurious and rebellious men within the state must be executed by coercive force, it was necessary to set up in the state a military or warrior part."[247] O'Donovan highlights that in "Marsilius's conception we may observe the first stirrings of that outlook which has come to be called 'realism': [where] the coercive act is a voiceless complement to an otherwise impotent word."[248] For his part, John Wyclif postulated that "it would be the best form of government for a people to be ruled solely through the law of God by judges. Within the constraints of our fallen state, the nearer a form of government comes to the state of innocence, the better and more wholly satisfactory it is."[249] In this case O'Donovan notes that "here we encounter a form of the 'idealist' tradition, derived from Plato's famous conception of the rule of philosophers in the *Republic*, where the whole action of government is contained in its expression of wisdom and rationality."[250] Admittedly, Wyclif conceded that coercive force as deployed by secular authority was necessary; for instance, though "no one should be subject to a sentence of death; yet with so many cases meriting the extreme penalty, it is more expedient that there should be kings to impose it. From evil, therefore, comes the usefulness that kings of the earth and their laws possess."[251]

O'Donovan goes on to highlight the pros and cons of each approach.[252] Thus, the idealist approach privileges rationality, though it cannot avoid falling back on force as a last resort. Also, that the idealist tradition may deploy an apologia for coercion under the banner of rationality is something to

---

247. Marsilius of Padua, *Defensor Pacis* 1.5.8, cf. 1.5.1; in O'Donovan and O'Donovan, *From Irenaeus to Grotius*, 428.

248. O'Donovan, *Ways of Judgment*, 14.

249. John Wyclif, *Civil Lordship* 1.27.62, in O'Donovan and O'Donovan, *From Irenaeus to Grotius*, 506.

250. O'Donovan, *Ways of Judgment*, 14.

251. John Wyclif, *Civil Lordship* 1.27.65, in O'Donovan and O'Donovan, *From Ireneaus to Grotius*, 508.

252. cf. O'Donovan, *Ways of Judgment*, 15.

reckon with which presents a problem of its own. On the other hand, the realist approach is more transparent about the role of coercion in the task of government. And when these approaches critique each other, "the realist critique of idealism is that it fails to acknowledge the brutal rupture implied in the transition from speech to action. [Whereas] The idealist critique of realism is that it allows too little distinction between rational force and irrational violence."[253] O'Donovan sounds his own note of caution given the limited though truthful nature of our judgment, reminding us that "it lacks final authority."[254] In other words, "human action is always subject to limits that make it fall short of its intellectual conception, and the action of political authorities, despite the illusion of being able to transcend limits, is peculiarly subject to them."[255]

All in all, O'Donovan's model of political authority, with its theo-political theorem and its inevitable corollary, seems to accommodate the Apocalypse's own construal of divine authority, just as it is also predicated on the resurrection and exaltation of Jesus. It also locates itself within a kind of middle ground between the idealist and realist poles of Western political thought, anticipated by Platonic and Roman models of authority. O'Donovan does this because he recognizes that the gap between human judgment's speech and action is bridged by force. Certainly, he is not a pacifist as he sees war within the scope of judgment enacted by political authority.[256] He also advocates a threefold (Aristotelian) constitution with an international orientation and the rule of *sub judice* to set healthy boundaries between the three powers, offering a prospective of Ciceronian political stability. O'Donovan's model presupposes a (liberal) democratic context where political authority draws legitimacy from the process of election by the people. Following a Pauline lead he also envisages this as a tax-funded political authority (as Plato's guardians). But, above all, he sees political authority as contrasted against divine authority, making it clearly limited and not final.

---

253. O'Donovan, 15.
254. O'Donovan, 28.
255. O'Donovan, 29.
256. cf. O'Donovan, *Just War Revisited*, 10–63.

5.4 Critique from Divine Authority

Plato, Cicero, Augustus, the Apocalypse's John, and most recently O'Donovan, along with those they refer or allude to (the Old Testament, Aristotle, Augustine, Thomas Aquinas, Marsilius of Padua, Hugo Grotius, among others), all witness to the ubiquity of the concept and reality of (political) authority, whether divine or human, as rightly observed by O'Donovan. Following his lead on how Western (theo-)political thought has tended to focus around the two poles anticipated by the Greek and Roman traditions, which are respectively characterized by their idealist and realist tendencies, we have considered various models as well as O'Donovan's own construal. Admittedly, the Apocalypse's own construal differs from these models, and yet just as the narrative of the book of Revelation itself allows for a counter-narrative (Rev 13, 17, for instance) that defies the main thrust of the apocalyptic story (§3.5, §3.6, §3.7), so we also have considered these contrasting models of authority. In what follows, however, we will expose them to the critique and contrast of the Apocalypse's construal of authority as we have understood it.

First, Plato's multifaceted guardian, whether portrayed as warrior, judge, king, philosopher or educator, highlights the accomplished type of authority that Plato desired for his imagined polis. This represents a thick, monolithic view of authority in stark contrast to, say, the more diffused model of authority shared by three differentiated powers that O'Donovan postulates, for instance. However, it is Plato's higher view of authority that most resonates with the multifaceted figure of the exalted Jesus in the Apocalypse, who is portrayed as Son of God, Lamb, Messiah and divine King, as does Augustus's self-portrayal of a multi-titled figure of authority. More importantly, it would appear this strand of "heavyweight" authority was construed according to a soteriological *telos*, that is the saving of the polis in Plato's account, the liberation of the *res publica* in Augustus's writings, and the buying/redeeming of an international people for God who are to take part in the Fellowship of the Throne in the Apocalypse. Understandably, O'Donovan's christological construal of a downsized remit of human authority pursues a more modest goal within the secular-as-time, an authority that is mediated through institutions mainly (i.e. the executive, the judiciary, the legislature).

Unique to Plato's construal is the epistemological nature of the ascension (i.e. enthronement) of the king as opposed to Augustus's purchase on *bellium* (war) as the means of empowerment. As the Platonic guardian reaches a level of understanding that transcends the shadows of reality to reality itself (i.e. "the form of the good"), he is considered ready to rule, and his attainment of *sophia* (wisdom) is to be mediated to the city through *paideia* (education). In fact, the Hebrew/Israelite tradition, which is the theological matrix of the Apocalypse and whose construal of the king as the Son of God has been previously discussed (§4.1.2),[257] records a historical episode regarding a king uniquely bestowed with wisdom (חָכְמָה) by YHWH.[258] The reign of "King Solomon [who] excelled all the kings on earth in wealth and in wisdom,"[259] arguably took place between "971/970 – 931/930" BC,[260] a few centuries earlier than Plato's time, but failed to perpetuate its achievements, and the Hebrew/Israelite theo-political tradition took on an eschatological messianic orientation (§4.4.1), where a descendant of King David would be endowed with YHWH's sevenfold Spirit, in particular, the Spirit of Wisdom.[261]

In contrast to the Platonic immanent and idealistic pursuit of wisdom (*sophia*), which is then conveyed to others through education (*paideia*), the exalted Jesus, in his apocalyptic portrayal as both "the one who has the seven spirits of God" and the Lamb (§4.1.2, §4.2.2),[262] is depicted as being invested with this the fullest pneumatological expression as the Isaianic figure of the Messiah. This pneumatological epistemology is transcendent, from above, as opposed to the Platonic immanent epistemology, from below so to speak. Also within the same epistemological remit, if in the Platonic account "the form of the good" is the ultimate epistemological source depicted as a sun irradiating light, then within the Apocalypse's construal of authority, which we have titled the Fellowship of the Throne, it is the Lord God who sheds light upon the servants of the Lamb (i.e. the liturgical sociality).[263] Thus, if epistemology has a place in the construal of political authority and in the

---

257. cf. 2 Sam 7:12–14.

258. 1 Kgs 5:26 (5:12 ET); cf. 5:9 (4:29 ET); 10:24; 2 Chr 1:11–12; 9:23.

259. 1 Kgs 10:23 JPS Tanakh translation; cf. 2 Chr 9:22.

260. Kitchen, *Reliability of the Old Testament*, 83; on the historical Solomon see Kitchen, 85–88; 107–137.

261. Isa 11:2; cf. 11:1.

262. Rev 3:1 and 5:6, respectively.

263. This echoes Augustine's idea of "the heavenly wisdom which comes down from the Father of Lights." Augustine, *On Christian Doctrine* 4.5 (NPNF1/2).

salvation and sustaining of the polis, then in the Apocalypse's this is transcendent and divine in nature.

As regards Roman theo-political thought, we find that the Ciceronian *res publica*, with its delicate and mixed balance, became sandwiched between the two strong monarchical construals of authority of King Romulus and Princeps Augustus, to the point it was squeezed out altogether and rendered irrelevant, except for the cosmetic role it played in keeping up appearances within Augustus's *imperium*. And yet, the Ciceronian ideal of allowing each component of the *res publica* (i.e. the monarchical *rex*, the aristocratic *consilium* and the democratic *plebs*), a share in the business of the *civitas* resonates with the Apocalypse's construal of the Fellowship of the Throne. On the one hand, divine authority as symbolized by the throne has undergone a christological shift where the one who sits on the throne and the exalted Jesus now share in this throne, as amply discussed in chapter 4, where it was explained as a correlation of power and divine status between the one who sits on the throne and the exalted Jesus. On the other hand, divine authority does not squeeze out or render irrelevant the role of the (international) people whom the Lamb had bought for God, and which we have called the liturgical sociality. On the contrary, they are intended to rule,[264] and as a result a space is opened for them within the existing structure of authority, leading to the advent of the Fellowship of the Throne, where they take their place and reign along with the two figures already sharing the throne.[265] "In the Eastern Church they speak more commonly of theosis or 'divinization', emphasizing the advance beyond simple restoration to communion with the divine nature."[266] In other words, divine authority allows for a diffused/democratized and flat (there is arguably no hierarchy among them) human authority, where the latter remains aligned with the former through the mediation of the exalted Jesus. In this sense, the Fellowship of the Throne resembles both the *politeia* (Greek) and the *res publica* (Roman) with an Augustinian caveat,[267] and presents us with the ultimate horizon of the political.

---

264. cf. Rev 5:10; cf. also 2:26–28; 3:21; 20:4.

265. cf. Rev 22:5.

266. O'Donovan, *On the Thirty-Nine*, location 708.

267. See Augustine, *City of God* 19.24; cf. 10.32; Justin Martyr, *Dialogue with Trypho* 42 (ANF/1); Tertullian, *Apology* 38 (ANF/3); Origen, *Against Celsus* 3.7; 8.5 (ANF/4); Origen, *Commentary on the Gospel of John* 2.4 (ANF/9).

Augustus's model for the retaining of *potestas* (power) and the exercising of *auctoritas* (authority) relied heavily on *bellum* (war) in order to *subicio* (to subject) enemies from within or foreign peoples. Out of war emerges a new order, the *imperium* (empire),[268] at times saluted as the *Pax Augusta*,[269] with the Roman *civitas* (city) as its locus.[270] On this O'Donovan observes that the "Romans did no wrong to the nations they ruled in ruling them, since they governed them by the same laws that they governed themselves. The wrong of the Roman empire lay in the violent conquest, driven by unbridled ambition and lust for glory, through which it was achieved."[271] By contrast, the Apocalypse's construal of divine authority offers a very subversive account of power and war. On the one hand, in stark contrast to empire by war, what we are presented with is a slaughtered Lamb who buys a truly international people for God rather than for himself (§4.2.2).[272] The exalted Jesus recovers for God what was his property by virtue of them being his creatures.[273] Though this is a violent and deadly transaction, yet it is only the buyer, the victor, who receives or absorbs the violence ("were their Lord was crucified"),[274] rather than inflicting it on potential subjects as Augustus did.

On the other hand, as opposed to the *Pax Augusta* born of war that underpins the Roman city, the Apocalypse gives us the divine King, who, though displaying the paraphernalia of warfare, speaks rather than launching into war. After all, he is the Word of God. And though there is a strong imagery of warfare, yet this is a war spoken by the the King of kings as a forensic logos. The outcome however is the desired one: he dethrones the kings of the earth (a divine prerogative pope Gregory VII dared to claim) and clears the space for the advent of a new order (new heaven and a new earth), a new city, a new *res publica*, which is the Fellowship of the Throne (§4.4.3). This apocalyptic double-subversion of war as a priori discourse enabling the peaceful installation of a new order/city in some way anticipates Augustine's critique

---

268. cf. Augustus, *Res Gestae* 13.
269. cf. Augustus, *Res Gestae* 12.2.
270. cf. Ovid, *Fasti* 2.683–684.
271. O'Donovan, *Ways of Judgment*, 212.
272. cf. Rev 5:6, 9.
273. cf. Rev 4:11; 10:6; 14:7; 21:5.
274. Rev 11:8.

of the Roman empire,[275] of which John Milbank notes that its "main gist . . . is that these [pagan] virtues were hopelessly contaminated by a celebration of violence."[276] In addition, the Apocalypse's divine King as Word of God resolves the O'Donovanian tension between idealist and realist modes of authority, since as he judges he also enacts the judgment.

In the same imperialistic vein, Augustus's promotion of his own claim to authority raises the question of the possibility of a world-wide authority, as considered in O'Donovan's model. In fact, Augustus unashamedly opens his *Res Gestae* affirming that he has subjugated the whole world (*orbis terrarium*); he equally concludes with a claim to world-wide authority by referring to the unique title awarded to him (i.e. *Pater Patriae*), with all its theo-political connotations, in addition to referring to himself as the *Maximus Pontifex*. According to his own account, he rules the world and mediates on behalf of it to the gods, that is to say, he bridges heaven and earth. A less pretentious view of a Roman emperor's authority is articulated by Eusebius regarding Constantine, the first Christian to hold this office: "our divinely favored emperor, receiving, as it were a transcript of the Divine sovereignty, directs, in imitation of God himself, the administration of this world's affairs."[277] After that, it would be popes who would recover and elaborate on this tradition of arrogating to themselves claims to some sort of world-wide authority. For instance, *The Donation of Constantine* states that

> since he [i.e. Peter] is seen to have been set up as the vicar of God's Son on earth, the pontiffs who act on behalf of that prince of the apostles should receive from us and our empire a greater power of government than the earthly clemency of our imperial serenity is seen to have conceded to them . . . And inasmuch as our imperial power is earthly, we have decreed that it shall venerate and honour his most holy Roman Church and that the

---

275. cf. Augustine, *City of God* 3.10.
276. Milbank, *Theology and Social Theory*, 289. In fact, following Augustine's lead, Milbank articulates a critique of Postmodernism's purchase on ontological violence (cf. Milbank, 278), which he counteracts "with an alternative mythos, equally unfounded, but nonetheless embodying an 'ontology of peace,'" Milbank, 279.
277. Eusebius, *Oration in Praise of the Emperor Constantine* 1.6 (NPNF2/1).

sacred see of the blessed Peter shall be gloriously exalted above our empire and earthly throne.[278]

Self-aggrandizing human authority predicated on immanent terms is recurrently portrayed in the biblical tradition as degenerating into a non-human form, usually into some sort of animal being, as exemplified in the story about the dream and metamorphosis of King Nebuchadnezzar (Dan 4), which in turn also anticipated Daniel's vision about the four beasts emerging from the sea (Dan 7). It is precisely this sort of distorted form of human authority (the beast), predicated on an heterodox theology and promoting a public liturgy based on it, who is exposed, criticized and disempowered in the Apocalypse (§3.6). At the same time, the sociality referred to as the great city, which somehow operates as a pivot on which the cities of the nations revolve,[279] develops a symbiotic relationship with the distorted form of human authority known as the beast.[280]

To a distorted form of human authority corresponds an equally distorted form of sociality, whether portrayed as the great city, a high-class prostitute, (ancient) Babylon or alluding to Rome.[281] This apocalyptic correlation appears to mirror the existing one between Augustus's self-aggrandizing claims regarding his own authority and the propaganda concerning Rome's imperial claims as articulated by Ovid, for instance. The Apocalypse also portrays local and diffused modes of authority (i.e. the kings of the earth), as being subsumed into that symbiotic relationship between the distorted form of authority (beast) and the distorted form of sociality (great city).[282] Yet this relationship proves unstable, since distorted authority suffocates distorted sociality in anticipation of the city's final annihilation, the enactment of divine judgment.[283] The divine King of the Apocalypse goes on to dethrone all existing modes of human authority that are complicit in any distorting,

---

278. *The Donation of Constantine* in O'Donovan and O'Donovan, *From Irenaeus to Grotius*, 229; cf. Gregory VII, *Dictatus Papae* in O'Donovan and O'Donovan, *From Irenaeus to Grotius*, 242–243.
279. Rev 16:19; 17:18.
280. Rev 17:3, 7.
281. Rev 17:1, 5, 9, 15, 18; 18:10, 21.
282. Rev 17:18; 19:19.
283. Rev 17:16; 18:21.

heretical, self-aggrandizing claim.[284] In short, world-wide authority tends to become immanentized (i.e. to lose its external referent to the divine King) and idolatrous, and its leaning towards totalitarianism is a source of instability for the sociality it sustains. In this regard, O'Donovan's construal of authority agrees with the Apocalypse's.

Admittedly, though the Apocalypse's and O'Donovan's construals of authority agree on the non-viability of world-wide authority, they appear at odds over their conceptuality of mundane human political authority. On the one hand, O'Donovan's christologically downsized model, which sees human authority as reduced to the enactment of judgment, presupposes an authorized agent willing to comply with the new theo-political rules of the game, so to speak. The Apocalypse's construal of divine authority, however, factors in a deliberate challenge to the exalted Jesus, as discussed in the previous two points. In other words, notwithstanding the reality of the exalted Jesus, the Apocalypse takes a more realist view by depicting human authority as resisting the boundaries defined by O'Donovan and continuing on its set course unabated. In the Apocalypse this resistance among human authorities to the divine authority is signalled by the use of "the kings of the earth" tag, which represents a more mundane mode of authority to that of the beast, who stands a priori for a distorted form of human authority with self-aggrandising and heretical claims, as discussed in the previous point.

The first time the tag of "the kings of the earth" features in the Apocalypse, it conveys the proper relationship between Jesus the Messiah and those it is used for (i.e. he is the ruler [ἄρχων] of the kings of the earth).[285] Then, in the vision where the Lamb opens the sixth seal of the scroll (§3.3) "the kings of the earth" are attempting to hide in caves and rocks because they are unable to withstand the sight or revelation (an apocalypse indeed) of the one who sits on the throne and the wrath of the Lamb.[286] In other words, so far this mode of authority, mundane and local, seems to conform to O'Donovan's construal of authority, since "the kings of the earth" acknowledge who the exalted Jesus is. Next, in a scene that, as we have argued (§3.3, §4.2.2), brings closure to the vision of the sixth seal, "the kings of the earth" feature again.

---

284. Rev 19:19–21.
285. Rev 1:5.
286. cf. Rev 6:15–17.

However, this time they come with their armies and in alliance with the beast ready to wage war against the divine King.[287] How does the narrative of the book of Revelation account for this metamorphosis of "the kings of the earth," who now appear to have assimilated the beast's own imperialistic discourse of war? Though there are intimations that they may have neglected the prophetic word,[288] we are left in no doubt that "the kings of the earth" have in fact been subsumed into the kingdom of the great city.[289] That is to say, they ceased to align themselves with the exalted Jesus, as in the beginning of the apocalyptic text, and instead their identity is now defined by the symbiotic relationship between the distorted form of authority (the beast) and the distorted form of sociality (the great city). This is where O'Donovan's model stops working in the face of the Apocalypse's more realist view of a mundane human authority. However, after their dethronement because of their alliance with the beast and the great city, "the kings of the earth" are welcomed into the holy city to which they contribute their honour/glory,[290] in anticipation of the materialization of the Fellowship of the Throne.[291] In other words, "the kings of the earth" voluntary submit (arguably) to the holy city instead of to the annihilated great city.

Finally, as opposed to the detailed nature of Plato's and O'Donovan's models of (mundane) human political authority, what the Apocalypse does is present us with a negative example, portraying what human political authority should not be (i.e. the beast) or should not do in the secular-as-time. In other words, it is not intended to furnish the reader with practical detail. Instead (i) it presents the reality of a stark choice for any human authority between aligning itself with Jesus the Messiah or with the kingdom of the great city; and (ii) highlights the importance of attentiveness to the prophetic word in order to avoid the entanglement of the great city, which is portrayed as an improper sexual relationship[292] and that leads human authority into conflict against the divine King.

---

287. cf. Rev 19:19.
288. cf. Rev 10:11.
289. cf. Rev 17:18; cf. 17:2; 18:3, 9.
290. cf. Rev 21:24.
291. cf. Rev 22:3–5.
292. cf. Rev 17:2; 18:3, 9.

5.5 Conclusion

The agenda for a political theology influenced by the Christ-event, says O'Donovan, is to criticize any notion of the political good, ancient or modern, including any understandings of political authority. And this is precisely what we have sought to do in this chapter by allowing our framework of divine authority as redefined by the exalted Jesus, previously articulated in chapter 4, to offer its own critique of ancient construals of political authority as well as by contrasting it with O'Donovan's own model. In this exercise we have followed O'Donovan's lead regarding the two poles of tradition that have shaped the developments of theo-political thought over time, and we have considered in some detail three ancient models of political authority: Plato's model as put across is his *Republic*, Cicero's construal in his *Res Publica*, and Augustus's self-interested ideas in his *Res Gestae Divi Augusti*.

What has emerged from our efforts is a new understanding of the Apocalypse's relevance and originality in terms of its own construal of authority, which displays some surprising common ground with all three of the ancient models of political authority that we have considered. It also shows that O'Donovan's model is mostly compatible with the Apocalypse's, and yet we find that in relation to the issue of human authority O'Donovan's construal fails to match up to the book of Revelation's perspective on it, and to the role it is given in the advent of the holy city that in turn allows for the Apocalypse's construal of the Fellowship of the Throne, which we have argued has now become the ultimate horizon of the political.

Part III

Society

CHAPTER 6

The Liturgical Sociality

"When the Jews of the First Temple period used to sing the refrain *Yhwh malak*, 'Yhwh is king,'"[1] observes O'Donovan, they were joining in "a liturgical act in which political and religious meanings were totally fused,"[2] that is to say that "the link which ties the exercise of Yhwh's kingly rule to the praise of his people is that as the people congregate to perform their act of praise, the political reality of Israel is displayed."[3] This programmatic statement for O'Donovan's political theology highlights the liturgical vocation of YHWH's chosen people with divine authority as its focal point, so that when the sociality of God's people lives up to its vocation in doxological relation to him, its political identity becomes transparent. This liturgical turn in O'Donovan's political theology is highly relevant when considering the Apocalypse and now drives us to explore in this chapter how the Apocalypse itself conveys the construal of its liturgical sociality, which we find is represented in spatial terms, both as sacred space and as a city (polis).

From the very introduction to this study (§1.2) we have highlighted the sequence of images deployed in the last vision of the Apocalypse (21:9–22:5), beginning with the bride on her way to her nuptials or the consummation of her marriage, and ending with the locus of the throne of God and of the Lamb. In between these, we see a walled city described as the ultimate sacred space and also as a place of pilgrimage, which then becomes a primeval garden or

---

1. O'Donovan, *Desire of the Nations*, 32.
2. O'Donovan, 32.
3. O'Donovan, 47. "The church as a political entity finds its constitutive and restitutive act in worship, which is the central praxis of the 'fellow citizens of the saints (Eph. 2:19)" Wannenwetsch, "Liturgy," 76.

paradise, and we have argued that this progressive yet seamless sequence of images point us to the construal of the Fellowship of the Throne. It is this aspect of the apocalyptic discourse (i.e. the liturgical space),[4] envisioned both as a sacred space and as a holy city, which we now aim to revisit in order to understand how the Apocalypse's "spatial ecclesiology"[5] conveys a liturgical sociality predicated on the (mediated) presence of the exalted Jesus in its midst, in other words, a liturgical sociality predicated on divine authority. This exegetical and theological task requires a retracing of the manifestations of the liturgical space to the very first vision of the narrative, in order that we may appreciate their relevance as overarching themes and their confluence in the materialization of the Fellowship of the Throne in the final vision of the narrative. Before that, however, a few words on the meaning of liturgy would illuminate our exegetical and theological task.

6.1 Archeology and Enactment of Liturgy

In classical Greek, "liturgy" (λειτουργία) was either "any public service or work" or "public service of the gods."[6] So Lysias could ask his audience "to remember my public services [λειτουργία] to the State,"[7] whereas Aristotle would suggest that a part of the common territory (in a city, arguably) "should be for public service [λειτουργία] relating to the gods."[8] Bernd Wannenwetsch observes that "the word *leitourgia* belongs to the constitutional vocabulary of the Greek city-states . . . [and that] It will hardly be by chance that, in taking

---

4. On the ancient Near Eastern concept of a sacred space see Walton, *Ancient Near Eastern Thought*, 118–123. In addition, "space" as an exegetical category for New Testament studies and ancient history appears to be undergoing a sort of revival after the so-called "spatial-turn," see Balch, and Weissenrieder, *Contested Spaces*, vi; cf. Ewald, and Noreña, *Emperor and Rome*, 11–24. Equally, "space" as a theo-political category of analysis is (increasingly) deployed by some theologians, e.g. Milbank, *Word Made Strange*, 268–292; Pickstock, *After Writing*; Cavanaugh, *Theopolitical Imagination*, 53–95, and, *Migrations of the Holy*, 46–67; O'Donovan, "Loss of a Sense of Place," 296–320.

5. The present writer is borrowing the phrase "spatial ecclesiology" from Dr. Angus Paddison, as it came across during the oral examination of this PhD dissertation on 20 January 2014.

6. LSJ 1036.

7. Lysias, *Speeches* 21.19 (LCL).

8. Aristotle, *Politics* 7.10.11 (1330a13).

over the term for the practice of worship, the Church adopted the use of the Septuagint, which preferred this term for Temple worship rather than *ourgia*."⁹

Yet, it should be noted that the Septuagint deploys "liturgy" (λειτουργία) and its related semantic domain to translate the Hebrew stem שרת (to serve),¹⁰ which for the Israelites was a flexible term meaning either the service rendered by (i) a priest to YHWH in his temple,¹¹ or by (ii) a particular person to the king.¹² We find it used with an Isaianic eschatological expectation, deeply messianic, to refer to the restored people of God as "priests to YHWH" and "ministers [λειτουργοι (LXX)] of our God,"¹³ in what would seem a recovery of their original covenantal vocation as granted by YHWH (i.e. to be for him "a kingdom of priests and a holy people").¹⁴ Therefore, and since the international people bought by the exalted Jesus in the Apocalypse are also given a vocation to be priests and a kingdom for God the Father (§3.3, §4.2.2),¹⁵ we may be exegetically authorized to use the term "liturgical sociality" in allusion to this Old Testament tradition,¹⁶ since a "sociality itself is not a bare empirical datum, but a historical and eschatological destiny."¹⁷

There is, however, a wider understanding of liturgy, as argued by Catherine Pickstock, who considers it a political category when predicated on a theological ground that then inevitably engages in a critique of modernity.¹⁸ What is more, this correlation between liturgical theory and practice is necessarily conveyed in spatial terms, as Pickstock illustrates with Christian medieval

---

9. Wannenwetsch, *Political Worship*, 160. Admittedly, liturgy (λειτουργία) features six times in the New Testament, and a quick survey of those references clearly render it meaning more than service in the temple (Luke 1:23; Heb 9:21). It may equally mean service in terms of welfare or care for others (2 Cor 9:12), service to the faith by those in Philippi (Phil 2:17), service for Paul the apostle (Phil 2:30), and the service or ministry of the exalted Jesus (Heb 8:6), arguably.

10. HALOT 1662.

11. e.g. 1 Kgs 8:11 || 2 Chr 5:14; cf. 2 Chr 13:10.

12. e.g. 1 Kgs 1:4, 15; 1 Chr 28:1; 2 Chr 17:19.

13. Isa 61:6 (MT/LXX). Precisely, "ministers of God" are those authorised agents in the key Pauline text on which O'Donovan's construal of human authority is predicated, as noted in §5.3.

14. Exod 19:6; cf. *Jubilees* 16.17–18; 33.20 (OTP/2); *2 Maccabees* 2.17.

15. Rev 5:10; cf. 1:6; 20:6; cf. 1 Pet 2:5, 9.

16. cf. Fekkes, *Isaiah and Prophetic Traditions*, 113–116; Aune, *Revelation 1–5*, 47–49.

17. O'Donovan, *Ways of Judgment*, 241.

18. cf. Pickstock, "Liturgy and Modernity," 139.

liturgy,[19] about which she notices its construal of the liturgical city as "avowedly semiotic. Its lineaments, temporal duration, and spatial extension are entirely and constitutively articulated through the signs of speech, gesture, art, music, figures, vestments, colour, fire, water, smoke, bread, wine, and relationality."[20] Or, in the words of Wannenwetsch, "worship is *place* (*topos*), a temporal-spatial extension, the site and current form of the political. In it the peaceful coexistence of men and women, the goal of politics, is not impossible . . . nor is it possible . . . it is simply *there*."[21]

6.2 Sacred Space

Earlier, in section §3.2 (Rev 1:9–3:22), we noted the interplay between the two spaces inhabited by both John the seer and his interlocutor, the exalted Jesus, respectively. These two spaces appear to be construed in allusion to a stylized version of the Old Testament's mobile tent of meeting and/or of the institutionalised royal temple. What follows is the evidence that supports this claim.[22]

First, John reports the following in his inaugural vision:

> I heard behind me a loud voice like a trumpet-sound . . .
> And I turned around to see the voice that was speaking to me
> and as I turned I saw seven golden lampstands [λυχνία]
> and in the middle of the lampstands like a son of man
> wearing a robe reaching to the feet [ποδήρης] and girding a
>   golden sash [ζώνη] by the breast . . .[23]

As already observed, "like a son of man" inhabits his "own" space of the seven golden lampstands (λυχνία) or menorahs (1:12–13; 2:1), which signal the

---

19. cf. Pickstock, *After Writing*, 228–233.
20. Pickstock, 169.
21. Wannenwetsch, *Political Worship*, 26.
22. As Annette Weissender sets to the task of understanding Paul's temple imagery in 1 Corinthians, she considers three hermeneutical paths: (1) a sort of spiritualization of the imagery, (2) a metaphorical approach, or (3) a framework resourced by textual (e.g. Vitrubius, *On Architecture*) and numismatic evidence, mainly. She opts for route (3), which in a sense is our method as well, since we rely mainly on allusions to the Old Testament; see Weissenrieder, "Do You Not Know," 377–381.
23. Rev 1:10, 12–13.

seven congregations (1:20) to whom John is ordered to convey a message in written form (1:11, 19; 2:1, 8, 12, 18; 3:1, 7, 14). Here we register allusions to the Exodus story of the Old Testament, when YHWH asked Moses to instruct the children of Israel to put together a sacred place/sanctuary (מִקְדָּשׁ) for him, so he might dwell in their midst.[24] This is the basic theological concept of a relationship, or better still, a fellowship between YHWH and his people that underpins the whole notion of a sacred space.[25] This sacred place was mostly referred to as the tabernacle or dwelling-place (מִשְׁכָּן),[26] or more fully as the tabernacle (מִשְׁכָּן) of the tent (אֹהֶל) of meeting (מוֹעֵד),[27] since the tabernacle included a tent.[28] Admittedly, the idea that YHWH (or God) wanted to dwell in the midst of his people had already been hinted at earlier in the Exodus story,[29] though this is a motif that runs across the Old Testament.[30] More importantly, within that sacred space YHWH would meet Moses and speak to him so that he might relay all YHWH's commands to the children of Israel.[31]

The sacred place, that is to say, the tent,[32] had two main sections, the holy of holies (קֹדֶשׁ הַקֳּדָשִׁים) and the Holy Place (קֹדֶשׁ), which were separated by a veil or curtain.[33] Within the holy of holies were the ark of the testimony/covenant with two golden cherubim over it,[34] that would eventually come to be regarded as a kind of throne or throne-room of YHWH's,[35] a point we elaborated in §4.2.1. There was also a lampstand (מְנוֹרָה) or menorah, made

---

24. Exod 25:1–2, 8; cf. 4Q11 f24_30i.1.

25. This Old Testament theologoumenon on sacred space resonates with the wider ancient Near East view on it, e.g. "I am Hammurabi, Enlil's chosen shepherd who heaps up plenty and abundance supplying Nippur, where earth and heaven meet, with whatever it needs, the devoted provider for Ekur." *Hammurabi's Laws*, P4.

26. Exod 25:9; cf. 4Q11 f24_30i.2.

27. Exod 39:32, 40; 40:2, 6, 29; 1 Chr 6:17. In fact, these three terms (sacred space, tabernacle, and tent of meeting), featured in Numbers 3:38 referring to the same spatial entity, arguably; cf. 4Q394 f3_7ii.16.

28. e.g. Exod 26:7; 35:11.

29. Exod 15:17; cf. 4Q14 6.40–41.

30. See Exod 25:8; 29:45–46; Num 5:3; 35:34; 1 Kgs 6:13; Ezek 43:7, 9; Zech 2:14–15; 8:3; cf. 8:8.

31. Exod 25:22; cf. Num 7:89; 4Q22 27.32–33; Durham, *Exodus*, 353.

32. cf. Exod 28:43; 29:30; 4Q22 33.6–7.

33. Exod 26:33; cf. 4Q11 f30ii_34.7–8.

34. Exod 25:22; 26:33–34; 40:21; cf. Num 7:89; 1 Kgs 8:6–7; 4Q22 27.33.

35. 1 Sam 4:4; 2 Sam 6:2; 1 Chr 13:6; cf. 2 Kgs 19:15; Isa 37:16; Ps 80:2; 99:1; cf. Keel, *Symbolism of the Biblical World*, 166–171; HALOT 85.

of pure gold,[36] placed outside the veil or curtain (i.e. in the Holy Place), opposite the table on which was placed bread before the presence of YHWH.[37] The lampstand/menorah had six branches, three to each side of its stem,[38] and held seven lamps,[39] which were meant to provide a permanent light before YHWH.[40] Later, when Solomon built a house (בַּיִת) for YHWH[41] (i.e. the temple), he had ten lampstands/menorahs made, which were placed in front of the inner sanctuary (דְּבִיר),[42] five on each side. The inner sanctuary was the holy of holies.[43]

As to the instructions given to Moses regarding the tabernacle,[44] they also specified that, from among the children of Israel, Moses's brother Aaron and his sons should serve YHWH as priests,[45] and that sacred vestments were to be produced for the priests,[46] of which two specific items were the robe (מְעִיל), a "sleeveless, cloak-like outer garment,"[47] and the girdle or sash (אַבְנֵט),[48] which the LXX renders as ποδήρης (foot-length robe) and the ζώνη (belt, girdle), respectively.[49] Other sources such as Josephus and Philo refer to these two items as part of the sacred garments of the high priest.[50]

Second, after John's interlocutor ends the dictation of the messages for the seven congregations, the transition to a new vision is described in the following way:

---

36. Exod 25:31; cf. 4Q22 28.10.
37. Exod 25:30; 26:35; 40:24; cf. 4Q11 f30ii_34.9-10; 4Q17 f2ii.21-22.
38. Exod 25:32–34; cf. 4Q22 28.11–15.
39. Exod 25:37; 35:14; Num 4:9. Carol Meyers suggests that the "significance of the lampstand . . . lies more in its iconic value than in its pragmatic function, as the details of its fabrication suggest." Meyers, *Exodus*, 232.
40. Lev 24:4; cf. 4Q24 f20ii+22_25.9–10.
41. 1 Kgs 6:1, 37.
42. 1 Kgs 7:49; cf. 2 Chr 4:7.
43. 1 Kgs 6:16; 8:6; 2 Chr 5:7.
44. Exod 25:9.
45. Exod 28:1, 4, 41; 29:44; 30:30; cf. 4Q11 f37.4–5; 4Q22 36.14.
46. Exod 28:2, 4; cf. Lev 16:4; 4Q22 31.19–20; 11Q1 fGii+M.5–7.
47. HALOT 612.
48. Exod 28:4; Lev 8:7; 4Q22 31.20. Interestingly enough, the Mishna regarded those two items as those being worn by the high (גָּדוֹל) priest (כֹּהֵן) (*Yoma* 7.5).
49. Exod 28:4 LXX; cf. BDAG 431, 838; LSJ 759, 1426.
50. Josephus, *Antiquities of the Jews* 3.7.4 (3.159); 8.3.8 (8.93); and Philo, *On the Life of Moses* 2.143.

> After these [things] I saw
> and look a door [θύρα] has been opened in heaven
> and the first voice that I heard as a trumpet-sound is speaking
> > to me saying:
> "Come up here, and I will show you what has to come about
> > after these [things]."
> Immediately I became in the Spirit
> and look, a throne [θρόνος] was lying in heaven
> and on the throne [one] sitting [on it][51]

Here we would highlight three aspects in connection with the tent/tabernacle/temple as discussed in the previous point: (i) when Solomon built a house for YHWH (the temple), the entrance (פֶּתַח) to the inner sanctuary or holy of holies was made of doors (דֶּלֶת).[52] (ii) John's interlocutor, referred to as one who speaks with a trumpet-sound-like voice, is clearly able to move from one side of the door, John's space, to the other, heaven itself, thus being able to lay his right hand on John (1:17) and also to lead him up into heaven (4:1). (iii) More importantly, in keeping with the details of the tabernacle/temple, the first thing John sees when he goes through the door is what is signalled by the furniture of the holy of holies, YHWH's throne.

Third, following from the above, we can ascertain that heaven is in fact the locus of the tent/tabernacle/temple's furniture, an altar of incense, arguably,[53] and the ark of the covenant.[54] Most importantly, "the temple [ναός] of God . . . is in heaven";[55] or, using an expression that merges the two models of sacred space used in the Old Testament, the rudimentary and mobile tent of meeting,

---

51. Rev 4:1–2.

52. 1 Kgs 6:31–32. "The motif connecting divine epiphanies with a heavenly door is particularly important in southwest Asia Minor in the Hellenistic and Roman periods" (Aune, *Revelation 1–5*, 281). On the opening of temple doors see Aune, *Revelation 6–16*, 676–677, 876.

53. Rev 8:3, 5; 9:13; cf. Exod 30:1, 27; 31:8; 35:15; 37:25; 39:38; 40:5. On the unusual altar of incense in heaven see Aune, *Revelation 6–16*, 511; on the meaning of incense see Beale, *Book of Revelation*, 456–457.

54. Rev 11:19. "This is the only explicit reference in early Jewish and early Christian literature to a heavenly ark of the covenant" (Aune, *Revelation 6–16*, 677).

55. Rev 11:19.

and the sophisticated and royal temple: "the temple [ναός] of the tent [σκηνή] of testimony/meeting [μαρτύριον]" is in heaven.[56]

Fourth, at this point the narrative envisions the temple of God, the altar, and those who worship within the temple as protected, while the external courtyard remains vulnerable, since it has been temporarily given over to the nations.[57] "John's vision is of a space for God, restricted in scope, the outer margins of which do not belong, at least in the short term, to God and are not, therefore, to be measured. [However,] No such restriction will apply in Rev 21:15."[58]

Fifth, with the advent of the holy city, a new heaven and a new earth is envisioned, where

> The tent [σκηνή] of God [is] among the human beings
> and he will dwell among them,
> and they will be his people,
> and he, God, will be among them (their God)[59]

Here, the basic theological concept that shaped the Old Testament notion of a sacred space (i.e. God wanting to dwell among his people),[60] is realized. Most importantly, as already noted (§1.2, §3.7) the holy city that comes down from heaven is in fact a "holy of holies" of immense proportions, and "its length and width and height are equal"[61] as in Solomon's temple, where the inner sanctuary (דְּבִיר), or holy of holies,[62] was literally a cube "20 cubits long, 20 cubits wide, and 20 cubits high."[63] However, we find that there is no temple in this apocalyptic city since "the Lord God all-powerful is her temple, and

---

56. Rev 15:5; cf. 15:1; *Wisdom of Solomon* 9.8; Eupolemos, *Fragment 2* 34.5 (OTP/2); Justin Martyr, *Dialogue with Trypho* 36 (ANF/1). See Aune's discussion of ναός in Aune, *Revelation 6–16*, 877.

57. Rev 11:2.

58. Rowland, "Book of Revelation," 642; cf. Beale and McDonough, "Revelation," 1118–1119.

59. Rev 21:3.

60. See Exod 25:8.

61. Rev 21:16; cf. Caird, *Revelation of St. John*, 273; Boxall, *Revelation of Saint John*, 304.

62. 1 Kgs 6:16; 8:6; 2 Chr 5:7.

63. 1 Kgs 6:20.

the Lamb [too],"⁶⁴ and "the glory of God gave light to the city, and its lamp [is] the Lamb."⁶⁵

We have therefore found that, throughout the narrative of the book of Revelation, there gradually emerges a liturgically construed spatial order built on the theological foundation that God, and the exalted Jesus, want to dwell among and have fellowship with God's people,⁶⁶ as exemplified by the Old Testament's mobile sanctuary/tabernacle,⁶⁷ and by the institutionalized royal temple.⁶⁸ In this new construal of spatial order, heaven is the holy of holies, where the throne, surrounded by its distinctive "cherubim" (i.e. the four living beings)⁶⁹ and the ark of the covenant are found.⁷⁰ Here the seven congregations or two witnesses are the Holy Place, since they are consistently depicted as lampstands/menorahs,⁷¹ and a door in heaven signals the divide between the two spaces.⁷² We also find that God's authorized/anointed agent, the Son of God, is the one who wears the vestments that signal a priestly or (more specifically, it would appear) a high-priestly role,⁷³ and as such, he is able to move freely between the two sacral spaces.⁷⁴ In addition, God's international people, the liturgical sociality, are also called to be priests and a kingdom.⁷⁵ Outside this sacred space lie the (historical) Greek/Roman cities,⁷⁶ or the

---

64. Rev 21:22.
65. Rev 21:23.
66. Rev 1:12–13, 20; 2:1; 21:3; 22:3–4; cf. 13:6.
67. Exod 25:8–9.
68. 1 Kgs 6:1, 11–13.
69. The four (τέσσαρες) living beings (ζῷον) in Revelation (4:6, 8; 5:6, 8, 14; 6:1, 6; 7:11; 14:3; 15:7; 19:4) allude to the four (אַרְבַּע) living beings (חַיָּה) featured in the Ezekiel's report of an inaugural vision of the throne (i.e. Ezek 1:5, 15; cf. 1:26; 4Q385 f6.6; Ezek 1:5, 15 LXX). What is more, in a second vision of the throne (Ezek 10:1), Ezekiel referred to cherubs or cherubim (כְּרוּב) linked to this throne (Ezek 10:1), four in number (Ezek 10:9, 14). Most importantly, he reported that the living beings of the first throne-vision are in fact the cherubs or cherubim of the second throne-vision (Ezek 10:15, 20).
70. Rev 11:19.
71. Rev 1:12, 13, 20; 2:1, 5; 11:4.
72. Rev 4:1.
73. Rev 1:13; cf. Victorinus of Petovium, *Commentary on the Apocalypse* 1.4 (ACT/L).
74. cf. Victorinus of Petovium, *Commentary on the Apocalypse* 1.2; 4.1 (ACT/L).
75. Rev 5:10; cf. 1:6; 20:6.
76. Rev 1:11; cf. 1:4.

symbolic great city,[77] which remain the loci of an alternative and heretical theological and liturgical order.

The above, however, does not constitute the ultimate liturgical spatial order. Instead this order collapses with the advent of the new heaven and new earth, within which only a holy of holies is conceived as the new sacred space.[78] As a result, the whole of the holy city now stands for the holy of holies,[79] and all the symbols and signposts of the previous order are overtaken and now point to the new reality. In this reality the tent of God is found among human beings,[80] and the one who sits on the throne and the exalted Jesus are both a temple and light for the city,[81] where God's people serve them (liturgically speaking).[82] Finally, the holy of holies becomes the locus from whence healing flows to the nations.[83] The diagram below illustrates this argument:[84]

---

77. Rev 11:8; 16:19; 17:18; 18:10, 16, 18, 19, 21; cf. 11:2.
78. Rev 21:1–2, 10.
79. Rev 21:16; cf. 1 Kgs 6:19–20.
80. Rev 21:3; cf. Beale, *Temple and the Churc's Mission*, 25.
81. Rev 21:22–23.
82. Rev 22:3. It should be said that the Apocalypse joins other New Testament documents that redefined what God's tent or temple means. Strikingly, the Letter to the Hebrews shows a remarkable closeness to the Apocalypse's perspective on this issue, since it also argues for a tent (σκηνή) set up by the Lord, where an authorized high-priest (ἀρχιερεύς), i.e. "one who sits at the right of the throne of the Majesty in the heavens" (Heb 8:1; cf. Ps 110:1, 4), is a minister (λειτουργός) there (Heb 8:1–2). This exalted high priest is identified in the letter as "Jesus the Son of God," who has passed through the heavens (Heb 4:14; cf. 3:1; 6:20; cf. Rev 2:18). When describing the (Old Testament) tent with its two main spaces, the Holy Place and the holy of holies (Heb 9:2–5), which it regards as a symbol for the present time (Heb 9:9), it refers to the greater and perfect non hand-made tent (σκηνή), which the Messiah (Χριστός), having appeared as high-priest, through his own blood (αἷμα) entered into the holy of holies, once for all, obtaining eternal redemption (Heb 9:11–12; cf. Rev 5:9–10; 1:5). Again, in the gospels Jesus envisioned a new kind of temple (John 2:19, 21; cf. Matt 26:61; 27:40; Mark 14:58; 15:29); whereas Paul regards the church as God's temple (1 Cor 3:16–17; 2 Cor 6:16; Eph 2:13–22).
83. Rev 22:2. Alternative understandings of a liturgical redefinition of space conveyed by the Apocalypse have been developed by Barbara Snyder, whose view is summarized in Beale, *Book of Revelation*, 141–144; and Gregory Beale in Beale, *Temple and the Church's Mission*, 313–331. In addition, Annette Weissenrieder, in her analysis of Paul's imagery relating to God's temple in 1 Corinthians, notes that numismatic evidence there may be seen as "an equivalence between physical and sacred space in the ancient world [that] can be understood so to speak as two sides of the same coin." Weissenrieder, "Contested Spaces," 400.
84. A standard graphical representation of the tabernacle's configuration of sacred spaces includes, from east to west, (i) the courtyard, (ii) the holy place, and (iii) the holy of holies. This is represented in many academic sources (e.g. Wenham, *Exploring the Old Testament*, 75) and even reproduced pictorially in more general sources (e.g. *The Accordance Bible Lands PhotoGuide 3*, paragraphs 2029–2044); and we are just adapting that standard configuration in order to convey our understanding of the Apocalypse's liturgical spaces.

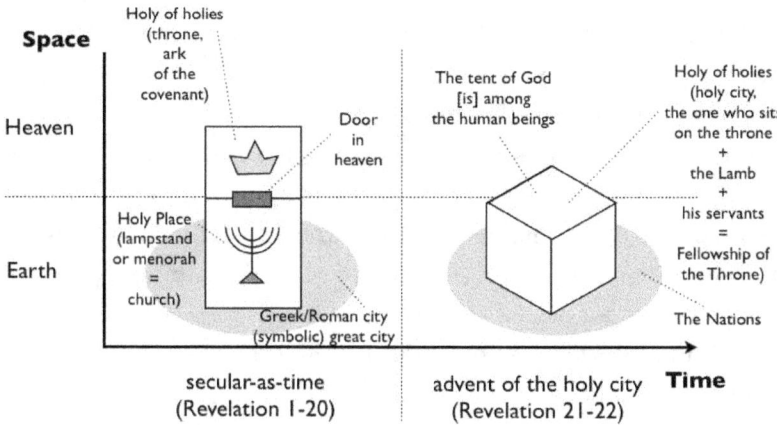

Figure 2. Liturgical Spaces

6.2.1 Mediated Presence

Once the Apocalypse's construal of the liturgical sacred space has been established, it makes exegetical sense to address the question of the presence of the exalted Jesus, since he features prominently in the very first vision and throughout the narrative as indispensable to the dynamics of the space. Let us start our discussion with the first and last messages to the (angels of the) churches of Ephesus and Laodicea respectively. To begin with, the first message to the (angel of the) church in Ephesus (Rev 2:1–7) carries a warning that its (golden) lampstand may be removed from its place "if you do not repent" (2:5). The realization of this warning would bring down to six the number of golden lampstands in the original vision, undermining the fullness or wholeness attached to the number/symbol "seven" in the narrative,[85] also disrupting the balance between the seven angels in the hand of the exalted Jesus and the corresponding seven churches in whose midst he walks. More importantly, if this warning is read in ontological terms, the coming of the

---

85. e.g. seven churches (Rev 1:4, 11, 20); seven spirits (1:4; 3.1; 4:5; 5:6); seven golden lampstands (1:12, 20; 2:1); seven stars (1:16, 20; 2:1; 3:1); seven torches of fire (4:5); seven seals (5:1, 5; 6:1); seven horns (5:6); seven eyes (5:6); seven angels (8:2, 6; 15:1, 6, 7, 8; 16:1); cf. 17:1; 21:9); seven trumpets (8:2, 6); seven thunders (10:3, 4); seven heads (12:3; 13:1; 17:3, 7, 9); seven diadems (12:3); seven plagues (15:1, 6, 8; 21:9); seven bowls (15:7; 16:1; 17:1; 21:9); seven mountains (17:9).

exalted Jesus to this church to remove its lampstand would mean (ironically) that (i) no church would be left in Ephesus (lampstand = church)[86] or, interchangeably, that (ii) his presence would no longer be available in that church (also a possibility faced by the church in Laodicea).

For its part, the final message to the (angel of the) church in Laodicea (3:14–22) poses a challenge and offers a reward linked to the idea of the presence of this exalted figure. Here, however, the exalted Jesus has taken on the symbolic image of an outsider – a foreigner or stranger, perhaps[87] – knocking at the door of a (church?) house possibly,[88] waiting to see if those who dwell in it are willing to open the door and entertain him with a meal, which would signify the beginning of a fellowship between them (3:20).[89] As O'Donovan puts it, "the sharing of food may constitute a shared meal, a sign of fellowship; as a sign of fellowship, the meal may be an affirmation of common understanding or purpose; as an affirmation of purpose, it may be a pledge of loyalty, and so on."[90] Clearly John's interlocutor has become too distant to this church, or has been alienated by it, so much so that the current state of affairs is portrayed in these terms.[91]

In between these initial and final messages to the churches we find the idea of the ruling presence of the exalted Jesus to be a recurrent one, featuring in the messages to each church (excepting the one for Smyrna). Accordingly, some in Pergamum might experience Jesus's presence negatively through judgment and death (2:16; cf. 19:15, 21); for their part, those in Thyatira are encouraged to keep going until the presence of Jesus is no more a future event (2:25); in Sardis the church is called upon to repent and return to what it

---

86. cf. Aune, *Revelation 1–5*, 147.

87. cf. Aune, 261.

88. It should be said that the New Testament offers evidence that in the early days, houses were the venues where churches met, (e.g. Rom 16:5; 1 Cor 16:19; Phlm 2). What is more, presumably early in Laodicea there was a woman Nympha whose house was the meeting place of a church there (Col 4:15). "There is neither literary evidence nor archeological indication that any house church was converted into an extant church building." Snyder, *Ante Pacem*, 128.

89. The gospel story of Jesus and Zacchaeus, as narrated in Luke 19:1–10, is the closest we could get to illustrate the point of a guest coming to a house, with a meal signalling a new sort of relationship between host and guest. See in particular Luke 19:5–9; cf. 17:8; 22:20; 1 Cor 11:25.

90. O'Donovan, *Ways of Judgment*, 250.

91. cf. Jer 7:3, where YHWH asked to the people of Judah to mend their ways so that both YHWH and the people of Judah could live together in the temple (i.e. YHWH's house), and presumably in the whole land (of Judah). The whole text of Jeremiah 7:1–7 contributes to the appreciation of this point.

was taught lest they experience Jesus's presence unexpectedly and negatively with the possible outcome of losing their membership as God's people (3:3, 5); and finally, the church in Philadelphia is also encouraged to persist until the presence of Jesus is actualised (3:11).

What we have found is that the presence of the exalted Jesus, pictured initially walking amidst the golden lampstands, is conveyed within a spectrum which goes from realized presence, as he stands knocking at the door, to imminent conditioned presence in either (i) a negative mode by bringing judgment on a church that fails to repent,[92] or in (ii) a positive mode, as an encouragement for other churches. In addition, we would also highlight the paradox of the presence of Jesus in connection with the church of Ephesus, which though arguably the most orthodox, is nonetheless in danger of losing its lampstand. Whereas the church of Laodicea, in spite of having alienated the exalted Jesus, is at the point of being able to (re)establish intimacy with him. In our view, the construal of the liturgical space discussed above provides a hermeneutical framework with which to interpret the presence of the exalted Jesus in the midst of his church, during the secular-as-time, as the recurrent interplay of sacred spaces exemplified in John's own experience at Patmos with the pneumatological proviso of "in the Spirit" (1:10).[93] From this configuration of the liturgical space as sacred space inhabited by the priestly presence of the exalted Jesus we turn to another mode of liturgical space as conveyed by the holy city.

6.3 Holy City

"The city, that pregnant symbol of all political life,"[94] has featured as a multivalent symbol across the narrative of the book of Revelation thus far, and we have recurrently referred to it in our work (e.g. §1.2, §3.6, §3.7). At present, however, we are interested in the ecclesiological overtones of this political

---

92. "In four of the letters there is a conditional threat that, if there is not repentance or watchfulness, Christ will come in judgment; and this seems strangely out of keeping with a belief in an imminent Parousia." Caird, *Revelation of St. John*, 27.

93. cf. Matt 18:20; 28:18, 20, where the motif of the presence of Jesus in the midst of or along his disciples features, even after his exaltation, on which see Wright, *Jesus and the Victory*, 297; Wright, *Resurrection*, 642–645.

94. O'Donovan, "History and Politics," 34.

symbol as it is theologically construed as the "holy city." In particular, we will focus on its stage as city-in-the-making, which brings out a christological feature of its design (i.e. its boundary markers).

6.3.1 Landscapes

Overall, the theological construal of the city is greatly determined by its landscape, that is the narrative context of any particular vision which informs the meaning of this urban symbol. A survey of the motif of the city across the Apocalypse's narrative allows us to suggest four different landscapes that may help us understand the theological construal of the city.

A historical landscape, since John the seer is asked to write to seven churches, each one located in a corresponding first-century Greek city under Roman rule.[95] This is a very materialist and immanent construal of the city which highlights its physicality as opposed to any metaphysical portrayal of it. The historical city holds or contains an expression of the liturgical sociality (i.e. the church [ἐκκλησία]), and in that sense it offers a (real) space for its nourishment and development, and for the advancement of its mission or the consummation of its teleology. At the same time, however, the historical city is, potentially, the source of adversity for the liturgical sociality, a space for compromise, and a threat to orthodoxy.[96]

An agonistic landscape, which becomes evident as each of the seven seals of the scroll is opened by the Lamb (§3.3). In the midst of the confrontation between the (political and military) earthly elite on the one hand, and the one who sits on the throne, together with the Lamb and his army on the other, the theological character of the city as it is being re-built by the Lamb gradually emerges,[97] on which we will elaborate below. In this landscape the (holy) city has metamorphosed into a sheltering space, a home for the refugee, a place of healing, despite the surrounding conflict. However, it also appears to have lost any space-time particularized referents, as opposed to the historical city, and instead anticipates the Fellowship of the Throne (§3.7).

---

95. Rev 1:11; 2:1, 8, 12, 18; 3:1, 7, 14; cf. 1:4. On the seven cities see Hemer, *Letters to the Seven Churches*; Jones, *Cities of the Eastern Roman*.

96. e.g. Rev 2:14, 20; cf. 17:2; 18:3, 9.

97. Rev 7:9–17.

It is perhaps not surprising that within this agonistic landscape another city, antagonistic to the first one, is also construed. It is the "great city" (§3.4),[98] the setting for the clash between the two witnesses and the beast, where the two witnesses are martyred,[99] and which is symbolically and simultaneously called Sodom and Egypt. And though it is also identified as the setting where the Lord of the two witnesses was crucified, yet it is where the two witnesses are infused with the divine breath of life and taken to heaven in an exalted manner. Thus, "the political institution [i.e. the great city] which appears as the embodiment of opposition to the truth may, below the level of appearances, be something else: it may be the holy city given over to desecration . . . We are at least permitted to anticipate that the politics of conquest may be countered by an alternative politics of worship."[100]

A forensic landscape, as the city is suddenly and unexpectedly annihilated by God's judgment (§3.6).[101] Up to this point, the city itself is construed variously as a high-class prostitute, a politically well-connected socialite who epitomises hostility towards God and his people;[102] and also as an oppressive imperial city,[103] with its suggestive code name Babylon,[104] the former city-empire, or through allusive geographical details linking it with Rome, the Apocalypse's contemporary city-empire.[105] The totalizing nature of this city, aptly described by its more general name "the great city,"[106] makes it the default locus of (political) power, commerce, and culture.[107] And yet, this construal of the city also renders it as the anti-city where God's people are concerned, since the blood of many of them has been shed in it,[108] and the survivors are told to depart from it for their own safety.[109]

---

98. Rev 11:8; cf. 16:19; 17:18; 18:10, 16, 18, 19, 21.
99. Rev 11:1–13.
100. O'Donovan, "History and Politcs," 34; cf. Aune, *Revelation 6–16*, 619.
101. Rev 18:21; cf. 18:10, 16, 18, 19.
102. Rev 17, in particular 17:18.
103. Rev 18.
104. Rev 18:10, 21; cf. 16:19.
105. cf. Rev 17:9; *Sibylline Oracles* 2.18 (OTP/1).
106. Rev 17:18; 18:10, 16, 18, 19, 21; cf. 11:8; 16:19.
107. cf. Ovid, *Fasti* 4.857–859; see also Bauckham, *Climax of the Prophecy*, 338–383.
108. Rev 18:24; cf. 17:6; 19:2.
109. Rev 18:4.

An artistic landscape (§3.7), as a new heaven and a new earth are created by the one who sits on the throne, and a new city is seen coming down out of heaven from God.[110] Within this newly created and creative landscape the city is construed as bridging the gap between the physical and metaphysical, the setting where the immanent and the transcendent meet harmoniously in the same ontological space. The new city becomes a haven for God's people, with no vestige of evil, in particular death, found within it.[111] Symmetrical dimensions and luxurious building materials highlight the divine origin of the city, though a memorial wall does feature some human contribution. Overall, the city is construed as a gift from God. However, some of these features also point to the utterly liturgical nature of the city (i.e. its shape as that of a new holy of holies of unprecedented dimensions). Also, the city is briefly construed as an engaged woman on the verge of entering into a covenantal marriage with the Lamb;[112] or as a benevolent imperial city, the new locus of power and worship to which kings, peoples and nations bring their glory.[113] The new city shares, or better put, reflects its God-given light to the nations,[114] and becomes a source of healing for them.[115] It is also the setting for a permanent *koinonia* of the the one who sits on the throne, the Lamb and his servants, that is to say, it is the setting for the Fellowship of the Throne. In short, the new holy city becomes the antithesis of the great city, and enables eschatological consummation.

It should be said that Old Testament literature provides a rich theological background for the apocalyptic construals of the city as envisioned by John the seer. From the first city (עִיר) built by Cain,[116] through the mythical Babel (בָּבֶל),[117] the iconic royal city of David,[118] bureaucratic Jerusalem (יְרוּשָׁלַםִ)[119]

---

110. Rev 21:1–22:5; cf. Heb 11:10, 16; 12:22; 13:14.
111. Rev 21:4.
112. Rev 21:2, 9; cf. 19:7; 22:17.
113. Rev 21:24, 26. Equally, we have regarded this city/holy of holies as a place of pilgrimage where again the kings of the earth and the nations bring their glory.
114. Rev 21:24.
115. Rev 22:3–4.
116. Gen 4:17; cf. O'Donovan, "Loss of Sense of Place," 312. For an alternative reading of Gen 4:17 see Wenham, *Genesis 1–15*, 111.
117. Gen 11:9; cf. 11:4–5, 8.
118. 2 Sam 5:7, 9.
119. 1 Kgs 3:1, 15; 8:1; 11:13.

and the imperial Babylon (בָּבֶל),[120] all the way to the eschatological Zion (צִיּוֹן),[121] these previous construals of the city somehow contemplate the contingent nature and unfinished status of its immanent, materialist, particularized teleology. In fact, to some extent, the Jerusalem of the Old Testament foreshadows the whole apocalyptic trajectory of the construal of the city as envisioned by John. That is, its founding as royal locus of God's people; its bureaucratic institutionalization; its social oppression, elitist excesses, and theological deviations; its spatial annihilation by a foreign power as a result of divine judgment; its rebuilding unfinished; and its eschatological hope of urbanized consummation.[122] In short, this trajectory may be summed up with three Ezekielian statements: Jerusalem was set in the midst/centre of the nations by YHWH,[123] was sent into exile among the nations,[124] and would arguably return to dwell in the midst/centre of the nations.[125]

6.3.2 Re-building the City

From the previous survey of the city motif and its assumed identity within each narrative landscape, we would like to focus on the theological construal of the city as being rebuilt (Rev 7:9–17), portrayed this way within the agonistic landscape. Our interest lies mainly in the christological purchase of the construal, which allows us to consider some additional aspects concerning our idea of the liturgical sociality. At this point, however, it is worth highlighting some (textual/thematic) similarities between Revelation 7:9–17, on the one hand, and 21:3–7 and 22:3–6 on the other, especially since the last two texts are unambiguously framed within the advent and materialization

---

120. e.g. 2 Kgs 24:1, 7, 10–12, 15–17, 20; 25:1, 6–8, 11.
121. e.g. Isa 51:3; 52:1, 7; Zech 2:14 (2:10 ET); 8:3.
122. See collection of essays in Hess, and Wenham, *Zion*; cf. Ollenburger, *Zion*.
123. Ezek 5:5; cf. Walton, *Ancient Near East Thought*, 174.
124. cf. Ezek 5:12.
125. Ezek 38:12. To turn to other theo-political traditions, without ignoring the influential Greek (§5.1) and Roman (§5.2) traditions on the *polis* and *civitas*, respectively, it is worth noticing that post-apostolic Christian tradition embraced and further developed the theological construal of the city. In particular, Augustine's interplay between the "City of God" and the "Earthly City" as recorded in his magisterial *The City of God against the Pagans*, is a case in point; cf. Augustine, *City of God* 14.28. It should be noted that Augustine's theological constructs of these two cities owes more to the Old Testament, in particular, Jeremiah 29, as conveyed in *City of God* 19.26, a point Luke Bretherton expands and updates within the Christian ethos underlying Augustine's mammoth work, see Bretherton, *Christianity and Contemporary Politics*, 3–6; cf. O'Donovan, "Political Thought."

of the holy city (21:2, 10, 14, 15, 16, 18, 19, 21, 23). Thus, we may notice (i) that God will dwell (σκηνόω) among "his people" (7:15; 21:3); (ii) that he will wipe away every tear from their eyes (7:17; 21:4); (iii) that the Lamb will guide the numberless great crowd to springs of water (7:17), while God will give freely to the thirsty from the springs of the water of life (21:6); (iv) that the numberless great crowd will liturgically serve (λατρεύω) day and night in God's temple (7:15), whereas the Lamb's servants will liturgically serve (λατρεύω) the Lamb, and through him we may presume the one who sits on the throne (22:3), (v) the ubiquitous presence of the throne (7:9, 10, 11, 15, 17; 21:3, 5; 22:1, 3), along with the one who sits on it (7:10, 15; 21:5) or God (7:10, 11, 12, 15, 17; 21:2, 3, 7, 10, 11, 22, 23; 22:1, 3, 5, 6), and the Lamb (7:9, 10, 14, 17; 21:9, 14, 22, 23, 27; 22:1, 3).

In addition, though scholars may generally agree that, because of its echoes of Isaiah 49:10 and 25:8, Revelation 7:9–17 as a whole alludes to the Old Testament motif of Israel's restoration from exile,[126] we would like to suggest that it is in fact the more nuanced Old Testament motif of the re-building of YHWH's city that we see here.[127] This expectation, which assimilates the idea of restoration from exile, would, when fulfilled, make it possible for YHWH to once more dwell among his people.[128] Our suggestion is reinforced when the similarities between this vision and that of the advent of the holy city, are factored in together with the fact that in the vision of the advent of the holy city, the city as such is finished, complete, whereas in the vision in 7:9–17 it is under construction, still in the making, so to speak. We would also note, however, that the motif of the re-building of Zion/Jerusalem/the holy city with the result that YHWH would once more dwell (שכן) in its midst, can be seen as a reworking of an older motif, that of YHWH dwelling or living (שכן) in the midst of his people after their exodus from Egypt (§6.2).[129] The motif seen here, however, was developed during the exile with the expectation

---

126. e.g. Fekkes, *Isaiah and Prophetic Traditions*, 172; Beale, *Book of Revelation*, 424.

127. The motif of the rebuilding of the city is highlighted by John Watts as he comments on Isaiah 49:5-12, see Watts, *Isaiah 34-66*, 730-739.

128. For an instance of the deployment of a variant of this motif (i.e. the return of YHWH to dwell among his people as they come back from exile) in reading of the gospels, see Wright, *Jesus and the Victory*, 615-624, who even provides references to other Jewish sources in addition to Old Testament prophetic literature, mainly from Isaiah.

129. E.g. Exod 29:46; 40:35; Num 35:34; Deut 12:5.

that YHWH's city would be re-built (בנה),[130] and therefore, YHWH would return to Zion,[131] along with those ransomed by him[132] to dwell/live (שׁכן) in Jerusalem.[133] YHWH's city,[134] that is to say, Jerusalem,[135] is rebuilt as he gathers those in exile.[136] Interestingly enough, Zion (צִיּוֹן), Jerusalem (יְרוּשָׁלַם), and the compound term holy (קֹדֶשׁ) city (עִיר) are all linked and seem to point to the same entity.[137]

What is more, Isaiah 49:10 is part of the wider vision regarding the mission of YHWH's servant to return Jacob to him, to gather or assemble Israel to him,[138] to return the preserved of Israel.[139] Isaiah 49:10 also envisions a time when they would be neither hungry nor thirsty,[140] nor would they be smitten by burning heat/parched ground or by the sun.[141] In addition, the one who has compassion on them would drive or lead them; he would lead them to springs of water.[142] When this prophecy is compared to John of Patmos' vision (7:16–17; cf. 21:6), the degree of similarity is remarkable; in fact, David Aune regards 7:16 as "the longest allusion to an OT passage found in Revelation."[143] Furthermore, Isaiah 25:8 picks up some of these expectations as part of a poem of praise to YHWH following the destruction of a city into a heap of stones,[144] presumably referring to Moab.[145] These words of praise draw attention to a "covering" that will be destroyed or swallowed up by YHWH,

---

130. Isa 45:13.
131. Zech 8:3.
132. Isa 35:10; 51:11.
133. Zech 1:16; 8:3.
134. Isa 45:13; cf. Ps 102:17 (102:16 ET).
135. Isa 44:28.
136. Ps 147:2.
137. Isa 52:1; cf. Watts, *Isaiah 1–33*, 8–13.
138. Isa 49:5.
139. Isa 49:6.
140. cf. Rev 7:16. Being hungry (רעב) and thirsty (צמא), among other "curses," would be the consequences of neglecting the covenant with YHWH (Deut 28:48), or the state of those nations that wage war against Zion (Isa 29:8).
141. cf. Rev 7:16.
142. cf. Rev 7:17; 21:6.
143. Aune, *Revelation 6–16*, 477.
144. Isa 25:2. Broadly speaking, this is a fate shared by the "great city" of the Apocalypse (cf. Rev 16:19; 18:19, 21).
145. Isa 25:10–12.

the covering on all the people,[146] which signifies death,[147] and which will be destroyed perpetually.[148] As well as bringing about the destruction of death, YHWH also wipes away tears from all faces.[149] As the praise continues, however, it becomes apparent that the destruction of death and the wiping away of tears is seen as more immediately actualized with the deliverance from Moab, which takes place on the same mount as the destruction of death.[150]

Overall, these allusions to Old Testament expectations about the re-building of a city to which God's people return from other (usually hostile) lands, as in the exile, and in the midst of which YHWH returns to dwell bringing about healing for his people, make up the dominant story in this apocalyptic vision (i.e. Rev 7:9–17). And yet, the christological reshaping of those expectations is evident, as it is the Lamb who shepherds the people, rather than God or any other messianic and royal figure from the past. Ascribing this divine/messianic prerogative to the Lamb is a feature consistent with other portrayals of the exalted Jesus in the Apocalypse, where he is also said to shepherd (i.e. rule) the nations,[151] whether as Son of God (§4.1.2),[152] Messiah (§4.3.2),[153] or divine King (§4.4.1).[154] More importantly, it is the Lamb that sets the boundaries regarding those who become part of this city-in-the-making, a point we will explore next.[155]

6.3.3 Theological Boundaries

Every theological construal of the city raises the question, either tacitly or explicitly, of who belongs to the city, or alternatively, who is excluded from it. More importantly, perhaps, the issue must be addressed of who decides

---

146. Isa 25:7. Death (מָוֶת) has a long pedigree in the biblical narrative that goes back to the garden of Eden (Gen 2:17; 3:3, 4), and its "covering" effects were felt by Adam himself (Gen 5:5).

147. Isa 25:8.

148. Isa 25:8; cf. Rev 21:4; Watts, *Isaiah 1–33*, 391–392.

149. Isa 25:8; cf. Rev 7:17; 21:4.

150. Isa 25:7, 9, 10; cf. Watts, *Isaiah 1–33*, 393–395. In Jer 31:16, no more tears from eyes is a signal that YHWH's people are returned from enemy's land, presumably an end to the exile (cf. Jer 28:4), to celebrate a new covenant with YHWH (Jer 31:31).

151. Ps 2:8–9 LXX.

152. Rev 2:27.

153. Rev 12:5.

154. Rev 19:15.

155. At times it appears that it is "people" that is meant by the term city, e.g. Isa 48:2; 60:14; 62:12.

and/or what criteria applies to distinguish between those two groups. In the Apocalypse it becomes evident that the exalted Jesus plays a pivotal role in defining who is in and who is out, so to speak. In the vision where the city is construed as being rebuilt within an agonistic landscape, as seen above, three features which we would highlight in relation to this issue are (i) the impossibility of putting a number on the quantity of people who make up the countless great crowd,[156] (ii) the heterogeneous mix and international origin of the people,[157] and more importantly, (iii) the blood of the Lamb as the defining common denominator for those present,[158] as a passport to this city-in-the-making. In fact, in this scenario, the Christian community,[159] which we have so far referred to as the liturgical sociality, stands for the already-and-not-yet transcendent city, the city-in-the-making, the city as being rebuilt.[160]

However, this view of the city – where its boundaries in relation to membership remain quantitatively imprecise and at the same time soteriologically fixed by the blood of the Lamb[161] – gives way to a theological correlation where on the one hand, membership in the Christian community/liturgical sociality is a divine gift[162] (i.e. a salvation or deliverance [σωτηρία]) worked out both by God and the Lamb,[163] who in this vision are located in the midst of the heavenly throne;[164] and on the other hand, the cosmopolitan people must have appropriated that gift, or as the oxymoronic analogy puts it, must

---

156. Rev 7:9; cf. 19:1, 6.

157. Rev 7:9; cf. 5:9; 11:9; 13:7; 14:6.

158. Rev 7:14; cf. 1:5; 5:9; 12:11. In the rest of the New Testament we encounter "the blood of Jesus" (Heb 10:19; 1 John 1:7), "the blood of the Messiah/Christ" (1 Cor 10:16; Eph 2:13; Heb 9:14), "the blood of Jesus the Messiah/Christ" (1 Pet 1:2; 1 John 5:6), and "the blood of the Lord" (1 Cor 11:27).

159. "The group must be identified as Christians" Aune, *Revelation 6–16*, 445.

160. For a survey of alternative views see Aune, *Revelation 6–16*, 445–447; equally see Beale, *Book of Revelation*, 432–439; Rowland, "Book of Revelation," 624–625.

161. It should be noted that there is an Old Testament precedent in equating a people with a city. In the prophetic tradition at least, there was the expectation that after the traumatic experience of the exile, the people of Israel would be called the "City [עִיר] of YHWH," i.e. "Zion [צִיּוֹן] (of) the Holy (One) of Israel." (Isa 60:14). Or implicitly, the holy people (of Israel) are equated to a city not forsaken (Isa 62:12).

162. A comprehensive view of gift as a theological category is explained by John Milbank in, *Being Reconciled*, ix.

163. Rev 7:10; cf. 12:10; 19:1.

164. Rev 7:17.

have whitened their robes in the blood of the Lamb.[165] Interestingly enough, in the vision of the advent of the holy city, which gives way to the Fellowship of the Throne, the question of "boundaries" is also raised, not least because it is a walled city.[166] Within that vision, there are those whose place is in "the lake of fire and sulphur,"[167] they are those whose names were not found written in the book of life when facing the judgment of the great white throne and the one who sits on it.[168] Or phrased positively, only those whose names were written in the book of life of the Lamb are able to enter into the city,[169] since in this new city there is no place for anything under (divine) curse.[170] Some further detail is given in a list of "profiles" of those who have no place in the new city,[171] as opposed to the overarching description of "the one who conquers" and therefore enters the city[172] – though, it should be said, the latter's profile was elaborated in the first apocalyptic vision.[173] Overall, the various profiles of those left out of the new holy city relate to issues already addressed in other parts of the narrative, but are mentioned here in order to further contrast between the two groups of people on either side of the city's boundaries.[174]

And yet, in what would appear a complication of this city's boundaries, or alternatively a cause for hope, the kings of the earth are said to bring their

---

165. Rev 7:14; cf. Rowland, "Book of Revelation," 624.
166. Rev 21:12, 14, 15, 17, 18, 19.
167. Rev 21:8.
168. Rev 20:11–15.
169. Rev 21:27.
170. Rev 22:3.
171. Rev 21:8, 27; 22:14–15; cf. 14:9–11.
172. Rev 21:7.
173. Rev 2:7, 11, 17, 26; 3:5, 12, 21; cf. 12:11; 15:2.
174. Thus, everyone is called to conquer (Rev 2:7, 11, 17, 26; 3:5, 12, 21; 12:11; 15:2), to be faithful to the point of death (2:10), to not deny the faith of the exalted Jesus (2:13). Then, the prophetess nicknamed Jezebel and the party of the Nicolaitans are rebuked because of their theological and liturgical compromise (2:14, 20). The pseudo-apostles (2:2; cf. 18:20; 21:14) and pseudo-Jews (2:9; 3:9) are spotted as instances of falsehood within and outside the Christian community. And though the holy ones claimed for vengeance (6:10; cf. 19:2), they lay their claim at God's altar (6:9; cf. 8:3, 5; 11:1; 16:7). They are the victims not the murderers (2:13; 6:9–10; 11:7; 13:15; 16:6; 17:6; 18:24; 19:2). They rely on God and the Lamb (13:10; 14:12), therefore, they refuse to be seduced by the beast that relies on other than God to impress the wider world (13:3, 13–15; 17:8).

glory (δόξα) into the new holy city,[175] having for the most part of the narrative of Revelation remained stubbornly and politically resisting both God and the Lamb in alliance with the great city and with the beast.[176] This U-turn raises the question of when the kings of the earth realigned themselves with the reality of the exalted Jesus, given that he is described as the ruler/leader of the kings of the earth.[177] The key factor in this mystifying change in the relationship between the kings of the earth and the new holy city lies in their action of bringing glory (δόξα) and honour (τιμή) into the holy city.[178] The significance of this gesture is clear because of the benefit of it as a source for the healing of the nations.[179] It is in fact this genuine liturgical act addressed to the one who sits on the throne and the Lamb that becomes a complementary guarantee of access into the new holy city. In other words, to give or ascribe *doxa* to God and the exalted Jesus is what is required to attain citizenship, thus confirming the liturgical link between authority and society.[180]

---

175. Rev 21:24.
176. Rev 6:15; 17:2, 18; 18:3, 9; 19:19.
177. Rev 1:5.
178. Rev 21:26.
179. Rev 22:2.
180. This is a motif that runs across the narrative of the book of Revelation as follows: (1) in the concentric heavenly throne setting, (a) the four composite beings give glory to the Lord God (i.e. the one who sits on the throne, or the one who lives for the ages of ages), for who he is (ontotheology, Rev 4:8–9), whereas (b) the twenty-four elders ascribe glory to the Lord God for what he had made (creation, 4;10–11), then (c) the countless myriad of angels ascribed glory to the Lamb, the one who has been slaughtered (soteriology, 5:11–12), and finally everything that is created ascribed glory to the one who sits on the throne and to the Lamb (5:13), a doxology endorsed by the four composite beings and enacted by the (twenty-four) elders (5:14). (2) In the vision we have called city-in-the-making, where all the angels surround the heavenly throne, the (twenty-four) elders and the four composite beings, they (i.e. the angels) ascribe glory to their God (7:11–12). Incidentally, the Lamb is in the midst of the throne (7:17; cf. 7:9–10). (3) At the end of the vision of the two witnesses, once their testimony was finished in the great city and were killed by the abyss-beast, God's breath of life came into them and they ascended into heaven as their enemies looked at them (i.e. those who dwell on earth) (11:3–12). Then a great earthquake followed suit, and those who survived it gave glory to the God of heaven (11:13). (4) The eternal gospel to proclaim to those who dwell on earth is summed up as "fear God and give him glory," since he is the Creator and the time for his judgment has come (14:6–7). (5) Yet, presumably those human beings who have the mark of the beast and worshipped its image, did not change their mind in order to give glory to God, rather they blaspheme his name (16:9; cf. 16.2). (6) Once the great city was annihilated as a result of God's judgment, a heavenly multitude ascribed glory to God (19:1). (7) Another undefined multitude give glory to the Lord God because the Lamb's marriage has taken place and his wife is ready (19:7). (8) In the final vision, the holy city has God's glory (21:11), in fact, God's glory gives light to the city, which makes redundant any natural or human-made source of light; besides, the Lamb is the lamp of this city (21:23). Precisely in this new holy city, the

6.4 Liturgical Space as Theo-Political Category

So far, we have traced back two strands that contribute to our understanding of liturgical space (i.e. the sacred space and the holy city), and we have shown how the confluence of both strands with each other in the final vision of the Apocalypse climaxes in the materialization of the Fellowship of the Throne (§1.2). Our exegetical inquiry has equally shown how the Apocalypse, through its many and various allusions to the Old Testament, recovers and further elaborates, with a clear christological orientation, the basic Israelite theologoumenon about sacred and liturgical space, adumbrated in the garden of Eden but materialized in the mobile tent of meeting and the institutionalized royal temple (i.e. YHWH's desire to dwell in the midst of his people and to have fellowship with them).[181] The traumatic experience of the exile raised the expectations of the re-building of a city where YHWH would return to dwell once more in the midst of his people. But it is the apocalyptic transformation of a holy city into a totalized holy of holies in order that it may give way to the materialization of the Fellowship of the Throne that provides the distinctive spatial ecclesiology conveyed by the Apocalypse. Here this sacred space is envisioned as the organic union of the churches addressed by the exalted Jesus, who inhabits this space, sustains the churches and seeks fellowship with them. Alternatively, the city-in-the-making is composed of a countless international crowd of individuals holding to a christological soteriology, engaging in liturgical enactment and enjoying the shepherding of the exalted Jesus. Then with the advent of the holy city, the liturgical sociality joins in the Fellowship of the Throne through the mediation of the exalted Jesus.

This apocalyptic construal of society as a liturgical space with a markedly christological orientation poses a theo-political challenge to and critiques other ancient models, pagan in nature, which articulated a view of society and their correlation to some other mode of authority. We will explore some of

---

kings of the earth bring their glory (21:24), presumably to God and the Lamb, as do nations (21:26). To be sure, John ascribes glory to Jesus the Messiah, as he introduces his narrative to his readers (1:6). One additional reference to God's glory in the narrative of Revelation takes place in 15:8, where the heavenly temple was filled by the cloud of God's glory as the seven angels prepare to pour out seven plagues from seven bowls. In view of the above, we may say that the ultimate human liturgical act is to give glory to God and the Lamb, and as a result of that, enter into *koinonia* or fellowship with them in the holy city.

181. On the thesis of the garden of Eden seen as an archetypal sanctuary see Wenham, "Sanctuary Symbolism," 19–25.

these in the next chapter. Before that, however, we would like to highlight how this theological construal of the liturgical challenges and critiques the alternative and heterodox mode of authority (the sea-beast), liturgical enactment (the earth-beast) and immanent sociality (the great city) also developed in the narrative of the Apocalypse, as noted in §3.6.[182] The great city, in particular, when personified as a high-class prostitute and a politically well-connected socialite (§6.3.1) discloses its totalizing nature as it exerts influence on or sustains a sociality described in terms almost identical to those deployed to refer to the countless crowd which we have termed "the city-in-the-making."[183] This city-woman "sits" on many waters,[184] which are "peoples and crowds and nations and languages,"[185] and "has a kingdom on the kings of the earth."[186] Here it is clear to see how a liturgical space with a christological orientation (i.e. the apocalyptic spatial ecclesiology) is in opposition to an alternative social space with an immanent and heterodox orientation.[187]

In the same way, when seen in the light of the political and liturgical legacy of the Roman Augustan era (§1.2), the subversive and polemical nature of our

---

182. See also §3.8.
183. cf. Rev 7:9.
184. Rev 17:1.
185. Rev 17:15; cf. 18:3, 23.
186. Rev 17:18; cf. 17:2; 18:3, 9.
187. Our construal of the Apocalypse's spatial ecclesiology poses an alternative to Joseph Mangina's account of the church in the book of Revelation, which takes its lead from George Lindbeck's view of the church as "the messianic pilgrim people of God typologically shaped by Israel's story." As quoted in Mangina, "God, Israel, and Ecclesia," location 1984. So, for Mangina, the church is "Israel, but precisely the messianic Israel, her identity shaped by God's and the Lamb's victory." Mangina, location 2180+. Additionally, "Revelation opens with . . . the church as we know it, in the form of the seven churches of Asia, and concludes with . . . the glorious New Jerusalem, the bride of the Lamb. The book describes a transformation." Mangina, location 2200+. Accordingly, (i) "The churches of Asia are seven real assemblies, located in seven actual cities of Asia Minor" (Mangina, location 2051); then, (ii) despite the fact that the term "church" does not feature in Revelation 4:1 – 22:5, yet "John (or the Spirit) reserves *ekklēsia* for the audience of the work . . . The point of the visions is to show them what they must *become*." Mangina, location 2197+. So, whether as 144,000 or a white-robed army of martyrs (7:1–17), the "two witnesses" (11:1–13), or the 144,000 with the Lamb on Mount Zion (14:1–4), "the people of God occupy a position of penultimacy – before the seventh seal, before the seventh trumpet, before the seven bowls representing God's definitive judgment. . . . The place of the church is not in the last things but in the things-before-the-last." (Mangina, location 2211+). In addition, the book of Revelation "sees the church as a locus of power . . . and that the people of God are called to rule." (Mangina, location 2337+). However, Mangina observes the Apocalypse shows a limited concern with the relations within the church(es), which he refers to as "an 'ethic of communal solidarity.'" Mangina, location 2377.

construal of the liturgical space with its christological orientation becomes apparent. Augustus claimed in his *Res Gestae* that "he made the world subject to the rule of the Roman people";[188] Ovid would say, in his *Fasti*,[189] that

> A city arose destined to set its victorious foot upon the neck of
>   the whole earth;
> who at that time could have believed in such a prophecy?
> Rule the universe, O Rome, and mayest thou ever be subject to
>   great Caesar,
> and mayest thou often have several of that name,
> and whensoe'er thou standest sublime in a conquered world,
>   may all else reach not up to thy shoulders![190]

In other words, the totalizing nature of this imagined spatial order, equally confessional,[191] is also transparent and opposed to our construal as above.

Here we should note the early attempts by some church fathers to articulate an ecclesiology with an explicitly and markedly christological orientation incorporating some spatial overtones in their discourse.[192] For instance, though Ignatius's ecclesiology redefined the bishopric from a ministerial role to a sort of *sine qua non* for the ontology of the local church, nonetheless, he predicated the whole universal, (or global) church on the exalted Jesus: "Wherever the bishop appears, there let the congregation be; just as wherever

---

188. Augustus, *Res Gestae Divi Augusti* heading.

189. "Ovid's *Fasti* is, after the *Aeneid*, the longest extant poem to reflect a contemporary's view of the ideology of the Augustan regime. It is the only work to reveal a living witness's interpretation of the mature Augustus' own view of his place in Roman history, and of the mythology created in the late Augustan Principate." Herbert-Brown, *Ovid and the Fasti*, vii.

190. Ovid, *Fasti* 4.857–862. On the penultime line of this quotation ("whensoe'er thou standest sublime in a conquered world") Elaine Fatham notes that "Rome is seen standing on the globe set beneath her feet . . . towering head and shoulders over all." Fantham, *Ovid*, 254; cf. Rev 17:1, 15.

191. Precisely, C. Green has attempted, "based on a re-examination of Varro's *Rerum Divinarum*, to reconstruct the religious thought that lies behind Ovid's *Fasti*, a work which, despite the sensitive and complex readings of the most recent scholarship, nevertheless remains difficult, because its true subject, Roman religion, has not been adequately engaged as such . . . It is my contention that, even from the relatively few surviving fragments of the RD, we can derive at least part of a recognizable Roman theology – that is, a *ratio*, an accounting of the divine from a specifically Roman perspective – and that this theology underlies Ovid's elegiac poem on the calendar." Green, "Varro's Three Theologies," 71.

192. For overall accounts of incipient ecclesiologies after the first-century AD see, for instance, Kelly, *Early Christian Doctrines*, 189–220, 401–421; Osiek, "Self-Defining Praxis," 274–292; Hall, "Ecclesiology Forged," 470–483.

Jesus Christ is, there is the catholic church."[193] More influential has proved Augustine's construal of the city in his magnum opus the *City of God against the Pagans*, as already noted (§6.3.1), where he conveys his view of two modes of sociality that share the same ontological space yet are predicated on different theological grounds and pursue diverging teloi.[194] Accordingly,

> two cities, the Heavenly and the earthly . . . are mingled together from the beginning to the end. One of them, the earthly, has made for itself such false gods as it wished, from whatever source it chose – even creating them out of men – in order to serve them with sacrifices. But the other, the Heavenly, a pilgrim in this world, does not make false gods. Rather, that City is itself made by the true God, and is itself to be His true sacrifice. Both cities alike make use of the good things, or are afflicted with the evils, of this temporal state; but they do so with a different faith, a different hope, a different love, until they are separated by the final judgment, and each receives its own end, to which there is no end.[195]

It should be noted that for Augustine the city of God is christologically predicated, since it is made "by the redeemed family of the Lord Christ and by the pilgrim city of Christ the King."[196] In relation to this, O'Donovan points out that "there is no true *tertium quid* between the two cities, no neutral space on which they meet as equal partners."[197] In other words, it seems that for Augustine "true Christians were never true Romans (in the sense of being part of the Roman imperial project) nor false Christians true members of the church (in the sense of being part of a pilgrim society)."[198] What is more,

---

193. Ignatius, *To the Smyrnaeans* 8.2. For the original purview of a bishop within the (Ephesian) church, see Acts 20:28, for instance.

194. cf. Augustine, *City of God* 10.32; 11.1; 14.1, 4, 13, 28; 15.1, 5, 15, 20, 21, 22; 16.3; 18.1, 2, 54; 19.1, 26; 21.1.

195. Augustine, *City of God* 18.54.

196. Augustine, 1.35; cf. 14.13.

197. O'Donovan, "Politcal Thought," 59.

198. O'Donovan, 59. For his part, John Milbank argues for a kind of triad of cities in Augustine's *City of God*, that is to say, the City of God, and the City of this World, which is split into two further polities; see Milbank, *Beyond Secular Order*, 228–236.

"Rome [as a figure of the earthly city] is not the name of a 'state', but of a *civitas* or 'city', which is a concrete and morally determined body of citizens."[199]

Over time Augustine's model has been recovered and elaborated, more recently by John Milbank and William Cavanaugh, who engage in a critique of modern liberal politics and the construal of the nation state, respectively, specifically deploying "space" as a theo-political category for their analyses. With reference to Milbank, he acknowledges that theology "has frequently sought to borrow from elsewhere a fundamental account of society or history, and then to see what theological insights will cohere with it."[200] This he calls "the pathos of modern theology,"[201] the positioning of theology by secular reason, leading theology to suffer "two characteristic forms of confinement. Either it idolatrously connects knowledge of God with some particular immanent field of knowledge – 'ultimate' cosmological causes, or 'ultimate' psychological and subjective needs. Or else it is confined to intimations of a sublimity beyond representation, so functioning to confirm negatively the questionable idea of an autonomous secular realm, completely transparent to rational understanding."[202]

However, Milbank argues that "no such fundamental account, in the sense of something neutral, rational and universal, is really available."[203] Rather, it is "theology itself that will have to provide its own account of the final causes at work in human history, on the basis of its own particular, and historically specific faith."[204] For Milbank, this account is necessarily ecclesiological in nature, a metadiscourse,[205] a kind of Christian social theory that offers an explanation of the church's practice, "which arose in certain precise historical circumstances, and exists only as a particular historical development."[206] This account would therefore take a narrative form rather than a foundational approach based on presuppositions that buy into universal reason, for instance.[207]

---

199. O'Donovan, "Politcal Thought," 59; cf. Augustine, *City of God* 5.14; 15.5.
200. Milbank, *Theology and Social Theory*, 382.
201. Milbank, 1.
202. Milbank, 1.
203. Milbank, 382.
204. Milbank, 382.
205. cf. Milbank, 1.
206. Milbank, 382.
207. cf. Milbank, 384–391.

The Liturgical Sociality 215

More importantly, for Milbank this account would retrieve and elaborate Augustine's account as conveyed in his *City of God against the Pagans*. "A re-reading of the *Civitas Dei* will allow us to realize that political theology can take its critique, both of secular society and of the Church, directly out of the developing Biblical tradition, without recourse to any entirely alien implementation."[208] In this account the church "is emphatically not, on a theological conception, a kind of 'extra' religious organisation which some people happen to belong to; it is, rather, the *sine qua non* for the existence of human society as such, and so for the existence of humanity as such."[209]

When this Milbankian political theology engages in a critique of modernity, it also would appear to take a spatial turn. For instance, Milbank conceives two spatial construals to convey two forms of "competing totalitarianisms."[210] On the one hand, there is the "complex space hierarchized and recruited to the service of crude mythologies, whose quasi-religious yet essentially secular imaginings of untrammelled energy obliquely disclose that corporatist fantasy has not really obliterated the formal emptiness of the modern state and market."[211] On the other hand, "simple space articulated between the controlling centre and the controlled individuals, [is] an articulation whose supposedly 'social' character barely disguises the fact that this is *still* the simple space of liberal modernity."[212] For Milbank, a migration fuelled by the Enlightenment has taken place from complex space to simple space. Within the narrative of the Enlightment, the past was regarded "as a time of illusion and confusion dominated by the power of the imagination. Yet imagination is also seen as a surrogate for reason, even as the necessarily confused beginnings of reason, which is only fully exercised in the clarity of the present."[213]

However, argues Milbank, "after the decay of complex and exotic mythical hierarchies, that political reality is a 'simple space' suspended between the mass of atomic individuals on the one hand, and an absolutely sovereign centre on the other. Despite the merely contractual origins of the state, its actual functioning demands an organic, bodily coordination of the centre and

---

208. Milbank, 391.
209. Milbank, *Beyond Secular Order*, 240.
210. Milbank, *Word Made Strange*, 272.
211. Milbank, 272.
212. Milbank, 272.
213. Milbank, 275.

the individual components."²¹⁴ As a result, any "bodies intermediate between the state and the individual – guilds, religious associations, universities – tend to suffer reduced autonomy, or else total extirpation."²¹⁵ What Milbank suggests, then, is a return to a variant of a complex space, which he calls gothic. "The interest in 'complex bodies', wherein parts are in turn wholes, and not simply subordinate to the greater whole . . . by contrast exhibits a way in which mediaeval exemplars were thought to manifest a crucial aspect of freedom – the freedom of groups – that modernity tends to obliterate."²¹⁶ More importantly, this configuration of space where "the whole exceed the sum of the parts . . . [and] the parts escape the totalizing grasp of the whole"²¹⁷ alludes to a medieval "linguistic and symbolic reconstrual of space as Christ's body. The Church as a whole was not an enclosed, defensible terrain like the antique *polis*, but in its unity the heavenly city and Christ its head, infinitely surpassed the scope of the state, and the grasp of human reason."²¹⁸

That brings us on to William Cavanaugh's political theology, whose critique of the construal of the modern nation-state also relies on the category of liturgical space. For Cavanaugh, "Politics is a practice of imagination."²¹⁹ To illustrate this premise, Cavanaugh asks "how does a provincial farm boy become persuaded that he must travel as a soldier to another part of the world and kill people he knows nothing about?"²²⁰ Surely, "he must be convinced of the reality of borders and imagined himself deeply, mystically, united to a wider national community that stops abruptly at those borders."²²¹ Therefore, for him "the nation-state is . . . one important and historically contingent type of 'imagined community' around which our conceptions of politics tend to gather."²²² In fact, pushing this idea further, it may be argued that "the state as such does not exist. What exist are building and aeroplanes and tax forms

---

214. Milbank, 275. Arguably, William Cavanaugh makes the same point when he analyzes torture sanctioned by the state, see Cavanaugh, *Torture and Eucharist*, 3.
215. Milbank, *Word Made Strange*, 275.
216. Milbank, 276.
217. Milbank, 276.
218. Milbank, 277.
219. Cavanaugh, *Theopolitcal Imagination*, 1.
220. Cavanaugh, 1.
221. Cavanaugh, 1.
222. Cavanaugh, 1.

and border patrols. What mobilizes these into a project called 'nation-state' is a disciplined imagination of a community occupying a particular space with a common conception of time, a common history and a common destiny of salvation from peril."[223] Thus, for Cavanaugh "the political imagination is simply the condition of possibility for the organization of bodies in society."[224]

More importantly, Cavanaugh offers a counter-intuitive archeology of this imagined space whose design is correlated to the modern construal of religion. At least in Western societies, "the attempt to create a transhistorical and transcultural concept of religion that is essentially prone to violence is one of the foundational legitimating myths of the liberal nation-state."[225] This myth suggests that the state came out of the so-called wars of religion in Europe, in the sixteenth and seventeenth centuries, as a necessary peacemaker between the parties in conflict, and therefore, a sort of new saviour of Europe, secluding religion to a private space, and developing a sense of loyalty to the state from the individual.[226] This immanent soteriology, according to Cavanaugh, conceals the fact that these wars were actually "the birthpangs of the state."[227] To put it another way, "There is a great deal of evidence to suggest that the transfer of power to the emergent state was a cause, not the solution, to the wars of the sixteenth and seventeenth centuries."[228] This is because "the process of state building, [that] begun well before the Reformation, was inherently conflictual. Beginning in the late medieval period, the process involved the internal integration of previously scattered powers under the aegis of the ruler, and the external demarcation of territory over against other, foreign states."[229] Therefore, "the creation of religion, and thus the privatization of the Church, is correlative to the rise of the state."[230] In addition, "The modern construction of religion interiorizes it, and makes religion only a motivating

---

223. Cavanaugh, 2.

224. Cavanaugh, 2.

225. Cavanaugh, *Myth of Religious Violence*, 4.

226. cf. Cavanaugh, *Theopolitical Imagination*, 9–42; Cavanaugh, *Myth of Religious Violence*, 125–180.

227. Cavanaugh, *Theopolitical Imagination*, 22.

228. Cavanaugh, *Myth of Religious Violence*, 162; cf. *Torture and Eucharist*, 5; *Theopolitcal Imagination*, 28.

229. Cavanaugh, *Myth of Religious Violence*, 162. For an alternative theo-political account of the nation-state see O'Donovan, "Nation, State, and Civil Society," 276–295.

230. Cavanaugh, *Theopolitical Imagination*, 31.

force on bodily political and economic practices. The modern Church thus splits the body from the soul and purchases freedom of religion by handing the body over the state."[231]

As a result, modern politics, according to Cavanaugh, offer us an assymetric correlation between two poles, the one and the many, that is to say, the one nation-state and the many individuals contractually linked to the nation-state. "The politics of the nation-state appears as a universal, encompassing all citizens regardless of their other affiliations."[232] In this configuration the church features as "a particular association, one of many that inhabit civil society. To base a politics in the church would be to set politics on a particularist and sectarian footing. Therefore, the church may make some contribution to the larger political life, but is not itself a political body."[233] How to break this relegation, then? In another exercise of the imagination inspired by Augustine's *City of God*,[234] Cavanaugh suggests "the church must constitute itself as an alternative social space, and not simply rely on the nation-state to be its social presence."[235] He therefore explores two ways in which the church may seek to overcome its secluded condition. On the one hand, there is what he calls "politically indirect ecclesiology" in which some political theologies "claim to influence the state only through the activities of Christian citizens in civil society."[236] However, this option renders the church as politically "bodyless," buying precisely into the modern construal of politics.[237] On the other hand, he proposes a "reimagining of the political as a direct response to God's activity in the world, a return to the Augustinian conviction that politics is truly politics only when mapped onto salvation history."[238] In addition, "central to this reimagining is the conviction that the church is at the heart of God's plan of salvation."[239] In Augustine's account, "neither city is a space with clearly defined boundaries, but both are sets of practices or dramatic performances,

---

231. Cavanaugh, 87.
232. Cavanaugh, *Migrations of the Holy*, 123.
233. Cavanaugh, 123.
234. cf. Cavanaugh, 55–68.
235. Cavanaugh, 42.
236. Cavanaugh, 131.
237. cf. Cavanaugh, 134.
238. Cavanaugh, 136.
239. Cavanaugh, 136.

one tragic, the other comic, broadly speaking."²⁴⁰ Within this horizon, what the church must do is "to interrupt the violent tragedy of the earthly city with the comedy of redemption, to build the city of God, beside which the earthly city appears to be not a city at all."²⁴¹

6.5 Mexican Liturgical Space

With reference to my own Mexican context, the apocalyptic construal of the liturgical space as seen above, offers a framework with which to critique what may be called the Mexican liturgical space. As already mentioned in the the introduction to this work, the secular turn that took place in Mexico, and which can be traced back to roughly the mid-nineteenth century onwards, took place in spite of Mexicans' innate inclination to embrace a view of reality infused with a concern for the transcendent, as evidenced from the Mayans and Aztecs of the past to the 90.2 percent of the current population who identify themselves in one way or another as Christian. Thus, as religion was banished from the public square and confined into a private space, a self-declared immanent and autonomous secular view of reality monopolized public life. This asymmetric correlation between a totalized secular political discourse and the marginilized religious voice of the majority may be seen as Milbank's simple space or as Cavanaugh's contractual correlation between the one and the many. If this secular stance is presupposed in the Mexican constitution, it is unashamedly conveyed in the Mexican law about religious associations and public worship (i.e. "El estado mexicano es laico" [the Mexican state is secular]).²⁴²

However, just as the Apocalypse unveils the theological yet heterodox nature of an immanent mode of authority (the sea-beast), sustained by public liturgy (the earth-beast) that in turn sustains a mode of sociality (the great city), which all together offer or impose an alternative to the divine authority (God and the exalted Jesus's throne) and the liturgical sociality (sacred space/

---

240. Cavanaugh, 63.
241. Cavanaugh, 63. Yet, this theological reorientation is still waiting for a more elaborated political theology from Cavanaugh, as he himself acknowledges, cf. Cavanaugh, *Migrations of the Holy*, 6.
242. *Ley de Asociaciones Religiosas y Culto Público*. Texto Vigente (17 Dec 2015). Artículo 3. This document is available at http://www.diputados.gob.mx/LeyesBiblio/pdf/24_171215.pdf.

holy city), so we find that the secular space in Mexico is deeply liturgical in nature. This becomes totally transparent in the so called *Ley sobre el Escudo, la Bandera y el Himno Nacionales* (law regarding the Nation's coat of arms, flag, and national anthem),[243] which may be thought of as a secular liturgy indeed. This law has seven chapters, with an additional special chapter and a record of the amendments made since the time of its publication. Chapter 1 (article 1) acknowledges the coat of arms, the flag and the national anthem as patriotic symbols of Mexico; chapter 2 (articles 2–4) describes the features of each symbol, of which it is worth noting that the coat of arms' design alludes to the foundational story of the Aztecs as narrated by Hernando de Alvarado Tezozomoc in his *Crónica Mexicana*;[244] chapter 3 (articles 5–6) regulates the usage of the coat of arms; chapter 4, the longest (articles 7–37), concerns the usage, displaying and honours to the Mexican flag; chapter 5 (articles 38–49) regards the performance of the national anthem; chapter 6 (articles 50–54 bis) deals with specific settings in connection with the patriotic symbols; chapter 7 (articles 55–56) deals with the issue of punishment as a result of dishonouring the patriotic symbols (i.e. a sort of penance); lastly, the special chapter offers the canonical words and music of the national anthem.

Above all, it is "el culto a la bandera" (the cult to the national flag) that discloses the liturgical nature of the Mexican secular public space.[245] Thus, "during civic festivities or official ceremonies where the national flag is present, honours will be paid to it . . . which will at the very least include a simultaneous civil salute by everyone present."[246] In addition, "within the federal institutions and civilian sections of the public administration at state and municipal levels of government, it is mandatory to pay honours to the national flag on 24 February, 15 and 16 September, and 20 November of each year, which must take place in accordance with this law."[247] What is more, "Official educational authorities at federal, state and municipal levels will ensure that

---

243. *Ley sobre el Escudo, la Bandera y el Himno Nacionales*. Texto Vigente (30 Nov 2018). This document is available at http://www.diputados.gob.mx/LeyesBiblio/pdf/213_301118.pdf.

244. cf. Hernando de Alvarado Tezozomoc, *Crónica Mexicana*, 1.

245. cf. *Ley sobre el Escudo, la Bandera y el Himno Nacionales*. Texto Vigente (30 Nov 2018). Artículos 7, 21, 51.

246. *Ley sobre el Escudo, la Bandera y el Himno Nacionales*. Texto Vigente (30 Nov 2018). Artículo 9. Translated from the Spanish by the author.

247. *Ley sobre el Escudo, la Bandera y el Himno Nacionales*. Texto Vigente (30 Nov 2018). Artículo 11. Translated from the Spanish by the auhor.

primary, secondary and higher education institutions pay honours to the national flag every Monday morning, either at the beginning of the student's day or at some point during the morning, as well as at the start and end of the academic cycle."²⁴⁸ Therefore, what we see in the Mexican setting is that, where there was previously a religious liturgy (trascendent in orientation and theologically orthodox), there is now a secular liturgy (immanent in nature and therefore theologically heterodox) that has replaced traditional religion in the public square. As Cavanaugh puts it, "the supposedly 'secular' world invents its own liturgies, with pretensions every bit as 'sacred' as those of the Christian liturgy, and these liturgies can come to rival the church's liturgy for our bodies and our minds."²⁴⁹ In other words, "modern societies are every bit as 'liturgical' as traditional ones."²⁵⁰

6.6 Conclusion

O'Donovan's understanding of the liturgical as a way to convey the political reality of God's people has provided us with a theo-political framework through which to ascertain how the Apocalypse envisions the liturgical sociality in spatial terms. We have found that it does so both as sacred space and/or holy city; a space inhabited throughout the narrative by the divine authority, the exalted Jesus, and at its climax by the Fellowship of the Throne. In connection with this, our preference for the term liturgy was exegetically justified drawing from the Septuagint's usage of it, and also considering its usage in classical Greece.

We also established that the apocalyptic liturgical sociality envisioned as a sacred space alludes to the Old Testament theologoumenon on sacred space (i.e. the point of meeting and fellowship between YHWH and his people), exemplified in the mobile tent of meeting or in the institutionalized temple. Either spatial configuration always presented two interconnected spaces, the Holy Place and the holy of holies. We have shown that at present (i.e. the secular-as-time), the church as the liturgical sociality enacts a sort of

---

248. *Ley sobre el Escudo, la Bandera y el Himno Nacionales*. Texto Vigente (30 Nov 2018). Artículo 15. Translated from the Spanish by the author.

249. Cavanaugh, *Migrations of the Holy*, 115.

250. Cavanaugh, 116. Cavanaugh offers an account of what he calls the liturgies of the American nation-state in Cavanaugh, *Migrations of the Holy*, 115–122.

Holy Place, whereas heaven as the holy of holies is the locus of the divine throne, and the exalted Jesus moves between these two sacred spaces. We concluded, however, that with the advent of a holy city in John's Apocalypse (which presupposes a new heaven and a new earth) the two-tier sacred space collapses into a whole sacred space, or better still, the Holy Place gives way to a totalized holy of holies. In this new reality, the holy city is in fact a holy of holies and becomes the locus of the Fellowship of the Throne. As for the motif of the city, this is better appreciated when it is seen in its urban narrative context, whether historic, agonistic, forensic or artistic. We have also seen how the interplay between the holy city and its rival, the great city, is gradually disclosed throughout the narrative. We focused particularly on the city-in-the-making, which adumbrates the advent of the holy city and the materialization of the Fellowship of the Throne. Equally, we noted the christological purchase of this city in the making.

This liturgical space with a christological orientation (i.e. a liturgical sociality predicated on the exalted Jesus) may be regarded as an apocalyptic spatial ecclesiology; indeed, it can be seen as an alternative to Joseph Mangina's account of the church in the Apocalypse, for instance. This construal of the liturgical space with a christological orientation also functions as a theo-political category that enables critical interaction with alternative liturgical spatial construals, whether ancient or modern. The Apocalypse itself critiques the liturgical sociality (the great city) predicated on an immanent mode of authority (the sea-beast) sustained by a heterodox theology and liturgy (the earth-beast). It equally provided a framework with which to critique the historical political and liturgical legacy of the Roman Augustan era. In a similar vein, Augustine's interplay of two socialities with different ontological grounds each pursuing a different *telos* yet sharing the same space, encourages John Milbank in criticism of modern liberal politics and William Cavanaugh in the critique of the nation-state, both of which formulate their views in spatial terms. In the same way, the Apocalypse, Augustine, Milbank and Cavanaugh have informed the present writer in the critique of the liturgical nature of the Mexican secular space, which becomes transparent in its mandatory (and heterodox) cult to the Mexican flag.

CHAPTER 7

Models of Society

"On the relation between the 'people' and the authority that summons it, hangs the delicate question of political representation,"[1] observes O'Donovan. In fact he considers that "the moment of collective self-discovery, in which the sociality of the people, reflected in the person of its representative, dawns to its recognition"[2] can amount to a kind of cathartic experience, to the extent that "ancient societies reckoned, one might say, to fall in love with their ruler's image. The thought that the king marries his kingdom is found in folk narrative of every provenance, and is taken up in the eschatological visions of the Apocalypse."[3] This illustration of the relationship between sociality and authority was included in our considerations in chapter 6, where we explored the Apocalypse's construal of the liturgical sociality whose identity is predicated on and determined by the exalted Jesus, and noted that this analogy of the marriage between the Lamb and his bride, can be seen as the liturgical act that makes transparent the Fellowship of the Throne, that is to say, the correlation between divine authority and society.

However, given O'Donovan's view that a people is "a community constituted by participation in the common good,"[4] other construals of sociality where elements like tradition,[5] space or territory,[6] and the need for defence,[7] play a

---

1. O'Donovan, *Ways of Judgment*, 149.
2. O'Donovan, 163.
3. O'Donovan, 161. However, O'Donovan opts to illustrate his point using the biblical story of David and Abigail as recorded in 1 Sam 25:2–42; see O'Donovan, *Ways of Judgment*, 161–162.
4. O'Donovan, *Ways of Judgment*, 149.
5. cf. O'Donovan, 150.
6. O'Donovan, 150.
7. cf. O'Donovan, 154.

role in defining its identity must be considered in addition to the Apocalypse's own construal. In fact, the issue of how a society is defined is considered by O'Donovan as "the chief point at issue in the theories of constitution,"[8] since it feeds into speculation about either the ontological priority of political authority (government) over political society, an approach known as contractarian, or the ontological priority of political society over political authority, an approach known as constitutionalist.[9] It should be noted that our accounts of Greek (Platonic, §5.1), and Roman (§5.2) construals of political authority presupposed an idea of society. However, in this chapter we will revisit these ancient traditions to briefly consider how they defined society and to what extent this definition impinged upon their construal of authority. This in turn will help us appreciate O'Donovan's threefold view of the church as (i) a political society ruled by the exalted Jesus, (ii) a post/counter-political society enacting the *koinonia* of Holy Spirit, and (iii) a moral society under the authority of Scripture. There will follow a critique of the above construals resulting from our understanding of the Apocalypse's own construal, since a "political theology must have something to say about society and something to say about rule, and the two must be coordinated."[10]

7.1 Ancient Society

It may be said that Plato's idea of the polis or city, as conveyed in his *Republic*, set in motion a dialectic on the subject, given that when Aristotle later articulated his ideas for the city in *Politics*, he did so explicitly in the light of the *Republic*,[11] and given also that Cicero deliberately wrote his *On the Commonwealth* in the light of the *Republic*,[12] though it was Aristotle he sided with when he offered a definition of the *res publica*.[13] Drawing on our previous

---

8. O'Donovan, 154.

9. cf. O'Donovan, 154–157. "The conception of society as a human product and therefore 'historical' remains one of the basic assumptions of secular social science, although it has always been aporetically crossed . . . by the accompanying reflection that human beings are the product of society." Milbank, *Theology and Social Theory*, 11.

10. O'Donovan, *Desire of the Nations*, 193.

11. e.g. Aristotle, *Politics* 2.1.3 (1261a+); though admittedly, Aristotle also refers to Plato's *Laws* in *Politcs* 2.6.1 (1264b+), for instance see, Rowe, "Aristotelian constitutions," 368.

12. e.g. Cicero, *On the Commonwealth* 2.3, 21–22, 51; 4.4; cf. 1.65, 68.

13. cf. Zetzel, *Cicero*, 128.

accounts of Platonic and Roman models of political authority, we now move on to consider their ideas about a polis or *res publica* in order to see how society is imagined there.

First, as noted in §5.1, the idea of the Socratic (and therefore Platonic) polis is framed within an overarching discussion on the nature of justice. This imagined city, Socrates observes, "comes to be because none of us is self-sufficient, but we all need many things."[14] Basic human needs like food, shelter, clothes, and those who provide them, like a farmer, a builder, a weaver,[15] lead many people to "gather in a single place to live together as partners and helpers. And such a settlement is called a city."[16] As a result, this Platonic society, we may say, is a need-driven community where each member satisfies the need of another, and at the same time, their need is satisfied by someone else. However, this materialistic aspect of the society can be seen negatively since "the city originates in selfishness rather than in friendship or sympathy,"[17] and is referred to in the dialogue as a "city for pigs."[18] Be that as it may, the city requires a space in which it may dwell; a space which, when further non-basic needs are considered, must be enlarged in order to satisfy the need for more land to plough. The need for more land may lead the now "*luxurious* city"[19] to seize it from its neighbours,[20] but it may also expose the city to a similar aggression, which in turn highlights another need: the need for an army, a professional army to protect the city,[21] i.e. the guardians,[22] who then are construed as the rulers of the city, as shown in §5.1. Thus, in Plato's *Republic* an initial notion of authority is not introduced until the city goes beyond its basic needs;[23] therefore, a sophisticated society precedes authority, so to speak.

Second, and by contrast, Aristotle opens his *Politics* without any narrative frame and straightforwardly states that "every city [πόλις] is some sort

---

14. Plato, *Republic* 2.369b.
15. cf. Plato, *Republic* 2.369d.
16. Plato, *Republic* 2.369c.
17. Rosen, *Plato's Republic*, 73.
18. Plato, *Republic* 2.372d.
19. Plato, *Republic* 2.372e.
20. cf. Plato, *Republic* 2.372e-373d.
21. cf. Plato, *Republic* 2.373e-374d.
22. cf. Plato, *Republic* 2.374e.
23. cf. Rosen, *Plato's Republic*, 80.

of community [κοινωνία], and that every community is constituted for the sake of some good [ἀγαθός],"[24] adding that "the community that is most authoritative of all and embraces all the others does so particularly, and aims at the most authoritative good of all. This is what is called the city or the political [πολιτικός] community."[25] This Aristotelian framing of the polis with its teleological orientation towards the common good[26] is then located within a story of origin (an archeology in this sense) that traces the natural development of the household,[27] "the community constituted by nature for the needs of daily life,"[28] into a village,[29] with the grouping of several villages constituting a city.[30] "Every city, therefore, exists by nature, if such also are the first communities. For the city is their end, and nature is an end."[31] Timothy Chappell observes that "the largest natural unit of political association is the one that meets *every* human need, and when we reach this we have reached the natural terminus of the process of political development: so the polis is natural because it is self-sufficient."[32]

Yet, in what may be described as an aporetic move, Aristotle notes that "the city is thus prior by nature to the household and to each of us. For the whole must of necessity be prior to the part."[33] This move is somehow required to allow for Aristotle's anthropology, since in his view "man is by nature a political animal"[34] and must belong to a city. For Aristotle, an individual "who is incapable of sharing [κοινωνέω] or who is in need of nothing through being self-sufficient is no part of a city, and so is either a beast or a god."[35] Within his model, members of the city are citizens, or to put in another way, "the

---

24. Aristotle, *Politics* 1.1.1 (1252a1).
25. Aristotle, *Politics* 1.1.1.
26. cf. Aristotle, *Politics* 2.8.17 (1268b+); 3.13.20 (1284b+).
27. For the various Aristotelian nuances of the term "nature" and its semantic domain see Chappell, "'Naturalism,'" 382–397.
28. Aristotle, *Politics* 1.2.5 (1252b+).
29. Aristotle, *Politics* 1.2.5.
30. cf. Aristotle, *Politics* 1.2.8 (1252b+).
31. Aristotle, *Politics* 1.2.8 (1252b+).
32. Chappell, "'Naturalism,'" 387–388.
33. Aristotle, *Politics* 1.2.12-13 (1253a+).
34. Aristotle, *Politics* 1.2.9 (1253a+).
35. Aristotle, *Politics* 1.2.14 (1253a+). Paul Cartledge notes that "the polis as [Aristotle] construed it was a natural organism within which alone could generic man attain his intrinsic natural end of living the good life." Cartledge, *Ancient Greek Political Thought*, 14.

city is a certain multitude of citizens,"[36] a citizen being someone "defined by no other thing so much as by partaking [μετέχω] in decision [κρίσις] and office [ἀρχή]."[37] However, though every member of the polis was expected to participate in judgment and rule, Aristotle seems to concede that "the ruler [ἄρχων], whether one person or more, should be authoritative with respect to those things about which the laws are completely unable to speak precisely on account of the difficulty of making clear general declarations about everything."[38] The Aristotelian polis develops therefore out of the *oikos*, however, his anthropology requires him aporetically to set the primacy of the polis over the human being, since the latter must by nature belong to the former. Within this construal, a member of the city is both a judge and a ruler who must participate in the pursuit of the common good.

Third, Cicero's definition of the *res publica* is conveyed within a narrative frame similar to Plato's, as noted in §5.2. However, in his case he offers a sort of political maxim as follows: "the commonwealth is the concern of the people [*est . . . res publica res populi*]."[39] Regarding this maxim James Zetzel suggests that "'Political organization is the organization of the people' is close to the sense of the phrase, but loses the etymological play."[40] In addition, Cicero explains that this res populi "is not any group of men assembled in any way, but an assemblage [*coitus*] of some size associated with one another through agreement [*consentio*] on law [*jus*] and community [*communio*] of interest."[41] Cicero's *res publica* therefore reveals an Aristotelian bent in that the sociality finds cohesion in a sort of common good with a legal orientation, and also in that his archeology of the assemblage is traced back to the house [*domicilium*], a large grouping of which would become a walled city [*urbs*].[42] However, "Aristotle's state is an agglomeration of individual citizens, while [Cicero's] belongs to the populus viewed as a single whole."[43] Also, Cicero categorically affirms that every *res publica*, that is to say, every *populus* constituted as a

---

36. Aristotle, *Politics* 3.1.2 (1275a+).
37. Aristotle, *Politics* 3.1.6 (1275a+).
38. Aristotle, *Politics* 3.11.19 (1282b+).
39. Cicero, *On the Commonwealth* 1.39.
40. Zetzel, *Cicero*, 127.
41. Cicero, *On the Commonwealth* 1.39.
42. cf. Cicero, *On the Commonwealth* 1.41.
43. Zetzel, *Cicero*, 128.

civitas, "needs to be ruled by some sort of deliberation in order to be long lived,"[44] though in Rome's case it was up to Romulus, as founder of the city, to establish a commonwealth.[45]

As we have seen above, Plato introduces authority only when his construal of the polis becomes more elaborate and complex giving way to what he calls the luxurious polis, whereas for Cicero authority is a *sine qua non* of the *res publica*. Aristotle's construal of the polis, however, is predicated on citizens' ability to judge and rule, and could be seen as the middle ground between Plato and Cicero's models. Also, if the polis (society) preceded authority, whether by an act of the imagination (Plato) or nature (Aristotle), in the Ciceronian account it is authority that preceded the *res publica* (i.e. the res populi).[46]

Further insights offered by Plato and Augustus into the dynamics between authority and society are worth noting here. On the one hand, Plato raises the question of unity within the city, so as to prevent the fracture of it into two or more groups in dispute – for instance rich against poor[47] – which for Plato constitutes the greatest evil for a city, "that which tears it apart and makes it many instead of one."[48] In fact, Plato argues that the size of the city is correlated to its unity: "As long as it is willing to remain *one* city, it may continue to grow, but it cannot grow beyond that point."[49] Out of this concern, Plato (that is to say, Socrates in the dialogue) proposes that the guardians of the city (i.e. authority) must take a bold step to preserve the unity of the city, so in addition to their education regime and upbringing, "marriage [γάμος],

---

44. Cicero, *On the Commonwealth* 1.41.
45. Cicero, 2.4.
46. The backcloth of Platonic, Aristotelian and Ciceronian coordinates of authority and society allow us to locate influential construals within political thought such as (1) Thomas Hobbes's sombre view of coercive power as a *sine qua non* of a commonwealth predicated on an anthropology that sees a human being as in need of protection from any other human being, see Hobbes, *Leviathan* 17; (2) John Locke's approach to human beings as free, equal and independent, but willing to give up this natural condition to join other human beings and form a community whose power is "the will and determination of the *majority*." Laslett, *Locke, Two Treatises of Government* II.8.96; (3) Jean Jacques Rousseau's understanding of human beings as a free individual that enters into a social contract with other human beings whereby they submit to the general will of this association, and in turn they and their goods are protected, see Rousseau, *Of the Social Contract* 1.6.4–9, in Gourevitch, *Rousseau*.
47. cf. Plato, *Republic* 4.422e-423b.
48. Plato, *Republic* 5.462a.
49. Plato, *Republic* 4.423b.

the having of wives, and the procreation of children must be governed as far as possible by the old proverb: Friends possess everything in common."[50] In other words, Plato proposes a redefinition of marriage as a way to achieve the greatest good for the city, which for him is "that which binds it together and makes it one."[51] Stanley Rosen notes that "[this] rule clearly has to do with the goal of unity, and the unification of the feeling of brotherhood and family with love of the city."[52]

But exactly how would this Platonic proposal work? To begin with, Socrates suggests in connection with the guardians that "the best men must have sex with the best women as frequently as possible,"[53] and their offspring have the right to be reared. Arguably, a kind of lottery would determine which man and which woman would have sexual intercourse.[54] However, in order to avoid the moral charge of promiscuity, since "promiscuity is impious in a city,"[55] Plato introduces the utilitarian idea of a "sacred marriage" where the guardians participating in this scheme would be regarded as brides and grooms and their marriages would be sanctioned by law and public liturgy, so to speak.[56] "Socrates defines 'holy' as what is useful to the city, not what the gods wish."[57] However, no guardian, man or woman, would be able to claim any child as his or her own. On the contrary, "a man will call all the children born in the tenth or seventh month after he became a bridegroom his sons, if they're male, and his daughters, if they're female, and they'll call him father."[58] Nurses would take "every precaution to insure that no mother knows her own child,"[59] effectively enabling the ultimate goal of this policy (or law, as Plato put it) to be realized, that is, to prevent any privatization, whether of pleasure or pain, that would "dissolve the city."[60] For Plato, "the

---

50. Plato, *Republic* 4.423e-424a; cf. 5.457c-d.
51. Plato, *Republic* 5.462a.
52. Rosen, *Plato's Republic*, 135.
53. Plato, *Republic* 5.459d.
54. cf. Plato, *Republic* 5.460a, 461e; Rosen, *Plato's Republic*, 189.
55. Plato, *Republic* 5.458d-e.
56. cf. Plato, *Republic* 5.458e, 459e-460a, 461a-b.
57. Rosen, *Plato's Republic*, 187. "In the Socratic city, religion becomes an instrument of lying, not truth telling." Rosen, 187.
58. Plato, *Republic* 5.461d.
59. Plato, *Republic* 5.461c.
60. Plato, *Republic* 5.462b.

best-governed city [is] the one in which most people say 'mine' and 'not mine' about the same things in the same way."[61]

On the other hand, Augustus also registers an innovation in his *Res Gestae Divi Augusti* in connection with the tradition of *sacramentum*, the oath of allegiance sworn by the (Roman) army to their commander.[62] An instance of its use was recorded in the midst of the civil war between Julius Caesar and Pompey. In this case, when the army of an ally of Pompey, Domitius, found out that their leader was planning to abandon them because they were under siege by Caesar's army, they took Domitius and offered him to Caesar alive, and from that moment took orders from Caesar alone.[63] Following this, however, Caesar ordered these soldiers "to take the oath of allegiance to himself."[64] In his various war campaigns Augustus obviously continues with this tradition, and highlights in his treatise that "there have been roughly 500,000 Roman citizens under oath of allegiance [*sacramentum*] to me."[65] However, before he engages in war against Antony at Actium, he notes that "the whole of Italy of its own accord swore [*juro*] an act of allegiance to me and demanded me as its commander for the war in which I conquered at Actium."[66] Presumably, Antony's army did the same in regard to him.[67]

Augustus's innovation concerning this oath, however, relates to its use among civilians, "perhaps . . . all adult male citizens in Italy and non-citizens in the western provinces. This oath, therefore, cannot be explained solely in terms of military *coniuratio* [a union or alliance]."[68] In addition, extant evidence like the bronze inscription found in Baetica (a province in modern

---

61. Plato, *Republic* 5.462c. "This is a hasty inference, since it could apply to a complete tyranny in which everyone agrees with the tyrant as to what is theirs and not theirs." (Rosen, *Plato's Republic*, 192). For his part, Aristotle's sustained explicit critique of Plato's idea of unity conveyed as a "sacred marriage" is registered in Aristotle, *Politics* 2.1, 2, 3, 4 (1260b25–1262b36). With reference to Cicero, there is a veiled and laconic critique of Plato's idea of holding everything in common, in line with the overall Roman disregard of Greek customs, see Cicero, *On the Commonwealth* 4.4, 5b, a point perhaps echoed in Lactantius, *Epitome of the Divine Institutes* 38 (ANF/7), cf. Zetzel, *Cicero*, 81n9.

62. cf. Cooley, *Res Gestae Divi Augusti*, 118.

63. cf. Julius Caesar, *Civil War* 1.20.

64. Julius Caesar, *Civil War* 1.23.

65. Augustus, *Res Gestae* 3.3.

66. Augustus, *Res Gestae* 25.2.

67. cf. Cassius Dio, *Roman History* 50.6.6.

68. Cooley, *Res Gestae Divi Augusti*, 215; cf. Crook, "Augustus," 115.

Seville, Spain) refers to "an oath to Augustus and the male members of his family."[69] Dated 6/5 BC, this inscription, argues Julián González, demonstrates

> an official attitude influencing all the towns of the Empire, whether they have a privileged status or were peregrinae, to pay close attention to major events in the life of the Imperial family and to the honours gained by its members, and the [sic] each provincial community had to decide the exact form of its own reaction, and expression of loyalty.[70]

Alison Cooley also suggests that "the oath of 32 BC foreshadows a later development, whereby Augustus used oath swearing as a way of reinforcing the loyalty of the provinces to himself and his heirs."[71]

The significance of both Plato's radical redefinition of marriage and parenthood for the sake of the city's unity, and Augustus's expanded use of the military *sacramentum* as a means of ensuring loyalty from his subjects, lies in the deployment of the liturgical act by the authority to seek the unity of society, or by society to bind itself to authority, thus highlighting the power of liturgy as a means of establishing a correlation between authority and society/sociality, and bringing it into the realm of the political.

7.2 The Church as Society

The above accounts of how society is construed and what the nature of its relationship with authority is, naturally interact with O'Donovan's view that a "theological account of how this world is ruled . . . must proceed from and through an account of the church."[72] But what this account may be, as understood by O'Donovan, is the task we now set for ourselves in this section. Here we will consider O'Donovan's understanding of the church by using the three theological categories that he lays out: (i) christologically speaking, the church is a political society whose identity is predicated on the exalted Jesus;

---

69. González, "First Oath," 114.
70. González, 123.
71. Cooley, *Res Gestae Divi Augusti*, 216. For alternative and more complex models regarding the dynamics between the Roman emperor and his subjects, specially after Augustus, see for instance Ando, *Imperial Ideology*; Noreña, *Imperial Ideals*.
72. O'Donovan, *Desire of the Nations*, 159.

(ii) pneumatologically speaking, the church is a post/counter-political society that enacts the *koinonia* of the Holy Spirit, and (iii) scripturally speaking, the church is a moral community under the authority of Scripture. Let us then consider each ecclesiastical portrait in turn.

7.2.1 The Church as Political Society

O'Donovan asserts that "the true character of the church as a political society" is found in that, as opposed to any contemporary nation-state, the church "is brought into being and held in being, not by a special function it has to fulfil, but by a government that it obeys in everything. It is ruled and authorised by the ascended Christ alone and supremely; it therefore has its own authority; and it is not answerable to any other authority that may attempt to subsume it."[73] Obviously, this is a case where authority preceded society, in contrast with ancient Greek construals of the political as seen in the previous section. This assertive account of the church as a political society mirrors ancient Israel's structure (exilic or post-exilic) as a society under "dual authority,"[74] living with the overlap between divine rule and earthly imperialistic, foreign rule. However, within O'Donovan's perspective the dynamics of this "duality assumes a conflictual, aggressive note, as the rule of Christ within the church presses back upon the old and withering authority of empire. It was not protection that was needed, but that the secular authority should give way."[75]

More significant, perhaps, is the theological rationale offered by O'Donovan in order to justify his account of the church as a political society exclusively authorized by the exalted Jesus, a rationale he predicates on the mediation of the Holy Spirit. For O'Donovan "Pentecost authorised the church by uniting it with the authorisation of Christ. It belongs, therefore, immediately to the moment of authorisation, Christ's exaltation,"[76] and it "can be seen as the moment at which the church comes to participate in the authority of the ascended Christ."[77] What is more, O'Donovan argues that since

---

73. O'Donovan, 159.

74. cf. O'Donovan, 82–88.

75. O'Donovan, 158; cf. 83, 158–159, where O'Donovan briefly considers other construed models of the dynamics of this duality of authority, in particular Augustine's two cities and Pope Gelasius I's two rulers.

76. O'Donovan, *Desire of the Nations*, 161.

77. O'Donovan, 162.

the exaltation of Jesus somehow sums up the whole Christ-event, Pentecost enables the church, as a political community, to participate in each stage of the event, which for O'Donovan unfolds as advent, passion, restoration and exaltation.[78] "In Christ [the church] is represented in that event, [and] in the Spirit it participates in it."[79]

O'Donovan concedes, however, that at present the political character of the church remains "hidden, to be discerned by faith as the ascended Christ who governs it is to be discerned by faith."[80] Though this "hiddenness" has been acknowledged since early times,[81] O'Donovan highlights the recurrent historical attempt by those within the Christian community to counter that hidden feature. In his words,

> the temptation besets the church to make its hidden government visible by a representative icon of the ruling Christ. Charged to realise the premonarchical confidence of Israel that it had no king but Yhwh, the church compromises itself when it asserts from its midst a ruling entity to act on Christ's behalf, matching the claims of secular rulers with counterclaims. If Erastianism is an instance of the first mistake, papalism is a striking example of this one.[82]

Yet, O'Donovan is at pains to point out that his criticism is not aimed at any church hierarchy, order or structure that engages with secular powers; rather, "the mistake is quite simply to posit an order of ministry, of whatever sort, and to deduce the identity of the church from it, as though *that* were the rule of Christ, and what it encompassed were the true form of Christ's bride!"[83] To be sure, "the identity of the church is given wholly and completely in the relation of its members to the ascended Christ independently of church ministry and organisation. Of no political community can it be said that it retains its identity irrespective of how, or by whom, it is governed."[84]

---

78. cf. O'Donovan, 133–146.
79. O'Donovan, 161.
80. O'Donovan, 166.
81. For example Epistle to Diognetus 4.6–5.5, in *The Apostolic Fathers*.
82. O'Donovan, *Desire of the Nations*, 166.
83. O'Donovan, 168.
84. O'Donovan, 169.

However, to resolve the tension between these two elements that define the political character of the church (i.e. its exclusive authorization by the exalted Jesus conferred at Pentecost, and the hidden nature of its relationship to the exalted Jesus which bypasses any contingent ecclesial order), O'Donovan deploys sacramental theology. For O'Donovan the sacraments are badges that communicate the political character of the church to the watching world in liturgical terms, "it is not the order of the church's ministry which announces with formal clarity the fact that this is Christ's community; it is the church's sacramental order which does so."[85] In addition, O'Donovan argues that the sacraments provide institutional stability to the church, and that "without [the sacraments] the church could be a 'visible' society, without doubt, but only a rather intangible one, melting indeterminately like a delicate mist as we stretched our arms to embrace it. In these forms we know where the church is and can attach ourselves to it."[86]

At this point it is worth observing that O'Donovan distinguishes between the catholicity and the order of the church; the former he understands as the ongoing outcome of the Spirit's continual mission to enlarge the church, whereas the latter is a contingent and particularized feature.

> The catholic identity of the church derives from the progress of the Spirit's own mission. It is therefore always larger than its ordered structures, taking its shape from the new ground that the Spirit is possessing. It remains for the church's structures to catch up with this mission, to discern what the Spirit has done, and to construct such ordered links of community as will safeguard brotherly love.[87]

As for the sacraments needed to communicate the political identity of the church, O'Donovan occupies a middle ground between the maximalist Lombardian position, which holds that there are seven sacraments, and the minimalist Reformed position, which identifies only two sacraments.[88] O'Donovan's own inventory of the sacraments includes baptism, the Eucharist,

---

85. O'Donovan, 172.
86. O'Donovan, 172.
87. O'Donovan, 169–170.
88. cf. O'Donovan, 173; McGrath, *Christian Theology*, 402–405.

the keeping of the Lord's Day, and the laying on of hands.[89] Crucial to his sacramental theology is the correlation he establishes between each of the stages of the Christ-event (advent, passion, restoration, exaltation) and the sacraments that define the church as a political society. In this way, the Christ-event becomes "the structuring principle for all ecclesiology, holding the key both to the church's spontaneous 'catholic' existence and to its formal structure."[90] The christological-sacramental correlation looks as follows:

(i) Advent. In this christological stage the church is seen as a gathering community since "it continually adds to its membership from all existing political and natural communities, as the recognition of Jesus as the Christ is communicated throughout the world."[91] The confession of Jesus as Lord and Messiah,[92] enacted in the baptism of the believer,[93] becomes both the criterion of church's membership and the boundary maker of the church as a political society.[94]

(ii) Passion. The church is seen as a suffering community when this stage of the Christ-event is considered.[95] In particular, "the authority conferred upon the suffering church . . . is the authority to confront and overcome resistance to God's saving will by enduring suffering in whatever form."[96] More importantly, the church is called to be a witness or martyr,[97] and as it enacts the Eucharist,[98] it participates in the passion of the Lord Jesus.[99]

(iii) Restoration. To counter any risk of developing a pathological fixation with martyrdom and a culture of victimization, this christological stage allows the church to become a glad community. "When we say that the church is

---

89. O'Donovan, *Desire of the Nations*, 173. And yet, in his *The Ways of Judgment*, O'Donovan seems to resort to a minimalist sacramental view when referring to the "signs of the church," i.e. baptism and the Eucharist, since "these are the primary authorizing marks of the church" (O'Donovan, *Ways of Judgment*, 266).

90. O'Donovan, *Desire of the Nations*, 174–175.

91. O'Donovan, 175.

92. e.g. Matt 16:16; Acts 11:17; 16:31; Rom 10:9; 1 Cor 6:11; 12:3; 1 John 3:23; 4:2; 2 John 7.

93. cf. Matt 28:19; Acts 2:38; 8:12, 16; 10:48; 19:5; Rom 6:3; 1 Pet 3:21.

94. cf. O'Donovan, *Desire of the Nations*, 176–178.

95. cf. O'Donovan, 178.

96. O'Donovan, 179.

97. cf. Acts 4:33; 6:3; 23:11; 1 Cor 15:15; 1 John 1:2; 4:14; Rev 1:9; 11:7; 20:4.

98. cf. Matt 26:27 || Mark 14:23 || Luke 22:17, 19; 1 Cor 11:24; Ignatius, *To the Philadelphians* 4.1; *To the Smyrnaeans* 6.2; 8.1; *The Didache* 9.1, 5; Justin Martyr, *Apology* 1.66 (ANF/1).

99. cf. O'Donovan, *Desire of the Nations*, 180–181.

glad in the resurrection of Christ, we point to the meaning of that event as the *recovery of creation order*. Gladness belongs essentially to the creature, as glory belongs to the creator."[100] As a result, the keeping of the Lord's Day is modelled on the keeping of the Sabbath, though with the elements of consummation brought by the resurrection of Jesus[101] (i.e. the completion and vindication of creation), on the one hand, and the forging of a communal identity as the church participates in (eschatological) fulfilment, on the other.[102]

(iv) Exaltation. This christological stage gives the church the role of mediating God's words, so that "the church speaks God's words in prophecy and in prayer."[103] Divine discourse in prophetic mode is mediated by the church to the world, enabled by charismata, whereas prayer is addressed to God in weakness. Within this context the laying-on of hands conveys the role of mediation as healing, ordination or even as the granting of the Holy Spirit.[104] "The wider use of the laying-on of hands . . . could do much to maintain the right relation of the individual believer to the community, and protect the church against the dangers of institutionalism and clericalism."[105]

7.2.2 The Church as Post-Political Society

In a move that may be seen in aporetic tension with the above, O'Donovan postulates that the church is also a post-political society, or a counter-political society.[106] On the one hand he explains this change in his construal of the church by focusing on the iconoclastic effect of the Christ-event on political authority as understood from Colossians 2:14–15, for example, where the cross of Jesus is portrayed as disarming rulers and stripping the authorities.[107] That this in itself is a divine political act is not to be questioned.[108] According to him, "the cross challenges the *exclusion* by which the rules and authorities

---

100. O'Donovan, 181.

101. cf. Mark 16:2; Luke 24:1; John 20:1; Justin Martyr, *Dialogue with Trypho* 41 (ANF/1).

102. cf. O'Donovan, *Desire of the Nations*, 186; Acts 20:7; Rev 1:10; Ignatius, *To the Magnesians* 9.1; *The Didache* 14.1; Justin Martyr, *Apology* 1.67 (ANF/1).

103. O'Donovan, *Desire of the Nations*, 187.

104. cf. Acts 6:6; 8:17; 9:12, 17; 13:3; 19:6; 28:8; 1 Tim 5:22; Irenaeus, *Against Heresies* 4.38.2 (ANF/1).

105. O'Donovan, *Desire of the Nations*, 190.

106. cf. O'Donovan, *Ways of Judgment*, 240.

107. cf. O'Donovan, 231.

108. cf. O'Donovan, 234.

define their identities . . . They exclude those who do not belong to them, and they exclude those who, while belonging, incur their condemnation."[109] As seen in §5.3, the Christ-event effects a downsized political authority which is however still able to enact judgment within the secular-as-time, its "God-given right of judgment within the world."[110] The church in turn must continue to show "deference to that right, not usurping the privileged sphere of secular judgment."[111]

On the other hand, O'Donovan explains that the cross "as a visible emblem . . . has drawn men, women, and children into a universal community of attention, overreaching the bounds of their national, tribal, and family identities,"[112] but that, in another political act derived from the cross, this community shows deference to the political authority's right of judgment following the evangelical imperative "do not judge, so that you may not be judged" (Matt 7:1).[113] It should be noted that a

> society that refrains from judging is not a society without judgment, persisting in primal innocence before the knowledge of wrong. Not-judging is not detachment from judgment . . . On the contrary, it is a society that has felt the need for judgment, has cried to God for judgment, and has seen it revealed in Christ; and believing what it has seen, it has judged for itself. A society that refrains from judgment does so because it has the judgment of God to defer to.[114]

It is in this sense that the church is a post-political society or a counter-political society with a markedly eschatological orientation, since they now live with the horizon of God's judgment in view, acknowledging that "all human judgment is merely interim, waiting for the judgment that is to come."[115]

The emergence of this post/counter-political society gives O'Donovan's political theology a new perspective with which to map out a short history

---

109. O'Donovan, 233.
110. O'Donovan, 239.
111. O'Donovan, 240.
112. O'Donovan, 232.
113. cf. O'Donovan, 233.
114. O'Donovan, 238.
115. O'Donovan, 238.

of a political society with a clear christological divide. Thus, at one end (i.e. the beginning) we find the pre-political society of God's creation, not yet knowing good and evil in their primeval and innocent condition;[116] and at the other end we see the post/counter-political society, "the bearer of a discourse that defers judgment, seeking further reflection and a discourse 'between the times' in the moment of God's patience. This discourse is its life, both as an announcement and as a lived display."[117] In "between the times" there is also political judgment, "a moment in parentheses between the two, an interim service that is a 'definite something,' with its defined beginning and its defined end."[118] Within this framework, the political reorientation of the church is materialized by the Spirit.

According to O'Donovan "the counter-political moment takes effect as the church takes form as a *koinonia* of the Holy Spirit in the midst of society's communications."[119] In other words, "the church is the community within which the Spirit is 'given,' representing the eschatological identity of humankind, and embodying it provisionally for all to see and enter."[120] This *telos* of the church as anticipating "the final form of human society" is grounded in the Apocalypse's final vision where

> the revelation of the church as *polis*, living immediately under the rule of God, coincides with the revelation of the church as *bride*, in marital fellowship with God. The completion and finalization of political order under the free and worshipping embrace of God's rule coincides with the completion and finalization of social order in complete and uncoerced fellowship with God.[121]

This eschatological horizon gives O'Donovan's political theology a ground on which to posit the concept of pure social theory as an "account of what it means for human beings to live together without judging, an account,

---

116. cf. Gen 2:9, 17; 3:5, 22; Deut 1:29; O'Donovan, *Ways of Judgment*, 238.
117. O'Donovan, *Ways of Judgment*, 240.
118. O'Donovan, 238.
119. O'Donovan, 293; cf. 2 Cor 13:13.
120. O'Donovan, 240.
121. O'Donovan, 240.

prescinding from political authority and judgment, of the social humanity that the world is summoned by the Spirit of God to become."[122]

Admittedly, for O'Donovan the church is the *koinonia* of the Holy Spirit, a concept he abstracts from the Pauline trinitarian "grace" at the end of 2 Corinthians, but which he opts to render as "communication" instead of community, communion (or even fellowship, as in our apocalyptic construal, i.e. the Fellowship of the Throne).[123] "To 'communicate' is to hold some thing as common, to make it a common possession, to treat it as 'ours,' rather than 'yours' or 'mine.'"[124] This dynamic does not mean to give up wholly (this mine is yours),[125] neither does it signify an exchange (this mine is yours, this yours is mine).[126] Instead, "the logic of communication sets the idea of 'mine' alongside that of 'ours.'"[127] This logic is best illustrated within the *koinonia* of the Spirit as follows: "Within the church the spiritual endowments and contributions of individual members converge upon a common life and a common confession, 'Jesus is Lord' (1 Cor. 12:3), and individual communications of various kinds are 'distributions' (*diaireseis*, 12:4–6), particular performances within the divine operation of a single organic whole."[128]

Now, within a community there are various spheres of communication that must be included in any consideration about the community itself, and which are closely linked to the concept of space.[129] O'Donovan argues that to understand the concreteness of particular societies we must identify them "in terms of the *place* in which they are situated. Place is the social communication of space,"[130] and the "determinant of society, [which] enables the division of our concerns into *public* and private."[131] For him two key places

---

122. O'Donovan, 240. "Christian social theory . . . is first and foremost an *ecclesiology*, and only an account of other human societies to the extent that the Church defines itself, in its practice, as in continuity and discontinuity with these societies." (Milbank, *Theology and Social Theory*, 382).

123. He founds his translation on the etymology of *koinonia* and on scholastic precedent, see O'Donovan, *Ways of Judgment*, 242–244.

124. O'Donovan, *Ways of Judgment*, 244.

125. cf. O'Donovan, 244.

126. cf. O'Donovan, 245.

127. O'Donovan, 249.

128. O'Donovan, 243.

129. cf. O'Donovan, 252–253.

130. O'Donovan, 255.

131. O'Donovan, 255.

in society are the market, which allows for exchange and "the sharing of a common space to move around in, a neighbourhood," and the household.[132] In the ancient world, it was presumed that the polis and the *oikos* (household) were the equivalent to public and private spheres of communication,[133] though the oikos was not "private" in the modern sense since it was "the social space where the aspirations of ordinary people to develop their engagements could find expression, sometimes experimentally."[134] However, according to O'Donovan, the nascent church was able to move around the two spatial spheres, public and private, that is to say, temple and household (oikos).[135] "From the beginning, then, the church took form as a city and as households. It had its *res publica* and its *res privata*, constituted by the two objects of its sharing, the bread of common life that human beings eat and the speech that human beings address to God. The households were independent centers of *koinonia*."[136]

"Domestic *koinonia*," however, "could not give form to the church on its own. Its material communicativeness – 'they had all things in common' – had to lead out into liturgical all-inclusiveness – 'they were together in one place' (Acts 2:43)."[137] In other words, "the church was not merely the sum of its households, but had its political center."[138] O'Donovan highlights two pneumatological implications for the church within these two spatial spheres: (a) with reference to the polis, it gave Christians the opportunity to present themselves before God. "In its central meeting the sovereignty of God's word was celebrated, attended to, and responded to. The city became a liturgy of praise."[139] It is a "liturgical word" that defines the city because of the apostles' teaching and the (responsive) prayer.[140] What is more, as Christians meet in the temple, the universality of the church is conveyed while they remain a

---

132. O'Donovan, 255.
133. cf. O'Donovan, 267.
134. O'Donovan, 268.
135. Acts 2:46; 5:42; cf. O'Donovan, *Ways of Judgment*, 269. This link between *oikos* and polis is also discussed in Wannenwetsch, *Political Worship*, 133–159.
136. O'Donovan, *Ways of Judgment*, 269.
137. O'Donovan, 269.
138. O'Donovan, 269.
139. O'Donovan, 271.
140. O'Donovan, 271.

local church. And yet, "the apostles' teaching, in the form of Holy Scripture and the sacraments of the Gospel, will still be the universal point of reference, holding all these particular churches together as one holy, catholic, and apostolic church."[141] (b) As for the *oikos*, it has undergone a social transformation to become "a sphere of social formation and mutual service open to participation."[142] That is to say, both master and slave were now standing on the same terms of dignity;[143] also, "economic management is practiced in the interests of *all* the household members."[144] However, O'Donovan also registers the gradual collapse of these two spatial poles as owners of oikos and land sell them and the proceeds are laid at the apostles' feet.[145] As a result, the city "now begins to assume some of the tasks of the household, and the first steps are taken which will eventually lead to the disappearance of the household as a unit of *koinonia*."[146]

The above brings us on to another aspect of the *koinonia* of the Spirit, which is the services or ministries (diakonia) of the church.[147] As the polis assimilated the *oikos*, the apostles' response was to bifurcate the *diakonia* of the church into the pastoral (the ministry of the tables) and doctrinal (ministry of the word, i.e. teaching and prayer) spheres of communication.[148] According to O'Donovan "ministry [*diakonia*] is the essence of the church's mutual relations in communication,"[149] and since there are a variety of ministries given by the Spirit,[150] he suggests these should be categorized according to their relevance to (a) "*the visible life of the universal church*,"[151] in all times and places, (b) "*the essential communications of the church*,"[152] which include the core sacramental signs of the church (baptism and Eucharist) as well as pastoral, didactic and missionary practices; and (c) "*the testimony of*

---

141. O'Donovan, 272.
142. O'Donovan, 272.
143. cf. O'Donovan, 273; Eph 6:9; Col 4:1.
144. O'Donovan, 273; cf. 1 Tim 6:2.
145. Acts 4:34.
146. O'Donovan, *Ways of Judgment*, 282.
147. cf. O'Donovan, 262.
148. cf. O'Donovan, 283–284, 286; Acts 6:2–4.
149. O'Donovan, 284.
150. cf. 1 Cor 12:4–11.
151. O'Donovan, *Ways of Judgment*, 264.
152. O'Donovan, 266.

the apostolic church, the church of the New Testament,"¹⁵³ though admittedly we cannot replicate this unique New Testament ecclesial model within our contemporary setting. Part of the apostles' response in the organizing of *diakonia* (ministry) into pastoral and doctrinal, was to establish *episkope* (oversight) for each sphere.¹⁵⁴ "Oversight . . . is a reflexive role, a special task that will protect the practice of ministry."¹⁵⁵ However, the composite term *diakonia-episkope* which had initially applied to both pastoral and doctrinal spheres underwent a redefinition and was subsequently divided into two roles of oversight: *episkopos* (bishop) and *diakonos* (minister),¹⁵⁶ with the bishop later taking the primacy within the church.¹⁵⁷ Within this context O'Donovan sees the role of a bishop as mediating "the opening of the local to the universal church on the only possible terms: agreement in the universal truth of the Gospel."¹⁵⁸

According to O'Donovan the current episcopal office must therefore look after the integrity of the *koinonia* in a particular place (inward focus), while also looking after the integrity of the koinonia in relation to the universal church (outward focus).¹⁵⁹ The impact of this local expression of the *koinonia* of the Spirit with a proper episcopal office in a particular political society should (a) restrain any attempt to universalize the locality (experiences, perspectives) of this society,¹⁶⁰ (b) question local traditions, (c) challenge "patterns of social standing and honour,"¹⁶¹ and also (d) help to advance "the social good which they exist to defend."¹⁶² In this kind of prophetic role, the church also displays its nature as a post or counter political society.

---

153. O'Donovan, 267.

154. cf. O'Donovan, 284, 286–287. Admittedly, Acts 6:3 deploys the verb ἐπισκέπτομαι (look at, examine, look after, BDAG 378).

155. O'Donovan, *Ways of Judgment*, 284.

156. cf. O'Donovan, 287; Phil 1:1; 1 Tim 3:2, 8, 12; Titus 1:7; *1 Clement* 42.4–5. At this stage, a bishop (*episkopos*) and an elder (*presbuteros*) were synonymous, cf. Acts 20:17, 28.

157. e.g. Ignatius, *To the Trallians* 2.1; *To the Philadelphians* 4.1; cf. O'Donovan, *Ways of Judgment*, 287.

158. O'Donovan, *Ways of Judgment*, 289.

159. O'Donovan, 288–289.

160. cf. O'Donovan, 291.

161. O'Donovan, 292.

162. O'Donovan, 292.

In the midst of this *koinonia* of the Spirit as construed by O'Donovan individuals have still a part to play in that as they live subject to the overlap of "two political realms, present and future, [they] judge for themselves."[163] That is to say, each individual anticipates, though privately, the judgments deployed by the political authority, and in this sense shows their support for the institutions of judgment. Equally, the individual judges themself and may pronounce on what they owes to their adversary,[164] since "[to] judge of oneself is the very heart of faith in God."[165] In fact, "faith in the crucified and risen Christ involves conformity to his cross; it means sharing his isolation and rejection,"[166] and it is the sharing of this moment, which marks "the initiation into the Christian community,"[167] it is also at this moment that "the individual emerges decisively as the primary agent."[168] For O'Donovan it is a conversion experience that inaugurates the ongoing meeting of God and the soul within the self, so that "the individual believer, filled with the Holy Spirit, participates directly and subjectively in the life of God."[169] Within this construal therefore "the saving history of Jesus Christ is not mediated to the believer uniquely through participating in the sacraments, but it takes its own reflected form in the hidden interior struggle for moral and spiritual integrity."[170]

In fact, if modernity construes human being as in a state of introspection, led by a "resolute and inexhaustible self-doubt,"[171] this is not the kind of reflection the Christian believer engages in. Instead, according to O'Donovan, the believer "withdraw[s] from the world to be conformed to the image of a self-communicating God, and so become[s] similarly self-communicative."[172] Within this context, the Christian believer that judges themself also anticipates the eschatological redundancy of political authority as known within

---

163. O'Donovan, 293.
164. cf. O'Donovan, 293.
165. O'Donovan, 294.
166. O'Donovan, 294.
167. O'Donovan, 294–295.
168. O'Donovan, 294.
169. O'Donovan, 296.
170. O'Donovan, 296. Ben Quash questions this "role of the individual believing heart as the privileged site of ecclesial transformation of the world" in Quash, "Life Beyond Judgment," 316–317.
171. O'Donovan, *Ways of Judgment*, 308.
172. O'Donovan, 310.

the secular-as-time.[173] What we find instead, in O'Donovan's construal is a correlation between the individual believer (the subject) and the church where "the subject is realized in the church, [and] the church completed in the subject."[174] This correlation is actualised in apocalyptic terms by O'Donovan as follows: "Here is the anonymous 'conqueror' of the letters to the churches in the Apocalypse, a figure very much in the singular, alone and without the support of the community, but who turns out to have a social identity after all."[175]

7.2.3 The Church as a Moral Society

For O'Donovan, the church is also a moral community under the authority of Scripture. This argument is based on the resurrection of Jesus and its implications,[176] in particular two aspects: "one is the decisive once-for-all achievement of the conquest of death, the other its ongoing consequences, the remoulding of the human race in the image of the risen Christ."[177] Within this christological framework and drawing from an Aristotelian model that splits reasoning into theoretical (or contemplative) and practical, respectively,[178] O'Donovan offers a moral account of the church in which the link between the resurrection of Jesus and practical reason is the restoration of the latter out of the former, which at the same time reshapes the social condition of the human being. Thus, "the greater Easter season is about restored practical reason and about a restored human fellowship. These two go together. As practical reason is healed, community is healed, and many agents can act as one."[179] Out of a restored practical reason, then, flow a will and desire that leads to (communal) action. This rationale takes an Augustinian turn when O'Donovan introduces the concept of "common objects of love" as the force that shapes communal identity and action.[180] Accordingly, "loving is the corporate function that determines and defines the structure of the political

---

173. cf. O'Donovan, 312.
174. O'Donovan, 317; cf. 314.
175. O'Donovan, 318–319. He is alluding to Rev 3:12.
176. O'Donovan, "What Kind of Community," 172, 178.
177. O'Donovan, 172.
178. cf. O'Donovan, *Common Objects of Love*, 2–3; O'Donovan, *Self, World, and Time*, 22–23; Aristotle, *Nicomachean Ethics* 6.2 (1139a+); 6.5 (1140a, 1140b).
179. O'Donovan, "What Kind of Community," 172.
180. cf. Augustine, *City of God* 19.24.

society; it is the key to its coherence and its organization. Loving *things*, not loving *one another*."[181]

Here O'Donovan argues that if "morality is man's participation in the created order," it follows that "Christian morality is his glad response to the deed of God which has restored, proved and fulfilled that order, making man free to conform to it."[182] As a result, "the Church has to be a *moral* community, because any community must be a moral community in some sense, [and] must have common objects of love."[183] What is more,

> the Church is committed to a comprehensive account of, and pursuit of, the human good, not just on its own behalf, but on behalf of the human race as a whole. Christians who believe that God has raised Jesus believe that he has restored the human community of desire and love. In the person of the Last Adam, he has granted us to live together in the world that was made for us, to desire together the good that is prepared for us to walk in.[184]

A further element in O'Donovan's account of the church takes us back to the notion of authority, though here arrived at via his construal of the church as a community; and this within his understanding of community as communication (i.e. "the exercise of sharing things or transmitting them among two or more people").[185] When communication is also seen as an event with a beginning and an end, it inevitably becomes subject to contingencies of various kinds, like interruptions.[186] These contingencies, whether quantitative, since "communities have a limited reach; they cannot share everything with everybody,"[187] or qualitative, since the community's common object of love "is not only affection for what we have in common, but desire for what we do not have,"[188] mean that the community of the church, with its in-built limitations, must live with a permanent tension between the outer and inner

---

181. O'Donovan, *Common Objects of Love*, 26.
182. O'Donovan, *Resurrection and Moral Order*, 76.
183. O'Donovan, "What Kind of Community," 181.
184. O'Donovan, 181.
185. O'Donovan, *Common Objects of Love*, 26; cf. O'Donovan, "What Kind of Community," 173.
186. Cf. O'Donovan, "What Kind of Community," 182.
187. O'Donovan, 182.
188. O'Donovan, 183.

form of its identity, whether expressed as visible vs invisible, consummation vs promise, local vs universal or generational vs cross-generational.[189]

However, here we find that "every element of the Church's outer forms is under criticism, subordinate to the identity of a community called into being by the Gospel proclamation of the Kingdom of God in Christ."[190] In fact, "to get the relation between the inner and the outer right is to see why *reformation* is a perpetually open question in the Church."[191] It is at this point that O'Donovan introduces Scripture as the divinely authorized agent to mediate in this ecclesial tension: "The supreme authority of *Scripture*, judging, correcting, criticizing the practices of the Church, assures the criticism under which the Church lives . . . out of the authoritative Word of God."[192] For O'Donovan, a church shaped by the Scriptures and submitted to the authority of the Scripture is the one that reads, interprets, and obeys it. And since "obedience is a task of practical reasoning,"[193] it follows that "Scripture is given us to guide and to discipline our practical reasoning; it sets us free to engage in clear-sighted deliberation leading to decision,"[194] arguably equipping us in ethics.[195] This in turn gives the church stability, since a "church living perpetually under the critical authority of Holy Scripture is protected from those hectoring voices that arise with shocking suddenness to propose radically new formal arrangements."[196]

All in all, O'Donovan's quasi trinitarian account of the church, given that the church is predicated on the authority of the exalted Jesus, is the *koinonia* of the Holy Spirit, and is under the authority of Scripture (God's word), proves to be politically highly charged. Its condition as political society is made transparent by a liturgical discourse, mainly sacramental; whereas its status as a post/counter-political society in the midst of the institutions of political judgment is conveyed by the pneumatological twofold ministry of liturgical word (teaching and prayer) and pastoral care, enabling it to be

---

189. cf. O'Donovan, 185–187.
190. O'Donovan, 187.
191. O'Donovan, 187.
192. O'Donovan, 188.
193. O'Donovan, 191.
194. O'Donovan, 192.
195. cf. O'Donovan, 191.
196. O'Donovan, 193.

light and salt within its local community, a role facilitated by the episcopal office of oversight. Within this construal individuals are initiated into the church the moment they judge themselves and put their faith in God and the exalted Jesus. This conversion experience leads the individual, infused by the Spirit, into an ongoing reflective life where God and the soul meet within the self in a dynamic greatly contrasting with the modern individual introspection that leads to self doubt. The church is also construed as moral community that is experiencing restoration of (the Aristotelian) practical reason because of the resurrection of Jesus, and that is therefore made free to pursue its (Augustinian) common objects of love guided by and under the authority of Scripture.

7.3 Critique from Liturgical Sociality

In *The Future of Love* John Milbank observes that "political theory and ecclesiology must . . . be then of one piece,"[197] a point of view we share and which has in many ways been self-evident throughout our theological inquiry into society and its relationship with authority, or vice versa. Whether we are presented with the Platonic luxurious polis, the Aristotelian natural polis, the Ciceronian *res publica*, or variants of these by Thomas Hobbes, John Locke and Jean-Jacques Rousseau, we find that the question of society (§7.1) is indeed a theological question when examined through the lenses of O'Donovan's understanding of the church (§7.2),[198] or through the Apocalypse's construal of the liturgical sociality (chapter 6). In what follows we will engage in a critique of these models, including O'Donovan's, from the perspective of the Apocalypse's own construal of society as we have understood it, since a christological political theology "must criticise existing notions of political good and necessity, not only classical republican notions but imperial and theocratic notions too, in the light of what God has done for the human race and the human soul."[199]

To begin with, there is the overall issue of how society is construed and whether it precedes authority or not, which may be seen as an attempt to

---

197. Milbank, *Future of Love*, xv.
198. cf. Milbank, *Theology and Social Theory*, 9–25.
199. O'Donovan, *Desire of the Nations*, 122.

answer what O'Donovan called the conundrum for political theory (i.e. that non-reciprocal or asymmetric relation where the ruler exerts authority and the subject responds with submission),[200] as noted in §5.3. Some, such as Hobbes and Rousseau tried, through contractarian theories, "to justify the non-reciprocal relation by deriving it from reciprocality . . . Political subjection was owed not to the rulers themselves but to the collective whole; consequently, everybody owed precisely the same to everybody else."[201] Within these models, the concept of "the people" "is imaginatively envisaged when and as its common good is in need of defense. The idea of the people and the idea of the authority that summons it to defend its common good arise together."[202] However, within these construals the idea of the people "is not the same as that of a juridical or law-based entity with a political order. Political authority does not 'make' a people; it 'finds' it."[203] What is more, humanity "is communal by virtue of God's creation, not by political invention. Political order discovers and defends the social order; it does not construct it."[204] So far it is clear to us that the Apocalypse would allow for a critique of those views in similar terms to those of O'Donovan.

In our reading of the Apocalypse, it is christological love ("to the one who loves us") conveyed soteriologically through a market transaction ("bought with his blood") that enables the constitution of the liturgical sociality ("a kingdom and priests") with a divine orientation ("to God the Father").[205] Clearly this construal does not reflect the Platonic need-driven polis or the naturally gregarious Aristotelian polis, and has little in common with the Hobbesian, Lockean or Rousseauian contractarian societies. However, Revelation's liturgical sociality displays some points of contact with the Ciceronian *res publica* à la Romulus and with the Aristotelian idea that every citizen of the polis is a judge and ruler, given the apocalyptic construal of the liturgical sociality as both a kingdom and as priests who will reign. It is, however, most emphatically the exalted Jesus (as the Lamb) that takes centre

---

200. cf. O'Donovan, *Ways of Judgment*, 127–128.
201. O'Donovan, 128.
202. O'Donovan, 154.
203. O'Donovan, 154.
204. O'Donovan, 156; cf. 297.
205. Rev 1:5–6; 5:9–10; cf. 3:9; 20:9.

stage and shepherds or rules the liturgical sociality;[206] equally, it is the exalted Jesus (this time portrayed as like a son of man/Son of God) that holds the liturgical sociality in his right hand signifying its unity and sustains it (§6.2.1). Clearly this figure is not the Platonic guardian, the Aristotelian citizen, or the Ciceronian consilium; it is neither the Hobbesian coercive power, the Lockean majority will, nor the Rousseauian general will – all of which remain purely immanent construals of authority, whether personal, corporate or diffused and impersonal. On the contrary, in the materialization of the Fellowship of the Throne, the divine authority and a liturgical sociality subordinated to the former through the mediation of the exalted Jesus become fully transparent.

With reference to the correlation between space (place) and liturgy articulated by O'Donovan, it is worth noting how this resonates with the Apocalypse's construal of the liturgical sociality as sacral space and city. For O'Donovan place is the social communication of space,[207] and when "space becomes inhabited as 'place,' it is assigned to various social uses, public, private, and a blend of the two,"[208] as illustrated by the interplay between market, polis and temple (all public) on the one hand, and *oikos* (private) on the other. In fact, he suggests that "the Garden of Eden is the first communication, the space where God and humankind are to be at home together."[209] Thus, in O'Donovan's account of the early church, the impact of "the presence of the Holy Spirit . . . upon the underlying bipolar social organization of city and household" was felt,[210] in the first instance, in the redefinition of the city as "a liturgy of praise" where "the sovereignty of God's word was celebrated, attended to, and responded to."[211] The gradual absorption of the oikos into the polis and its eventual disappearance, perhaps expanded the scope for liturgy (§6.1), but certainly reaffirmed the church's liturgical orientation, since the liturgical word (teaching and prayer) is the ministry of the word.[212] In general, O'Donovan's correlation between space and liturgy aligns with the Apocalypse's construal of the liturgical sociality as a sacred space (where the

---

206. Rev 7:17; cf. 2:27; 12:5; 19:15.
207. cf. O'Donovan, *Ways of Judgment*, 255.
208. O'Donovan, 257.
209. O'Donovan, 245.
210. O'Donovan, 270.
211. O'Donovan, 271.
212. cf. O'Donovan, 270, 271, 284, 285, 286.

ministry of the word is performed), a city-in-the-making, the holy city and holy of holies (where liturgical service and boundaries are highlighted),[213] as seen in §6.2 and §6.3. However, O'Donovan's liturgical construal of space is predicated on the Holy Spirit, whereas the Apocalypse's is construed around the (mediated presence of the) exalted Jesus and the divine authority. And yet, if the garden of Eden was the first communication, certainly the holy city/holy of holies is the ultimate communication, the liturgical space where the Fellowship of the Throne materializes.

Turning now to the role of liturgy as presented in the various accounts of sociality and authority, we would note that Plato deploys liturgy as a discourse to legitimize a new set of laws or policies regarding marriage (no longer an exclusive monogamous relationship), parenthood (no longer based on blood relation) and public morality (the charge of promiscuity is deflected by redefining marriage) with the sole aim of maintaining the unity of the polis. Augustus deploys liturgy as a means of asserting the non-reciprocal or asymmetric relation between authority and subject. Here it is worth highlighting that *sacramentum* (oath), especially among civilians, was the alternative to *bellum* (war) because of the emperor's zeal to exact *subicio* (to submit/subject).[214] O'Donovan argues that liturgical discourse conveyed by the sacraments is the means by which to communicate to the watching world the condition of the church as a political society predicated on the exalted Jesus. Also, when the pneumatological church is understood as a post/counter-political society, the ministry of the word (teaching, prayer) is a liturgical word.

It should be noted, however, that more recently O'Donovan has espoused a minimalist view of the sacraments (baptism and the Eucharist),[215] as opposed to his fourfold sacramental model (the keeping of the Lord's Day and the laying-on of hands, in addition to baptism and the Eucharist) which mirrored each stage of his construal of the Christ-event (advent, passion, restoration

---

213. "It was much more common to think of Jerusalem as a spiritual and liturgical center for the independent peoples of the world." (O'Donovan, *Ways of Judgment*, 211).

214. The liturgical overtones of *sacramentum*, according to Pliny the Younger, were equally displayed by Christians, who "were accustomed to assemble at dawn on a fixed day, to sing a hymn antiphonally to Christ as God, and to bind themselves by an oath [*sacramentum*]" Pliny the Younger, *Letters* 10.96.7.

215. e.g. O'Donovan, *Ways of Judgment*, 266, 266n7; O'Donovan, "What Kind of Community," 188.

and exaltation).[216] Be that as it may, the Apocalypse lacks any explicit or unambiguous sacramental discourse, if a minimalist view is considered,[217] in stark contrast to O'Donovan's multifaceted account of the church, a fact which explains the absence of sacramental referents within our construal of the Apocalypse's liturgical sociality. What we find instead is that the Apocalypse's liturgical discourse can be understood through alternative theological categories other than sacramental, for example aesthetics, revelation, Christology, soteriology, doxology. More importantly, the Apocalypse signifies what the sacraments are meant to signify,[218] for instance, fellowship with the exalted Jesus within the context of his mediating presence (§6.2), as in the Eucharist,[219] or the salvation/initiation of the individual into the church (§6.3.3), as in baptism.[220] Arguably, this hermeneutical gap between apocalyptic vision and sacrament was collapsed by Oecumenius (ca. 600 AD) in his *Commentary on the Apocalypse* where he interprets both Revelation 3:20 ("I will come in to you and eat with you and you with me") and 7:14 ("they washed their clothes and whitened them with the blood of the Lamb") as mere references to the sacraments of the Eucharist and baptism, respectively.[221]

O'Donovan uses his sacramental discourse, in particular as regards baptism, to set the boundaries of the Christian community. On the one hand, baptism is a very individual experience, since "it is *as* a believer that the individual is baptized, already conditioned by the faith which God has brought to birth in him or her,"[222] and on the other hand, "the individual, *qua* believer, is already of the church when he is joined to the church in baptism."[223] It is precisely in this corporate sense that baptism is "the sign that marks the gathering

---

216. cf. O'Donovan, *Desire of Nations*, 174–191; O'Donovan, *On the Thirty-Nine*, location 2605+.

217. However, when in Patmos John was in the Spirit on the Lord's Day (Rev 1:10), and there is expectation about the marriage of the Lamb and his bride (Rev 19:7; 21:9; cf. 19:9).

218. e.g. "in the sacrament of His body and blood He signified His will through the sense of taste" Augustine, *On Christian Doctrine* 2.3 (NPNF1/2).

219. We registered in §4.1.4 that O'Donovan considers a meal as a sign of fellowship (O'Donovan, *Desire of the Nations*, 250). For a brief discussion of the Eucharist and the presence of Jesus see McGrath, *Christian Theology*, 414–420.

220. cf. O'Donovan, *Ways of Judgment*, 313–314.

221. Oecumenius, *Commentary on the Apocalypse* Third Discourse, Fifth Discourse (ACT/G).

222. O'Donovan, *Ways of Judgment*, 314.

223. O'Donovan, 314.

community."²²⁴ However, as noted in §6.3.3, the blood of the Lamb becomes the soteriological threshold into the city in the making, one of the construals of the liturgical sociality of the Apocalypse; equally, we observed that in the vision of the advent of the holy city, the finished/complete city, *doxa*, understood as a liturgical act addressed to the divine authority becomes the requirement for entering into this holy of holies, the locus of the Fellowship of the Throne. Thus, despite the lack of explicit and unambiguous sacramental discourse to convey political status as society or initiation/incorporation into the church in the way argued by O'Donovan, the Apocalypse deploys alternative theological categories, still operating within a liturgical framework, that convey what those sacraments signify. After all, with the advent of the holy city and the materialization of the Fellowship of the Throne, "the sacraments themselves are to pass away in the fullness of sight."²²⁵

A final point to consider and contrast from O'Donovan's account of the church is his concern for the individual. For instance, he is deeply critical of "the pre-political individual of contractarian theory, the individual of Hobbes, Locke, and Rousseau . . . who is an underdetermined atom from which the molecular structures of society are constructed by processes of negotiation and compromise."²²⁶ Of this individual who lacks personality, identity and aspirations other than those relating to their basic needs, O'Donovan notes that "he encounters us simply as the bearer of 'human rights,' that tide of undifferentiated demands that relentlessly erodes the coasts of our social institutions."²²⁷ By contrast, "the believer within the church [does not] cease at any point to be the individual disciple who was first called to 'take up his cross . . . daily' (Luke 9:23)."²²⁸ This delicate balance which O'Donovan strikes between the individual and the community in his account of the church has much in common with the Apocalypse's own treatment of these issues.

From the outset in the first vision the liturgical sociality of the Apocalypse is portrayed as made up of individuals, churches and other groups. The one who conquers is unambiguously referred to as an individual (Rev 2:7, 11,

---

224. O'Donovan, *Desire of the Nations*, 177.
225. O'Donovan, *Ways of Judgment*, 319.
226. O'Donovan, 297.
227. O'Donovan, 297.
228. O'Donovan, 314.

17, 26; 3:5, 12, 21), together with the one who has an ear to listen to what the Spirit says to the churches (2:7, 11, 17, 29; 3:6, 13, 22). Other individuals singled out are Antipas as a witness (2:13), the prophetess nicknamed Jezebel (2:20), and the anonymous "each [of] you" (2:23) as well as "someone" who hears Jesus's voice and opens the door (3:20). There are also various groups referred or alluded to in the messages to the churches: those who call themselves apostles and are not (2:2); the Nicolaitans (2:6, 15) and those who hold to their teaching (2:15), also nicknamed as those who hold to the teaching of Balaam (2:14); those who the devil is going to throw into prison (2:10); Jesus's servants (2:20); those who "commit adultery" with Jezebel (2:22); Jezebel's children (2:23), and "the rest of you," those who have not known the "deep things of Satan" (2:24). Then we have the comprehensive expression "all the churches" (2:23) that implies the sum of individual churches (cf. 1:11), and the all-encompassing phrase "I scrutinize and discipline as many as I love" (3:19).

Throughout the greatest part of the narrative in Revelation, however, it is the holy ones[229] and the servants[230] who most feature and who are consistently portrayed as living in some degree of sociality as evident in the church of Thyatira (2:20; cf. 2:18), the beloved city (20:9), and the holy city (22:3). Other portrayals of the liturgical sociality are the priests (1:6; 5:10; 20:6); the souls of those that have been slaughtered (6:9) or beheaded (20:4); the countless great multitude (7:9); the rest of the descendants of the woman (12:17); those who keep the commands of God and the witness/faith of Jesus (12:17; 14:12); the prophets (10:7; 11:10, 18; 16:6; 18:20, 24; 22:6, 9); the two witnesses (11:3) and the witnesses of Jesus (17:6), and last but not least, the liturgical entity known as a kingdom (1:6, 9; 5:10). In fact, in the vision of the new heaven and new earth and the advent of the holy city, the individual and the sociality are kept in balance: there God will dwell with (the sociality of) human beings (21:3), while the one who conquers will (individually) be a son to God (21:7). And yet, the materialization of the Fellowship of the Throne highlights the corporate dimension of the liturgical sociality, that is the servants of the Lamb will liturgically serve him (22:3) and God will illuminate them as they rule (22:5) under the authority of the throne of God and the Lamb (22:3).

---

229. Revelation 5:8; 8:3–4; 11:18; 13:7, 10; 14:12; 16:6; 17:6; 18:20, 24; 19:8; 20:9.
230. Revelation 1:1; 2:20; 7:3; 11:18; 19:2, 5; 22:3, 6.

7.4 Conclusion

The political question of society, which we initially considered through ancient Greek and Roman political construals, becomes a theological question when understood through O'Donovan's threefold account of the church as political society (§7.2.1), post-political society (§7.2.2) and moral society (§7.2.3). In many ways this theological approach minimizes differences between O'Donovan's account of the church and our own construal of the liturgical society in the Apocalypse. The main point of divergence, as we have seen, is in their deployment of the sacramental discourse, which O'Donovan conveys in explicit and unambiguous terms, while the book of Revelation, unlike other New Testament documents, bypasses.

Here we argued, however, that the Apocalypse's construal of the liturgical sociality alludes to what the sacraments signify, and that, instead, alternative theological categories render in the Apocalypse's construal what O'Donovan's account of the church predicates on sacramental theology, in particular as regards the political identity, initiation and boundary makers of the church. What has become self-evident in this discussion is that the Apocalypse's construal of the liturgical sociality, with its alternative yet signifying discourse, anticipates the redundancy of the sacramental discourse with the advent of the holy city and materialization of the Fellowship of the Throne.

CHAPTER 8

Conclusions

8.1 "I, John . . . Was in the Isle Called Patmos . . . Was in (the) Spirit"[1]

One of the paradoxes of the real-life context of the present writer, a Mexican national, instigated this research into the renewed field of political theology and in some way gave this study a *raison d'etre*. It is the reality, as reported by the latest Mexican census, that though an overwhelming majority of the population identify themselves as Christians of some description, all aspects of public life in the Mexican state are ordered and sanctioned by a purely immanent and/or secular approach to life, as implied in the Mexican constitution and expressly conveyed in a law about religious associations. This present state of things is in stark contrast with a historic tendency to embrace a view of life infused with a concern for the transcendent which is evident on the streets of Mexico up and down the country. In chapter 1 of this work we gave an account of what this paradox of modern life in Mexico looks like and briefly traced the origins of the secular turn in public life. The reality is that the present immanent and secular approach to life now exerts a monopoly in the public square while also confining any religious or theological voices to the private sphere. It is this assymetric correlation between a totalized secular discourse and a marginalized religious and/or theological voice that led us to our theo-political inquiry into authority and society as conveyed by the narrative of the Apocalypse, guided by Oliver O'Donovan's scholarly

---

1. Rev 1:9–10.

theo-political framework. This study grew out of the expectation that it would offer the present writer a theological resource that may inform an appropriate response to his personal context. Our context, just as John the Seer's in the Apocalypse, has left its imprint on our thesis.

8.2 "The Marriage of the Lamb Has Come"[2]

Arguably, the apocalyptic analogy of marriage is an apt image to import into our vision of this project. This is so because, methodologically speaking, our work has brought together, in a not too common partnership, two separate fields of knowledge, biblical studies and theology, in order to interact with and inform each other throughout the trajectory of this thesis. This methodology is in some ways the hallmark of O'Donovan's political theology, who invariably looks to Scripture to inform and resource his theology in the search for the truths about the political, a strategy not often adopted by other practitioners.[3] In a similar way, in this project we have drawn specifically from the book of Revelation; and because of the enormous amount of allusions to the Old Testament within the Apocalypse's narrative, we have also looked to the Israelite/Jewish tradition, including (briefly) Qumranic and Second-Temple literature to assist our enterprise. In keeping with O'Donovan's agenda for a political theology, which we have surveyed in this project, we have been compelled to engage with his wider theological work, as well as with essential ancient literature on the political such as Plato's *Republic*, Aristotle's *Politics*, Cicero's *On the Commonwealth* and Augustus's *Res Gestae*. More occasionally we have referred to the work of early modern political theorists and noted the contribution of the Christian theo-political tradition. It is in this way that the marriage of Scripture and a theology resourced by the political tradition – whether ancient or modern, Christian or not – has metaphorically taken place throughout this project.

On the other hand, in terms of its structure, this project has endeavoured to draw together two lines of inquiry: the one relating to authority, and the

---

2. Rev 19:7; cf. 19:9.

3. John Milbank acknowledged this was the case with his *Theology and Social Theory*, see Milbank, *Theology and Social Theory*, xxxi–xxxii. To some extent, Milbank's method is exposed (or at least it transpires) in Milbank, *Future of Love*, 316–334.

other to society, both framed within the parameters of O'Donovan's methodology and choreographed by the overarching construal of the Fellowship of the Throne as explained in our introduction (chapter 1). Accordingly, we undertook this study in three parts, each part presenting two chapters. In part 1 we dealt with the questions of principles for engaging O'Donovan and of method and concepts discerned by O'Donovan from the narrative of Scripture (chapter 2) as well as the themes emerging from our own reading of the narrative of the Apocalypse (chapter 3). Part 2 covered our inquiry into the theo-political category of authority, whether divine (chapter 4) or human (chapter 5); and part 3 addressed the theo-political category of society, looking first at our understanding of the Apocalypse's construal of the liturgical society as both sacred space and holy city, assisted by the theo-political input on space by both John Milbank and William Cavanaugh (chapter 6), and followed by an overview of ancient models of immanent society (Plato, Aristotle, Cicero) and O'Donovan's ecclesiology (chapter 7). With this structure we have endeavoured to attain the coherence and balance between the various strands of this project, offering also in each part a critique of the category discussed from the corresponding counterpart as we have found it in the Apocalypse (chapters 5 and 7). In brief, we sought coherence between both disciplines (i.e. biblical studies and theology) and terms of inquiry (i.e. authority and society), by adopting O'Donovan's method and agenda for political theology within the structure of the thesis while allowing a critique of it from the Apocalypse's construal, which we have summed up in the Fellowship of the Throne. This is also the marriage of authority and society.

8.3 "Who Bore Witness . . . as Far as He Perceived"[4]

Our construal of the Fellowship of the Throne, we have argued, is predicated on two theo-political categories, divine authority and liturgical sociality, where the latter became subsidiary to the former through the mediation of the exalted Jesus. Guided by this christological connection between authority and society, we were able to engage in a three-step inquiry, (i) following O'Donovan's method of inquiry (chapter 2), we traversed the Apocalypse's narrative (chapter 3) noting how the Fellowship of the Throne is adumbrated

---

4. Rev 1:2.

from the very first vision, and developed as an overarching motif throughout its story and plot. (ii) Digging deeper around one of the strands of this overarching motif (i.e. divine authority, chapter 4) – which we argued was signified by the ubiquitous and most stable symbol in the narrative, that of the heavenly throne – we found that it had undergone a christological shift that may be postulated as the correlation of power and divine status between the one who sits on the throne (i.e. God) and the exalted Jesus. This is better conveyed in the last vision of the narrative as "the throne of God and the Lamb,"[5] which is in stark contrast to John's rendering of his first sighting of the heavenly throne as "look! a throne was standing in heaven, and on the throne one sitting there."[6]

This correlation of power, we found, continues to be conveyed in a markedly (and arguably standard) christological discourse, with the exalted Jesus featuring in major apocalyptic visions as the Son of God, the Lamb, the Messiah, and in the converging portrait of the divine King, whose persona draws on features from the three previous christological portraits. Continuing in our exploration, we noticed also how each major depiction of the exalted Jesus displayed a link with the liturgical sociality: whether adumbrating the fellowship between divine authority and sociality (as the Son of God); recovering a sociality for God by means of a market transaction (the Lamb); affirming the value of tradition and a teleological orientation of history (the Messiah); or clearing an ontological space for the advent of the holy polis by forensic means (the divine King). In addition, we noted the dragon's unsuccessful attempt to prevent this christological shift from taking place, which led to its downfall, opting here to maintain the integrity of this narrative strand rather than dividing it into two separate accounts. We also interpreted this event as modelled on the Old Testament and ancient Near Eastern motifs of political conspiracy, where a vassal or minor ruler plots against a superior imperial power, and having failed is seized, bound, and imprisoned or exiled, in short dethroned. To our knowledge no scholar has proposed this view. In this section we also argued that the portrayal of Jesus as the divine King is based on the "job description" associated with the king in ancient Israel (with

---

5. Rev 22:1, 3.
6. Rev 4:2.

an allusion to 1 Samuel 8 overlooked as of yet) from which later theological and eschatological traditions on the king developed.

(iii) The second of our theo-political categories intrinsic to the construal of the Fellowship of the Throne (i.e. the liturgical sociality, chapter 6), can be identified within the Apocalypse as both a sacred space and a holy city, in particular, a city in the making. It should be noted that these two images (sacred space and city) converge in the final vision of the narrative: the advent of the holy city, in which a succession of images, including a bride on her way to meet his bridegroom/husband, a walled city turned into a sacred space (in fact, an enormous holy of holies), and then a primeval garden or paradise all appear to signify the same reality. This convergence furnishes us with a hermeneutical purchase with which we can trace back these images (sacred space and city) to earlier visions within the narrative. The identifiable visual elements of these visions allow us to construe the spaces between which the exalted Jesus moves as a stylized version of the Old Testament tent of meeting and temple, not least because of the allusive nature of those elements to Old Testament sacred spaces, whether the holy of holies or the Holy Place. More importantly, in the Old Testament the whole notion of a sacred space was underpinned on the relationship and fellowship God wanted to have with his people. Thus, the construal of the liturgical sociality as a sacred space recovers this theologoumenon since it allows for the mediated presence of the exalted Jesus in the midst of his church, a hermeneutical move that offers a way forward for this exegetical conundrum in the very first vision of the narrative, since Jesus's presence goes from realized presence to imminent conditional presence in either negative or positive mode.

The liturgical sociality construed as a city in the making, we also judge to be a christological reworking of an Old Testament motif where a city (i.e. Jerusalem/Zion/the holy city) is rebuilt on the return of the people of God from exile in hostile lands, and as the place where God would return to dwell among his people once more, bringing also healing and wholeness. However, in this apocalyptic construal of the city in the making it is the exalted Jesus who takes over some of the Old Testament divine expectations, in particular, he shepherds this people. More importantly, it is the exalted Jesus who sets the boundaries of this city, that is to say, membership or citizenship in this city is necessarily christological, since those who come into the city do so because they whitened their clothes in the blood of the Lamb. The question of citizenship is addressed again in the vision of the advent of the finished or complete city (i.e. the holy city). Within that context, a liturgical act addressed to the divine authority becomes a complimentary means of gaining access into the city. In other words, it is genuine *doxa* ascribed to God and the exalted Jesus that confirms citizenship of the holy city, that is to say, as also discerned by O'Donovan, political identity is derived from an act of liturgy addressed to the divine authority. Overall, our spatial approach to the question of society as raised in the Apocalypse makes a new contribution to an upward trend among biblical scholars and theologians in which the concept of "space" becomes an exegetical and theological category of analysis.

8.4 "This Calls for Discernment"[7]

Our exploration into the Apocalypse's construal of divine authority (chapter 4), we found, provided us with a framework from which to critique the construal of human political authority (chapter 5), whether it be conveyed as *sophia* and *paideia* (Plato), *bellum* and *subicio* (Augustus), or as a downsized secular political authority only entitled to enact judgment (O'Donovan). As part of this apocalyptic framework there emerges a corollary of human authority conveyed in apophatic terms, that is to say, showing what a human political authority should not be (the sea-beast), which is a self-aggrandizing and immanent authority predicated on a heterodox theology and reinforced by an equally heretical public liturgy. It also communicates what a human authority (the kings of the earth) should not do, which is to move away from its christological point of reference to draw its identity instead from the symbiotic relationship between a distorted form of authority and a distorted form of sociality. This aspect (i.e. what a human authority should not do), we found to be absent from O'Donovan's model of political authority, which is predicated mainly on Romans 13.

As a result, the *kataphatic* (affirmative) construal of divine authority and the *apophatic* (negative) corollary on human authority of the Apocalypse create an expectation for the emergence of the ultimate horizon of the political realised in the Fellowship of the Throne. Central to Fellowship of the Throne, we have argued, is the divine authority signified by the throne, jointly

---

7. Rev 13:18 (BDAG 1101); cf. Rev 17:9.

shared by God and the exalted Jesus, which has drawn alongside itself a liturgical sociality in christological coordination and submission to the divine authority and yet sharing in its reign. Perhaps the most remarkable feature about this apocalyptic construal of divine authority is the fact that it does not suffocate, overwhelm or deny any notion of human authority per se. On the contrary, divine authority proactively opens a space for human authority as it did in the beginning, according to the account of creation in Genesis. We have found also that human authority, though immanent, does not walk away from its christological and transcendent referent; instead this sociality liturgically serves the divine authority. Other features of this construal of human authority include its diffused, plural, multicultural, cosmopolitan, cross-regional, cross-generational nature, since it is made up of those "from every tribe and language and people and nation,"[8] as opposed to a mode of authority concentrated in one single individual (as in the beast), or in a few (as in the kings of the earth).

As to the apocalyptic liturgical sociality construed in spatial terms as either a sacred space or a city in the making – with the two images merging in the final vision of the advent of the holy city – we have found that it enabled us to engage in a critique with Platonic, Aristotelian, Ciceronian and O'Donovanian construals of society and its relationship to authority (chapter 7). Thus, we found that for Plato, an imagined need-driven society precedes any notion of authority (i.e. the guardian), as it does for Aristotle's polis, though here its members (i.e. citizens) are able to participate with judgment and rule in the pursuit of common good. By contrast, in Cicero's historical account of the Roman *res publica* authority was a *sine qua non* of the *civitas*. We also noted other early modern contributions to the discussion (Hobbes, Locke, Rousseau), whose construal O'Donovan rightly faults on their misunderstanding of what is in fact an asymmetric or non-reciprocal relation between authority and subject, which they see instead as a reciprocal contractarian consensus among free, equal and independent human beings. Within this discussion we considered O'Donovan's threefold account of the church as (a) a political society predicated on the exalted Jesus, whose identity is conveyed to the watching world through a liturgical discourse based on

---

8. cf. Rev 5:9; 7:9.

the sacraments; (b) a post-political society enacting the koinonia of the Holy Spirit; and (c) a moral society under the authority of Scripture (God's word).

Also as part of this discussion we looked at the use of the liturgical discourse in Plato, Augustus, and O'Donovan's accounts of society. As we saw, Plato deploys liturgy to legitimize a radical redefinition of marriage and parenthood among its ruling class in order to guarantee the unity of his polis; whereas Augustus extended the use of the military *sacramentum* (oath) to include civilians in order to assert the non-reciprocal relation between authority and subject (*subicio*). For O'Donovan, liturgy mediated by the sacraments (mainly the Eucharist and baptism) conveys the christological political identity of the church; it also plays a part within the church as his pneumatological post-political society deploys the ministry of the word (teaching and prayer), which is a liturgical word. These three instances of the use of liturgical discourse to convey some aspect of the dynamics between authority and society, allow us to appreciate the distinctive character of the Apocalypse's own liturgical discourse, which in contrast to O'Donovan's understanding, and perhaps more strikingly to other New Testament documents, lacks explicit and unambiguous references to the Christian sacraments of the Eucharist and baptism. However, here we have argued that in fact the Apocalypse's liturgical discourse, as enacted by the construal of the liturgical sociality and discerned by a set of theological categories, signifies what the sacraments are meant to signify; and that fellowship with the exalted Jesus and his mediated presence, as signified by the Eucharist, is equally conveyed by the construal of the liturgical sociality as a sacred space, which as such adumbrates the Fellowship of the Throne. Also, initiation into the Christian community as signified by baptism is communicated by the construal of the liturgical sociality as both a city in the making where the blood of the Lamb becomes the soteriological threshold through which to enter into this city, and as the finished/complete city where the liturgical act of giving *doxa* to the divine authority allows access into the holy city, the locus of the Fellowship of the Throne. To put it another way, the apocalyptic liturgical discourse poses a question for any theological enterprise that invests heavily on the sacraments (e.g. the Eucharist) as the only way to point to what they signify.[9]

---

9. For instance, consider William Cavanaugh's view that "a Christian practice of the political is embodied in the Eucharist, the remembering of Jesus' own torture at the hands of

8.5 "If Anyone Has an Ear"[10]

Overall, this work makes a unique contribution to the fields of biblical studies on the Apocalypse and political theology as follows. (i) It offers an account of the narrative of the Apocalypse that does not bypass some of its key exegetical conundrums. In particular, it offers an exegetical framework, grounded in Old Testament allusions (and ancient Near Eastern's as well) to account for the correlation between the exaltation of the child-Messiah and the downfall of the dragon, which features as a twofold yet continuous story in the narrative of the Apocalypse (i.e. Rev 12, 20). (ii) Equally, it offers an exegetical account of the four christological portrayals of the exalted Jesus as Son of God, the Lamb, the Messiah and the divine King, where the latter sums up to some extent the previous representations of Jesus's persona in the Apocalypse. Again, this account of the divine King is grounded in Old Testament allusions. (iii) The Fellowship of the Throne has proved an original and very useful theological construal to account for the Apocalypse's ideas on authority and society and their correlation.[11] In turn, this new theo-political construal has enabled an easier interaction with ancient and (pre-)modern political theory, since at the end of the day, any text on political theory must say something about authority as well as society, and how the two are correlated. (iv) The deployment of space as a theo-political category of analysis, derived from our understanding of society in the Apocalypse, has equally resonated with an upward trend both in biblical studies and political theology where "space" gives the theo-political imagination a channel for new possibilities of thinking. In this sense, our own critique of the assymetric correlation between a totalized secular discourse and a marginalized religious and theological voice in present-day Mexico has been strengthened by this spatial theo-political analysis in line with the Apocalypse's, Augustine's, Milbank's and Cavanaugh's critiques of their respective contexts (chapter 6). We have attested that, despite appearances to the contrary, a secular space

---

the powers of this world. The Eucharist is the church's response to torture, and the hope for Christian resistance to the violent disciplines of the world." Cavanaugh, *Torture and Eucharist*, 2.

10. Rev 13:9; cf. 2:7, 11, 17, 29; 3:6, 13, 22.

11. During an abridged presentation of this thesis to an ordinary audience, one of the attendants (who holds a PhD in theology and directs the European Christian Mission) told the present writer that the title "Fellowship of the Throne" sums up appropriately what the book of Revelation is about.

is in need of a liturgy in order to sustain its own mode of sociality though it be of a purely immanent orientation. Here the case in point has been that of the Mexican secular state and its construal of a public liturgy around the mandatory cult of the national flag.

Further challenges to the Mexican context are posed by the understanding of authority and sociality as found in the Apocalypse, in particular with reference to the most prominent expression of Christianity in Mexico, which remains dominated by an extraordinary devotion to the Virgen de Guadalupe, the local version of Mary the mother of Jesus, who for centuries has been accorded an unusual exalted status.[12] Within this strand of Christianity the narrative of the gospel story is often reduced to Jesus's arrest, torture, and death by crucifixion,[13] while the fact of his resurrection and exaltation tends to be sidelined. In other words, this thesis poses a direct challenge to both a secular view of reality and a strand of Christianity that exalts the mother of Jesus rather than Jesus himself. The portrayals of Jesus as Son of God, the Lamb, the child-Messiah and the divine King must reshape the so called Mexican ethos, restrain and revert the secular grasp on public life, and redress the theological balance within this historic iteration of Christianity.

This study's contribution in the form of a critique of the Mexican national context, perhaps inevitably, offers obvious areas of opportunity for its own author's contribution to public life in his home country, as well as for the church's mission in Mexico:

(i) A theo-political voice must claim a place within the (secular) university, as argued by David Ford and Angus Paddison, for instance.[14]

(ii) A Mexican political theology must articulate an extensive account of an archeology or genealogy of the Mexican secular that has as referent John Milbank's *Theology and Social Theory*. Equally, it must deepen a theo-political account of the liturgical

---

12. cf. Brading, *Mexican Phoenix*, 288–310.

13. According to the Mexican Nobel prize winner Octavio Paz, "El mexicano venera al Cristo sangrante y humillado, golpeado por los soldados, condenado por los jueces, porque ve en él la imagen transfigurada de su propio destino." [The Mexican reveres the bleeding and humbled Christ, beaten by the soldiers, condemned by the judges, because in his image he recognises his own destiny]. Paz, *El Laberinto de la Soledad*, 100–101. Translated by the author.

14. cf. Ford, *Shaping Theology*, 3–26; Paddison, *Very Theological*, 122–144.

nature of the Mexican secular state as William Cavanaugh has done in connection with his home country, the United States, in his *Migrations of the Holy*. In a sense, this study has sown the seeds for both theo-political projects.

(iii) At the same time, immanent voices from within the secular who have expressed a concern about the limits of secular reason, such as Jurgen Habermas's and William Connolly's,[15] must be relayed within the Mexican secular establishment.

(iv) Additionally, an effort to educate Christian believers on biblical hermeneutics must be made. In particular, believers should be taught how to "read" the Bible from "left-to-right" time-wise, that is to say, taking into account the historical and theological emergence, flow and development of ideas or concepts such as the "Son of God," which at present tend to be read from "right-to-left" time-wise, that is to say, from a sort of Nicene or post-Nicene perspective that impinges upon the biblical text. This educational effort in the teaching of hermeneutics would also help to stem the tide of a (still prevalent) literalistic approach to the Bible.

On the whole, while this work already delivers a platform from which to articulate a theo-political critique of the Mexican secular discourse and identifies possible theo-political projects that would break the strong grasp of an immanent approach to public life in its author's home country, it also has a contribution to make to the rest of the world. As The Fellowship of the Throne (in the narrative of the Apocalypse) is recognized as the ultimate expression of divine and political authority as well as of human society (i.e. the ultimate horizon of the political), it offers (and may resource) a critique of every current mode of human authority and society as we know it, wherever it may be found. It also challenges the church, whatever its particular context, to recognize its own calling as God's people and as his liturgical space, and to live in the reality of the exalted Jesus's authority above all modes of human authority (i.e. "to conquer").

---

15. cf. Habermas, "Relations Between the Secular"; Connolly, *Why I Am Not a Secularist*.

Bibliography

A. Primary Sources

1. Bible

Aland, Barbara, Kurt Aland, Johannes Karavidopoulos, Carlo M. Martini, and Bruce M. Metzger, eds. *Novum Testamentum Graece* [New Testament in Greek]. Nestle-Aland, 28th edition. Stuttgart: Deutsche Bibelgesellschaft, 2012 (1898). Electronic version 1.2 by Accordance Bible, 2013.

Elliger, Karl, and Wilhelm Rudolph, eds. *Biblia Hebraica Stuttgartensia*. 5th edition. Stuttgart: Deutsche Bibelgesellschaft, 1997 (1977). Electronic version 1.4 by Accordance Bible, 2010.

Rahlfs, Alfred, ed. *Septuaginta*. Editio altera by Robert Hanhart.Stuttgart: Deutsche Bibelgesellschaft, 2006. Electronic version 5.0 by Accordance Bible, 2012.

TANAKH: A New Translation of THE HOLY SCRIPTURES According to the Traditional Hebrew Text [JPS]. N/a: The Jewish Publication Society, 1985. Electronic version 2.9 by Accordance Bible.

2. Other Jewish Texts

1 Enoch. Translated by E. Isaac. In *The Old Testament Pseudepigrapha*, volume 1, edited by James H. Charlesworth. New Haven, CT: Yale University Press, 1983. Reprinted by Hendrickson Publishers, 2009.

2 Baruch. Translated by A. F. J. Klijn. In *The Old Testament Pseudepigrapha*, volume 1, edited by James H. Charlesworth. New Haven, CT: Yale University Press, 1983. Reprinted by Hendrickson Publishers, 2009.

2 Enoch. Translated by F. I. Andersen. In *The Old Testament Pseudepigrapha*, volume 1, edited by James H. Charlesworth. New Haven, CT: Yale University Press, 1983. Reprinted by Hendrickson Publishers, 2009.

4 Ezra. Translated by B. M. Metzger. In *The Old Testament Pseudepigrapha*, volume 1, edited by James H. Charlesworth. New Haven, CT: Yale University Press, 1983. Reprinted by Hendrickson Publishers, 2009.

Apocalypse of Abraham. Translated by R. Rubinkiewicz. In *The Old Testament Pseudepigrapha*, volume 1, edited by James H. Charlesworth. New Haven, CT: Yale University Press, 1983. Reprinted by Hendrickson Publishers, 2009.

Apocalypse of Elijah. Translated by O. S. Wintermute. In *The Old Testament Pseudepigrapha*, volume 1, edited by James H. Charlesworth. New Haven, CT: Yale University Press, 1983. Reprinted by Hendrickson Publishers, 2009.

Charlesworth, James H., ed. *The Old Testament Pseudepigrapha [OTP]*. 2 vols. New Translations from Authoritative Texts with Introductions and Critical Notes by an International Team of Scholars. New Haven, CT: Yale University Press, 1983. Reprinted by Hendrickson Publishers, 2009.

Eupolemus. *Fragments*. Translated by F. Fallon. In *The Old Testament Pseudepigrapha*, volume 2, edited by James H. Charlesworth. New Haven, CT: Yale University Press, 1983. Reprinted by Hendrickson Publishers, 2009.

Joseph and Aseneth. Translated by C. Burchard. In *The Old Testament Pseudepigrapha*, volume 2, edited by James H. Charlesworth. New Haven, CT: Yale University Press, 1983. Reprinted by Hendrickson Publishers, 2009.

Josephus. *Works* (with morphological tagging). The Greek text is based on the 1890 Niese edition. Morphological tagging by Jean-Noel Aletti, A. Gieniusz and Michael Bushell. Electronic version 2.3 by Accordance Bible, 2005.

Life of Adam and Eve (Apocalypse of Moses). Translated by M. D. Johnson. In *The Old Testament Pseudepigrapha*, volume 2, edited by James H. Charlesworth. New Haven, CT: Yale University Press, 1983. Reprinted by Hendrickson Publishers, 2009.

Mishna. Based upon the Kaufmann A 50 manuscript. Grammatical tagging supervised by Martin Abegg. Electronic version 2.5 by Accordance Bible, 2009.

Nickelsburg, George W. E., and James C. VanderKam. *1 Enoch: A New Translation*. Based on the Hermeneia Commentary. Minneapolis: Fortress, 2004.

Philo. *Works* (with morphological tagging). The Norwegian Philo Concordance Project. Morphological tagging by Rex A. Koivisto further revised with the help of Marco V. Fabbri. Electronic version 3.0 by Accordance Bible, 2009.

Qumran. Dead Sea Scrolls Biblical Corpus (Canonical order). Grammatical tagging by Martin Abegg, James E. Bowley, and Edward M. Cook with Casey Toews. Electronic version 2.4 by Accordance Bible, 2009.

———. Dead Sea Scrolls Biblical Corpus (Manuscript order). Grammatical tagging by Martin Abegg, James E. Bowley, and Edward M. Cook with Casey Toews. Electronic version 2.4 by Accorandance Bible, 2009.

———. *Judean Desert Manuscripts*. Judean text and grammatical tags by Martin G. Abegg, Jr. Electronic version 2.1. by Accordance Bible, 2009.

———. *Qumran Non-biblical Manuscripts*. Qumran text and grammatical tags by Martin G. Abegg, Jr. Electronic version 3.5 by Accordance Bible.

Sibylline Oracles. Translated by J. J. Collins. In *The Old Testament Pseudepigrapha*, Vol. 1, edited by James H. Charlesworth. New Haven: Yale University Press, 1983. Reprinted by Hendrickson Publishers, 2009.

Testament of Abraham. Translated by E. P. Sanders. In *The Old Testament Pseudepigrapha*, Vol. 1, edited by James H. Charlesworth. New Haven: Yale University Press, 1983. Reprinted by Hendrickson Publishers, 2009.

Testaments of the Twelve Patriarchs (Reuben, Simeon, Levi, Judah, Issachar, Zebulon, Dan, Naphtali, Gad, Asher, Joseph, Benjamin). Translated by H. C. Kee. In *The Old Testament Pseudepigrapha*, Vol. 1, edited by James H. Charlesworth. New Haven: Yale University Press, 1983. Reprinted by Hendrickson Publishers, 2009.

3. Other Early Christian and Related Texts

1 Clement. In *The Apostolic Fathers*. Greek Texts and English Translations, edited and translated by Michael W. Holmes. Grand Rapids, MI: Baker Academic, 2006.

Andrew of Caesarea. *Commentary of the Apocalypse*. In *Ancient Christian Texts: Greek Commentaries on Revelation*, translated by William C. Weinrich, edited by Thomas C. Oden. Downers Grove, IL: IVP Academic, 2011.

Apocalypse of Peter. Translated by C. Detlef G. Müller. In *New Testament Apocrypha*. Vol. 2, edited by Wilhem Schneemelcher. Cambridge: James Clark & Co.; Louisville, KY: Westminster John Knox, 1991–1992 (1989–1990).

Augustine. *Against Lying*. In *A Select Library of the Nicene and Post-Nicene Fathers of the Christian Church: First Series*. Vol. 3, edited by Philip Schaff. Edinburgh: T&T Clark; Grand Rapids, MI: Eerdmans, 1887.

———. *Letters*. In *A Select Library of the Nicene and Post-Nicene Fathers of the Christian Church: First Series*. Vol. 1, edited by Philip Schaff. Edinburgh: T&T Clark; Grand Rapids, MI: Eerdmans, 1887.

———. *On Christian Doctrine*. In *A Select Library of the Nicene and Post-Nicene Fathers of the Christian Church: First Series*. Vol. 2, edited by Philip Schaff. Edinburgh: T&T Clark; Grand Rapids, MI: Eerdmans, 1887.

———. *On the Catechising of the Unstructed*. In *A Select Library of the Nicene and Post-Nicene Fathers of the Christian Church: First Series*. Vol. 3, edited by Philip Schaff. Edinburgh: T&T Clark; Grand Rapids, MI: Eerdmans, 1887.

———. *On the Merits and Forgiveness of Sins, and on the Baptism of Infants*. In *A Select Library of the Nicene and Post-Nicene Fathers of the Christian Church:*

First Series. Vol. 5, edited by Philip Schaff. Edinburgh: T&T Clark; Grand Rapids, MI: Eerdmans, 1887.

———. *On the Psalms.* In *A Select Library of the Nicene and Post-Nicene Fathers of the Christian Church: First Series.* Vol. 8, edited by Philip Schaff. Edinburgh: T&T Clark; Grand Rapids, MI: Eerdmans, 1887.

———. *Reply to Faustus the Manichaean.* In *A Select Library of the Nicene and Post-Nicene Fathers of the Christian Church: First Series.* Vol. 4, edited by Philip Schaff. Edinburgh: T&T Clark; Grand Rapids, MI: Eerdmans, 1887.

———. *The City of God against the Pagans.* Translated and edited by R. W. Dyson. Cambridge Texts in the History of Political Thought. Cambridge: Cambridge University Press, 1998.

Bede the Venerable. *The Exposition of the Apocalypse.* In *Ancient Christian Texts: Latin Commentaries on Revelation*, translated by William C. Weinrich, edited by Thomas C. Oden. Downers Grove, IL: IVP Academic, 2011.

Caesarius of Arles. *Exposition on the Apocalypse.* In *Ancient Christian Texts: Latin Commentaries on Revelation*, translated by William C. Weinrich, edited by Thomas C. Oden. Downers Grove, IL: IVP Academic, 2011.

Epistle to Diognetus. In *The Apostolic Fathers.* Greek Texts and English Translations, edited and translated by Michael W. Holmes. Grand Rapids, MI: Baker Academic, 2006.

Eusebius. *Ecclesiastical History.* In *A Select Library of the Nicene and Post-Nicene Fathers of the Christian Church: Second Series.* Vol. 1, edited by Philip Schaff and Henry Wace. Edinburgh: T&T Clark; Grand Rapids, MI: Eerdmans, 1890.

———. *Oration in Praise of the Emperor Constantine.* In *A Select Library of the Nicene and Post-Nicene Fathers of the Christian Church: Second Series.* Vol. 1, edited by Philip Schaff and Henry Wace. Edinburgh: T&T Clark; Grand Rapids, MI: Eerdmans, 1890.

Gospel of Thomas. Translated by Beate Blatz. In *New Testament Apocrypha.* Vol. 1, edited by Wilhem Schneemelcher. Cambridge: James Clark & Co; Louisville, KY: Westminster John Knox, 1991–1992 (1989–1990).

Hippolytus. *Treatise on Christ and Antichrist.* In *The Ante-Nicene Fathers*: The Writings of the Fathers Down to A.D. 325. Vol. 5, edited by Alexander Roberts and James Donaldson. Edinburgh: T&T Clark; Grand Rapids, MI: Eerdmans, 1885.

Holmes, Michael W., trans and ed. *The Apostolic Fathers in English.* 3rd edition. Grand Rapids, MI: Baker Academic, 2006.

Ignatius. *To the Magnesians.* In *The Apostolic Fathers.* Greek Texts and English Translations, edited and translated by Michael W. Holmes. Grand Rapids, MI: Baker Academic, 2006.

———. *To the Philadelphians*. In *The Apostolic Fathers*. Greek Texts and English Translations, edited and translated by Michael W. Holmes. Grand Rapids, MI: Baker Academic, 2006.

———. *To the Smyrnaeans*. In *The Apostolic Fathers*. Greek Texts and English Translations, edited and translated by Michael W. Holmes. Grand Rapids, MI: Baker Academic, 2006.

———. *To the Trallians*. In *The Apostolic Fathers*. Greek Texts and English Translations, edited and translated by Michael W. Holmes. Grand Rapids, MI: Baker Academic, 2006.

Irenaeus. *Against Heresies*. In *The Ante-Nicene Fathers*. The Writings of the Fathers Down to A.D. 325. Vol. 1, edited by Alexander Roberts and James Donaldson. Edinburgh: T&T Clark; Grand Rapids, MI: Eerdmans, 1885.

Jerome. Letters. In *A Select Library of the Nicene and Post-Nicene Fathers of the Christian Church: Second Series*. Vol. 6, edited by Philip Schaff and Henry Wace. Edinburgh: T&T Clark; Grand Rapids, MI: Eerdmans, 1890.

Justin Martyr. *Apology*. In *The Ante-Nicene Fathers*. The Writings of the Fathers Down to A.D. 325. Vol. 1, edited by Alexander Roberts and James Donaldson. Edinburgh: T&T Clark; Grand Rapids, MI: Eerdmans, 1885.

———. *Dialogue with Trypho*. In *The Ante-Nicene Fathers*. The Writings of the Fathers Down to A.D. 325. Vol. 1, edited by Alexander Roberts and James Donaldson. Edinburgh: T&T Clark; Grand Rapids, MI: Eerdmans, 1885.

Martyrdom and Ascension of Isaiah. Translated by M. A. Knibb. In *The Old Testament Pseudepigrapha*. Vol. 2, edited by James H. Charlesworth. New Haven, CT: Yale University Press, 1983. Reprinted by Hendrickson Publishers, 2009.

Oden, Thomas C., ed. *Ancient Christian Texts: Greek Commentaries on Revelation. Oecumenius and Andrew of Caesarea*. Translated by William C. Weinrich. Downers Grove, IL: IVP Academic, 2011.

Oecumenius. *Commentary of the Apocalypse*. In *Ancient Christian Texts: Greek Commentaries on Revelation*, translated by William C. Weinrich, edited by Thomas C. Oden. Downers Grove, IL: IVP Academic, 2011.

Origen. *Against Celsus*. In *The Ante-Nicene Fathers*. The Writings of the Fathers Down to A.D. 325. Vol. 4, edited by Alexander Roberts and James Donaldson. Edinburgh: T&T Clark; Grand Rapids, MI: Eerdmans, 1885.

———. *Commentary on the Gospel of John*. In *The Ante-Nicene Fathers*. The Writings of the Fathers Down to A.D. 325. Vol. 9, edited by Alexander Roberts and James Donaldson. Edinburgh: T&T Clark; Grand Rapids, MI: Eerdmans, 1885.

Roberts, Alexander, and James Donaldson, eds. *The Ante-Nicene Fathers [ANF]. The Writings of the Fathers Down to A.D. 325*. 8 vols. Edinburgh: T&T Clark; Grand Rapids, MI: Eerdmans, 1885. Original electronic text from the

Christian Classic Ethereal Library. Electronic text hypertexted, corrected and prepared by Oak Tree Software, Inc. Version 2.1.

The Didache. In *The Apostolic Fathers*. Greek Texts and English Translations, edited and translated by Michael W. Holmes. Grand Rapids, MI: Baker Academic, 2006.

The Shepherd of Hermas. In *The Apostolic Fathers*. Greek Texts and English Translations, edited and translated by Michael W. Holmes. Grand Rapids, MI: Baker Academic, 2006.

Schaff, Philip, ed. *A Select Library of the Nicene and Post-Nicene Fathers of the Christian Church: First Series*. (NPNF1). 14 vols. Edinburgh: T&T Clark; Grand Rapids, MI: Eerdmans, 1887. Original electronic text from the Christian Classic Ethereal Library. Electronic text hypertexted, corrected and prepared by Oak Tree Software, Inc. Version 2.2.

Schaff, Philip, and Henry Wace, eds. *A Select Library of the Nicene and Post-Nicene Fathers of the Christian Church: Second Series*. (NPNF2). 14 vols. Edinburgh: T&T Clark; Grand Rapids, MI: Eerdmans, 1890. Original electronic text from the Christian Classic Ethereal Library. Electronic text hypertexted, corrected and prepared by Oak Tree Software, Inc. Version 2.2.

Schneemelcher, Wilhem, ed. *New Testament Apocrypha*. 2 vols. Revised edition. English translation edited by R. McL. Wilson. Cambridge: James Clark & Co.; Louisville, KY: Westminster John Knox, 1991–1992 (1989–1990).

Tertullian. *Apology*. In *The Ante-Nicene Fathers*. The Writings of the Fathers Down to A.D. 325. Vol. 3, edited by Alexander Roberts and James Donaldson. Edinburgh: T&T Clark; Grand Rapids, MI: Eerdmans, 1885.

Thomas Aquinas. *The Summa Theologica*. Translated by Fathers of the English Dominican Province. N/a: Benziger Bros., 1947. Electronic version 2.3 by OakTree Software Inc.

Victorinus of Petovium. *Commentary of the Apocalypse of the Blessed John*. In *The Ante-Nicene Fathers*. The Writings of the Fathers Down to A.D. 325. Vol. 7, edited by Alexander Roberts and James Donaldson. Edinburgh: T&T Clark; Grand Rapids, MI: Eerdmans, 1885.

Weinrich, William C., ed. *Latin Commentaries on Revelation: Victorinus of Petovium, Apringius of Beja, Caesarius of Arles and Bede the Venerable*. Translated by William C. Weinrich. Downers Grove, IL: IVP Academic, 2011.

4. Pagan Texts

de Alvarado Tezozomoc, Fernando. *Crónica Mexicana*. Linkuga Historia 19. Barcelona: Linkgua Ediciones, 2008.

Aristotle. *Nicomachean Ethics*. Translated and edited by Roger Crisp. Cambridge: Cambridge University Press, 2000.

———. *Poetics*. In *The Complete Works of Aristotle*. Vol. 2, edited by Jonathan Barnes. The Revised Oxford Translation. Bollingen Series 71.2. Princeton, NJ: Princeton University Press, 1984.

———. *Politics*. Translated by Carnes Lord. 2nd edition. Chicago: University of Chicago Press, 2013 (1984).

———. *Politica*. Edited by W. D. Ross. Oxford: Clarendon Press, 1957. Online edition available at http://www.perseus.tufts.edu/hopper/text?doc=Perseus%3Atext%3A1999.01.0057%3Abook%3D1%3Asection%3D1252a as of 13 September 2013.

———. *Rethoric*. In *The Complete Works of Aristotle*. Vol. 2, edited by Jonathan Barnes. The Revised Oxford Translation. Bollingen Series 71.2. Princeton: Princeton University Press, 1984.

———. *The Complete Works of Aristotle*. Edited by Jonathan Barnes. 2 vols. The Revised Oxford Translation. Bollingen Series 71.2. Princeton: Princeton University Press, 1984.

Athanassakis, Apostolos N., trans. *The Homeric Hymns*. 2nd edition. Baltimore: John Hopkins University Press, 2004.

Bierhorst, John, trans. *History and Mythology of the Aztecs: Codex Chimalpopoca*. Tucson: University of Arizona Press, 1992.

Caesar. *The Civil Wars, together with The Alexandrian War, The African War, and The Spanish War by other Hands*. Translated by Jane F. Gardner. Penguin Classics. London: Penguin Books, 1967.

Cicero. *De Re Publica: Selections*. Edited by James Zetzel. Cambridge: Cambridge University Press, 1995.

———. *Epistulae ad Familiares* [Letters to his Friends]. Translated and edited by Evelyn S. Shuckburgh, 1900. Available online http://artflsrv02.uchicago.edu/cgi-bin/perseus/citequery3.pl?dbname=LatinSept18&query=Cic.%20Fam.&getid=1

———. *On the Commonwealth and On the Laws*. Translated and edited by James Zetzel. Cambridge Texts in the History of Political Thought. Cambridge: Cambridge University Press, 1999.

———. *Pro Sestio*. Translated and edited by C. D. Yonge. London: George Bell & Sons, 1891. Available online, http://perseus.uchicago.edu/perseus-cgi/citequery3.pl?dbname=PerseusLatinTexts&query=Cic.%20Sest.&getid=1.

———. *The Letters of Cicero*. Translated by Evelyn S. Shuckburgh. London: George Bell and Sons, 1909. Available online http://www.perseus.tufts.edu/hopper/text?doc=Perseus%3atext%3a1999.02.0022.

———. *The Orations of Marcus Tullius Cicero: Literally Translated by C. D. Yonge*. Vol. 2. Translated by C. D. Young. 1852. Available online, http://lexundria.com/cic_cat/0/y.

Cooper, John M., ed. *Plato: Complete Works*. Indianapolis: Hackett, 1997.

Cooley, Alison E., trans., and ed. Augustus. *Res Gestae Divi Augusti*. Cambridge: Cambridge University Press, 2009.

Dalley, Stephanie, ed. and trans. *Myths from Mesopotamia: Creation, the Flood, Gilgamesh, and Others*. Revised edition. Oxford World's Classics. Oxford: Oxford University Press, 2000.

Cassius Dio. *Roman History*. Translated by Earnest Cary and Herbert Baldwin Foster. 9 vols. Loeb Classical Library. Cambridge, MA: Harvard University Press, 1927.

Edwards, Catharine. *Suetonius: Lives of the Caesars*. Oxford World's Classics. Oxford: Oxford University Press, 2000.

Florus. *Epitome of Roman History*. Translated by E. S. Forster. Loeb Classical Library. Cambridge, MA: Harvard University Press, 1929. Available online, http://penelope.uchicago.edu/Thayer/E/Roman/Texts/Florus/Epitome/home.html.

Fyfe, W. H., trans. *Tacitus: The Histories*. Revised edition, edited by D. S. Levene. Oxford World's Classics. Oxford: Oxford University Press, 1997.

Gibson, John C. L. *Canaanite Myths and Legends*. Originally edited by G. R. Driver. New York: T&T Clark, 1978.

Grayson, Albert Kirk, trans. *Assyrian and Babylonian Chronicles*. Winona Lake, Indiana: Eisenbrauns, 2000.

Herodotus. *The Histories*. Translated by A. D. Godley. Cambridge: Harvard University Press, 1920. Available online http://www.perseus.tufts.edu/hopper/text?doc=Perseus%3atext%3a1999.01.0126.

Hesiod. *Theogony, Works and Days, Testimonia*. Translated and edited by Glenn W. Most. Loeb Classical Library. Cambridge, MA: Harvard University Press, 2006.

Lewis, C. Day, trans. *Virgil: The Aeneid*. Oxford World's Classics. Oxford: Oxford University Press, 1986.

Livy. *The History of Rome, Volume I: Books 1-2*. Translated by Benjamin Oliver Foster. Loeb Classical Library. Cambridge, MA: Harvard University Press, 1919. Available online, http://www.perseus.tufts.edu/hopper/text?doc=Perseus%3atext%3a1999.02.0151%3abook%3d1.

Lysias. *Speeches*. Translated by W. R. M. Lamb. Cambridge, MA: Harvard University Press, 1930. Available online, http://perseus.uchicago.edu/perseus-cgi/citequery3.pl?dbname=GreekFeb2011&query=Lys.&getid=1.

Morris Hall, Clayton, trans. *Nicolaus of Damascus's Life of Augustus: A Historical Commentary Embodying a Translation*. 1923. Kindle edition of public domain.

Olmos, Andrés de. *Huehuetlahtolli: Testimonios de la Antigua Palabra*. Edited by Miguel León-Portilla. Translated by Librado Silva Galeana. México: Comisión Nacional Conmemorativa del V Centenario del Encuentro de Dos Mundos, 1988.

Ovid. *Fasti*. Translated by James George Frazer. 6 vols. 2nd edition, revised by G. P. Goold. Loeb Classical Library. Cambridge, MA: Harvard University Press, 1989.

Plato. *Laws*. Translated by Trevor J. Saunders. In *Plato: Complete Works*, edited by John M. Cooper, 1318–1616. Indianapolis: Hackett, 1997.

———. *Republic*. Translated by G. M. A. Grube, and revised by C. D. C. Reeve. In *Plato: Complete Works*, edited by John M. Cooper, 971–1223. Indianapolis: Hackett, 1997.

Pliny the Elder. *The Natural History*. Translated by John Bostock and H. T. Riley. London: Taylor & Francis, 1855. Available online, http://www.perseus.tufts.edu/hopper/text?doc=Plin.+Nat.+toc.

Polybius. *The Histories*. Translated by W. R. Paton. Loeb Classical Library. Cambridge: Harvard University Press, 1922–1927. Available online, http://penelope.uchicago.edu/Thayer/E/Roman/Texts/Polybius/home.html.

Quintilian. *Institutio Oratoria*. Translated by Harold Edgeworth Butler. Loeb Classical Library. Cambridge: Harvard University Press, 1920. Available online, http://penelope.uchicago.edu/Thayer/E/Roman/Texts/Quintilian/Institutio_Oratoria/home.html.

Richardson, Mervyn E. J., trans. *Hammurabi's Laws: Text, Translation and Glossary*. Sheffield: Sheffield Academic Press, 2000.

Smith, Mark S., and Wayne T. Pritard, eds. *The Ugaritic Baal Cycle. Volume II. Introduction with Text, Translation and Commentary of KTU/CAT 1.3–1.4*. Leiden: Brill, 2009.

Strabo. *Geography*. Translated by H. L. Jones. London: William Heinemann, 1924. Available online, http://perseus.uchicago.edu/perseus-cgi/citequery3.pl?dbname=GreekFeb2011&query=Str.&getid=2.

Tedlock, Dennis, trans. *Popol Vuh: The Mayan Book of the Dawn of Life*. Revised edition. New York: Simon & Schuster, 1996.

Trzaskoma, Stephen M., R. Scott Smith, and Stephen Brunet, eds. *Anthology of Classical Myth: Primary Sources in Translation. Edited and Featuring New Translations*. With additional translations by other scholars and an appendix on Linear B sources by Thomas G. Palaima. Indianapolis: Hackett Publishing Company, 2004.

Wiseman, D. J., trans. *Chronicles of Chaldean Kings (626–556 B.C.) In the British Museum*. London: British Museum, 1956.

Wlash, P. G. *Pliny the Younger: Complete Letters*. Oxford World's Classics. Oxford: Oxford University Press, 2006.

Yardley, J. C., trans. *Tacitus, The Annals: The Reigns of Tiberius, Claudius, and Nero*. Introduction and notes by Anthony A. Barrett. Oxford World's Classics. Oxford University Press, 2008.

5. Early Modern Political Thought

Tuck, Richard, ed. *Hobbes: Leviathan*. Revised student edition. Cambridge Texts in the History of Political Thought. Cambridge: Cambridge University Press, 1996.

Laslett, Peter, ed. *Locke: Two Treatises of Government*. Student edition. Cambridge Texts in the History of Political Thought. Cambridge: Cambridge University Press, 1988.

Gourevitch, Victor, trans and ed. *Rousseau: The Social Contract and Other Later Political Writings*. Cambridge Texts in the History of Political Thought. Cambridge: Cambridge University Press, 1997.

6. Mexican Constitutions and Laws

Constitución de 1824. Available online at http://www.diputados.gob.mx/biblioteca/bibdig/const_mex/const_1824.pdf.

Constitución de 1857. Available online at http://www.juridicas.unam.mx/infjur/leg/conshist/pdf/1857.pdf.

Constitución de 1917. Available online at http://www.diputados.gob.mx/LeyesBiblio/ref/cpeum/CPEUM_orig_05feb1917.pdf.

Constitución Política de los Estados Unidos Mexicanos. Texto vigente (6 March 2020). Available at http://www.diputados.gob.mx/LeyesBiblio/pdf/1_060320.pdf

Ley de Asociaciones Religiosas y Culto Público. Texto Vigente (17 Dec 2015). Available online at http://www.diputados.gob.mx/LeyesBiblio/pdf/24_171215.pdf

Ley sobre el Escudo, la Bandera y el Himno Nacionales. Texto Vigente (30 Nov 2018). Available online at http://www.diputados.gob.mx/LeyesBiblio/pdf/213_301118.pdf

B. Secondary Literature

Abbott, H. Porter, ed. *The Cambridge Introduction to Narrative*. 2nd edition. Cambridge: Cambridge University Press, 2008.

―――. "Story, Plot, and Narration." In *The Cambridge Companion to Narrative*, edited by David Herman, 39–51. Cambridge: Cambridge University Press, 2007.

Adams, Edward. *The Stars Will Fall from Heaven: 'Cosmic Catastrophe' in the New Testament and Its World*. London: T&T Clark, 2007.

Alcalá Alvarado, Alfonso. "Las misiones de los dominicos, agustinos y otras órdenes." In *Historia General de la Iglesia en América Latina*. Vol. 5, *México*, edited by Enrique Dussel, 49–54. Mexico City: Sígueme, 1984.

Allen, Leslie C. *Jeremiah: A Commentary*. The Old Testament Library. Louisville, KY: Westminster John Knox, 2008.

Allen, R. Michael. "Theological Commentary." In *Theological Commentary: Evangelical Perspectives*, edited by R. Michael Allen, 1–9. New York: T&T Clark, 2011.

Ando, Clifford. *Imperial Ideology and Provincial Loyalty in the Roman Empire*. Berkeley: University of California Press, 2000.

Annas, Julia. *Plato: A Very Short Introduction*. Oxford: Oxford University Press, 2003.

Atkins, E. M. "Cicero." In *The Cambridge History of Greek and Roman Political Thought*, edited by Christopher Rowe and Malcolm Schofield, 477–516. Cambridge: Cambridge University Press, 2005.

Aune, David E. *Prophecy in Early Christianity and the Ancient Mediterranean World*. Grand Rapids, MI: Eerdmans, 1983.

———. *Revelation 1–5*. Word Biblical Commentary 52. Waco, TX: Word Books, 1997.

———. *Revelation 6–16*. Word Biblical Commentary 52B. Waco, TX: Word Books, 1998.

———. *Revelation 17–22*. Word Biblical Commentary 52C. Nashville: Thomas Nelson, 1998.

Balch, David L., and Annette Weissenrieder, eds. *Contested Spaces: Houses and Temples in Roman Antiquity and the New Testament*. Tübingen: Mohr Siebeck, 2012.

Balthasar, Hans Urs von. *Theo-Drama*. Volume 4, *The Action*. Translated by Graham Harrison. San Francisco: Ignatius Press, 1994.

Barnadas, Joseph M. "The Catholic Church in Colonial Spanish America." In *The Cambridge History of Latin America*. Volume 1, *Colonial Latin America*, edited by Leslie Bethell, 511–540. Cambridge: Cambridge University Press, 1984.

Barr, David. "The Apocalypse as a Symbolic Transformation of the World: A Literary Analysis." *Interpretation* 38, no. 1 (1984): 39–50.

———. *Tales of the End: A Narrative Commentary on the Book of Revelation*. Salem, OR: Polebridge Press, 2012. Kindle edition.

———. "Using Plot to Discern Structure in John's Apocalypse." *Proceedings of the Eastern Great Lakes and Midwest Biblical Societies* 15 (1995): 23–33.

———. "Waiting for the End that Never Comes: The Narrative Logic of John's Story." In *Studies in the Book of Revelation*, edited by Steve Moyise, 101–112. Edinburgh: T&T Clark, 2001.

Barrett, Charles K. *The Gospel According to St. John: An Introduction with Commentary and Notes on the Greek Text*. 2nd edition. London: SPCK, 1978.

Barth, Karl. *The Doctrine of Creation*. Vol. 3.1 of *Church Dogmatics*. Edited by G. W. Bromiley and T. F. Torrance. Edinburgh: T&T Clark, 1958.

———. *The Doctrine of the Word of God*. Vol. 1.1 of *Church Dogmatics*. 2nd edition. Edited by G. W. Bromiley and T. F. Torrance. Translated by G. W. Bromiley. Edinburgh: T&T Clark, 1975.

———. *The Doctrine of the Word of God*. Vol 1.2 of *Church Dogmatics*. Edited by G. W. Bromiley and T. F. Torrance. Translated by G. T. Thomson and Harold Knight. Edinburgh: T&T Clark, 1956.

Barthes, Roland. "Introduction to the Structural Analysis of Narratives." In *Image Music Text: Essays Selected and Translated by Stephen Heath*, 79–124. London: Fontana Press, 1977.

Bartholomew, Craig G. "Introduction." In *A Royal Priesthood? The Use of the Bible Ethically and Politically: A Dialogue with Oliver O'Donovan*, edited by Craig Bartholomew, Jonathan Chaplin, Robert Song, and Al Wolters, 1–45. Grand Rapids, MI: Zondervan, 2002.

Bartholomew, Craig, Jonathan Chaplin, Robert Song, and Al Wolters, eds. *A Royal Priesthood? The Use of the Bible Ethically and Politically: A Dialogue with Oliver O'Donovan*. Grand Rapids, MI: Zondervan, 2002.

Barton, John. "Disclosing Human Possibilities: Revelation and Biblical Stories." In *Revelation and Story: Narrative Theology and the Centrality of Story*, edited by Gerhard Sauter and John Barton, 53–60. Aldershot: Ashgate, 2000.

Bastian, Jean Pierre. "La primera ola de la penetración protestante en México (1869–1914)." In *Historia General de la Iglesia en América Latina*. Vol. 5, *México*, edited by Enrique Dussel, 296–310. Salamanca: Sígueme, 1984.

Bauckham, Richard. *The Climax of the Prophecy: Studies on the Book of Revelation*. London: T&T Clark, 1993.

———. *Jesus and the God of Israel: God Crucified and Other Studies on the New Testament's Christology of Divine Identity*. Milton Keynes: Paternoster, 2008.

———. "Revelation." In *The Oxford Bible Commentary*, edited by John Barton and John Muddiman, 1287–1306. Oxford: Oxford University Press, 2001.

———. *The Theology of the Book of Revelation*. New Testament Theology. Cambridge: Cambridge University Press, 1993.

Bazant, Jan. "Mexico from Independence to 1867." In *The Cambridge History of Latin America*. Vol. 3, *From Independence to c. 1870*, edited by Leslie Bethell, 423–470. Cambridge: Cambridge University Press, 1985.

Beale, G. K. *The Book of Revelation: A Commentary on the Greek Text*. The New International Greek Testament Commentary. Grand Rapids, MI: Eerdmans, 1999.

———. *John's Use of the Old Testament in Revelation*. London: Bloomsbury, 1998.

———. "The Origin of the Title 'King of Kings and Lord of Lords' in Revelation 17:14." *New Testament Studies* 31, no. 4 (1985): 618–620.

———, ed. *The Right Doctrine from the Wrong Texts? Essays on the Use of the Old Testament in the New*. Grand Rapids, MI: Baker Books, 1994.

———. *The Temple and the Church's Mission: A Biblical Theology of the Dwelling Place of God*. New Studies in Biblical Theology. Leicester: Apollos, 2005.

———. *The Use of Daniel in Jewish Apocalyptic Literature and in the Revelation of St. John*. Lanham, NY: University Press of America, 1984.

Beale, G. K., and Sean M. McDonough. "Revelation." In *Commentary on the New Testament Use of the Old Testament*, edited by G. K. Beale and D. A. Carson, 1081–1161. Grand Rapids, MI: Baker Academic, 2007.

Bebbington, David W. *Evangelicalism in Modern Britain: A History from the 1730s to the 1980s*. New York: Routledge, 1989.

Berger, Peter L. "The Desecularization of the World: A Global Overview." In *The Desecularization of the World: Resurgent Religion and World Politics*, edited by Peter L. Berger, 1–18. Grand Rapids, MI: Eerdmans, 1999.

Bethell, Leslie. "A Note on the Church and the Independence of Latin America." In *The Cambridge History of Latin America*. Vol. 3, *From Independence to c. 1870*, edited by Leslie Bethell, 229–234. Cambridge: Cambridge University Press, 1985.

Biggar, Nigel. "On Defining Political Authority as an Act of Judgment: A Discussion of Oliver O'Donovan's *The Ways of Judgment* (Part I)." *Political Theology* 9, no. 3 (2008): 273–293.

Black, Antony. *A World History of Ancient Political Thought*. Oxford: Oxford University Press, 2009.

Bloom, Harold, ed. *Satan*. Philadelphia, PA: Chelsea House, 2005.

Boring, M. Eugene. "Narrative Christology in the Apocalypse." *The Catholic Biblical Quarterly* 54, no. 4 (1992): 702–723.

———. *Revelation*. Interpretation: A Bible Commentary for Teaching and Preaching. Louisville, KY: Westminster John Knox, 1989.

Boxall, Ian. *The Revelation of Saint John*. Black's New Testament Commentaries. New York: Continuum, 2006.

Brading, D. A. *Mexican Phoenix: Our Lady of Guadalupe: Image and Tradition across Five Centuries*. New York: Cambridge University Press, 2002.

Brandwood, Leonard. "Stylometry and Chronology." In *The Cambridge Companion to Plato*, edited by Richard Kraut, 90–120. Cambridge: Cambridge University Press, 1992.

Bretherton, Luke. *Christianity and Contemporary Politics: The Conditions and Possibilities of Faithful Witness*. Oxford: Wiley-Blackwell, 2010.

———. "Introduction: Oliver O'Donovan's Political Theology and the Liberal Imperative." *Political Theology* 9, no. 3 (2008): 265–271.

Bruce, F. F. "The Earliest Latin Commentary on the Apocalypse." *Evangelical Quaterly* 10 (1938): 352–366.

———. *Paul: Apostle of the Heart Set Free*. Grand Rapids, MI: Eerdmans, 1977.

Brueggemann, Walter. *A Commentary on Jeremiah: Exile and Homecoming*. Grand Rapids, MI: Eerdmans, 1998.

Caird, G. B. *The Revelation of St. John the Divine*. 2nd edition. London: Black, 1984.

Carson, D. A. *The Gospel According to John*. Grand Rapids, MI: Eerdmans, 1991.

———. "Theological Interpretation of Scripture: Yes, But . . ." In *Theological Commentary: Evangelical Perspectives*, edited by R. Michael Allen, 187–207. New York: T&T Clark, 2011.

Cartledge, Paul. *Ancient Greek Political Thought in Practice*. Cambridge: Cambridge University Press, 2009.

———. "Greek Political Thought: The Historical Context." In *The Cambridge History of Greek and Roman Political Thought*, edited by Christopher Rowe and Malcolm Schofield, 11–22. Cambridge: Cambridge University Press, 2005.

Cavanaugh, William T. *Migrations of the Holy: God, State, and the Political Meaning of the Church*. Grand Rapids, MI: Eerdmans, 2011.

———. *The Myth of Religious Violence: Secular Ideology and the Roots of Modern Conflict*. Oxford: Oxford University Press, 2009.

———. *Theopolitical Imagination: Discovering Liturgy as a Political Act in an Age of Global Consumerism*. New York: Bloomsbury, 2002.

———. *Torture and Eucharist: Theology, Politics, and the Body of Christ*. Oxford: Blackwell, 1998.

Cavanaugh, William T., Jeffery W. Bailey and Craig Hovey, eds. *An Eerdmans Reader in Contemporary Political Theology*. Grand Rapids, MI: Eerdmans, 2012.

Chadwick, Henry. *Augustine of Hippo: A Life*. Oxford: Oxford University Press, 2009.

Chaplin, Jonathan. "Political Eschatology and Responsible Government: Oliver O'Donovan's 'Christian Liberalism.'" In *A Royal Priesthood? The Use of the Bible Ethically and Politically: A Dialogue with Oliver O'Donovan*, edited by Craig Bartholomew, Jonathan Chaplin, Robert Song, and Al Wolters, 265–308. Grand Rapids, MI: Zondervan, 2002.

Chappell, Timothy. "'Naturalism' in Aristotle's Political Philosophy." In *A Companion to Greek and Roman Political Thought*, edited by Ryan K. Balot, 382–398. Oxford: Blackwell, 2009.

Chatman, Seymour. *Story and Discourse: Narrative Structure in Fiction and Film*. Ithaca, NY: Cornell University Press, 1978.

Chauvet, Fidel. "Las misiones franciscanas." In *Historia General de la Iglesia en América Latina*, Vol. 5, *México*, edited by Enrique Dussel, 28–48. Salamanca: Sígueme, 1984.

Childs, Brevard S. *Isaiah: A Commentary*. Louisville, KY: Westminster John Knox, 2001.

Clements, Ronald E. *Isaiah 1–39*. New Century Bible Commentary Based on the Revised Standard Version. Grand Rapids, MI: Eerdmans, 1980.

Clines, David J. A. *Interested Parties: The Ideology of Writers and Readers of the Hebrew Bible*. Sheffield: Sheffield Academic Press, 1995.

Collins, John J. "Apocalypse." In *Dictionary of Early Judaism*, edited by John J. Collins and Daniel C. Harlow, 341–345. Grand Rapids, MI: Eerdmans, 2010.

———. *The Apocalyptic Imagination: An Introduction to Jewish Apocalyptic Literature*. 2nd edition. Grand Rapids, MI: Eerdmans, 1998.

———. "Introduction: Towards the Morphology of a Genre." *Semeia* 14 (1979): 1–20.

———. "The King as Son of God." In *King and Messiah as Son of God: Divine, Human, and Angelic Messianic Figures in Biblical and Related Literature*, edited by Adela Yarbro Collins and John J. Collins, 1–24. Grand Rapids, MI: Eerdmans, 2008.

Connolly, William E. *Why I Am Not a Secularist*. Minneapolis, MN: University of Minnesota Press, 1999.

Crook, J. A. "Augustus: Power, Authority, Achievement." In *The Cambridge Ancient History: Volume X: The Augustan Empire, 43 B.C. – A.D. 69*, edited by Alan K. Bowman, Edward Champlin and Andrew Lintott, 113–146. Cambridge: Cambridge University Press, 1996.

Culler, Jonathan. "Defining Narrative Units." In *Style and Structure in Literature: Essays in the New Stylistics*, edited by Roger Fowler, 123–142. Ithaca, NY: Cornell University Press, 1975.

Danker, Fredrick W., ed. *A Greek-English Lexicon of the New Testament and other Early Christian Literature [BDAG]*. 3rd edition. Chicago: University of Chicago Press, 2000.

Dannenberg, Hilary P. "Plot." In *Routledge Encyclopedia of Narrative Theory*, edited by David Herman, Manfred Jahn, and Marie-Laure Ryan, 435–439. New York: Routledge, 2005.

Day, John. *God's Conflict with the Dragon and the Sea: Echoes of a Canaanite Myth in the Old Testament*. Cambridge: Cambridge University Press, 1984.

———. *Psalms*. Sheffield: Sheffield Academic Press, 1990.

———. *Yahweh and Gods and Goddesses of Canaan*. London: Sheffield Academic Press, 2002.

de Vries, Hent, and Lawrence E. Sullivan, eds. *Political Theologies: Public Religions in a Post-Secular World*. New York. Fordham University Press, 2006.

DeMoss, Matthew S. *Pocket Dictionary for the Study of New Testament Greek*. Downers Grove, IL: InterVarsity Press, 2010.

Dunn, James D. G. *Christology in the Making: An Inquiry into the Origins of the Doctrine of the Incarnation*. 2nd edition. London: SCM Press, 1989.

Durham, John I. *Exodus*. Word Biblical Commentary 3. Waco, TX: Word Books, 1987.

Duyfhuizen, Bernard. "Framed Narratives." In *Routledge Encyclopedia of Narrative Theory*, edited by David Herman, Manfred Jahn and Marie-Laure Ryan, 186–188. New York: Routledge, 2005.

Eck, Werner. *The Age of Augustus*. Translated by Deborah Lucas Schneider. New material by Sarolta A. Takács. Oxford: Blackwell, 2003.

Ekins, Richard. "Secular Fundamentalism and Democracy." *Journal of Markets & Morality* 8, no. 1 (2005): 81–93.

Elliot, J. H. "The Spanish Conquest and settlement of America." In *The Cambridge History of Latin America*. Vol. 1, *Colonial Latin America*, edited by Leslie Bethell, 149–206. Cambridge: Cambridge University Press, 1984.

Eskola, Timo. *Messiah and the Throne: Jewish Merkabah Mysticism and Early Christian Exaltation Discourse*. Tübingen: Mohr Siebeck, 2001.

Ewald, Björn C., and Carlos F. Noreña, eds. *The Emperor and Rome: Space, Representation, and Ritual*. Yale Classical Studies 35. Cambridge: Cambridge University Press, 2010.

Fantham, Elaine, ed. *Ovid: Fasti, Book IV*. Cambridge: Cambridge University Press, 1998.

Fekkes, Jan, III. *Isaiah and Prophetic Traditions in the Book of Revelation: Visionary Antecedents and their Development*. Sheffield: Sheffield Academic Press, 1994.

Ferrari, Giovanni R. F., ed. *The Cambridge Companion to Plato's Republic*. Cambridge: Cambridge University Press, 2007.

Fine, Gail, ed. *The Oxford Handbook of Plato*. Oxford: Oxford University Press, 2008.

Fiorenza, Elisabeth Schüssler. *The Book of Revelation: Justice and Judgment*. Philadelphia: Fortress, 1985.

Fokkelman, J. P. *Narrative Art and Poetry in the Books of Samuel: A Full Interpretation Based on Stylistic and Structural Analyses*. Vol. 4, *Vow and Desire (I Sam. 1-12)*. Assen: Van Gorcum, 1993.

Ford, David. "Epilogue: Twelve Theses for Christian Theology in the Twenty-first Century." In *The Modern Theologians: An Introduction to Christian Theology Since 1918*, edited by David Ford, 760–761. 3rd edition. Malden, MA: Blackwell, 2005.

———. *Shaping Theology: Engagements in a Religious and Secular World*. Oxford: Blackwell, 2007.

France, R. T. *The Gospel of Mark*. The New International Greek Testament Commentary. Grand Rapids, MI: Eerdmans, 2002.

Frei, Hans W. *The Eclipse of Biblical Narrative: A Study in Eighteenth and Nineteenth Century Hermeneutics*. New Haven, CT: Yale University Press, 1974.

Furnish, Paul Victor. "How Firm a Foundation? Some Questions about Scripture in The Desire of the Nations." *Studies in Christian Ethics* 11, no. 2 (1998): 18–23.
Garnsey, Peter. "Introduction: the Hellenistic and Roman Periods." In *The Cambridge History of Greek and Roman Political Thought*, edited by Christopher Rowe and Malcolm Schofield, 401–414. Cambridge: Cambridge University Press, 2005.
Genette, Gérard. *Narrative Discourse: An Essay in Method*. Translated by Jane E. Lewin. Ithaca, NY: Cornell University Press, 1980.
Goldingay, John E. *Daniel*. Word Biblical Commentary 30. Nashville: Thomas Nelson, 1989.
González, Julián. "The First Oath *Pro Salute Augusti* Found in Baetica." *Zeitschrift für Papyrologie und Epigraphik* 72 (1988): 113–127.
Gordon, Robert P. *1 & 2 Samuel*. Sheffield: JSOT Press, 1984.
———. *I & II Samuel: A Commentary*. Exeter: Paternoster, 1986.
Green, C. M. C. "Varro's Three Theologies and their Influence on the Fasti." In *Ovid's Fasti: Historical Readings at its Bimillennium*, edited by Geraldine Herbert-Brown, 71–100. Oxford: Oxford University Press, 2002.
Green, Joel B. "The (Re-)Turn to Theology." *Journal of Theological Interpretation* 1, no. 1 (2007): 1–3.
———. "Scripture and Theology: Uniting the Two So Long Divided." In *Between Two Horizons: Spanning New Testament Studies and Systematic Theology*, edited by Joel B. Green and Max Turner, 23–43. Grand Rapids, MI: Eerdmans, 2000.
Gunkel, Hermann. *The Psalms: A Form-Critical Introduction*. With an Introduction by James Muilenburg. Translated by Thomas M. Horner. Philadelphia: Fortress, 1967.
Gurval, Robert Alan. *Actium and Augustus: The Politics and Emotions of Civil War*. Michigan: University of Michigan Press, 1995.
Guthrie, Donald. *New Testament Introduction*. Downers Grove, IL: InterVarsity Press, 1990.
Gutiérrez Baqueiro, Oscar. "Influencia de la Biblia." In *Historia General de la Iglesia en América Latina*. Vol. 5, *México*, edited by Enrique Dussel, 288–295. Salamanca: Sígueme, 1984.
Gutiérrez Casillas, José. "La organización de la Iglesia en la Nueva España." In *Historia General de la Iglesia en América Latina*. Vol. 5, *México*, edited by Enrique Dussel and, 55–93. Salamanca: Sígueme, 1984.
Habermas, Jürgen. "On the Relations Between the Secular Liberal State and Religion." In *Political Theologies: Public Religions in a Post-Secular World*, edited by Hent de Vries and Lawrence E. Sullivan, 251–260. New York. Fordham University Press, 2006.

Hahn, Scott W. *Kingdom of God as Liturgical Empire: A Theological Commentary on 1–2 Chronicles*. Grand Rapids, MI: Baker Academic, 2012.

Hall, Stuart George. "Ecclesiology Forged in the Wake of Persecution." In *The Cambridge History of Christianity*. Vol. 1, *Origins to Constantine*, edited Margaret M. Mitchell and Frances M. Young, 470–483. Cambridge: Cambridge University Press, 2006.

Hamnett, Brian R. *A Concise History of Mexico*. 2nd edition. Cambridge: Cambridge University Press, 2006.

Hardy, Daniel W. "Karl Barth." In *The Modern Theologians: An Introduction to Christian Theology Since 1918*, edited by David Ford, 21–42. 3rd edition. Oxford: Blackwell, 2005.

Hays, Richard B. "Reading the Bible with Eyes of Faith: The Practice of Theological Exegesis." *Journal of Theological Interpretation* 1, no. 1 (2007): 5–21.

Hemer, Colin J. *The Letters to the Seven Churches of Asia in their Local Setting*. Sheffield: JSOT Press, 1986.

Hengel, Martin. *Studies in Early Christology*. Edinburgh: T&T Clark, 1995.

Herbert-Brown, Geraldine. *Ovid and the Fasti: An Historical Study*. Oxford: Clarendon Press, 1994.

Hess, Richard S., and Gordon J. Wenham, eds. *Zion, City of Our God*. Grand Rapids, MI: Eerdmans, 1999.

Hurtado, Larry W. *Lord Jesus Christ: Devotion to Jesus in Earliest Christianity*. Grand Rapids, MI: Eerdmans, 2003.

Instituto Nacional de Estadística y Geografía (México) [INEGI]. *Panorama de las religiones en México 2010*. Aguascalientes, Meixco: INEGI, 2011.

Johns, Loren L. *The Lamb Christology of the Apocalypse of John: An Investigation into Its Origins and Rhetorical Force*. Tübingen: Mohr Siebeck, 2003.

Jones, A. H. M. *The Cities of the Eastern Roman Provinces*. 2nd edition. Amsterdam: Adolf M. Hakkert Publisher, 1983.

Kaiser, Otto. *Isaiah 1–12: A Commentary*. 2nd edition. Translated by John Bowden from the German *Das Buch des Propheten Jesaja, Kapitel 1–12*. Philadelphia, PN: Westminster Press, 1983.

Katz, Friedrich. "Mexico: Restored Republic and Porfiriato, 1867–1910." In *The Cambridge History of Latin America*. Vol. 5, *c. 1870 to 1930*, edited by Leslie Bethell, 3–78. Cambridge: Cambridge University Press, 1986.

Keel, Othmar. *The Symbolism of the Biblical World: Ancient Near Eastern Iconography and the Book of Psalms*. Reprint edition. Translated by Timothy J. Hallett. Winona Lake, IN: Eisenbrauns, 1997.

Kelly, J. N. D. *Early Christian Doctrines*. 5th edition. New York: Bloomsbury, 1977.

Kirwan, Michael. *Political Theology: A New Introduction*. London: Darton, Longman and Todd, 2008.

Kitchen, Kenneth A. *On the Reliability of the Old Testament*. Grand Rapids, MI: Eerdmans, 2003.

Koehler, Ludwig, and Walter Baumgartner. *The Hebrew and Aramaic Lexicon of the Old Testament [HALOT]*. Translated and edited under the supervision of M. E. J. Richardson. Leiden: Brill, 2000 (1994). Electronic text hypertexted and prepared by OakTree Software, Inc. Version 3.1.

Kraus, Hans-Joachim. *Psalms 1-59: A Commentary*. Translated by Hilton C. Oswald. Minneapolis: Augsburg, 1988.

Lane, Melissa. "Socrates and Plato: An Introduction." In *The Cambridge History of Greek and Roman Political Thought*, edited by Christopher Rowe and Malcolm Schofield, 155-163. Cambridge: Cambridge University Press, 2005.

Larsen, Timothy. "Defining and Locating Evangelicalism." In *The Cambridge Companion to Evangelical Theology*, edited by Timothy Larsen and Daniel J. Treier, 1-14. Cambridge: Cambridge University Press, 2007.

Lauderville, Dale. *Piety and Politics: The Dynamics of Royal Authority in Homeric Greece, Biblical Israel and Old Babylonian Mesopotamia*. Grand Rapids, MI: Eerdmans, 2003.

Liddell, Henry George, and Robert Scott. *A Greek-English Lexicon [LSJ]*. Revised and augmented throughout by Sir Henry Stuart Jones with the assistance of Roderick McKenzie. 9th edition. Oxford: Oxford University Press, 1940. Accordance edition hypertexted and formatted by OakTree Software, Inc. Version 1.1

Lilla, Mark. *The Stillborn God: Religion, Politics, and the Modern West*. New York: Vintage Books, 2007.

Lintott, Andrew. "The Crisis of the Republic: Sources and Source-Problems." In *The Cambridge Ancient History*. 2nd edition. *Volume IX: The Last Age of the Roman Republic, 146-43 B.C.*, edited by J. A. Crook, Andrew Lintott, and Elizabeth Rawson, 1-15. Cambridge: Cambridge University Press, 1992.

Lowe, Walter. "Why We Need Apocalyptic." *Scottish Journal of Theology* 63, no. 1 (2010): 41-53.

Lynch, John. "The Catholic Church in Latin America, 1830-1930." In *The Cambridge History of Latin America*. Vol. 4, *c. 1870 to 1930*, edited by Leslie Bethell, 527-595. Cambridge: Cambridge University Press, 1986.

———. "Latin America: The Church and National Independence." In *The Cambridge History of Christianity*. Vol. 8, *World Christianities c. 1815 to c. 1914*, edited by Sheridan Gilley and Brian Stanley, 395-411. Cambridge: Cambridge University Press, 2006.

Mangina, Joseph L. "Apocalypticizing Dogmatics: Karl Barth's Reading of the Book of Revelation." *Journal of Theological Interpretation* 1, no. 2 (2007): 193-208.

———. "God, Israel, and Ecclesia in the Apocalypse." In *Revelation and the Politics of Apocalyptic Interpretation*, edited by Richard B. Hays and Stefan Alkier, location 1951–2390. Kindle edition. Waco, TX: Baylor University Press, 2012.

———. *Revelation*. Brazos Theological Commentary on the Bible. Grand Rapids, MI: Brazos Press, 2010.

Mansfeld, Jaap. "Theology." In *The Cambridge History of Hellenistic Philosophy*, edited by Keimpe Algra, Jonathan Barnes, Jaap Mansfeld, and Malcolm Schofield, 452–478. Cambridge: Cambridge University Press, 1999.

Marshal, Howard, Stephen Travis, and Ian Paul. *Exploring the New Testament: Volume 2: A Guide to the Letters and Revelation*. 2nd edition. Downers Grove, IL: InterVarsity Press, 2011.

Martin, David. *Tongues of Fire: The Explosion of Protestantism in Latin America*. Oxford: Blackwell, 1990.

McConville, James Gordon. *God and Earthly Power: An Old Testament Political Theology, Genesis-Kings*. New York: T&T Clark, 2006.

McGrath, Alister E. *Christian Theology: An Introduction*. 5th edition. Oxford: Wiley-Blackwell, 2011.

Medina Ascensio, Luis. "La iglesia ante la emancipación de la Nueva España." In *Historia General de la Iglesia en América Latina*, Vol. 5, *México*, edited by Enrique Dussel, 167–229. Salamanca: Sígueme, 1984.

Mendenhall, George E., and Gary A. Herion. "Covenant." In *The Anchor Yale Bible Dictionary: Volume 1 A-C*, edited by David Noel Freedman, 1.1194–1195. New York: Doubleday, 1992.

Meyer, Jean. "Mexico: Revolution and Reconstruction in the 1920s." In *The Cambridge History of Latin America*. Vol. 5, *c. 1870 to 1930*, edited by Leslie Bethell, 155–194. Cambridge: Cambridge University Press, 1986.

Meyers, Carol. *Exodus*. New York: Cambridge University Press, 2005.

Milbank, John. *Being Reconciled: Ontology and Pardon*. Abingdon: Routledge, 2003.

———. *Beyond Secular Order: The Representation of Being and the Representation of the People*. Oxford: Wiley Blackwell, 2013.

———. *The Future of Love: Essays in Political Theology*. London: SCM, 2009.

———. *Theology and Social Theory: Beyond Secular Reason*. 2nd edition. Oxford: Blackwell, 2006.

———. *The Word Made Strange: Theology, Language, Culture*. Oxford: Blackwell, 1997.

Millar, William R. *Isaiah 24–27 and the Origin of Apocalyptic*. Missoula, MT: Scholar Press, 1976.

Miller, Patrick D., Jr. *Interpreting the Psalms*. Philadelphia: Fortress, 1986.

Moberly, R. W. L. "The Use of Scripture in *The Desire Of The Nations*." In *A Royal Priesthood? The Use of the Bible Ethically and Politically: A Dialogue with*

Oliver O'Donovan, edited by Craig Bartholomew, Jonathan Chaplin, Robert Song and Al Wolters, 46–64. Grand Rapids, MI: Zondervan, 2002.

———. "What Is Theological Interpretation of Scripture?" *Journal of Theological Interpretation* 3, no. 2 (2009): 161–178.

Mowinckel, Sigmund. *The Psalms in Israel's Worship*. Volume 1. Translated by D. R. Ap-Thomas. Oxford: Blackwell, 1962.

Nickelsburg, George W. E. *1 Enoch: A Commentary on the Book of 1 Enoch, Chapters 1–36; 81–108*. Hermeneia – A Critical and Historical Commentary on the Bible. Minneapolis: Fortress, 2001.

Noreña, Carlos F. *Imperial Ideals in the Roman West: Representation, Circulation, Power*. Cambridge: Cambridge University Press, 2011.

O'Donovan, Joan Lockwood. "Nation, State, and Civil Society in Western Biblical Tradition." In *Bonds of Imperfection: Christian Politics, Past and Present*, by Oliver O'Donovan and Joan Lockwood O'Donovan, 276–295. Grand Rapids, MI: Eerdmans, 2004.

O'Donovan, Oliver. *Begotten or Made?*. Oxford: Clarendon, 1984.

———. *Common Objects of Love: Moral Reflection and the Shaping of Community*. Grand Rapids, MI: Eerdmans, 2002.

———. *A Conversation Waiting to Begin: The Churches and the Gay Controversy*. London: SCM, 2009.

———. *The Desire of the Nations: Rediscovering the Roots of Political Theology*. Cambridge: Cambridge University Press, 1996.

———. "Government as Judgment." In *Bonds of Imperfection: Christian Politics, Past and Present*, by Oliver O'Donovan and Joan Lockwood O'Donovan, 207–224. Grand Rapids, MI: Eerdmans, 2004.

———. "History and Politics in the Book of Revelation." In *Bonds of Imperfection: Christian Politics, Past and Present*, by Oliver O'Donovan and Joan Lockwood O'Donovan, 25–47. Grand Rapids, MI: Eerdmans, 2004.

———. *The Just War Revisited*. Cambridge: Cambridge University Press, 2003.

———. "Karl Barth and Paul Ramsey's 'Uses of Power.'" In *Bonds of Imperfection. Christian Politics, Past and Present*, by Oliver O'Donovan and Joan Lockwood O'Donovan, 246–275. Grand Rapids, MI: Eerdmans, 2004.

———. "The Loss of a Sense of Place." In *Bonds of Imperfection: Christian Politics, Past and Present*, by Oliver O'Donovan and Joan Lockwood O'Donovan, 296–320. Grand Rapids, MI: Eerdmans, 2004.

———. *On the Thirty-Nine Articles: A Conversation with Tudor Christianity*. 2nd edition. Kindle edition. London: SCM, 2011.

———. "The Political Thought of *City of God* 19." In *Bonds of Imperfection: Christian Politics, Past and Present*, by Oliver O'Donovan and Joan Lockwood O'Donovan, 48–72. Grand Rapids, MI: Eerdmans, 2004.

———. "Response to Gordon McConville." In *A Royal Priesthood? The Use of the Bible Ethically and Politically: A Dialogue with Oliver O'Donovan*, edited by Craig Bartholomew, Jonathan Chaplin, Robert Song and Al Wolters, 89–90. Grand Rapids, MI: Zondervan, 2002.

———. "Response to Respondents: Behold, The Lamb!" *Studies in Christian Ethics* 11, no. 2 (1998): 91–110.

———. *Resurrection and Moral Order: An Outline for Evangelical Ethics*. 2nd edition. Grand Rapids, MI: Eerdmans, 1994.

———. *Self, World, and Time: Ethics as Theology*. Vol. 1. Grand Rapids, MI: Eerdmans, 2013.

———. *The Ways of Judgment*. Grand Rapids, MI: Eerdmans, 2005.

———. "What Kind of Community is the Church? The Richard Hooker Lectures 2005." *Ecclesiology* 3, no. 2 (2007): 171–193.

———. *The World in Small Boats: Sermons from Oxford*. Edited by Andy Draycott. Grand Rapids, MI: Eerdmans, 2010.

O'Donovan, Oliver and Joan Lockwood O'Donovan. *Bonds of Imperfection: Christian Politics, Past and Present*. Grand Rapids, MI: Eerdmans, 2004.

———, eds. *From Irenaeus to Grotius: A Sourcebook in Christian Political Thought 100–1625*. Grand Rapids, MI: Eerdmans, 1999.

Ollenburger, Ben C. *Zion, the City of the Great King: A Theological Symbol of the Jerusalem Cult*. Sheffield: JSOT Press, 1987.

Osiek, Carolyn. "The Self-Defining Praxis of the Developing of Ecclesia." In *The Cambridge History of Christianity*. Vol. 1, *Origins to Constantine*, edited by Margaret M. Mitchell and Frances M. Young, 274–292. Cambridge: Cambridge University Press, 2006.

Oswalt, John. *The Book of Isaiah Chapters 1–39*. The New International Commentary of the Old Testament. Grand Rapids, MI: Eerdmans, 1986.

———. *The Book of Isaiah Chapters 40–66*. The New International Commentary of the Old Testament. Grand Rapids, MI: Eerdmans, 1998.

Paddison, Angus. *Scripture: A Very Theological Proposal*. New York: T&T Clark, 2009.

Pataki, András Dávid. "A Non-Combat Myth in Revelation 12." *New Testament Studies* 57, no. 1 (2011): 258–272.

Paul, Ian. "Ebbing and Flowing: Scholarly Developments in Study of the Book of Revelation." *The Expository Times* 119, no. 11 (2008): 523–531.

Paz, Octavio. *El Laberinto de la Soledad*. México: Fondo de Cultura Económica, 1959.

Pew Research Centre. *Global Christianity: A Report on the Size and Distribution of the World's Christian Population*. Washington, DC: Pew Research Centre, 2011.

Phillips, Elizabeth. *Political Theology: A Guide for the Perplexed*. London: T&T Clark, 2012.
Pickstock, Catherine. *After Writing: On the Liturgical Consummation of Philosophy*. Oxford: Blackwell, 1998.
———. "Liturgy and the Senses." In *Paul's New Moment: Continental Philosophy and the Future of Christian Theology*, edited by John Milbank, Slavoj Žižek and Creston Davis, Location 1517–1778. Kindle edition. Grand Rapids, MI: Brazos Press, 2010.
———. "Liturgy and Modernity." In *An Eerdmans Reader in Contemporary Political Theology*, edited by William T. Cavanaugh, Jeffrey W. Bailey and Craig Hovey, 139–155. Grand Rapids, MI: Eerdmans, 2012.
Price, S. R. F. *Rituals and Power: The Roman Imperial Cult in Asia Minor*. Cambridge: Cambridge University Press, 1984.
———. "The Place of Religion: Rome in the Early Empire." In *The Cambridge Ancient History: Volume X: The Augustan Empire, 43 B.C. – A.D. 69*, edited by Alan K. Bowman, Edward Champlin, and Andrew Lintott, 812–847. Cambridge: Cambridge University Press, 1996.
Provan, Iain, V. Philips Long, and Tremper Longman III. *A Biblical History of Israel*. Louisville, KY: Westminster John Knox, 2003.
Quash, Ben. "Hans Urs von Balthasar." In *The Modern Theologians: An Introduction to Christian Theology Since 1918*, edited by David Ford with Rachel Muers, 106–123. 3rd edition. Oxford: Blackwell, 2005.
———. "Life Beyond Judgment: Communication. Response to Section III of *The Ways of Judgment* by Oliver O'Donovan." *Political Theology* 9, no. 3 (2008): 309–318.
Rawson, Elizabeth. "The Aftermath of the Ides." In *The Cambridge Ancient History: Volume IX: The Last Age of the Roman Republic, 146–43 B.C.*, edited by J. A. Crook, Andrew Lintott and Elizabeth Rawson, 468–490. Cambridge: Cambridge University Press, 1992.
Resseguie, James L. *Narrative Criticism of the New Testament*. Grand Rapids, MI: Baker Academic, 2005.
———. *The Revelation of John: A Narrative Commentary*. Grand Rapids, MI: Baker Academic, 2009.
———. *Revelation Unsealed: A Narrative Critical Approach to John's Apocalypse*. Leiden: Brill, 1998.
Roberts, John, ed. *Oxford Dictionary of the Classical World*. Oxford: Oxford University Press, 2007.
Robinson, John A. T. *Redating the New Testament*. London: SCM Press, 1976.
Rosen, Stanley. *Plato's Republic: A Study*. New Haven: Yale University Press, 2005.

Rowe, Christopher. "Aristotelian Constitutions." In *The Cambridge History of Greek and Roman Political Thought*, edited by Christopher Rowe and Malcolm Schofield, 366–389. Cambridge: Cambridge University Press, 2005.

———. "Introduction." In *The Cambridge History of Greek and Roman Political Thought*, edited by Christopher Rowe and Malcolm Schofield, 1–6. Cambridge: Cambridge University Press, 2005.

Rowe, Christopher, and Malcolm Schofield, eds. *The Cambridge History of Greek and Roman Thought*. Paperback edition. Cambridge: Cambridge University Press, 2005.

Rowland, Christopher. "Apocalypticism." In *Dictionary of Early Judaism*, edited by John J. Collins and Daniel C. Harlow, 345–348. Grand Rapids, MI: Eerdmans, 2010.

———. "The Apocalypse and Political Theology." In *A Royal Priesthood? The Use of the Bible Ethically and Politically: A Dialogue with Oliver O'Donovan*, edited by Craig Bartholomew, Jonathan Chaplin, Robert Song, and Al Wolters, 241–254. Grand Rapids, MI: Zondervan, 2002.

———. "Apocalypticism: The Disclosure of Heavenly Knowledge." In *The Mystery of God: Early Jewish Mysticism and the New Testament*, edited by Christopher Rowland and Christopher R. A. Morray-Jones, 13–32. Leiden: Brill, 2009.

———. "The Book of Revelation." In *The New Interpreter's Bible*. Vol. 12, *Hebrews to Revelation*, edited by Leander E. Keck, 501–743. Nashville: Abingdon, 1998.

———. *The Open Heaven: A Study of Apocalyptic in Judaism and Early Christianity*. London: SPCK, 1982.

———. "The Vision of the Risen Christ in Rev.i.13 ff.: The Debt of an Early Christology to an Aspect of Jewish Angelology." *Journal of Theological Studies* 31, no. 1 (1980): 1–11.

Ryan, Marie-Laure. "Toward a Definition of Narrative." In *The Cambridge Companion to Narrative*, edited by David Herman, 22–35. Cambridge: Cambridge University Press, 2007.

Schofield, Malcolm. "Approaching the Republic." In *The Cambridge History of Greek and Roman Political Thought*, edited by Christopher Rowe and Malcolm Schofield, 190–232. Cambridge: Cambridge University Press, 2005.

———. *Saving the City: Philosopher-Kings and Other Classical Paradigms*. London: Routledge, 1999.

Scott, Peter, and William T. Cavanaugh, eds. *The Blackwell Companion to Political Theology*. Malden, MA: Blackwell, 2004.

Sigurdson, Ola. "Beyond Secularism? Towards a Post-Secular Political Theology." *Modern Theology* 26, no. 2 (2010): 177–196.

Shortt, Rupert. *God's Advocates: Christian Thinkers in Conversation*. London: Darton, Longman and Todd, 2005.

Smith, James K. A. *Introducing Radical Orthodoxy: Mapping a Post-Secular Theology*. Grand Rapids: Baker Academic, 2004.

———. "Secularity, Globalization, and the Re-enchantment of the World." In *After Modernity? Secularity, Globalization and the Re-Enchantment of the World*, edited by James K. A. Smith, 3–13. Waco, TX: Baylor University Press, 2008.

———. *Who's Afraid of Postmodernism?: Taking Derrida, Lyotard, and Foucault to Church*. Grand Rapids, MI: Baker Academic, 2006.

———. "Will the Real Plato Please Stand Up? Participation versus Incarnation." In *Radical Orthodoxy and the Reformed Tradition: Creation, Covenant, and Participation*, edited by James K. A. Smith and James H. Olthuis, 61–72. Grand Rapids, MI: Baker Academic, 2005.

Snyder, Graydon F. *Ante Pacem: Archeological Evidence of Church Life Before Constantine*. Macon, GA: Mercer University Press, 2003.

Stanton, Graham N. "Presuppositions in New Testament Criticism." In *New Testament Interpretation: Essays on Principles and Methods*, edited by I. Howard Marshall, 60–71. Exeter: Paternoster, 1985.

Stone, Michael Edward. *Fourth Ezra: A Commentary on the Book of Fourth Ezra*. Hermeneia – A Critical and Historical Commentary on the Bible. Minneapolis, MN: Fortress, 1990.

Stuckenbruck, Loren T. *Angel Veneration and Christology: A Study in Early Judaism and the Christology of the Apocalypse of John*. Tübingen: Mohr, 1995.

———. *1 Enoch 91–108*. Commentaries on Early Jewish Literature. Berlin: Walter de Gruyter, 2007.

———. "Revelation." In *Eerdmans Commentary on the Bible*, edited by James D. G. Dunn and John W. Rogerson, 1535–1572. Grand Rapids, MI: Eerdmans, 2003.

Taylor, Charles. *A Secular Age*. Cambridge, MA: Harvard University Press, 2007.

Turner, Max. *The Holy Spirit and Spiritual Gifts: Then and Now*. Carlisle: Paternoster, 1999.

———. *Power from on High: The Spirit in Israel's Restoration and Witness in Luke-Acts*. Sheffield: Sheffield Academic Press, 2000.

United Nations Office on Drugs and Crime (UNODC). *World Drug Report 2010*. Vienna: United Nations, 2010.

Vanhoozer, Kevin J. *Is there a Meaning in This Text?: The Bible, The Reader, and the Morality of Literary Knowledge*. Grand Rapids, MI: Zondervan, 1998.

———. "What is Theological Interpretation of the Bible?" In *Dictionary for Theological Interpretation of the Bible*, edited by Kevin J. Vanhoozer, 19–25. Grand Rapids, MI: Baker Academic, 2005.

Walton, John H. *Ancient Near Eastern Thought and the Old Testament: Introducing the Conceptual World of the Hebrew Bible*. Grand Rapids, MI: Baker Academic, 2006.

Wannenwetsch, Bernd. "Liturgy." In *The Blackwell Companion to Political Theology*, edited by Peter Scott and William T. Cavanaugh, 76–90. Oxford: Blackwell, 2004.

———. *Political Worship: Ethics for Christian Citizens*. Translated by Margaret Kohl. Oxford: Oxford University Press, 2004.

Ward, Graham. "In the Economy of the Divine: A Response to James K. A. Smith." *PNEUMA: The Journal of the Society for Pentecostal Studies* 25, no. 1 (2003): 115–120.

———. *Theology and Contemporary Critical Theory*. 2nd edition. Basingstoke: Macmillan, 2000.

Watts, John D. W. *Isaiah 1–33*. Revised edition. Word Biblical Commentary 24. Nashville: Thomas Nelson, 2005.

———. *Isaiah 34–66*. Revised edition. Word Biblical Commentary 25. Nashville: Thomas Nelson, 2005.

Webster, John. "Introduction: Systematic Theology." In *The Oxford Handbook of Systematic Theology*, edited by John Webster, Kathryn Tanner and Iain Torrance, 1–15. Oxford: Oxford University Press, 2007.

Weinrich, William C., ed. *Revelation*. Ancient Christian Commentary on Scripture. New Testament 12. Downers Grove, IL: InterVarsity Press, 2005.

Weissenrieder, Annette. "Contested Spaces in 1 Corinthians 11:17–33 and 14:30." In *Contested Spaces*, edited by David L. Balch and Annette Weissenrieder, 59–108. Tübingen, Germany: Mohr Siebeck, 2012.

———. "'Do You Not Know That You Are God's Temple?' Towards a New Perspective on Paul's Temple Image in 1 Corinthians 3:16." In *Contested Spaces*, edited by David L. Balch and Annette Weissenrieder, 377–411. Tübingen, Germany: Mohr Siebeck, 2012.

Wells, David F. "Evangelical Theology." In *The Modern Theologians: An Introduction to Christian Theology Since 1918*, edited by David Ford, 608–609. 3rd edition. Malden, MA: Blackwell, 2005.

Wells, Samuel, and Ben Quash. *Introducing Christian Ethics*. Malden, MA: Blackwell, 2010.

Wenham, Gordon J. *Genesis 1–15*. Word Biblical Commentary 1. Nashville: Thomas Nelson, 1987.

———. *Genesis 16–50*. Word Biblical Commentary 2. Nashville: Thomas Nelson, 1994.

———. "Sanctuary Symbolism in the Garden of Eden Story." *Proceedings of the Ninth World Congress of Jewish Studies*, 19–25. Division A: The Period of the Bible; Jerusalem: World Union of Jewish Students, 1986.

Wiedemann, Thomas. "Reflections of Roman Political Thought in Latin Historical Writing." In *The Cambridge History of Greek and Roman Political Thought*, edited by Christopher Rowe and Malcolm Schofield, 517–531. Cambridge: Cambridge University Press, 2005.

Winton, Richard. "Herodotus, Thucydides and the Sophists." In *The Cambridge History of Greek and Roman Political Thought*, edited by Christopher Rowe and Malcolm Schofield, 89–121. Cambridge: Cambridge University Press, 2005.

Witherington III, Ben. *Revelation*. The New Cambridge Bible Commentary. Cambridge: Cambridge University Press, 2003.

Wilson, J. Christian. "The Problem of the Domitianic Date of Revelation." *New Testament Studies* 39, no. 4 (1993): 587–605.

Wolterstorff, Nicholas. "A Discussion of Oliver O'Donovan's *The Desire of the Nations*." *Scottish Journal of Theology* 54, no. 1 (2001): 87–109.

———. *The Mighty and The Almighty: An Essay in Political Theology*. Cambridge: Cambridge University Press, 2012.

Womack, John, Jr. "The Mexican Revolution, 1910–1920." In *The Cambridge History of Latin America*. Vol. 5, *c. 1870 to 1930*, edited by Leslie Bethell, 79–153. Cambridge: Cambridge University Press, 1986.

Woodhead, Linda. "Editorial." *Studies in Christian Ethics* 11, no. 2 (1998): ix–x.

Wright, N. T. *Jesus and the Victory of God*. Christian Origins and the Question of God, volume 2. London: SPCK, 1996.

———. "Narrative Theology: The Evangelists' Use of the Old Testament as an Implicit Overarching Narrative." In *Biblical Interpretation and Method: Essays in Honour of John Barton*, edited by Katharine J. Dell and Paul M. Joyce, 189–200. Oxford: Oxford University Press, 2013.

———. *The New Testament and the People of God*. Christian Origins and the Question of God, vol. 1. London: SPCK, 1992.

———. "Paul and Caesar: A New Reading of Romans." In *A Royal Priesthood? The Use of the Bible Ethically and Politically: A Dialogue with Oliver O'Donovan*, edited by Craig Bartholomew, Jonathan Chaplin, Robert Song and Al Wolters, 173–193. Carlisle: Paternoster; Grand Rapids, MI: Zondervan, 2002.

———. *Paul and the Faithfulness of God: Parts III and IV*. Christian Origins and the Question of God, volume 4. London: SPCK, 2013.

———. *The Resurrection of the Son of God*. Christian Origins and the Question of God, vol. 3. London: SPCK, 2003.

Yarbro Collins, Adela. "The Early Christian Apocalypses." *Semeia* 14 (1979): 61–121.

Zetzel, James, trans. and ed. *Cicero: On the Commonwealth and On the Laws*. Cambridge Texts in the History of Political Thought. Cambridge: Cambridge University Press, 1999.

Index of Names

A
Abbott, H. Porter 85
Adams, Edward 21
Annas, Julia 147
Apringius of Beja 20
Aquinas 175
Aristotle 138, 169, 172, 173, 175, 188, 226–228, 256, 257, 261
Atkins, E. M. 18, 154, 155
Augustine 12, 18, 88, 175, 178, 213, 214, 222, 263
  City of God 215, 218
Augustus 7, 19, 22, 144, 158–161, 166, 173, 175, 178–180, 228, 230, 231, 250, 256, 260, 262
  Res Gestae 143, 183, 230
Aune, David E. 79, 81, 93, 100, 104–106, 193, 205, 207

B
Barnadas, Joseph M. 2
Barr, David 56, 59, 60–62, 68, 93, 116
Barth, Karl 21
Bartholomew, Craig 31
Bauckham, Richard 58, 59, 61, 62, 68, 70, 75, 106, 117
Beale, Gregory K. 12, 57, 58, 61, 75, 76, 84, 127, 139
Boring, Eugene M. 56
Boxall, Ian 15, 93
Bretherton, Luke 28, 31
Brueggemann, Walter 128

C
Caird, G. B. 76, 103, 127, 199
Cartledge, Paul 16, 226
Cassius Dio 158, 161
Cavanaugh, William T. 33, 214, 216–219, 221, 222, 257, 263, 265
Chadwick, Henry 18
Chappell, Timothy 226
Chatman, Seymor 85
Childs, Brevard S. 131
Cicero 18, 22, 138, 143, 144, 154–157, 161, 175, 227, 228, 256, 257, 261
Clines, David J. A. 102
Connolly, William 265
Cooley, Alison E. 158, 159, 161, 230, 231
Crook, J. A. 158, 160, 161

D
Dannenberg, Hilary P. 85
Day, John 131
de Alvarado Tezozomoc, Hernando 220
Duyfhuizen, Bernard 63

E
Eusebius 179

F
Fantham, Elaine 212
Fekkes, Jan, III 67, 81, 189, 204

Fiorenza, Elisabeth Schüssler 59, 61
Ford, David 20, 264

G
Garnsey, Peter 17, 18
Genette, Gérard 64
Gibson, John C. L. 126, 127
Goldingay, John 95
González, Julián 231
Grayson, Albert Kirk 81, 126, 129, 130
Green, C. M. C. 212
Grotius, Hugo 171, 175
Gurval, Robert Alan 159

H
Habermas, Jürgen 265
Hahn, Scott W. 111
Hengel, Martin 105
Herbert-Brown, Geraldine 212
Hobbes, Thomas 247, 248, 252, 261
Hurtado, Larry 93, 116–118

I
Ignatius 212

J
Jerome 56
Johns, Loren L. 115
Josephus 192
Julius Caesar 18, 79, 157, 230

L
Lilla, Mark 28
Livy 157
Locke, John 169, 247, 252, 261
Lysias 188

M
Mangina, Joseph 211, 222
Marsilius of Padua 169, 172, 173, 175
McConville, J. Gordon 33, 34
McGrath, Alister E. 29
Meyer, Jean 4

Meyers, Carol 192
Milbank, John 6, 179, 214, 215, 219, 222, 247, 257, 263, 264
Montesquieu 169

O
O'Donovan, Oliver 5–10, 19, 20, 22–24, 27–32, 34–39, 41–46, 49–52, 55, 57, 86–89, 93, 109, 119, 132, 141, 143, 144, 159, 162–175, 178, 179, 181–183, 187, 198, 213, 221, 223, 231–234, 236–252, 254–257, 260–262
Oecumenius 123
Oswalt, John 105, 106
Ovid
  Fasti 212

P
Paddison, Angus 21, 188, 264
Paul, the apostle 61, 88, 97, 122, 165, 166
Paz, Octavio 264
Phillips, Elizabeth 17, 28
Philo 192
Pickstock, Catherine 189, 190
Plato 16, 22, 144, 146, 166, 172–175, 182, 227–229, 231, 250, 256, 257, 260–262
Pope Gregory VII 171
Price, S. R. F. 160, 161

Q
Quash, Ben 21, 145, 243

R
Richardson, Mervin E. J. 126, 133
Resseguie, James L. 56
Rosen, Stanley 225, 229, 230
Rousseau, Jean-Jacques 228, 247, 248, 252, 261
Rowland, Christopher 71, 93, 194

S
Smith, James K. A. 32, 149
Snyder, Graydon F. 198
Socrates 17, 144–148, 150–153, 225, 228, 229
Stuckenbruck, Loren 96, 98, 112

T
Tacitus 158, 159
Tertullian 71, 138, 139
Turner, Max 103, 104

V
Vanhoozer, Kevin J. 20, 22
Victorinus of Petovium 12, 56, 88

W
Wannenwetsch, Bernd 187–190
Watts, John D. W. 103
Weinrich, William C. 12, 20, 56, 71
Wenham, Gordon J. 33, 85
Wiedemann, Thomas 154
Wolterstorff, Nicholas 6, 10
Woodhead, Linda 31
Wright, N. T. 14, 31, 42, 44, 45, 82, 97, 199
Wyclif, John 172, 173

Z
Zetzel, James 17, 154, 155, 227

Index of Subjects

Numbers
the 144,000 68

A
abyss 71
Against Celsus (Origen) 139
Against Heresies (Irenaeus) 139
Against Marcion (Tertullian) 138
Ancient of Days 16, 42, 46, 48, 95, 97, 112
An Exact Exposition of the Orthodox Faith (John of Damascus) 139
angel 11, 77, 97, 118
  church 98, 100, 101, 197, 198
  Iaoel 97
  mighty 95
  of the Lord 97
  powerful 71
angels 67
  countless 69
  seven 69
Anointed One 80
Antiquities of the Jews (Josephus) 138
Apocalypse of Abraham 97
apophatic 260
ark of the covenant 72
Asia Minor 61, 64, 86
authority 8, 9, 14, 17–19, 23, 31, 33, 37, 39, 44, 45, 48, 52, 57, 65, 73, 79, 89, 133, 142, 161, 164–166, 169, 174, 179, 182, 183, 209, 210, 223, 228, 231, 232, 235, 245–247, 250, 253, 255, 256, 261–264
ancient models 162
Apocalypse's construal 143, 144, 176, 181
Augustus 160, 178
beast 86
centralization 157
concept of 29
corporate beast 79
divine 14, 15, 19, 20, 22, 23, 30, 34, 38, 84, 87, 93, 94, 108, 109, 118, 119, 124, 133, 142, 174, 177, 183, 187, 188, 219, 221, 250, 252, 257, 258, 260
divine King 79
dragon 76
dual 232
embodiment 155
from above 80
from below 80
God 164
heavenly 83
heretical construal 86
heterodox mode 211
human 139, 140, 144, 165, 180, 182, 183, 260
immanent 88, 219, 222, 249, 260
international 172
Jesus 42, 85
Messiah 75, 124, 125
modern construal 22

monarchical construal 177
Platonic 153, 154, 175, 225
political 11, 13, 37, 46, 52, 76, 102, 112, 132, 143, 158, 165–172, 174–176, 183, 224, 225, 236, 237, 239, 243, 265
rider of the pale horse 71
Roman senate 157, 159
Scripture 244, 246
secular 49, 50, 173, 232
Son of God 101, 103
Aztec 4
foundational story 220

B

baptism 20, 103, 234, 235, 241, 250, 251, 262
beast 14, 50, 78, 82, 118, 142, 180–182, 201, 209, 261
  abyss 71
  Aristotelian 226
  destruction 78
  dethronement 136
  earth 73, 76, 86, 132, 211, 219, 222
  sea 73, 74, 76, 80, 86, 132, 139, 211, 219, 222, 260
  throne 78
  tyranny 50
  worship 77, 132, 142
  worshippers 83
Bible 265
  shape of Protestant, evangelical communities 21
  theological interpretation 22
biblical studies 21, 31, 256, 257, 263
book of life 83
bride 84

C

Caesar 114, 159, 212
category 22, 142, 216, 257
  christological 93, 94
  epistemological 148
  political 7, 13, 55, 189

theological 67, 109, 231, 251, 252, 254, 260, 262
theo-political 8, 57, 87, 214, 222, 257, 259, 263
cave
  Platonic story 149
Cherubim (Philo) 138
Christ 5, 45, 46, 58, 119, 162–164, 166, 213, 216, 232, 234, 235, 237, 246
  ascended 9, 48, 232, 233
  child 50
  event 6, 10, 23, 45, 46, 52, 144, 183, 235, 236, 250
  exaltation 47, 48
  exalted 19, 105
  resurrection 6, 19, 93, 236
  risen 243, 244
  rule 57
Christendom 6, 49, 50, 171
Christianity 264
  Protestant, evangelical 21
  Protestant, Pentecostal 1
  reformed, evangelical 3
  Roman Catholic 1, 2
christological 6, 11, 19, 20, 45, 52, 59, 99, 106, 135, 139, 141, 200, 203, 206, 210, 212, 222, 238, 244, 257–261
  categories 93
  construal 94, 175
  ecclesiology 212
  liturgy 66
  love 248
  mutation of divine authority 108
  objective reality 164
  political identity 262
  political theology 247
  portrayals 263
  shift 108, 109, 118, 142, 177
  stage 235, 236
  turn 115
Christology
  theological category 67

Index of Subjects

church 2, 5–7, 9, 20, 24, 46, 48–50, 53, 86, 87, 89, 198–200, 213, 218, 221, 222, 231, 234, 236, 240–242, 244–247, 250–252, 254, 259, 261, 262, 264, 265
  apostolic 9, 44, 52
  authorized 48
  bride 9, 238
  counter-political society 232
  early 45, 249
  Ephesus 197, 199
  gathering community 235
  glad community 235
  global, universal 212
  koinonia of the Holy Spirit 238, 239
  Laodicea 198
  liturgical sociality 221
  local 212
  locus of social renewal 119
  mission 49
  modern 218
  moral community 232, 244, 245
  political character 233, 234
  politically bodyless 218
  political reorientation 238
  political society 231, 232, 254
  post-political society 236, 237
  Roman Catholic 3
  sacramental order 234
  seven churches 64, 65, 197
  society 10
  suffering community 235
  Thyatira 253
city 11, 12, 16, 17, 41, 51, 71, 77, 84, 101, 187, 201, 203, 205, 207, 208, 240, 249, 262
  anti-city 201
  Augustinian 213
  beloved 82, 88, 253
  boundaries 208
  construal(s) 202, 203, 213
  earthly 219
  giant cube 84
  God's 219
  great 14, 73, 74, 77–80, 86, 101, 132, 141, 180, 182, 196, 201, 209, 211, 219, 222
  fate 79
  Greek 172, 188, 200, 224–226, 228, 229, 231
  heavenly 216
  historical 200
  holy 11, 23, 53, 57, 64, 68, 74, 81, 83, 84, 86, 88, 140, 141, 182, 183, 188, 194, 196, 199–202, 204, 205, 208–210, 220–222, 250, 252–254, 257, 259, 261, 262
  advent 80
  imperial 201
  in the making 211, 222, 252, 259, 261
  Jerusalem 128, 137
  liturgical 190, 202
  new 87, 202
  Platonic 145–149, 151–153, 155, 176
  re-building 204, 206
  Roman 178
  Rome 156, 212
  symbol of all political life 199
  theological character 200
  theological construal 200, 206
  walled 12, 13, 187, 208, 227
  woman 79
City of God (Augustine) 213
civitas 214
Commentary on the Apocalypse (Oecumenius) 251
Commentary on the Gospel of John (Origen) 139
common good 168
cosmic commotion 67, 69
creation
  theological category 67
Crónica Mexicana 220

D

Decalogue (Philo) 138

diakonia 241, 242
diakonos 242
Dialogues (Theodoret) 139
Dialogue with Trypho (Justin Martyr) 138
discourse 73, 98, 100, 108, 139, 178, 188, 212, 238, 250, 254
  Augustan 162
  christological 258
  divine 236
  forensic 141
  imperialistic 182
  justice 79, 133, 141
  liturgical 246, 250, 251, 261, 262
  Logos 142
  narrative 55, 89
  Pauline 168
  sacramental 20, 251, 254
  Second Temple 106
  secular 5, 27, 219, 255, 263, 265
Divine Institutes (Lactantius) 139
divine name 136, 138, 139, 141, 142
doxa 209, 252, 260, 262
dragon 14, 75, 79, 86, 118, 126, 127, 133, 142, 258
  actions 127
  agents 76
  attempt à la Nebuchadnezzar 131
  Babylonian 128
  cosmic 60
  demise 82, 83
  dethronement 139
  downfall 73, 75, 81, 82, 88, 89, 119, 125, 131, 258, 263
    narrative thread 128
  fall 139
  heretical agenda 132
  hostility 62
  locus of evil 132
  mode of evil 132
  plot 128
  political conspiracy 82, 83, 119, 131
  political symbol 126
  serpent 120, 126, 127

Ugaritic 127
thrown from heaven 124
worship 132, 142
worshippers 81

E
earth 38, 40, 49, 50, 64, 66, 67, 69, 70, 72, 76, 77, 80, 82, 83, 88, 96, 99, 100, 106, 107, 110, 111, 113, 116, 117, 132, 135, 166, 179, 212
  elite 86
  new 83, 84, 140, 178, 194, 196, 202, 222, 253
earthquake 38, 62, 72, 82
  great 71, 77–79
ecclesiology 212, 235, 247, 257
  politically indirect 218
  spatial 188, 210, 211, 222
education 48, 147–149, 151–153, 166, 176
  Greek 146
  higher 221
  secular 3
  theological 146
ekklesia 16
emperor 250
  Augustus 143
  cult 17
  Roman 17, 113, 179
empire 41, 50, 179, 232
  analysis 53
  city 201
  collapse 51
  criticism 41
  imperium 178
  Mesopotamian 40
  monster-god 128
  rise 41
  Roman 122, 158–160, 178, 179, 231
  world 41
enmity, between serpent and woman 120
Enochic Judaism 131

Enuma Elish 127
episkopos 242
era
   Augustan 158, 211, 222
   Christendom 49
Erastianism 233
ethics 28, 30, 31, 246
Eucharist 20, 234, 235, 241, 250, 262
evil 14, 51, 87, 128–131, 166, 173, 202, 228, 238
   community 50
   located by Jesus 132
   political conspiracy 132
exaltation 45, 46, 52, 73, 102, 104, 121, 152, 153, 233, 236
   child-Messiah 75, 119, 263
   Christ 9, 232, 235, 251
   Jesus 163, 167, 174, 233, 264
   like a son of man 136
   liturgical 67
   philosopher-king 149
   scene 66
   slaughtered Lamb 66, 69, 70, 73
   Son of God 101, 124, 132
   YHWH's son 102
exegesis
   biblical 31
   literary 55
Exposition of the Christian Faith (Ambrose of Milan) 139

F
false prophet 14, 80, 82, 139, 142
Fellowship of the Throne 13, 14, 16, 19, 22–24, 57, 64, 65, 67–69, 72, 82, 84, 86, 87, 89, 94, 103, 105, 108, 118, 119, 140–142, 166–168, 175–178, 182, 183, 188, 200, 202, 208, 210, 221–223, 239, 249, 250, 252–254, 257, 259, 260, 262, 263, 265

G
garden
   city 12
   Eden 210, 249, 250
   primeval 12, 13, 84, 187, 259
God's people 44, 45, 66, 68, 72, 73, 79, 82, 187, 195, 196, 199, 201–203, 206, 221, 265
gospel 98, 242, 264
   eternal 77
   proclamation 246
   sacraments 241
   tradition 104
government 3, 4, 17, 18, 39, 41, 52, 106, 154, 166, 171, 173, 174, 179, 220, 224, 232, 233
   coercive 143
   confessionally Christian 7
   contemplative 143
   liberal 169
   secular 47, 49, 162
   three powers 172
   triad of powers 169
   world 171

H
heaven 11, 33, 37, 51, 57, 58, 60, 64, 65, 67–69, 71–73, 76, 80, 82, 83, 96, 97, 100, 101, 110, 111, 113, 117, 124, 125, 131–133, 136, 140, 141, 162, 179, 193–195, 201, 202, 258
   as holy of holies 195, 222
   creator 99
   door opened 65
   new 83, 84, 140, 178, 194, 196, 202, 222, 253
   portents 62, 73, 75, 78, 81, 120
   seven-layered view 109
   the one who made it 77
heresy 76, 103, 140
   beasts 77
hermeneutics 31–33, 55, 150, 265
history 5, 28, 29, 30, 33, 34, 36, 37, 39, 42, 49, 51, 52, 55, 94, 132,

142, 163, 165, 214, 217, 218, 237, 243, 258
Christendom 7, 171
ideas 171
immanent 28
Israel 30, 34, 43
political 29, 37, 52
salvation 37, 47, 50, 167
holy of holies 11, 84, 110, 191, 193–196, 202, 210, 221, 250, 252, 259
Homilies on 1 Thessalonians (John Chrysostom) 139

I

Isaianic Apocalypse 131

J

Jerusalem 36, 110, 128–130, 137, 203–205, 259
new 59, 65, 74, 83, 166
Jesus 7, 8, 13, 42–45, 52, 60, 82, 88, 97, 98, 103–106, 108, 114, 122, 181, 182, 235, 239, 243–245, 253, 264
cross 236
death 8, 45, 264
divine pre-existence 136
divine status 118
exaltation 6, 46, 167, 174
exalted 13, 19, 23, 52, 53, 84–87, 89, 93, 94, 105, 109, 118, 132, 141–144, 175–178, 181, 183, 188–190, 195–199, 206, 207, 209, 210, 212, 219, 221–224, 231, 232, 234, 246, 247–251, 257–259, 261–263, 265
from incarnation to exaltation 163
historical 97
incarnation 46
presence 198, 199
resurrection 6, 8, 9, 45, 46, 162, 236, 247, 264
Jezebel 253

children of 253
prophetess 101, 253
Joseph and Aseneth 96, 97
judgment 7, 14, 18, 35–38, 41, 43, 45, 46, 48, 51, 52, 58, 74, 77, 78, 82, 87, 130, 144, 162, 165, 166, 167, 170, 172, 174, 179, 181, 198, 199, 201, 208, 227, 237–239, 243, 246, 260, 261
divine 53, 72, 180, 203
final 213
human 174
visions 59
Judith 106
justice 14, 35, 67, 82, 88, 105, 133–135, 140–142, 145, 148, 165, 225
discourse 79
forensic language 139

K

kataphatic 260
king, philosopher 17, 149, 152, 166
King 17, 38, 78, 101, 102, 106, 117, 121, 122, 125–129, 131, 134–136, 155–158, 165, 166, 176, 189, 213
beast 79
divine 11, 23, 74, 79, 80, 85, 94, 98, 106, 107, 113, 139–142, 175, 178–180, 182, 206, 258, 263, 264
divinely authorized 80
Jesus 44
Logos 140–142
of kings 115, 136, 138, 139, 142, 178
YHWH 8, 15, 34, 35, 37, 40, 52, 99, 110, 111, 128, 134, 187
kingdom 9, 10, 13, 15, 42, 44, 46, 48, 66, 72, 73, 78, 86, 102, 105, 110, 116, 117, 121, 135, 137, 140, 182, 189, 195, 211, 223, 248, 253
liturgical 118

of God 6, 9, 13, 29, 42, 44, 45, 49, 52, 162, 246
kings of the earth 11, 80, 81, 136, 173, 178, 180, 181, 208, 209, 211, 260, 261
koinonia 13, 14, 202, 224, 232, 238–243, 246, 262

L

lake of fire 75, 82, 83, 136, 208
Lamb 11–13, 16, 23, 60, 67–70, 74, 76, 79–81, 83–86, 94, 106–109, 113, 115–119, 124, 136, 139, 141, 142, 175–177, 181, 187, 195, 200, 202, 204, 206, 209, 223, 248, 253, 258, 263, 264
  blood 89, 207, 251, 252, 259, 262
  servants 176, 204, 253
  slaughtered 66, 68–70, 72, 114–116, 118, 142, 178
landscape 200, 202, 203
  agonistic 200, 201, 203, 207
  artistic 202
  forensic 201
  historical 200
law 2, 35, 36, 38, 39, 41, 45, 151, 155, 166, 171, 173, 220, 227, 229, 248, 255
  boundary marker 43
  divine 169, 170
  natural 169
  positive 170
  studies 31
Letter of Agatho, Pope of Old Rome, to the Emperor 139
Letters 146 (Theodoret) 139
Ley sobre el Escudo, la Bandera y el Himno Nacionales 220
like a son of man 16, 57, 64, 72, 77, 95, 98, 136, 190, 249
linguistic markers 58, 61
Lion 66, 114

liturgy 45, 66, 67, 83, 109, 188, 190, 221, 231, 240, 249, 250, 260, 262, 264
  choreographed 66
  coercive 76, 80, 86, 132, 142
  heretical 260
  heterodox 222
  in classical Greek 188
  in the New Testament 189
  in the Septuagint 189
  pagan 103
  political category 189
  public 76, 180, 219, 229, 264
  religious 221
  secular 220, 221
  true 77, 86
  unorthodox 141

M

market transaction 119, 142, 248, 258
marriage 20, 80, 135, 187, 228, 256, 257
  analogy 223, 256
  covenantal 202
  Platonic redefinition 229, 231, 250, 262
Messiah 23, 51, 72, 73, 75, 76, 82, 85, 94, 104, 108, 122, 124, 125, 140–142, 175, 176, 206, 235, 258, 263
  advent 125, 132, 142
  child 62, 75, 81, 82, 88, 107, 119, 122, 125, 142, 263, 264
  enthronement 125, 132
  Jesus 98, 103, 105, 106, 108, 114, 122, 181, 182
Mexican 4, 221, 255
  census 1
  consensus 5
  constitution 4, 219, 255
  context 219, 264
  ethos 2, 264
  flag 220, 222
  law 219

political theology 264
secular 220, 222, 264, 265
state 2, 3, 219, 255, 264
Mexico 1–3, 219, 255, 263, 264
patriotic symbols 220
Protestant, evangelicals 21
Roman Catholicism 1
secular space 220
midheaven 77, 80, 141
modernity 216, 243
critique 189, 215
liberal 215

N

narrating voice 63, 64
narrative 14, 19, 46, 49, 53, 55–57, 59, 61, 62, 64–78, 81, 83–88, 94, 99, 101–103, 108, 109, 118–120, 131, 133, 134, 188, 194, 197, 200, 203, 214, 221–223, 225, 227, 258, 259
Apocalypse 22, 56, 57, 85, 87, 89, 106, 112, 115, 119, 120, 126, 200, 208, 211, 255–257, 263, 265
biblical 33
birth of Jesus 122
book of Revelation 14, 56, 57, 62, 63, 89, 93, 100, 112–115, 175, 182, 195, 199, 209, 253
counter 76
Genesis 120
gospel story 264
reading 23, 142
Scripture 257
the Enlightment 215
theory 56, 66
nation-state 216, 218, 232
assymetric correlation 218
construal 216
critique 222
foundational myths 217
number 4, symbolic meaning 66
number 7, symbolic meaning 197
number 12, symbolic meaning 66

O

oikos 227, 240, 241, 249
On the Commonwealth (Cicero) 17, 183, 224
On the Resurrection of the Flesh (Tertullian) 139
On the Trinity (Hilary of Poiters) 139

P

papalism 233
paradise 12, 84, 188, 259
Patmos 19, 49, 57, 58, 60, 64, 65, 95, 199
John of 48, 166, 205
plot 69, 79, 85, 127, 258
Apocalypse 85, 86, 89
book of Revelation 62, 63, 93
dragon 75
polis 16, 177, 187, 216, 225, 226, 240, 241, 249
Aristotelian 226–228, 247, 248, 261
church 9, 238
Greek 16, 18
holy 94, 258
Platonic 17, 153, 155, 175, 224, 225, 228, 247, 248, 250, 262
politeia
apocalyptic 118
Ciceronian 155
Greek 169, 177
Platonic 17, 153
political conspiracy 136, 139
ancient Near Eastern motif 129, 131, 258
dragon 82, 83, 132, 142
Old Testament motif 81, 129, 130
political theory 17, 31, 155, 168, 247, 248, 263
politics 1, 27–30, 47, 109, 153, 172, 190, 201, 214, 216, 218, 222
Politics (Aristotle) 224, 225
post-resurrection 19, 165, 166
potentia 157

absoluta 29, 34
ordinata 29
power 8, 9, 13, 14, 16, 35, 37, 42, 43, 45, 46, 50–52, 65, 67, 71–73, 75, 76, 81, 84, 86, 102–104, 109, 112, 115, 118, 125, 141, 147, 148, 150–152, 156–158, 160–162, 168, 170–172, 178, 179, 201–203, 215, 217, 231
  coercive 249
  correlation 23, 93, 94, 141–143, 177, 258
  de jure 159
  heretical construal 86
  imperial 42, 81, 121, 126, 129–131, 179, 258
  ultimate 85, 89
praise 8, 35–37, 44, 67, 126, 187, 205, 240, 249
providence 34
  divine 30, 37, 51
public square 1, 3, 4, 219, 221, 255

R

recapitulation, hermeneutical device 88
Reformation 217, 246
religion 1, 3, 217, 219, 221
  modern construal 217
Republic (Plato) 17, 143, 144, 154, 183, 224, 225
Res Gestae (Augustus) 159, 179, 212
res privata, church 240
res publica 155–159, 175, 225
  apocalyptic 118, 178
  church 240
  Ciceronian 17, 18, 143, 155, 177, 183, 224, 227, 228, 247, 248
  Roman 156, 169, 177, 261
resurrection 9, 19, 46, 50, 93, 104, 162, 167, 174, 236, 244, 247
  Jesus 44
rider on the white horse 79–81, 133, 135–141

Rome 17–19, 43, 61, 80, 138, 156, 158, 160, 161, 180, 201, 212, 214, 228
  founding myth 78

S

sacraments 20, 49, 234, 241, 243, 250–252, 254, 262
  Lombardian position 234
  minimalist Reformed position 234
salvation 5, 35, 37, 59, 124, 125, 177, 207, 217, 251
  history 37, 47, 50, 52, 167, 218
  political implication 35
  political vocabulary 5
Scripture 21, 22, 28, 29, 32, 52, 55, 93, 165, 246, 256
  authority 224, 232, 244, 246, 247, 262
  Holy 21, 28, 241, 246
  narrative 257
Second Temple Judaism 117, 137
secular 3–7, 50, 166, 167, 172, 173, 215, 219, 220, 222, 232, 233, 255, 260, 264, 265
  approach to life 2, 255
  as a domain 167
  as time 175, 182, 199, 221, 237, 244
  creed 1
  discourse 5, 27, 219, 255, 263, 265
  government 47, 49, 162
  reason 214
secularism 3
secularization theory 27
serpent 120, 126
  dragon 120, 126, 127
seven 59, 61, 62, 87, 192, 197, 220
  angels 69, 70, 78, 98, 197
  archangels 69
  bowls 62, 69, 73, 74, 78
  churches 49, 60, 64, 79, 87, 200
  cities 86
  communities 60

congregations 191, 192, 195
crowns 127
eyes 107
golden lampstands 64, 190
heads 78, 127
hills 78
horns 107, 115
kings 78
messages 58, 60, 72
mountains 78
plagues 69, 78
sacraments 234
seals 59, 66, 69, 72, 88, 89, 113, 140, 200
spirits 103, 104, 107, 116, 176
stars 69
thousand 71
trumpets 62, 69, 70, 72, 78, 88, 89
Sirach 100
sociality 14, 15, 17, 19, 79, 86, 88, 118, 132, 135, 141, 145, 180, 182, 211, 213, 219, 223, 227, 231, 250, 253, 260, 264
    human 34, 57, 119, 141
    liturgical 13–15, 19, 22, 23, 30, 72, 73, 84, 86, 87, 89, 94, 108, 116, 133, 142, 176, 177, 187–189, 195, 200, 203, 207, 210, 219, 221–223, 247–249, 251–254, 257–259, 261, 262
social theory 238
    Christian 214
society 5, 10, 31–33, 37, 39, 42, 49, 52, 57, 93, 132, 168, 169, 209, 213–215, 217, 218, 223–225, 228, 231, 234, 237–239, 247, 252, 254, 255, 257, 260–263, 265
    construal 22, 210, 247
    liturgical 254, 257
    moral 254, 262
    Platonic 225
    political 9, 23, 24, 48, 166, 224, 231, 232, 235, 242, 245, 246, 250, 254, 261
    post-political 236, 237, 246, 250, 254, 262
    theo-political category 257
Son of God 23, 64, 76, 85, 94, 98, 101, 103, 104, 106–108, 123, 125, 131, 132, 136, 141, 142, 166, 175, 176, 195, 206, 249, 258, 263–265
    as Solomon 111
    construal 102, 110, 123, 134
    Davidic 111, 128, 131
space 11, 32, 41, 53, 57, 64, 65, 94, 140, 162, 177, 178, 190, 193, 194, 200, 202, 213, 215–220, 223, 225, 239, 249, 258, 260, 261
    liturgical 188, 199, 210–212, 216, 219, 222, 250, 265
    sacral 23, 249
    sacred 11–13, 84, 110, 187, 188, 191, 193–197, 199, 210, 219, 221, 222, 249, 257, 259, 261, 262
    secular 3, 220, 222, 263
    social 41, 49, 211, 218, 240
    theo-political category 214, 263
Spain 231
    Islamic 2
spatial turn 215
Special Laws (Philo) 138
Spirit 11, 13, 14, 48, 58, 64, 65, 98, 103, 116, 117, 164, 193, 199, 233, 234, 238, 239, 247, 253
    Holy 7, 21, 122, 224, 232, 236, 238, 239, 243, 246, 249, 262
    koinonia 241–243
    role 103, 104
    YHWH 103, 176
story 9, 33, 34, 44, 46, 56, 59, 60–62, 64, 73, 75, 78, 81, 82, 85, 98, 100–102, 114, 123, 125, 132, 139, 140, 149, 150, 175, 180, 191, 206, 220, 226, 258, 263, 264
    book of Revelation 63, 87

time 69, 73, 79

T
Targum Isaiah 103
Testament of Abraham 106
The Divine Liturgy of James 139
The Divine Liturgy of Mark 139
theology 5, 6, 8, 17, 20, 22, 30, 36,
    77, 86, 132, 141, 180, 214, 222,
    256, 257, 260
  Christian 28, 45
  pathos 6, 214
  philosophical 34
  political 5–8, 10, 20, 22, 23,
    27–36, 44, 52, 53, 93, 132,
    144, 183, 187, 215, 216, 218,
    224, 237, 238, 247, 255–257,
    263, 264
  sacramental 172, 234, 235, 254
  systematic 21
theories of constitution 224
  constitutionalist 224
  contractarian 224
thousand years 82
throne 13, 15, 19, 46, 62, 65, 68, 69,
    75, 77, 78, 81–83, 86, 87, 102,
    105, 106, 108, 112, 114, 116,
    120, 123, 125, 130–132, 134,
    135, 177, 180, 193, 195, 204,
    219, 260
  Ancient of Days 112
  divine 20, 60, 107, 118, 222
  God and the Lamb 12, 13, 84, 108,
    187, 253, 258
  heavenly 62, 67, 69, 70, 85, 89,
    109, 207, 258
  the one who sits on it 23, 66–70,
    72, 76, 83, 85, 86, 89, 93, 94,
    100, 108, 109, 113, 116, 117,
    141–143, 177, 181, 193, 196,
    200, 202, 204, 208, 209, 258
  YHWH 16, 110, 111, 117, 123,
    137, 191, 193
Tobit 100

tradition 30, 37–39, 41, 45, 52, 94,
    119, 124, 126, 127, 132–135,
    141, 142, 168, 172, 173, 179,
    180, 183, 215, 223, 230, 258
  Christian 138, 170, 256
  church 21
  gospel 104
  Greek 16, 17, 143
  Hebrew/Israelite 15, 176
  Israelite/Jewish 8, 256
  messianic 103
  modern 27
  Old Testament 189
  political 162, 256
  Roman 17, 143
Treatise 12 (Cyprian) 139
two witnesses 49, 71, 72, 77, 86–88,
    195, 201, 253

W
war 18, 67, 69, 76, 81, 82, 105,
    113, 124, 133–135, 141, 145,
    147, 153, 157, 159, 161, 167,
    173–175, 178, 182, 230, 250
  forensic 141
  making 48, 166
  motif 68, 71, 73, 86, 159
woman 60, 62, 75, 78, 79, 82,
    120–124, 127, 131, 132, 137,
    202, 211, 229, 253
  great city 78
  Lamb 84
  pregnant 75, 120, 121, 125
  primeval 120, 132
Word of God 21, 80, 136, 139, 141,
    142, 178, 179, 246

Y
YHWH 8, 11, 15, 34–41, 43, 52,
    99–103, 110, 111, 115–117,
    120–126, 128–131, 134,
    136, 138, 165, 176, 187, 189,
    191–193, 203–205, 210, 221
  return 206

Index of Scripture

OLD TESTAMENT

Genesis
1 33
1:1 83
1–3 33
1–11 33
2:8 84
2:9 .... 12, 84
2:10 .... 12, 84
2:11–12 84
3 120
3:22 .... 12, 84
3:24 .... 12, 84
11 41
11:1–9 33
47:20 116
47:23 116
49:9 114

Exodus
3:15 15
7:1 15
12:5 114
12:6 114
12:7–8 115
12:12–13 115
12:14 115
14:13 35
14:14 15
14:25 15
15 124
15:2 35
15:16 116
15:18 15
19:4–6 15
19:8–10 15
19:16 62
20:2 117
20:2–5 15
20:3 117
20:5 117
20:16 15
20:19 .... 15, 38

Leviticus
4:32–33 115
14:11–13 115
14:25 115

Deuteronomy
6:4 15
10:16–17 138
10:17 138
34:10 15

Joshua
5:13–15 136
10:14 15

1 Samuel
2:1–10 125
8 259
8:20 15
12:12 15

2 Samuel
7 102
7:11–14 64
7:12–14 .... 102, 123, 134

1 Kings
1:46 110
6:5 11
6:19 11
6:20 .... 11, 84
8:6 11
16:31 117
22:17 137
22:19 137

2 Kings
17:16 117
17:34–35 117
17:35 117
22:54 117

1 Chronicles
16:31 15
29:20 .... 16, 117
29:23 .... 16, 110, 117

2 Chronicles
6:14 117

311

Ezra
7:12 138

Nehemiah
9:6 137

Psalms
2 .... 102, 123, 136
2:1 46
2:1–3 .... 80, 136
2:4–12 80
2:6–9 .... 64, 136
2:7 .... 39, 123
2:7–9 .... 101, 123
2:8 123
2:9 123
8 163
35:18 36
40:9–10 36
42:9 40
47:2–3 40
50:6 37
74:2 116
77:19 62
93 34
93:1 34
96:10 36
99:4 35
101 38
110:1 105
132:17 115
135:26 (LXX) 138
136 138
136:1 138
136:2 138
136:3 138

Isaiah
2:3 36
7 105
7:14 .... 121, 122
9 105
9:5–6 105
9:6 105
11:1 114
11:1–5 103
11:4 103
11:11 116
14:4–23 131
14:12–15 131
24:21–22 131
24:21–23 131
24–27 131
25:8 .... 204, 205
41:4 99
44:6 99
48:12 99
49:10 .... 204, 205
53:7 115
60 11
60:2 11
60:3 11
60:11 11
65:17 83
66:22 83

Jeremiah
10:10 99
17:10 .... 65, 100
29 41
51 128
51:6 128
51:24 128
51:34 .... 79, 127, 128
51:35 128
51:44 .... 79, 128

Lamentations
1 137
1:12 137
1:15 137

Ezekiel
2:8–3:4 71
5:2 70
26:7 138
38:2–6 82
38:8–9 82
38:22 82
39:6 82

Daniel
2:37 138
3:2 (LXX) 138
4 180
4:37b (LXX) 138
4:37 (LXX) 138
7 .... 41, 78, 95, 97,
                      136, 139, 180
7:3–8 76
7:7 79
7:9 95
7:11 .... 80, 136
7:11–12 78
7:13 95
7:13–14 136
7:17–25 76
7:19 79
7:23 79
7:26 .... 78, 80, 140
10 .... 95, 97
10:5 95
10:6 95

Micah
4:2 36

NEW TESTAMENT

Matthew
7:1 237
10:34–36 43
17 98
17:1–9 97
17:5 97
17:9 97
28:2 97
28:2–4 97

Index of Scripture

Mark
3:15 8
9:2–9 97
9:7 97

Luke
9:23 252
9:28–36 97
9:35 97

Acts
2:43 240

Romans
2:29 61
8:9 61
8:27 65
9:1 61
13 260
13:1 165
13:4 165
14:17 61
15–16 61

1 Corinthians
12:3 239
12:4–6 239

Ephesians
2:22 61
3:5 61
5:18 61
6:18 61

Colossians
2:14–15 236

1 Timothy
6:15 139

1 Peter
2:12 167

Revelation
1:1 .... 69, 88
1:1–8 59
1:3 58
1–3 60
1:4 64
1:5 .... 100, 104, 106
1:6 .... 13, 15, 253
1:9 .... 13, 14, 19, 63, 253
1:9–3:22 .... 58, 59, 94
1:9–10 58
1:10 .... 58, 64, 199
1:11 .... 64, 191, 253
1:12–13 190
1:12–20 59
1:13 .... 64, 95, 122
1:13–16 .... 64, 98
1:14 .... 95, 107
1:15 95
1:16 .... 95, 107
1:17 64
1:17–18 .... 64, 99
1:17–20 94
1:18 99
1:19 .... 61, 191
1:19–20 64
1:20 .... 122, 191
2:1 .... 65, 69, 99, 122, 190, 191
2:1–3:21 65
2:1–7 197
2:2 .... 65, 253
2:5 197
2:5b 123
2:6 253
2:7 ...... 12, 65, 84, 252, 253
2:8 ...... 65, 69, 99, 100, 191
2:10 .... 87, 253
2:11 .... 65, 252, 253
2:12 ... 65, 69, 99, 107, 191
2:13 .... 87, 253
2:14 253
2:15 253
2:16 198
2:17 .... 65, 253
2:18 .... 64, 65, 69, 76, 88, 98, 99, 101, 107, 123, 124, 134, 191, 253
2:19 65
2:20 .... 88, 253
2:22 253
2:23 .... 65, 87, 100, 253
2:24 .... 87, 253
2:25 198
2:26 .... 65, 76, 253
2:26–28 .... 85, 123
2:26–28a 101, 102
2:28 65
2:29 253
3:1 .... 65, 69, 99, 103, 107, 191
3:3 199
3:5 ..... 65, 69, 83, 199, 253
3:6 253
3:7 .... 65, 69, 99, 191
3:8 65
3:11 199
3:12 ...... 19, 64, 65, 83, 253
3:13 253
3:14 .... 65, 69, 99, 104–106, 191
3:14–22 198
3:15 .... 65, 105
3:19 253
3:20 ..... 109, 198, 251, 253
3:20–21 .... 19, 65
3:21 .... 65, 85, 105, 106, 108, 113, 253
3:22 253
4 .... 109, 112
4:1 .... 61, 65
4:1–2 58
4:1–9:21 59
4:2 .... 58, 65, 83
4:2–3 65
4:4 66
4–5 58
4:5a 62
4:6 66
4:8–11 .... 66, 118

4:9 .... 65, 100	6:12–17 .... 67, 81, 113, 140	9:13–21 71
4:10 .... 65, 100	6:16 .... 65, 67, 108	9:15 71
4:10–11 76	6–16 58	10:1 .... 61, 69, 98
4–11 60	7 61	10:1–10 71
5 .... 109, 112, 118	7:1 61	10:1–11 61
5:1 .... 61, 65	7:1–8 .... 68, 82	10:1–15:4 59
5:1–4 66	7:2 61	10:6 100
5:1–5 113	7:3 88	10:7 253
5:2 .... 61, 69	7:4 .... 68, 77	10:8–11 72
5:2–3 113	7:9 .... 61, 108, 204, 253	10:11 71
5:3 113	7:9–10 67	11:1–14 71
5:5 .... 66, 114	7:9-17 203	11:3 .... 72, 88, 253
5:6 .... 61, 66, 107, 113–115, 124	7:9–17 .... 68, 82, 203, 204, 206	11:7 .... 69, 71
5:6-8 70	7:10 .... 65, 108, 204	11:8 .... 71, 77, 88
5:7 65	7:11 204	11:10 253
5:7–10 66	7:12 204	11:11 71
5:8 .... 69, 70, 88, 124	7:13–17 84	11:12 .... 69, 71
5:8–12 116	7:14 .... 68, 89, 204, 251	11:13 .... 71, 77
5:8–14 76	7:15 .... 65, 68, 204	11:15 .... 13, 61, 69, 72, 124, 140
5:9 .... 68, 116	7:16 205	11:15–19 59
5:9–10 .... 67, 84, 85	7:16-17 205	11:16 70
5:9–14 100	7:17 .... 67, 68, 108, 204	11:16–18 72
5:10 ... 13, 15, 84, 116, 253	8:1 .... 61, 67, 68	11:18 .... 72, 83, 88, 253
5:11 .... 61, 69	8:2 .... 61, 69, 70	11:19 .... 62, 72
5:11–12 67	8:3 .... 69, 70, 72	12 .... 119, 263
5:12 .... 114, 124	8:3–4 88	12:1 .... 62, 73, 75, 120
5:13 .... 65, 67, 108, 114, 124	8:3–5 70	12:1–2 .... 75, 120
5:13–14 .... 113, 116, 118	8:4 .... 69, 70, 72	12:1–19:21 88
6:1 .... 61, 67, 113	8:5 .... 62, 69	12:3 .... 62, 73, 75, 120
6:1–8 67	8:6 70	12:3–4 .... 75, 120
6:1–8:1 .... 61, 67	8:7 .... 69, 70	12:4 .... 79, 81
6:1–12 140	8:8 .... 69, 70	12:5 .... 75, 108, 120, 122, 123
6:2 61	8:10 .... 69, 70	12:5a 123
6:3 .... 67, 113	8:12 .... 69, 70	12:5b 123
6:5 .... 61, 67, 113	8:13 61	12:7–9 .... 73, 75, 128
6:7 .... 67, 71, 113	9:1 .... 61, 69, 71	12:9 81
6:8 .... 61, 71	9:1–12 71	12:10 .... 13, 75, 76, 108, 124, 125, 132
6:9 .... 67, 69, 79, 82, 88, 113, 253	9:2 71	12:10–12 124
6:9–10 .... 67, 88	9:2–3 69	12:11 132
6:10 88	9:4 .... 71, 72	12:13 .... 75, 120
6:11 67	9:11 71	12–13 50
6:12 .... 61, 67	9:12 61	
	9:13 .... 61, 69	

12:17 .... 75, 82, 120, 133, 253	16:2 .... 78, 118	19:4 65
12–22 60	16:3 78	19:5 88
13 .... 17, 50, 175	16:4 78	19:5–10 80
13:1 .... 61, 74, 76, 132	16:6 .... 88, 253	19:6 98
13:2 .... 76, 131, 132	16:8 78	19:7 .... 11, 20, 84
13:3–4 118	16:10 .... 74, 78	19:8 88
13:4 .... 76, 81, 132	16:12 78	19:9 .... 11, 20, 84
13:5 76	16:13 61	19:9–10 .... 74, 118
13:5–6 76	16:17 78	19:9b–10 58
13:7 .... 76, 88	16:18 62	19:10 58
13:8 .... 76, 83, 114, 118	16:18–19 78	19:11 .... 15, 61, 67, 79, 80, 133
13:10 88	16:19 .... 74, 77, 132	19:11–16 59
13:11 .... 61, 76, 132	17 .... 50, 74, 175	19:11–21 .... 79, 113, 133, 138
13:12 .... 76, 118, 132	17:1 74	19:11–21:8 .... 58, 59
13:13 76	17:1–3 58	19:11–22:9 59
13:14 76	17:1–5 78	19:12 .... 98, 107
13:14–15 118	17:1–19:10 .... 58, 59	19:13 .... 80, 139
13:15–17 76	17:3 ...... 58, 61, 74, 78, 132	19:14 .... 80, 136
13–19 .... 73, 75	17:6 .... 61, 79, 88, 253	19:15 .... 80, 98, 107, 136, 137, 198
14:1 .... 61, 68, 76	17:7 .... 78, 132	19:16 .... 80, 115, 136, 138, 139
14:1–20 74	17:7–13 74	19:17 .... 61, 80
14:3 .... 68, 77	17:8 .... 78, 83, 132	19:17–21 67
14:4 77	17:9 78	19:19 .... 61, 80, 136
14:6 .... 61, 74, 77	17:10 79	19:19–20 .... 74, 80
14:8 .... 74, 77	17:11 78	19:19–21 11
14:9 .... 74, 118	17:12 .... 78, 79, 115	19:20 .... 118, 136
14:10–11 77	17:13 79	19:20–21 .... 80, 139
14:11 118	17:14 ... 115, 136, 138, 139	19:21 198
14:12 .... 88, 253	17:16 .... 74, 79	20 263
14:14 61	17:17 79	20:1 61
14:14–20 77	17:18 .... 78, 132	20:1–3 .... 73, 76, 81, 128, 131
14:19–20 137	17–18 50	20:1–10 .... 75, 119
15:1 .... 59, 61, 62, 73	17–19 17	20:3 61
15:2 61	18 74	20:4 ...... 61, 82, 84, 88, 253
15:2–4 .... 77, 78	18:1 61	20:6 .... 82, 84, 253
15:4 61	18:2 .... 74, 77	20:7 81
15:5 61	18:10 .... 77, 132	20:7–10 .... 73, 81
15:5–16:21 59	18:20 .... 88, 253	20:8 82
15:5–19:10 59	18:21 .... 77, 79, 132	20:9 .... 82, 88, 253
15:6 98	18:23 20	
15:7 .... 78, 100	18:24 .... 79, 88, 253	
15–16 78	19 74	
16 58	19:1 61	
16:1–21 .... 73, 74	19:1–2 124	
	19:2 .... 79, 88	20:10 .... 82, 118

20:11 .... 61, 65, 83	21:10 .... 11, 58, 64, 83, 84, 204	22:2 .... 12, 84
20:11–15........................ 83	21:11 204	22:3 .... 67, 88, 108, 113, 114, 116, 118, 204, 253
20:12 61	21:11–23................... 11, 84	
20:12–13........................ 83	21:14 204	22:3–5 .... 12, 13, 64, 67, 68, 84
20:14 83	21:15 .... 194, 204	
20:15 83	21:16 .... 11, 84, 204	22:3–6 203
21:1 .... 61, 83, 84	21:18 204	22:5 .... 84, 204, 253
21:1–22:5........................ 140	21:18–21........................ 84	22:6 .... 88, 204, 253
21:2 ...... 64, 80, 83, 84, 204	21:19 204	22:6–9 .... 58, 74
21:3 .... 68, 83, 204, 253	21:21 204	22:8–9 118
21:3–7 .... 68, 203	21:22 .... 11, 84, 204	22:9 .... 59, 253
21:4 204	21:23 204	22:10–22:21 59
21:5 .... 65, 204	21:23–24.................... 140	22:14 84
21:6 .... 204, 205	21:24 11	22:17 84
21:7 .... 15, 83, 204, 253	21:27 .... 11, 83, 204	22:19 .... 83, 84
21:9 ...... 11, 80, 83, 84, 204	22:1 .... 12, 67, 108, 204	
21:9–10.................... 58, 74	22:1-2........................ 12, 84	
21:9–22:9................. 58, 59		

ANCIENT TEXTS

1 Enoch............ 95, 97, 103, 131, 137, 138	3 Maccabees 106, 138	4Q405 138
	4 Ezra 80	*Psalms of Solomon* 103, 139
1QSb............................ 103	4Q112.......................... 138	
2 Baruch 80	4Q381.......................... 138	
2 Maccabees 138	4Q403.......................... 138	

Langham Literature, with its publishing work, is a ministry of Langham Partnership.

Langham Partnership is a global fellowship working in pursuit of the vision God entrusted to its founder John Stott –

> *to facilitate the growth of the church in maturity and Christ-likeness through raising the standards of biblical preaching and teaching.*

Our vision is to see churches in the Majority World equipped for mission and growing to maturity in Christ through the ministry of pastors and leaders who believe, teach and live by the word of God.

Our mission is to strengthen the ministry of the word of God through:
- nurturing national movements for biblical preaching
- fostering the creation and distribution of evangelical literature
- enhancing evangelical theological education

especially in countries where churches are under-resourced.

Our ministry

Langham Preaching partners with national leaders to nurture indigenous biblical preaching movements for pastors and lay preachers all around the world. With the support of a team of trainers from many countries, a multi-level programme of seminars provides practical training, and is followed by a programme for training local facilitators. Local preachers' groups and national and regional networks ensure continuity and ongoing development, seeking to build vigorous movements committed to Bible exposition.

Langham Literature provides Majority World preachers, scholars and seminary libraries with evangelical books and electronic resources through publishing and distribution, grants and discounts. The programme also fosters the creation of indigenous evangelical books in many languages, through writer's grants, strengthening local evangelical publishing houses, and investment in major regional literature projects, such as one volume Bible commentaries like the *Africa Bible Commentary* and the *South Asia Bible Commentary*.

Langham Scholars provides financial support for evangelical doctoral students from the Majority World so that, when they return home, they may train pastors and other Christian leaders with sound, biblical and theological teaching. This programme equips those who equip others. Langham Scholars also works in partnership with Majority World seminaries in strengthening evangelical theological education. A growing number of Langham Scholars study in high quality doctoral programmes in the Majority World itself. As well as teaching the next generation of pastors, graduated Langham Scholars exercise significant influence through their writing and leadership.

To learn more about Langham Partnership and the work we do visit **langham.org**

www.ingramcontent.com/pod-product-compliance
Lightning Source LLC
Chambersburg PA
CBHW070233240426
43673CB00044B/1776